The Pierrot Ensembles

Mary Thomas as Pierrot (Chris Davies / ArenaPAL)

Poetics of Music
Editor: Christopher Wintle

The Pierrot Ensembles

Chronicle and Catalogue 1912-2012

Christopher Dromey

Plumbago Books

in association with
Middlesex University

2012

Plumbago Books and Arts
26 Iveley Road,
London sw4 0ew

plumbago@btinternet.com
www. plumbago.co.uk

Distribution and Sales:
Boydell & Brewer Ltd.
PO Box 9
Woodbridge
Suffolk ip12 3df

trading@boydell.co.uk
tel. 01394 610 600
www.boydellandbrewer.com

Boydell and Brewer Inc.
668 Mount Hope Avenue
Rochester
ny 14620, USA

Christopher Dromey, *The Pierrot Ensembles: Chronicle and Catalogue 1912-2012*
Poetics of Music, Editor: Christopher Wintle

First published 2012
with the generous financial support of Middlesex University

isbn: 978-0-9566007-2-1 (hardback), 978-0-9566007-3-8 (softback)

Typeset in Adobe Minion Pro and Adobe Cronos Pro

Printed by MPG Books Group in the UK

Contents

Author's Preface

The idea to write this book first suggested itself during a memorable lecture given by the composer Sadie Harrison on the music of Peter Maxwell Davies. A group of musicians, Max included, had once banded together and named themselves the Pierrot Players, I learned. But it was an off-the-cuff comment, that composers today (i.e. in 2001) still wrote for the idiosyncratic forces of this long since disbanded group, which struck me. Modestly, the composer made no mention of her own works for 'Pierrot ensemble' – as the group is described henceforth – and it is probably no coincidence that the 2000 Brighton Festival and the Hoxton New Music Days had recently celebrated the medium. (Released the following year, NMC's disc *The Hoxton 13* featured a dozen new Pierrot ensemble pieces by emerging voices such as Tansy Davies and Jonathan Cole.) The evident pattern of this compositional tale was one thing; its chronology was quite another, for if my introduction to the topic was somewhat back to front, with Arnold Schoenberg's famous prototype, *Pierrot lunaire*, consigned to the background, it quickly became apparent that I was not alone. In the post-1945 years especially, a flourishing repertory for Pierrot ensemble upgraded its medium, once dangerously new, until it became that rare thing: a new standard in composition and concert life.

This book, then, chronicles and catalogues the implications of this modern phenomenon: for *Pierrot*, for historically important Pierrot ensembles configured around its line-up, and for the incredible amount of music written for and performed by such groups. The incubation period for the book's various ideas has been prolonged, if we count the eleven years since the aforesaid lecture was given at Goldsmith's College, University of London. In fact, my memory of it was revived several years later, when it became the starting point for my doctoral studies at King's College, London. I am deeply grateful to my supervisor, Christopher Wintle, for guiding me through the project since then. Always stimulating and encouraging, his suggestions never let me forget that the reader's eyes will see in ways other than mine do. Thanks are also due to other members of the Department of Music at King's College, London, especially Silvina Milstein and Rob Keeley for their generosity in reading and commenting on draft sections of the thesis. I owe the same debt to Christopher Mark, Robert Adlington, Keith Potter, Tim Davy and Chris Heaton. Several other musicologists kindly donated scores and recordings, advised on the whereabouts of long-lost Pierrot ensembles, or pored over the manuscript, for which I thank David Beard, Meirion Bowen, David Blake, Susie Harries, Thomas Ahrend, Philip Rupprecht and Michael Taylor.

I am indebted to the staff of various libraries and archives I have visited during my research: Eike Fess of the Arnold Schönberg Zentrum, Melissa Bromley and Kathleen Dickson of the British Film Institute, Paul Banks of the Centre for Performance History (Royal College of Music, London), Bettina Tiefenbrunner and David Sharpe of Universal Edition, Nick Clark at the Britten-Pears Archive in Aldeburgh, Richard Malton at the BBC, and everyone at the Paul Sacher Stiftung, the British Library Sound Archive and Music Section, and the British Music Information Centre. Many musicians, composers and ensemble administrators obliged my pleas for information, among them Anthony Gilbert, Tristram Cary, Bruce Cole, Richard Emsley, Lawrence Casserley, Duncan Druce, Alan Hacker, Jennifer Ward Clarke, Stephen Pruslin, James Murdoch, Judy Arnold, Jane Manning, Dorothy Dorow, Ed Dudley Hughes (New Music Players), Tim Williams (Psappha), Elizabeth Gilbert (London Sinfonietta), Louis Fujinami Conti (New York New Music Ensemble), Libby Rice (London Symphony Orchestra) and Stuart Robinson (Hallé Orchestra). Fiona Searle and members of Leonard Isaacs's family also gave their time generously.

Special thanks go to my colleagues at Middlesex University, especially Peter Fribbins and François Evans, and to former colleagues at the Performing Right Society and the University of Leicester: their help and understanding was crucial. I also gratefully acknowledge King's College, London, the Musica Britannica Trust and Middlesex University for their support of my doctoral studies, and the Society for Music Analysis for helping fund my postgraduate studies. Finally, to Helen I give the greatest thanks: she has lovingly accepted her fate to become an unsuspecting authority on the Pierrot ensemble these past seven years, and the book is dedicated to her.

Autograph scores of Britten's unpublished film music appear courtesy of the Britten-Pears Foundation; Harrison Birtwistle's score of *Some Petals from the Garland* and excerpts from his *Medusa* are included with the kind permission of the composer; the photo of Hugh Davies's shozyg is reproduced with the kind permission of Clive Graham; an extract from Hanns Eisler's *Palmström*, Op. 5, appears courtesy of Universal Edition A.G., Wien, and images of Mary Thomas and Roy Hart courtesy of ArenaPAL.

Editor's Preface

In the early 1970s I had the pleasure and genuine privilege of joining the then-rising composer Jonathan Harvey as co-director of a small mixed chamber group, The Ulysses Ensemble. Together we toured universities propagating modern British and American music, gave broadcasts and on one occasion appeared at the Queen Elizabeth Hall. On the British side the group featured works by, inter alia, Geoffrey Poole, Julian Rushton and Jonathan Harvey (the tape piece *Time Points* as well as the first of his *Inner Light* series), and on the American side works by Milton Babbitt, Claudio Spies, Peter Westergaard and the impressively fluent George Edwards (*Kreuz und Quer*). We also devoted an entire concert to the electronic music of Milton Babbitt, including the beautiful *Philomel*. Then came 1974 and the Arab oil crisis, and the flow of cash ended abruptly – which was a pity, as we were lining up a large piece (*Notturno*) by the immensely gifted Donald Martino.

Yet for all its commitment and energy, and despite the fact that some of its best players were to become London Sinfonietta 'stars', our group was never more than one among many. Nor can I claim that audiences came in droves to hear what even by the adventurous standards of the '60s and early '70s were demanding programmes. Yet the hard fact was that, for economic and artistic reasons, it was through the small mixed ensemble that composers conducted most of their ground-breaking musical thought – thought that released itself into line and counterpoint from the apparent confines of the harmonically-orientated string quartet or piano-singer duo. As the novelty of the music demanded familiarity and explanation, this also became the era of 'workshop' rehearsals, pre-performance talks and analysis seminars replete with numinously arithmetical 'magic squares'. (Now, in the second decade of the twenty-first century, the groups have dwindled, but the talks, if anything, have multiplied …) Since then, those of us involved have gone our different ways. Yet the memory of a blissful dawn remains: it was a time of high seriousness, when the quest for new means to match a new musical language was to the fore, and composers quarried the liberating words of fin-de-siècle poets and writers for their song-texts – Trakl, Virginia Woolf, Gerard Manley Hopkins among others.

Nevertheless, all groups drew their inspiration from the remarkable achievement of the Pierrot Players (later to become The Fires of London), founded by two composers of markedly different creative personalities: Peter Maxwell Davies and Harrison Birtwistle. I cannot remember how many Pierrot Players' concerts I went to, nor the full range of pieces played. Certainly, it epitomized the post-Webern era by playing very little – if any – Webern. Instead, 'Max's' theatricality was to the fore – Alan Hacker playing the shrill *Hymnos*, Randolph Stow talking to caged birds in *Eight Songs for a Mad King*, Simon McBurney miming in *The No. 11 Bus* – and above all Mary Thomas playing not just Pierrot but also many other roles that expanded the repertory of Schoenberg's *Kabarettliederkreis*. Not surprisingly, the concerts were well attended. *Pierrot lunaire* was inevitably the centre-piece of the first *Pierrot Players* concert in 1967, introduced by Davies's dapper *Antechrist* and including Birtwistle's *Monodrama* to a text by Stephen Pruslin (who also wrote *Punch and Judy*). About *Monodrama*, however, there is a story. The actor speaking the role of Choregos did indeed 'send up' the climax by emitting a blood-curdling cry through a loud hailer just as Pruslin describes (amid the laughter I heard Hugh Wood exclaim "Andy Pandy!", *AP* being a children's TV show); and amid a welter of hurt feelings, the piece was firmly withdrawn. So I am grateful to Stephen Pruslin for allowing us to reprint the text for the first time.

Christopher Dromey's *The Pierrot Ensembles* began as a PhD thesis. Although the aim was to analyze a few representative examples of works written for 'Pierrot Ensemble', it soon became clear that unless the repertory and context had first been established, there could be no responsible selection. So over several years Dromey worked diligently through archives here and abroad, interviewed 'main players', collected tapes and music, and compiled not just a chronicle but also a preliminary catalogue. Work of this kind is bedrock: without such an effort, the achievement of a whole generation of musicians would vanish into the mist of history. Doubtless, others will build on these foundations, the end of his work marking the beginning of theirs.

As both academic and publisher, I am grateful to colleagues who have read this work formally and contributed positively to its shaping: in particular Arnold Whittall (King's College London), Christopher Mark (University of Surrey) and Keith Potter (Goldsmiths' College London). I thank The Cosman Keller Art and Music Trust and David Hockney Inc. for kind permission to use their drawings; and although not all copyright-holders of photographs have replied to permission-requests, I nevertheless reproduce their work on the grounds that photographers expect iconic images to be seen. I am happy to meet any reasonable claim. As always, I am deeply indebted to my production team, notably Kate Hopkins for proof-reading and Julian Littlewood for type-setting.

Christopher Wintle

List of Examples

The Pierrot Ensembles: Chronicle

Roy Hart as the Mad King George (Boosey & Hawkes / ArenaPAL)

Prologue

Upon the death of Arnold Schoenberg in July 1951, Richard Capell, editor of *Music & Letters*, invited many of Britain's leading composers, musicians and critics to write obituaries. Their twenty-five replies were extraordinary for their diversity and vehemence.[1] Just one author was neither for nor against Schoenberg: the critic Eric Blom discussed only whether the twelve-note method should be taught in English schools, and even then reserved judgement. Otherwise, two factions emerged, with those broadly resistant to Schoenberg's artistic achievements narrowly outnumbering his supporters.[2] This may not surprise readers aware of the controversies Schoenberg's work aroused during his lifetime. But the general intensity of feeling reveals other assumptions about the composer. The topics that surfaced most frequently were the advent of serialism and the composition of *Pierrot lunaire*, Op. 21 (1912). Given the disparity between those who defended and derided Schoenberg, recollections of *Pierrot* were peculiar. Of the eight writers who cited the work, six gave their approval, a seventh, Egon Wellesz, offered no opinion (though his support for Schoenberg's early work was long established),[3] and Arthur Bliss made a coy slight on it by criticizing the 'inhuman lunar landscape' of Schoenberg's works.[4] There was broad consensus on *Pierrot*, then, and tellingly, half of those who spoke well of it had reached otherwise downbeat conclusions about the rest of Schoenberg's works and musical ideas. Although John Amis, Rollo Myers and Felix Aprahamian were reluctant to praise the piece – evocatively, the latter told how he had 'succumbed to [its] unholy spell of broken-glass noises'[5] – they nevertheless respected it.

If *Pierrot* had secured a special place in Schoenberg's oeuvre by the time of his death, it is worth remembering how its earliest critics were less willing to forgo their prejudices. François Lesure's selective compilation of press reviews up to, but not including, the Spanish premiere of *Pierrot* in 1925 has encouraged discussion of its reception.[6] David Metzer has also detailed the circumstances under which the work was premiered in the United States in 1923 and repeated in 1925.[7] His scrutiny of *Pierrot*'s reception in that country contrasts with broader chronicles of the work's early performance history, albeit in anthology (Lesure) or biography (Hans Heinz Stuckenschmidt).[8] From these we learn how one acerbic critic in the *New York Times* coined what would remain the most famous of derogatory epithets, describing *Pierrot* as the 'decomposition of the art' and the 'ecstasy of the hideous!'[9] Critical responses to each American concert, though mostly negative, reaffirmed the work's significance to concertgoers and the public. Alongside reactions in the British obituaries, these much earlier, unguarded responses to *Pierrot* point to its immediate allure: yet the global trajectory of *Pierrot* has not been documented comprehensively.

Multiple performances of *Pierrot* were guaranteed before its composition was even begun. Schoenberg shrewdly negotiated with his commissioner Albertine Zehme that its Berlin premiere, fronted by the well-known singer-cum-actress, would be the first leg of a national tour.[10] In its aftermath, most European countries would also host national premieres of *Pierrot* during the first quarter of the century, including a tour of seven Italian cities in 1924 that featured eight performances and a more modest, localised run of three concerts in consecutive days in different London venues a year earlier. A further consequence of the work's international magnetism was that even before the end of the 1920s, many more musicians than the eight of Schoenberg's original ensemble had performed the work.[11] *Pierrot*'s power to provoke critics was only as great as its ability to galvanise musicians and administrators. The League of Composers (USA) was even founded to present the work, and *Pierrot*'s repeated presence on the programmes of other concert societies, such as the *Corporazione delle Nuove Musiche* (Italy) and Schoenberg's own *Verein für musikalische Privataufführungen* (Austria, later also Czechoslovakia), made it an essential and defining part of their existence. Tracing the lineage of these early trans-Atlantic performances exposes the conditions of music-making and the place of contemporary – or, to adopt the multilingual parlance of the era, 'ultra-modern' – music in several countries. *Pierrot*'s mixed instrumentation only elevated its status as a piece that would epitomize modern music-making: its performances obliged fresh groups of players to convene, and often led to the formation of new and enduring groups based on or around the Pierrot ensemble.

What, then, is a Pierrot ensemble? In *Pierrot lunaire* it comprised the Sprechstimme (the speaking voice, source of ceaseless debate on its realization and reception) with a versatile accompaniment of flute doubling piccolo, clarinet doubling bass clarinet, piano, violin doubling viola, and cello. The line-up was certainly unprecedented: the closest historic match is an obscure Quintet in A Major, KWV 5113 (for piano, flute, clarinet, viola and cello) by Conradin Kreutzer, whose early nineteenth-century operas have outlasted his sideline in mixed chamber music. Yet, to generate companions for his hitherto exceptional work, Schoenberg sometimes encouraged new works from his former pupils, including Hanns Eisler's *Palmström*, Op. 5 (1924) and Anton Webern's transcription of the First Chamber Symphony, Op. 9 (1922-23). Their instrumentation varies, however. Eisler became the first composer to use the speaking voice with an accompaniment reminiscent of *Pierrot*, but *Palmström* omitted the piano. Webern reduced Schoenberg's lop-sided chamber symphony from its fifteen-strong force (eight woodwinds, two horns, five strings) to what we should call a Pierrot quintet, that is, without *Pierrot*'s speaking voice and instrumental doubling. Within this moderately brief timeframe, then, to recognize a musical lineage derived from the instrumentation of *Pierrot lunaire* appears to cloud the definition of what constitutes a Pierrot ensemble once we go beyond Schoenberg's seminal work.

Of course, a more probing response to this issue calls for consideration of a far larger sample of prospective Pierrot ensembles, composed over a much wider period of time, than the few works which emanated from Schoenberg's circle. At the same time, it is clear that music written for conventional chamber-music groupings has become increasingly rare since the early twentieth century, and that the preference of composers for more colourful and heterogeneous types of ensemble has grown. Because of these tendencies, the Pierrot ensemble could be popular but never absolutely fixed – as we shall see, virtually all Pierrot ensembles deviate in some way from Schoenberg's prototype. This fact probably explains why the phrase 'Pierrot ensemble' has been used so rarely, and only ever informally, to describe either relevant musical works or the groups that perform them. Interrogate a composer or critic on the subject and they are much likelier to summon up memories of The Fires of London (1970-87), a group of musicians led by Peter Maxwell Davies dedicated to a blend of concert music and music theatre. No group did more to exploit and experiment with the resources of *Pierrot*'s line-up, it is true, yet even this version of history risks obscuring the achievements of its first incarnation: the Pierrot Players (1967-70), the brainchild of Harrison Birtwistle and the clarinettist Alan Hacker, and co-directed by Davies and Birtwistle. Writing over fifty works for the players at their disposal, these two British composers not only became the most important figures after Schoenberg to score Pierrot ensemble pieces, but also thereby laid the foundation for the considerable reputation they enjoy today.

The focus of this study lies with these two groups. To explain how their pride of place was earned, later chapters examine how they established themselves on the concert scene in the late 1960s and 1970s. This exposes a number of subordinate issues, from the maturity of Davies's style, through Birtwistle's influence in the 1960s, to their primary attraction to the Pierrot ensemble itself. Before this, the opening chapters outline the subject's rich background, as *Pierrot*'s colourful concert history reveals the circumstances under which it first reached and later returned to Britain. The Epilogue revisits this international context to assess The Fires of London's legacy, especially the reciprocal influence the group exerted abroad. An underlying object of the study as a whole, then, is to introduce the term 'Pierrot ensemble' into the lingua franca of music criticism. It will uncover a lineage from Schoenberg to Davies and Birtwistle and beyond to examine what the term can really mean.

In general, this calls for an explanation of how it is that a remarkable, British-led repertory, crowned by Davies's Eight Songs for a Mad King (1969) and Ave Maris Stella (1975), arose. In the first chapter, a more immediate subtext is that of genre. The Pierrot ensemble repertory vied for attention with melodrama, commedia dell'arte, music theatre and the song cycle as soon as Pierrot's first performances had taken place. As new works for Pierrot ensemble were written, issues of taxonomy join those of style and aesthetic in mapping the field. Documenting how and why Schoenberg invented, or stumbled across, his line-up therefore provides the backdrop to this study's most far-reaching aim: to unearth, list and scrutinize Pierrot's progenies, be they renowned (e.g. Davies's aforementioned works) or largely, and perhaps unfairly, forgotten (e.g. Birtwistle's works for the Pierrot Players). For all their fascination, Benjamin Britten's cinematic Pierrot ensembles for the British Commercial Gas Association (1936) still belong firmly to the latter category. Yet, the opening chapters establish a link between Pierrot's international reception and Britten's local use, which in turn instigates the Pierrot ensemble's influential association with film, a conflation of genres maintained by Eisler, Davies and others and traced accordingly.

Tales of the devotion of performers, conductors and administrators to Pierrot and the Pierrot ensemble also pervade this study. Another of its aims, then, is to record their effect, beginning with Schoenberg and Zehme and continuing with such exiled Austrian musicians as Erwin Stein and Peter Stadlen. From their collaborations with British musicians with far less experience of atonal and serial styles new issues arise, for instance how revisions to William Walton's Façade, when programmed next to Pierrot, compounded the cultural tensions of the two works' performance and reception. Stein's accomplishments as a concert organizer, performer, conductor, editor and author are also reflected in the work of the British composer Humphrey Searle, who was no less a polymath. His administrative support for mixed chamber music, including Elisabeth Lutyens's first work for Pierrot ensemble, Concertante for Five Players (1950), encourages their comparison. During the same decade, Davies was equally passionate in criticizing the moribund behaviour of British composers and educators, as he saw it.[12] Hence, studying the Pierrot ensemble also suggests a new perspective on the mid-century schism within British music-making, and one that implicates second-generation serialists such as Searle and Lutyens, as well as a new, brasher generation of composers.

Davies's frustrations were a factor in the decision to join the Pierrot Players. The study proceeds to explain how this group's distinctive, durable engagement between composers and performers was forged. The Pierrot ensemble was to become especially pronounced in Britain; its growing momentum in the second half of the twentieth century only fastened its ties between composition and concert life and composition. This engagement of theory and practice pre-dates the Pierrot Players' first concerts (e.g. through the 1964/65 Wardour Castle Summer Schools) but it helps explain how the group went on to present themselves in the way they did and reach a new generation of concertgoers. Its innovations in composition, performance and, indeed, ensemble management rightly inform our understanding of the Pierrot ensemble, as concert and reception histories will again show. Yet, the Pierrot Players' interpersonal complications prompt other questions, for example over Birtwistle's apparent difficulties 'breaking through' with the group, or how the co-directors' roles and relationship changed during the time they worked together. Birtwistle's decision to leave the group is another watershed, focussing our attention on the artistic direction of the 'new' Fires of London. What is immediately apparent is that Davies's composition for ever more variegated Pierrot ensembles in the late 1970s and early 1980s, coupled with the diminishing influence of *Pierrot* itself, had a direct impact on a medium his earlier works had done so much to evolve. The Epilogue therefore revisits this issue from the post-Fires perspective in an attempt to make sense of the Pierrot ensembles' modern-day appearance and appeal.

Notes

1   'Arnold Schönberg 1874-1951', *Music & Letters* 32/4 (1951), 305-23. The authors of letters that were printed – it is not said how many others were questioned – were John Amis, Felix Aprahamian, Arnold Bax, Arthur Bliss, Eric Blom, Adrian Boult, Mosco Carner, Winton Dean, George Dyson, Scott Goddard, Herbert Howells, Gordon Jacob, Ivor Keys, G.H.M. Lockhart, Edward Lockspeiser, William Mann, Norman del Mar, Wilfrid Mellers, Herbert Murrill, Rollo H. Myers, Edmund Rubbra, Marion M. Scott, Humphrey Searle, Ralph Vaughan Williams and Egon Wellesz.

2   The brevity of Vaughan Williams's reply might suggest neutrality – 'Schönberg meant nothing to me – but as he apparently meant a lot to a lot of other people I daresay it is all my own fault' – but its faint praise scarcely conceals the bewilderment of its author. *Ibid.*, 321.

3   In one of the earliest essays on Schoenberg to be published in English, Wellesz had said of *Pierrot*, '[never] before have such fantastically extravagant and such tragi-comic scenes found a cognate genius to translate them into music.'

Egon Wellesz, 'Schönberg and Beyond', trans. Otto Kinkeldey, *Musical Quarterly* 2/1 (January, 1916), 93.

4   'Arnold Schönberg 1874-1951', 307.

5   *Ibid.*, 306.

6   Original newspaper and journal reviews of twenty-four of *Pierrot*'s earliest performances in concerts around the world, including its Berlin premiere and Austro-German tour of 1912, are collected in *Dossier de Presse: Press-book de Pierrot lunaire d'Arnold Schönberg*, ed. François Lesure (Geneva: Minkoff, 1985), 34-93. See also Reinhold Brinkmann (ed.), *Arnold Schönberg: Sämtliche Werke, Melodramen und Lieder mit Instrumenten*, vol. 1, *Pierrot lunaire, Op. 21, Kritischer Bericht – Studien zur Genesis – Skizzen – Dokumente* (Mainz: Schott; Vienna: Universal, 1995), 234-98.

7   See David Metzer, 'The New York Reception of *Pierrot lunaire*: The 1923 Premiere and Its Aftermath', *Musical Quarterly* 78/4 (Winter, 1994), 669-99.

8   See Hans Heinz Stuckenschmidt, *Arnold Schoenberg: His Life, World and Work*, trans. Humphrey Searle (Eng. edn., London: Calder, 1977), 134-42, 212-15, *passim*.

9   James Huneker, 'Schoenberg, Musical Anarchist, who has Upset Europe', *New York Times* (19 January 1913), repr. in: Lesure (ed.), 19-20. These durable soundbites notified New Yorkers of *Pierrot*'s European performances, although more than a decade would pass before the work was performed in the United States.

10   Schoenberg's contract with Zehme is reproduced in Brinkmann (ed.), 227.

11   This number includes Zehme, the composer and Hermann Scherchen, co-conductor of the 1912 tour.

12   See Peter Maxwell Davies, 'The Young British Composer', *The Score and I.M.A. Magazine* 16 (March, 1956), 84-5.

1 *Pierrot lunaire*

Pierrot offers us the refraction of an 'aesthetic' sensibility, with the aesthete in question an anarchic surrealist, playing with menace ... Ninety years after its composition, [the piece] is a cultural, creative phenomenon which is not simply talked about but performed, a permanent feature of a musical landscape from which composers, musicologists – and even cultural historians – continue to take their bearings.[1]   ARNOLD WHITTALL

Now a century old, Arnold Schoenberg's *Pierrot lunaire* still matters tremendously. The excesses of its make-believe world could never fail to shock, such as when Pierrot acts the priest, serving his own heart for Communion in 'Rote Messe', or when he bores open Cassander's skull, smoking tobacco from it in 'Gemeinheit' five numbers later. No single feature of this bizarre and blackly comic work, however, can entirely explain its draw. Of course, the effect of its grotesqueries is dampened through its 'concert' presentation; theatrical, costumed performances, with the instrumentalists hidden behind a screen – the conditions of *Pierrot*'s premiere – are much rarer. Besides, *Pierrot*'s haunted, moonstruck journeys through fantasy, blasphemy, violence and nostalgia are appreciable, or endurable, only through ironic distancing on the listener's part. Schoenberg's oft-quoted description of *Pierrot*'s 'light, ironic-satirical tone' (*leichten, ironisch-satirischen Ton*) would otherwise be groundless.[2]

Scholarship on *Pierrot*'s legacy has instead navigated around several related areas. By far the most contentious is the speaking voice, specifically how to unravel the intricate performing instructions Schoenberg gave in the preface to his score (ex. 1.1): the classic conundrum is that his ideal *Sprechsängerin* 'gives the pitch but immediately leaves it again by falling or rising ... [being] very careful not to adopt a *singsong* way of speaking.'[3] The uncertainty over this no man's land between speech and song led Darius Milhaud to brand *Sprechstimme* a 'properly insoluble' problem.[4] Milhaud had special cause to comment, having played a significant role in *Pierrot*'s early performance history, at a time when Albertine Zehme, Erika Wagner, Marya Freund and other *Sprechsängerin* (and one *Sprechsänger*, Karl Geibel) were forging its traditions, reportedly in very different ways. Nor was the speaking voice future-proof: Walter Frisch observes that melodrama – speech over music – was to prove 'a dead end, or ancillary activity' for most German modernists,[5] and with it went *Pierrot*'s entwined generic types of expressionism and declamatory naturalism focussed by the *Sprechstimme*.

Under the cloud of Schoenberg's indeterminate *Sprechstimme*, music-ologists have done surprisingly little work on *Pierrot*'s musical language, much less its motivicism at the macro-structural level.[6] The speaking voice removed one barrier (of expression, making possible *Pierrot*'s hallucinatory theatre) only to erect another that would provoke critics and frustrate those attempting to make sense of the work's atonality. Its musical language is at least broadly consistent, from the moment the distinctive seven-note motif of 'Mondestrunken' is heard, to the wilfully vain attempt to impose E major on 'O alter Duft'. Better understood is Schoenberg's use of counterpoint to clarify his work's structure, be it the passacaglia of 'Nacht' or the brilliantly audible canons of 'Parodie'. Such allusions to order – texturally, atonally – inevitably bring to mind the 'breakthrough' Schoenberg was to achieve with the serial style towards the end of the decade. In *Pierrot*, though, the relevant subject is its aggregate 'decet',[7] and how its patchwork of variable solos, duos, trios, quartets, quintets, and sextets bring its new Pierrot ensemble to life. Example 1.2 illustrates how these forces permute across *Pierrot*'s twenty-one numbers and five transitional passages. By dividing the numbers in this manner, my example follows Jonathan Dunsby's method, with three minor adjustments.[8] Besides 'Valse de Chopin' and 'O alter Duft', then, there are two further occurrences of doubling within *Pierrot* than is commonly realized. Given Schoenberg's meticulousness, and how his instrumental 'patchwork' so openly delineates the piece, such details surely mattered: all three alternative instruments accompany the macabre scene of 'Rote Messe', for example.[9]

The next most important issue is the work's *commedia dell'arte* heritage, embodied in the collection of fifty poems by the Belgian poet Albert Giraud, known through Otto Erich Hartleben's translation, from which Schoenberg drew just twenty-one (three times seven).[10] Their seminal depiction of the white-clad Pierrot as a detached, moonstruck artiste rather than the usual butt of jokes inspired a related conclusion first proposed by Susan Youens: that *Pierrot* is a stylised self-portrait.[11] Certainly, the poems' continual switching between the first and third person helps explain its confusing narrative, as does Hartleben's updating of Giraud's tense from past to present. The claim that 'Schoenberg imposed a coherent structure on those poems he chose' is exaggerated, for *Pierrot*'s expressionist allure partly lies in loosely piecing together its dissociated images.[12] As such, it is the most famous of many modern works to cast the *commedia*'s stock characters musically: Ferruccio Busoni's opera *Arlecchino* (1914-16), Richard Strauss's hybrid *Ariadne auf Naxos* (1911-12, rev. 1916), and Igor Stravinsky's ballets *Petrushka* (1910-11) and *Pulcinella* (1919-20), both with several instrumental derivatives.[13]

No one would claim that *Pierrot* has a special hold over these works, save perhaps for *Arlecchino*, given the composers' friendship and Busoni's role in *Pierrot*'s early performance history. (Busoni hosted an important private performance of the work in June 1913.) Indeed, the search for a 'genre of *Pierrot*', as Dunsby has put it, is the least concrete context to date for discussion of *Pierrot*'s influence:

> *Pierrot* established chamber music as a genre independent of the ghost of Beethoven's string quartets. No-one, from Mendelssohn to Carter, Debussy and Schoenberg themselves included, ever really thought they could write a string quartet better than Beethoven did ... Many composers since 1912 have been convinced that they can write in the genre of *Pierrot*, approximately, and have tried, probably in the same spirit.[14]

Although Dunsby does not attempt to define *Pierrot*'s legacy, the important implication here is that the *accumulative* invention of its genre warrants a more thorough investigation. It surely does, despite the suspicions the term sometimes carries. To some, genre '[denies] the uniqueness of the text' under scrutiny, as David Duff explains,[15] or must otherwise be reconciled with a strain of twentieth-century creativity that sought to loosen, re-invent or simply neglect generic frameworks. *Pierrot* has it both ways: its oracular *Sprechstimme* and structure emasculate the song cycle; yet, its conflation of more particular genres (barcarolle, waltz, serenade, fugue, passacaglia, polka, nocturne, canon), themselves set in wider generic contexts (melodrama, tragicomedy), is a faultless model of what Marina Lobanova dubbed a 'mixed genre ... the main tendency in the twentieth century ... [and] an extremely dynamic phenomenon, because the type of combination, the possibility of including this or that genre molecule[,] could vary greatly depending on artistic conception or individual style.'[16]

At the same time, no composer has ever given the title Pierrot Ensemble No. 1 (or so forth) to their piece, so, in this sense, the Pierrot ensemble's conventions cannot be codified as we might expect. Nevertheless, dozens of composers have turned either to the line-up or to very close derivatives of it, suggesting, at least, that its taxonomy, while divisible into several subcategories, has undergone a century of formation, variation and continuation (see the catalogue of Pierrot ensembles that accompanies

Vorwort

Die in der Sprechstimme durch Noten angegebene Melodie ist (bis auf einzelne besonders bezeichnete Ausnahmen) nicht zum Singen bestimmt. Der Ausführende hat die Aufgabe, sie unter guter Berücksichtigung der vorgezeichneten Tonhöhen in eine Sprechmelodie umzuwandeln. Dies geschieht, indem er

I. den Rhythmus haarscharf so einhält, als ob er sänge, das heißt mit nicht mehr Freiheit, als er sich bei einer Gesangsmelodie gestatten dürfte;

II. sich des Unterschiedes zwischen Gesangston und Sprechton genau bewußt wird: der Gesangston hält die Tonhöhe unabänderlich fest, der Sprechton gibt sie zwar an, verläßt sie aber durch Fallen oder Steigen sofort wieder. Der Ausführende muß sich aber sehr davor hüten, in eine »singende« Sprechweise zu verfallen. Das ist absolut nicht gemeint. Es wird zwar keineswegs ein realistisch-natürliches Sprechen angestrebt. Im Gegenteil, der Unterschied zwischen gewöhnlichem und einem Sprechen, das in einer musikalischen Form mitwirkt, soll deutlich werden. Aber es darf auch nie an Gesang erinnern.

Im übrigen sei über die Ausführung folgendes gesagt:

Niemals haben die Ausführenden hier die Aufgabe, aus dem Sinn der Worte die Stimmung und den Charakter der einzelnen Stücke zu gestalten, sondern stets lediglich aus der Musik. Soweit dem Autor die tonmalerische Darstellung der im Text gegebenen Vorgänge und Gefühle wichtig war, findet sie sich ohnedies in der Musik. Wo der Ausführende sie vermißt, verzichte er darauf, etwas zu geben, was der Autor nicht gewollt hat. Er würde hier nicht geben, sondern nehmen.

Example 1.1   Arnold Schoenberg's Preface to Pierrot lunaire, *Op. 21*

this chronicle). Exploring genre from this broader perspective is less straightforward. Certainly, *Pierrot* helped define a new epoch in chamber music, but charting its attraction over several decades reveals a very chequered history. Barren periods existed when either *Pierrot* was not performed or no Pierrot ensemble pieces were composed. Other years see a new incarnation so momentous that subsequent Pierrot ensembles pay homage to the newer work. Such is the case with Peter Maxwell Davies's *Eight Songs for a Mad King* (1969), a music-theatrical panoply – of madness, mockery, multiphonics, and so on – that cast George III as the alienated protagonist (rather than Pierrot).

Yet, the *Eight Songs* are also something of an anomaly, given their *Sprechstimme*-inspired, expressionist debt to Schoenberg: as we shall see, other Pierrot ensembles cannot be traced back to *Pierrot* so easily. Conversely, of course, *Pierrot* does not always exemplify features that were to become typical of the 'class' of Pierrot ensembles. It is still a prototype, for the non-standard character of *Pierrot*'s line-up is reflected in certain works that

Preface

The melody indicated by the notes for the speaking voice is *not* (save for a few specifically marked exceptions) meant to be sung. The task of the performer is to transform it into a *speech-melody*, taking into account the given pitch. This is achieved by:

I. Observing the rhythms accurately, as if one were singing, i.e. with no more freedom than would be allowed with a sung melody;

II. Becoming fully aware of the difference between *singing tone* and *speaking tone*: the singing tone maintains the pitch; the speaking tone gives the pitch but immediately leaves it again by falling or rising. However, the performer must be very careful not to adopt a *singsong* way of speaking. That is absolutely not intended. In no way should one strive for realistic, natural speech. On the contrary, the difference between ordinary speaking and the kind of speaking involved in a musical form should become clear. But it must also never be reminiscent of singing.

Incidentally, I would like to make the following comment on the performance:

It is never the task of the performers to recreate the mood and character of the individual pieces out of the meaning of the words, but solely out of the music. The extent to which the tone-painterly representation of the text's events and emotions were important to the composer is found in the music already. Where the performer finds it lacking, they should refrain from presenting something the author did not intend. They would not be adding, but detracting.

emulate Schoenberg on one level, yet, typically, strive not to be rule-bound on another. This paradox naturally affects the reality of modern concert life – how to run a viable mixed ensemble along these lines, for example. Hence, this issue also becomes a question of reception on the part of the public and, indeed, composers. The friction between these two groups is hardly new, but it is apt that Elliott Carter, who Dunsby cites for his string quartets (but who also wrote the influential Pierrot ensemble *Triple Duo*), was to rail against a public and profession 'caught, almost frozen in the rigid patterns of older musical thought as well as by the physical conditions of music-making, antiquated instruments, inadequate concert-halls and standardized instrumental groupings.'[17]

Let us, then, briefly reconsider one such grouping: the string quartet. Dunsby draws it into open competition with Schoenberg's modern upstart, but was *Pierrot*'s legacy really compelling enough both to challenge that venerated genre and, probably, to create another? Certainly, the constancy of the string quartet came under threat in the early twentieth century, for

	Ss.	fl	pic	A-cl	Bb-cl	bcl	pf	vn	va	vc
1. Mondestrunken	✓	✓					✓	✓		✓
2. Colombine	✓	✓		✓			✓	✓		
3. Der Dandy	✓		✓	✓			✓			
4. Eine blasse Wäscherin	✓	✓		✓				✓		
5. Valse de Chopin	✓	✓		✓		✓	✓			
6. Madonna	✓	✓				✓	✓	✓		✓
7. Der kranke Mond	✓	✓								
8. Nacht (Passacaglia)	✓					✓	✓			✓
9. Gebet an Pierrot	✓			✓			✓			
10. Raub	✓	✓		✓				✓		✓
[Transition]							✓			
11. Rote Messe	✓		✓			✓	✓		✓	✓
12. Galgenlied	✓		✓						✓	✓
13. Enthauptung	✓					✓	✓		✓	✓
[Transition]		✓		✓		✓			✓	✓
14. Die Kreuze	✓	✓		✓			✓	✓		✓
15. Heimweh	✓			✓			✓	✓		
[Transition]			✓	✓			✓			✓
16. Gemeinheit	✓		✓	✓			✓	✓		✓
17. Parodie	✓	✓	✓	✓			✓		✓	
[Transition]							✓			
18. Der Mondfleck	✓		✓		✓		✓	✓		✓
19. Serenade	✓						✓			✓
[Transition]		✓		✓			✓	✓		✓
20. Heimfahrt (Barcarole)	✓	✓		✓			✓	✓		✓
21. O alter Duft	✓	✓	✓	✓		✓	✓	✓	✓	✓

Example 1.2   Vocal and Instrumental Specification of Schoenberg's Pierrot lunaire

which Schoenberg and his associates were again partly responsible. In 1908, Schoenberg's Second String Quartet, Op. 10, controversially added a soprano to the ensemble, and its composition was buoyed by the belated success of another relative of the string quartet, *Verklärte Nacht*, Op. 4, a chamber-music tone poem written less than a decade earlier for the Brahmsian ensemble of two violins, two violas and two cellos.[18] Instrumental modifications aside, the quartet's own lineage would soon include the quasi-operatic architecture of Alban Berg's once secretly autobiographical *Lyric Suite* (1925-26) and Alfredo Casella's *Concerto per due violini, viola e violoncello*, Op. 40 (1923-24), a lesser-known work but one premiered alongside *Pierrot* in Italy. Whereas the first work quotes Richard Wagner and Alexander Zemlinsky, the second largely eschews instrumental cooperation in favour of soloistic writing. The titles of both quartets also avoid reference to their nominal genre, Casella's pointedly so, and foreshadow greater challenges to it at the tail end of the century, such as Luigi Nono's radical *Fragmente-Stille, an Diotima* (1979-80) and Karlheinz Stockhausen's airborne *Helikopter-Streichquartett* (1993).

Unlike the Pierrot ensemble, however, the quartet is naturally not a modern phenomenon, which is where the destinies of the two ensembles differ most: performers obviously draw on a colossal, pre-modern body of repertoire for string quartet, too. Experiments to subvert its genre have nevertheless afforded the quartet a lineage that bears comparison with that of the multifigured Pierrot ensemble. The premiere of Casella's *Concerto* alongside *Pierrot* first demonstrated how the performance histories of the string quartet and Pierrot ensemble might collide, but the uneconomical use of players probably thwarted any regular such programming. More prescient, then, is the indebtedness to *Pierrot* of Casella's attempts to foist upon his instrumentalists a modern, soloistic style comparable to Schoenberg's – a relationship Schoenberg was later to criticize.[19] Although their disagreement was largely political, debating the thorny issue of national style, the aesthetics of the quartet and the Pierrot ensemble as competing mediums was a tacit factor. With its spread-out registers, the quartet's configuration shaped a history of harmonic and textural practice that has been revered for well over two hundred years. Less compatible with such qualities, the Pierrot ensemble effectively reprioritised the musical elements themselves: hence Schoenberg's emphasis on rhythm in the preface to the score, the estranging effect of his speaking voice on pitch, the primacy of contrapuntal forms, and the unprecedented way in which timbre plots the dramatic structure.

In *Pierrot*, the connective potential of these last characteristics – counterpoint and colour – atoned for the loss of tonal and cyclical organization. Put simply, *Pierrot*'s mixed timbres enhanced its linearity. The consequences of this 'new energy' for the Pierrot ensemble as an evolving medium are arguably even greater because, more so than the quartet, the line-up offered a new freedom of instrumentation in itself, within, and even between different pieces of music. These initial conclusions help explain why *Pierrot*'s legacy was so precious to Schoenberg, who felt various composers and performers had misunderstood his intentions. In a 1949 essay 'This is My Fault' he toed a revisionist line by conceding (albeit with some sarcasm) that his instruction to performers to separate the meaning of the text from the execution of the speaking voice was nonsensical.[20] Yet, his true targets were unnamed composers who responded to *Pierrot*, as he saw it, by seizing upon this controversial area to excuse the expressionless state of their music. Schoenberg's declared intention in *Pierrot* was to absorb into his music the expressive and illustrative qualities of the Giraud-Hartleben text; the points of disagreement in performance arise over his downplaying of actual pitch in favour of tone colour and the relation of the voice to the polyphonic fabric.

This is not to suggest, conversely, that *Pierrot* shoulders responsibility for all future examples of similar writing. Nor was it the sole inspiration behind the modern revival of mixed, *concertante*-type ensembles: the original version of Schoenberg's First Chamber Symphony is acclaimed for similar feats (though it is less demanding for performers); and the work written immediately prior to *Pierrot*, *Herzgewächse*, Op. 20, shares with its neighbouring opus an unconventionally 'doctored' voice – a coloratura soprano – and another unprecedented ensemble of celesta, harmonium and harp (though its timbres and tessitura are more integrated than those of the Pierrot ensemble). Nevertheless, some of the twentieth century's most celebrated works for voice and mixed ensemble have diverted attention from a stricter lineage of Pierrot ensembles. The early compositional responses to *Pierrot*, Stravinsky's *Three Japanese Lyrics* (1912-13), Maurice Ravel's *Chansons madécasses* (1925-26), Pierre Boulez's *Le Marteau sans maître* (1953-55, rev. 1957) and Davies's *Revelation and Fall* (1965-66) have each been heralded as their composer's most seminal answer to *Pierrot*.

On the other hand, certain more recent works have been written for Pierrot ensemble without their composers being especially aware of *Pierrot lunaire*. Michael Torke, who wrote two pieces for Pierrot ensemble while still a student, makes an aesthetically credible denial of ever having studied *Pierrot* before writing *Ceremony of Innocence* (1983) and *The Yellow Pages* (1985).[21] Similarly, just as Schoenberg's work reached the height of its popularity in Britain, David Bedford wrote several works for Pierrot ensemble, including *Music for Albion Moonlight* (1965) for soprano and a Pierrot quintet whose piano was not doubled but joined by an alto-melodica, and *The Sword of Orion* (1970), an instrumental work in which Bedford replaced the piano with thirty-two percussion instruments. Despite its ensemble, and the expressionist temperament of Kenneth Patchen's poems, the composer admits no relationship between *Music for Albion Moonlight* and *Pierrot*.[22] And, remarkably, Judith Weir claims never to have heard *Pierrot lunaire* before completing her first work for Pierrot ensemble, *King Harald Sails to Byzantium* (1979).[23]

These cases, and others, query the Pierrot ensemble's more recent history. If not through *Pierrot*, how did the composers come to write for their respective ensembles? Is *Pierrot* really as dissociated, aesthetically or timbrally, from their works as they suppose? Only by tracing each work's context within the lineage can we properly answer these questions. Encouragingly, another writer has homed in on the origins of such problems. Glenn Watkins expresses surprise at the eclecticism of compositional responses to *Pierrot*, and questions what their (purportedly) elevated popularity means for the standing of Schoenberg's work:

> ... recognition that the *Pierrot* legacy found a larger audience in works by other composers than did the original itself forces consideration of the surprising degree to which this 'unloved' masterpiece served as a kind of authority figure for composers of vastly differing orientations over the remainder of the twentieth century.[24]

It is improbable that even the cumulative might of works in *Pierrot*'s shadow is really so potent that it outstrips their progenitor. It is also tenable that *Pierrot* should be held dear by such Schoenbergian descendants as Boulez and Davies, yet should remain 'unloved' or, indeed, barely known by other later composers.

This is also true of composers of works for Pierrot ensemble that exhibit little or no aesthetic adherence to *Pierrot*. But Davies, too, is a composer to whom we must look carefully when evaluating a likely 'rupture' in the lineage of Pierrot ensembles: he not only wrote dozens of such works, but also commissioned from his followers and contemporaries many more. If *Pierrot* is 'eclipsed' by even a fraction of these, a compliment is paid to Schoenberg nonetheless: their very being testifies to the power of the model. Questions of taxonomy persist, but even when a succession of Pierrot ensembles leads down an apparent cul-de-sac that loses sight of *Pierrot*, this universality endures, perhaps unknowingly for some composers. Torke, for example, was unapologetic about designing his two Pierrot ensembles to reach a mass audience. Over and above the works' post-minimalist language, this aim gelled with his impression of the similar line-ups he chose: that they were 'very common, easily assembled and so playable everywhere.'[25]

Circumstances were quite different for the previous generation of composers. Greater dedication was required to sustain the medium, and even this did not guarantee success. Birtwistle's departure from the Pierrot

Players in late 1970, for example, left Davies to write the bulk of Pierrot ensembles for The Fires of London over the next two decades. Despite their similar Lancastrian upbringings, Davies's youthful zest for composition contrasted with Birtwistle's more circuitous route to his eventual, full-time vocation: Birtwistle was principally a clarinettist until gradually, towards the end of the 1950s, composition prevailed. Had the pair not been the same age, certain suspicions that surfaced in the late 1960s citing Birtwistle's alleged inexperience might have appeared baseless.[26] Instead, such responses warrant further attention in part because they are symptomatic of the Pierrot Players' exceptional group dynamic. There are several conceivable reasons for Birtwistle's decision to leave, most of which the composers are unwilling to discuss. But at least one of these centres on his limited success within the group, which, given his co-leading role as composer, conductor, artistic director and commissioner, deserves to be reappraised. Ironically, Davies's sole leadership of The Fires of London would test the Pierrot ensemble's generic recognition more sternly. His first concert work for them, *From Stone to Thorn* (1971), cast aside the flute, violin and cello but introduced two timbral anomalies which, by now, were less unusual: a harpsichord, preferred to the piano, and a guitar – the latter redolent of *Serenade*, Op. 24 (1920-23), another of Schoenberg's works for mixed chamber ensemble.

Schoenberg's commitment to his Pierrot ensemble, a thirty-year association that stretched from the earliest, rigorous rehearsals of *Pierrot* to his recording of the work in 1942, is underrated. But his emigration to the United States distanced him from all but three players with whom he had performed the work. Coupled with his disinclination to repeat himself by composing for the Pierrot ensemble ever again, these circumstances meant his attachment to the ensemble was fleeting. By contrast, The Fires' pattern of engagement between composers, performers and composer-performers (and vice versa) was astonishingly durable and arguably more typical of the customs of popular music. So significant were their achievements that Birtwistle and Davies are usually cited as the original British composers to react to Pierrot. In fact, as we have already seen, the first British reaction came in an earlier generation still. For the British Commercial Gas Association, a young Benjamin Britten used instrumentation derived closely from *Pierrot*, and touched on problems in film composition that would not resurface, nor be studied in detail, until the composition of Eisler's second Pierrot ensemble, *Vierzehn Arten den Regen zu beschreiben*, Op. 70 (1940-41), also for a film (*Regen*, 1929). Because modern appreciation of this musico-cinematic heritage is scarce enough even today, most of its works remain unpublished and unacknowledged. Yet, their composition again exemplifies how *Pierrot*'s performance history elicited responses from composers: it is no coincidence that Britten's work closely followed two of its British performances in 1930 and 1933. Likewise, the British lineage of Pierrot ensembles from Britten to Birtwistle and Davies is much more diverse than might be imagined: Thea Musgrave, Bedford and, as mentioned, Lutyens each penned Pierrot ensemble pieces in the interim, as its growth became inexorable.

Pierrot may not have reached Britain until 1923, but this does not compare unfavourably with the United States, France, Italy or Spain. Germany might be considered the ensemble's natural home, as host to *Pierrot*'s first tour and birthplace to notable Pierrot ensemble composers such as Eisler and Hans Werner Henze. Yet, *Vierzehn Arten...* was written while the composer was exiled in the United States and Henze's *Der langwierige Weg in die Wohnung der Natascha Ungeheuer* (1971) and *Sonate für sechs Spieler* (1984) were respectively first recorded and performed by The Fires of London. Indeed, the group's bearing on the norms of domestic concert life tells only half the story: Birtwistle and Davies began to develop the Pierrot Players' international standing almost as soon as they founded the group – hence a work such as Franco Donatoni's *etwas ruhiger im Ausdruck* (1967) could receive its British premiere in the year it was written. Birtwistle's rapport with Morton Feldman later tempted the American to write *the viola in my life* (1970) for Pierrot ensemble.[27] The Fires' international stature also grew significantly, as they toured Australia and the Americas and collaborated with the likes of Carter, Peter Sculthorpe and others. Their works, together with those of Feldman, Henze, Michael Finnissy and dozens of others, attest to the ensemble's authority.

The Pierrot ensemble thus continued to stride the international stage decades after *Pierrot* had received its series of national premieres. The prolific success of the Pierrot Players and The Fires of London set a new benchmark by which the 'genre of *Pierrot*' would be understood. If they had a blind spot, it was to omit from their repertoire works written by their near contemporaries such as Lutyens and Musgrave – the group's tendency to commission younger composers and international figures precluded such obvious programming – plus most works written before 1967 except *Pierrot* itself and Webern's aforementioned chamber-symphonic transcription. As a 'personality'-driven group, rather than another of the 1960s 'repertoire' ensembles such as the Nash Ensemble (1964-) and the London Sinfonietta (1968-), the Pierrot Players under Birtwistle and Davies nonetheless showcased an ample variety of idioms in their programmes. *Pierrot lunaire*, their catalyst, has been freighted with all kinds of meanings by composers, performers, administrators, musicologists and critics. From a prototype already famed for its innovations in the fields of expressionism, instrumentation, music theatre, vocalisation and satire, a lineage of Pierrot ensembles of comparable multiformity was spawned. To trace its beginnings is to discover an unexpectedly rich context.

Notes

1   Arnold Whittall, '*Pierrot* in Context: *Pierrot* as Context' in: *Pierrot Lunaire: Albert Giraud – Otto Erich Hartleben – Arnold Schoenberg: A Collection of Musicological and Literary Studies*, ed. Mark Delaere and Jan Herman (Louvain: Peeters, 2004), 44-5.

2   Arnold Schoenberg, letter to Fritz Stiedry (31 August 1940), quoted in Reinhold Brinkmann, 'The Fool as Paradigm: Schönberg's Pierrot Lunaire and the Modern Artist' in: *Schönberg and Kandinsky: An Historic Encounter*, ed. Konrad Boehmer (Amsterdam: Harwood, 1997), 148.

3   '[*Der Sprechton*] *gibt sie zwar an, verläßt sie aber durch Fallen oder Steigen sofort wieder … [wobei müßte er sich] sehr davon hüten, in eine »singende« Sprechweise zu verfallen.*' Arnold Schoenberg, 'Vorwort' to *Pierrot lunaire* (Universal, 1914); emphasis his.

4   Darius Milhaud, *My Happy Life* (1974), trans. Donald Evans, George Hall and Christopher Palmer (Eng. edn., London and New York: Boyars, 1995), 111.

5   See Walter Frisch, *German Modernism: Music and the Arts* (Berkeley and Los Angeles: University of California Press, 2005), 59.

6   For a glimpse of how such analysis might be undertaken, see Jonathan Dunsby, 'Schoenberg's Pierrot Keeping his *Kopfmotiv*' in: *Pierrot Lunaire: Albert Giraud – Otto Erich Hartleben – Arnold Schoenberg: A Collection of Musicological and Literary Studies*, ed. Mark Delaere and Jan Herman (Louvain: Peeters, 2004), 67-76. See also Phyllis Bryn-Julson and Paul Mathews, *Inside Pierrot lunaire: Performing the Sprechstimme in Schoenberg's Masterpiece* (Lanham: Scarecrow Press, 2009), 98-100.

7   That is, including the *Sprechstimme* and counting the A- and B♭-clarinets separately, even though the latter is used just once, in 'Der Mondfleck'.

8   The second 'Transition' doubles the clarinet and bass clarinet, the third 'Transition' does not employ the violin, and 'Parodie' calls for the piccolo *and* flute (Schoenberg's published list of forces also omits the flute here). See Jonathan Dunsby, *Schoenberg: Pierrot lunaire* (Cambridge: Cambridge University Press, 1992), 23.

9   Often cited for its uniqueness, this 'reversal' of timbre in fact recurs at the end of 'O alter duft', so connecting the eleventh (middle) and twenty-first (final) numbers. One of Schoenberg's pupils gives evidence of his precision when considering the permutations available to him: '[Schoenberg] thinks it a good idea to list combinations … and thus have a better conception of your variety of resources. That is what he did for the instrumentation of *Pierrot Lunaire* and as a result in all the twenty-one pieces there is only one duplication of combination [by which Newlin means 'Die Kreuze' and 'Heimfahrt'].' Dika Newlin, *Schoenberg Remembered: Diaries and Recollections (1938-76)* (New York: Pendragon, 1980), 186-87.

10   Schoenberg's full title, once *Pierrot lunaire* was published, was *Dreimal sieben Gedichte aus Albert Girauds Pierrot Lunaire*.

11   See Susan Youens, 'Excavating an Allegory: The Text of *Pierrot Lunaire*', *Journal of the Arnold Schoenberg Institute* 8/2 (November, 1984), 96ff.

12 *Ibid.*, 96. In a similar vein, Richard Kurth has recently sought to refine Youens's hypothesis: '[The] sense of disorientation [in *Pierrot*] arises first from the discontinuous contrasts between the many black and white Pierrots that swerve through the poems, representing the obsessions of the modern psyche generally, not just the delusions of a single individual artist.' Richard Kurth, '*Pierrot lunaire*: Persona, Voice, and the Fabric of Allusion' in: *The Cambridge Companion to Schoenberg*, ed. Jennifer Shaw and Joseph Auner (Cambridge: Cambridge University Press, 2010), 123.

13 See Martin Burgess and John Swan, *The Triumph of Pierrot: The Commedia dell'Arte and the Modern Imagination* (New York: Macmillan, 1986), 195-232.

14 Jonathan Dunsby, *Schoenberg: Pierrot lunaire*, 75.

15 David Duff, *Modern Genre Theory* (Harlow: Longman, 2000), 1.

16 Marina Lobanova, *Musical Style and Genre: History and Modernity* (1979), trans. Kate Cook (Amsterdam: Harwood Academic Publishers, 2000), 174.

17 Elliott Carter, 'For Pierre on His Sixtieth' in: *Pierre Boulez: eine Festschrift zum 60. Geburtstag am 26. März 1985*, ed. Josef Häusler (Vienna: Universal Edition, 1985), 12.

18 Several composers had already written for this symmetrical, bass-heavy sextet: Luigi Boccherini and Louis Spohr, innovators of eighteenth- and nineteenth-century chamber music respectively, were two such exponents. More relevant to Schoenberg's *fin de siècle* example was Johannes Brahms's use of the same medium twice a generation earlier (Opp. 18 and 36). I have written about this in 'Zemlinsky's Surface Structures: *Maiblumen blühten überall* and the String Sextet Genre' in: *Zemlinsky Studies*, ed. Michael Frith (London: Middlesex University Press, 2007), 77-87.

19 See Arnold Schoenberg, '"Fascism is No Article of Exportation"' (c. 1935) in: Joseph Auner (ed.), *A Schoenberg Reader: Documents of a Life* (New Haven and London: Yale University Press, 2003), 268-75. See also Chapter 2, note 52.

20 See Arnold Schoenberg, 'This is My Fault' (1949) in: *Style and Idea*, ed. Leonard Stein, trans. Leo Black (3rd edn., London: Faber, 1984), 145-47.

21 Michael Torke, email communication with the author, 5 February 2004. For Torke, the pared-down Pierrot quintet of *The Yellow Pages* (1985) was a capricious choice – 'that cluster of instruments … seemed everywhere in the mid eighties' – which simply amplified his colourful, post-minimalist lacework. The work was so popular in the United States that *The Blue* and *The White Pages* were commissioned by Present Music, creating *The Telephone Book* (1985/95), replete with piccolo and bass clarinet alongside their doubling instruments.

22 David Bedford, interview with the author, 17 December 2004, excerpt quoted below:

CD In conversation with Cornelius Cardew [cf. *Musical Times*, 107/1477 (1966), 198-202], you strongly criticized the 'unadventurousness' of the contemporary music scene…

DB Yes, in those days there were only a couple of chamber groups who played contemporary music, but of course, thankfully, there are many more now.

CD Was it this conviction that led you to pursue different types of chamber groups at this time, especially those that seem to adapt the forces of Schoenberg's *Pierrot lunaire* (*Music for Albion Moonlight*, *A Horse, His Name was Hunry Fenceweaver Walkins* [1972], *The Sword of Orion*…)?

DB I included a melodica [in *Music for Albion Moonlight*] because I was teaching in schools at the time and I quite liked the sounds it made: an unusual sound between a harmonica and mouth organ, but slightly electronic, too. The work has expressionist elements – the singer screams into the piano on one occasion – but on the other hand there's no relationship with *Pierrot*, because it's not composed as rigorously and doesn't 'spot' the instruments of the ensemble in Schoenberg's clever way.

23   Judith Weir, roundtable discussion with Anthony Payne, Christopher Wintle, Julian Jacobson and Peter Maxwell Davies, held during a conference on '*Pierrot lunaire* and Its Legacy', 2 March 2006, Kingston University, London. The conference was convened by the singer Jane Manning who subsequently published her research into performing the lead role in *Pierrot Lunaire* as: *Voicing Pierrot* (Amarro, Australia, Southern Voices, 2012).

24   Glenn Watkins, *Pyramids at the Louvre: Music, Culture, and Collage from Stravinsky to the Postmodernists* (Cambridge, Mass. and London: Harvard University Press, 1994), 307.

25   Michael Torke, *op. cit.*

26   The reception of Birtwistle's works for Pierrot ensemble is a topic of Chapters 7 and 8.

27   Birtwistle had left the Pierrot Players before the work was premiered, but his departure did not jeopardize this fruitful Anglo-American relationship: Feldman wrote two more works for The Fires, *the viola in my life (2)* (1970) and *For Frank O'Hara* (1973).

2 The First Pierrot Ensembles

Arnold Schoenberg as Conductor and Composer

The first tour of Schoenberg's *Pierrot lunaire* in 1912 was a brilliant advertisement for the work and its composer. Framed by performances in Berlin, it stopped at thirteen other major cities in Germany and Austria (ex. 2.1-3), with news of the events reaching across Europe and the United States.[1] With Schoenberg listed among the touring party as conductor and composer, *Pierrot*'s earliest performances established him as a figurehead for progressive contemporary music. This was not the first time Schoenberg had stepped onto the podium to conduct his own work: since dallying with cabaret at Ernst von Wolzogen's Überbrettl Theater in 1901, he had taken *Pelleas und Melisande*, Op. 5, to audiences in Vienna, Berlin and Prague. His music had also caused controversy before, as reactions to the Five Orchestral Pieces, Op. 16, premiered in London only a month before *Pierrot*'s first tour, back through to the First Chamber Symphony, Op. 9, Second String Quartet, Op. 10, and, earlier still, *Verklärte Nacht*, Op. 4, attest.[2]

The premiere of *Pierrot lunaire* was different. Remembered as one of the century's seminal concerts, it was a *succès de scandale* that now ranks alongside the premiere of Igor Stravinsky's *Le Sacre du printemps*, held in Paris just seven months later. Only through their reception did these events come to be recognized as milestones, but *Pierrot*'s subsequent tours in the early 1920s (aided by its more portable ensemble) were unique. Its immediate reputation went before it so dramatically that even those still to hear the work were spurred into action: within months of *Pierrot*'s first tour Maurice Ravel had breathlessly lobbied the *Société de Musique Indépendante* (SMI) to support his 'stupendous project for a scandalous concert' to grant a French premiere to the 'work for which blood is flowing in Germany and Austria'.[3] Hyperbole did not help Ravel's cause: the premiere of *Le Sacre* gave Parisians their chance to rebel, but the still unpublished *Pierrot* would not arrive there for another decade.

Rather, Schoenberg and Albertine Zehme, the work's patron and original reciter, were the first driving forces behind *Pierrot*'s dissemination. A year

16 October 1912, 8pm –
Choralionsaal, Konzert-Bureau Emil Gutmann, Bellvuestrasse, Berlin

Arnold Schoenberg
"Lieder des Pierrot Lunaire" *
(Albert Giraud, trans. Otto Erich Hartleben), Op. 21 (1912) WP‡

Albertine Zehme (*Sprechsängerin*), Arnold Schoenberg (conductor)

Ensemble †

FLUTE / PICCOLO Hendrick W. de Vries	VIOLIN / VIOLA Jakob Maliniak
CLARINET / BASS CLARINET Karl Essberger	CELLO Hans Kindler
PIANO Eduard [Edward] Steuermann	

---

* "Lieder des Pierrot lunaire" was the advertised title. The more familiar *Dreimal sieben Gedichte aus Albert Girauds* Pierrot Lunaire was used when the work was published by Universal Edition in July 1914.
† Various reviews of the time refer to the performers as The 'Pierrot Lunaire' Ensemble, although there is no evidence that Schoenberg or his musicians used this title formally.
‡ WP signifies a world premiere.

Example 2.1   World Premiere of Schoenberg's Pierrot lunaire, *Op. 21*

earlier, Zehme had toured Germany singing Otto Vrieslander's *Lied* version of *Pierrot lunaire* (1904). The experience inspired her to tour again and to commission Schoenberg to set Albert Giraud's cycle in a different way. Schoenberg's Pierrot ensemble took shape gradually, however. Edward Steuermann, the pianist with Schoenberg's ensemble and several others thereafter, told of being given the manuscript of 'Gebet an Pierrot', the first number Schoenberg finished, to rehearse alone with Zehme.[4] Only halfway through sketching 'Mondestrunken', *Pierrot*'s opening number but the fifth to be composed, was the cello added.[5] For Schoenberg to include his own instrument (the cello) – first sketched beneath the word '*Dichter*', as Reinhold Brinkmann has outlined – gave further credence to *Pierrot*'s oft-discussed allegory.[6] Yet, it also reveals the first Pierrot ensemble to have grown from an intimate relationship with the text, rather than from some preconceived idea. Notably, this was not the case with *Pierrot*'s genre of melodrama, nor, consequently, its use of *Sprechstimme*, of which Anton Webern and Alban Berg were aware in the month before Schoenberg began the work.[7] Schoenberg had not yet breached the terms of his commission,

Example 2.2 The 'Pierrot Lunaire' Ensemble,
pictured in the Choralionsaal, Konzert-Bureau Emil Gutmann, Berlin
(left to right: Karl Essberger, Jakob Maliniak, Arnold Schoenberg,
Albertine Zehme, Edward Steuermann, Hans Kindler, Hendrick W. de Vries).

which called for 'piano accompaniment, possibly with accompaniment of two further instruments.'[8] But as staves for flute and piccolo, clarinet and bass clarinet, and violin and viola were added, he was obliged to approach Zehme to 'gradually encourage her to add one, two, three and finally four other instrumentalists, which she generously accepted.'[9]

Neither Schoenberg nor Zehme had originally planned for Hermann Scherchen, then only twenty-one, to make his debut co-directing *Pierrot*. Zehme funded the instrumentalists and took some responsibility for their recruitment. For the position of violinist/violist she sought Georg Göhler's advice. The Leipzig conductor recommended Scherchen and, on Zehme's behalf, invited him to join the ensemble. Inspecting the parts for violin, viola and, incidentally, *Sprechstimme*, Scherchen felt unable to take on such a virtuosic and prominent role.[10] Göhler also hoped Scherchen might help Zehme enlist *Pierrot*'s other players, and this led Scherchen to suggest that his friend, Jakob Maliniak, might suit the part. Reluctant not to participate in the project in some way, Scherchen asked to attend *Pierrot*'s rehearsals. Zehme agreed on both fronts.

Date	City	Conductor
16 October	Berlin (see ex. 2.1-2)	Schoenberg
19 October	Hamburg*	Schoenberg
24 October	Dresden	Schoenberg
25 October	Stettin	Schoenberg
28 October	Danzig	Scherchen
31 October	Breslau	Schoenberg
2 November	Vienna	Schoenberg
5 November	Munich	Scherchen
11 November	Stuttgart	Scherchen
14 November	Karlsrühe	Scherchen
15 November	Mannheim	Scherchen
17 November	Frankfurt	Scherchen
22 November	Graz	Scherchen
23 November	Leipzig	Schoenberg
1 December	Berlin	Scherchen
8 December	Berlin†	Schoenberg

*Notable members of the audiences included * Richard Dehmel, Otto Klemperer and † Igor Stravinsky. Schoenberg's proposal to share conducting duties with Hermann Scherchen is confirmed by a letter to Alban Berg (3 October 1912). The letter is reprinted in Joseph Auner (ed.), A Schoenberg Reader: Documents of a Life (New Haven and London: Yale University Press, 2003), 116. Scherchen (accurately) recalls how he was asked to direct around half of the performances on the tour. An early proposal would have seen Schoenberg and Scherchen strictly alternate their appearances. See Hermann Scherchen, Werke und Briefe, ed. Joachim Lucchesi (Berlin: Lang, 1991), 165. In the event, this was impractical since Schoenberg was absent from the tour for much of November, conducting the Concertgebouw Orchestra in their performances of his symphonic poem Pelleas und Melisande, Op. 5 on the 28th (Amsterdam) and 30th (The Hague).*

Example 2.3   *The First Tour of* Pierrot lunaire *(16 October to 8 December 1912)*

From then on, Scherchen witnessed Schoenberg coaching the ensemble at Zehme's home in Berlin's Zehlendorf district. When, one day, Schoenberg was too ill to coach his five costly musicians, Maliniak was asked to deputize.[11] He declined, and instead repaid the favour by nominating Scherchen, who had sat studying *Pierrot*'s score. Later, with the tour already planned but with Schoenberg hesitant to commit to it entirely, Scherchen was promoted to ensemble co-director.[12] At only twenty, another young musician, the Dutch-born Hans Kindler, was the group's cellist. Despite their low average age, and our ignorance of the professional expertise of the flautist Hendrick de Vries and violinist Maliniak,[13] this was no amateur ensemble: like the clarinettist Karl Essberger, Kindler had been hand-picked from one of the city's top orchestras (the Staatsoper and Berlin Philharmonic respectively); Steuermann's recruitment sprang from his introduction to Schoenberg some months earlier by Ferruccio Busoni, who gave Steuermann lessons on the piano and, later, in composition.[14]

As Zehme's coach before the premiere, Steuermann was an important intermediary between Schoenberg and the actress-cum-singer. Moreover, he left an outspoken account of how Zehme interpreted her part, recalling her 'strange idea [to identify] herself with the character of Pierrot'.[15] The suggestion is odd not because of the theatricality it implies – although Zehme's exaggerated onstage actions also caused some disquiet – rather because in composing the work, Schoenberg actually undermined the dramatic role of the speaking voice: first, his version of *Pierrot lunaire* was abridged, setting only twenty-one of Giraud's fifty poems and excluding the last, 'Cristal de Bohême' ('Böhmischer Krystall'), in which the poet reveals himself as Pierrot; second, Schoenberg re-ordered these to create his celebrated *dreimal sieben* (three times seven) structure, creating a narrative which is teleologically ambiguous at best; and third, in Otto Erich Hartleben's vivid translation, certain poems make first- and third-person references to other *commedia dell'arte* characters such as Harlequin, Colombine and Cassander. These are all poetic functions from which Zehme's more straightforward, overstated empathy with Pierrot was thought to detract.

Pierrot's Progenies?

Stravinsky was one of Zehme's fiercest critics. Two musical tours converged on Berlin in late 1912 as the Ballets Russes brought *Petrushka* to German audiences and *Pierrot* came full circle, returning to its original venue for two concerts held a week apart. The coincidence drew Stravinsky and Schoenberg together. It was the only time they were to meet. They also heard each other's music live, reportedly thanks to Serge Diaghilev: Schoenberg saw *Petrushka* on 4 December and Stravinsky attended a matinée of *Pierrot* four days later. These were historic, if fleeting, events; the composers' duopoly of modern music would ensue through their stubborn independence. Yet, from its 'instrumental substance' to the 'whole contrapuntal and polyphonic structure of this brilliant *instrumental* masterpiece', *Pierrot* apparently impressed Stravinsky greatly.[16] He was far less enamoured with Zehme:

> [She] accompanied her epiglottal sounds with a small amount of pantomime ... I was concentrating too closely on the copy of a score Schoenberg had given me to notice anything else ... I wanted Frau Zehme to be quiet ... so that I could hear the *music*.[17]

Its significance is disputed, but Stravinsky had already interrupted his composition of *Le Sacre* and within five months would complete his *Three Japanese Lyrics* with scoring which 'looks, and sometimes sounds, very like Schoenberg's': soprano, two flutes (one doubling piccolo), two clarinets (one doubling bass clarinet), piano and string quartet.[18]

Stravinsky was also one of the first commentators to speculate that *Pierrot* might one day be performed without its controversial speaking voice:

> I seem to remember having expressed the opinion [to Alma Mahler-Werfel] that *Pierrot lunaire* should be recorded without voice so that the record buyer could add the ululations himself [*sic*], a 'do-it-yourself' record.[19]

The ambition was realized, in concert if not on record, at Hans Keller's suggestion in 1969.[20] If Stravinsky's idea came with a characteristic air of mischief, then it is a clue that some of his criticisms of *Pierrot* were more strategic than others, and that his take on the rise of mixed ensembles in the early twentieth century was distinct from Schoenberg's. *The Soldier's Tale* (1918) would soon be scored for another small group of instruments, but, as much inspired by jazz as curbed by shoestring economics, its solo-instrumental style still invites comparisons with *Pierrot*'s.

Where the *Three Japanese Lyrics* had augmented the Pierrot ensemble, the later work's septet of clarinet, bassoon, cornet, trombone, violin, double bass and percussion was a better match for the *kleines Kammerorchester* label under which *Pierrot* had been speciously advertised in Berlin. This distinction is crucial, circumstantially and aesthetically. Once Stravinsky had inspired Ravel during their joint residence by Lake Geneva to write his *Trois poèmes de Stéphane Mallarmé* (1913) for the same line-up as his *Japanese Lyrics*, the newer, larger ensemble had a companion that pushed *Pierrot* into the margins. After all, Ravel knew of Schoenberg's work only through Stravinsky's memory. Ravel's emulation painted a very different picture of a putative lineage of Pierrot ensembles to that which we appreciate today. And when his plan to have the three works performed together collapsed, omitting only *Pierrot*, the division between the histories of the two ensembles was sealed.

Nationalist tensions that enveloped the three composers influenced the reception of their works; such were the divisions along Franco-Russian and Austro-German lines at the time. Certainly, this may help to explain Pierre Boulez's scornful attitude towards his compatriot's efforts in the otherwise popular *Trois poèmes*:

> ... even in the writing for instruments, the influence of *Pierrot lunaire* goes little further than the nomenclature, for if the use

> Schoenberg makes of the various elements – which he *chose* –
> derives from a need to express himself contrapuntally, that is from
> the individualizing of each instrumental component, Ravel uses
> the same formation – to some extent imposed on him – as a kind
> of restrained orchestra.[21]

The vision of a miniature orchestra again looms large here, and it is true that Ravel's adherence to traditional, familial units in his 'orchestration' was at odds with Schoenberg's unparalleled mixture of timbres as exhibited in *Pierrot*'s aggregate line-up and within each of its numbers. Nor was Boulez the first to commend Schoenberg's counterpoint and to correlate it with *Pierrot*'s unique ensemble.[22]

On the other hand, Boulez looked to debunk the 'mythology of renewal which crystallized around *Pierrot*', citing Ravel's 'harmonic misunderstanding' – as much a reference to his aping of various styles in the final setting, 'Surgi de la croupe et du bond', as to the more general differences between Ravel and Schoenberg.[23] This critique preceded *Le Marteau sans maître*, Boulez's own response to *Pierrot*. That he invented for this work a peculiar mirror image of the Pierrot ensemble (contralto, alto flute, guitar, xylorimba, vibraphone and viola) is one giveaway. His censure of *Pierrot*'s instrumental 'physicality' and its perceived disservice to Giraud's (not Hartleben's) verse is another. Because of their works' shared origins in the French language, this poetic aspect re-invokes the issue of national sensibility. Relatedly, Roger Marsh has recently argued for Giraud's text to be rehabilitated and has set all fifty *rondels bergamasques* in *Albert Giraud's Pierrot lunaire* (2002-06), a work that is by turn choral, orchestral and narrative.[24] Marsh's view bucks a dominant trend in *Pierrot*'s reception: even Schoenberg thought Giraud's text was 'scurrilous'.[25] Dunsby and Susan Youens followed suit, the latter citing Hartleben's 'immeasurably better' text to help expose *Pierrot*'s allegory.[26]

Hanns Eisler went even further, deriding Giraud's *Pierrot* as a 'weak copy of Verlaine by a third-class Belgian poet.'[27] Whatever the merits of these Symbolist originals, Eisler's outlook is significant because of his earlier composition of *Palmström*, Op. 5 for *Sprechstimme*, flute doubling piccolo, clarinet in A, violin doubling viola, and cello (ex. 2.4). It is ironic nonetheless that *Palmström*, commissioned by Schoenberg and 'obediently' subtitled *Studien über Zwölfton-Reihen*, should have taken its cue from Christian Morgenstern's anti-scholastic verse, itself inspired by English nonsense rhyme. Also rejecting the piano (the main protagonist in Schoenberg's melodramas), and both the florid and contemplative qualities of *Pierrot*'s expressionism, Eisler wrote a set of five coherently structured miniatures to match Morgenstern's wit. Every number except the third, 'L'art pout l'art'

	Ss.	fl	pic	A-cl	vn	va	vc
Venus Palmström	✓	✓		✓	✓		✓
Notturno	✓	✓		✓		✓	✓
L'art pour l'art	✓		✓	✓	✓		
Galgenbruders Frühlingslied	✓	✓	✓	✓	✓		✓
Couplet von der Tapetenblume	✓	✓		✓	✓		✓

Example 2.4   *Vocal and Instrumental Specification of Hanns Eisler's* Palmström, Op. 5

* Eisler: 'Als Couplet, wie im Kabaret vorzutragen: halb singend'

Example 2.5   *Hanns Eisler,* Palmström, V. 'Couplet von der Tapetenblume', *bars 6-15* (without cello), requires the whole group to perform; only in the fourth, 'Galgenbruders Frühlingslied', does a player 'double up' (flute and piccolo). Moreover, Eisler's instruction to the *Sprechsängerin* to 'half sing' the finale, 'Couplet von der Tapetenblume' (ex. 2.5), is a clear, probably satirical reference to Schoenberg's warning to avoid a 'singsong' manner in *Pierrot lunaire*.

The loose serial style and cabaret parody of this same number have also encouraged a familiar-sounding autobiographical interpretation of what Eisler meant by *Palmström*: the unruly pupil/autocratic teacher tension is especially popular as a portent of the real rift between the composers in the 1930s.[28] What Schoenberg made of *Palmström* is not known. Whether it was actually performed alongside *Pierrot* is also unclear.[29] We do know that Eisler, who was too young to have witnessed the 1912 tour, first heard *Pierrot* in 1921, probably in Vienna at the *Verein für musikalische Privataufführungen*.[30] Indeed, the detachment of *Pierrot lunaire* from Ravel, Stravinsky and others in the 1910s foreshadowed many of its first performances outside Austria and Germany in the following decade, giving rise to works such as Eisler's and, ultimately, a more credible, recognizable lineage of Pierrot ensembles.

Pierrot's Premieres and Revivals, 1921-25

At the beginning of the 1920s, *Pierrot* had not been heard anywhere since the outbreak of war. Given the voguish spectre of neo-Classicism and Schoenberg's decision not to publish from 1913 to 1923, these circumstances challenge the idea that '*Pierrot*'s place in the canon of modernist artworks has never been at risk.'[31] Schoenberg was also acutely wary of how and when *Pierrot* was performed, discouraging Alexander Siloti from performing it in St Petersburg (which did not happen) and more angrily refusing Edgard Varèse's proposal to give an American premiere (which went ahead anyway).[32] Yet *Pierrot*'s notoriety in the early 1920s brought with it a following that translated into premieres – and, more than once, speedy revivals and tours – not only in the United States, but also in the Netherlands, Czechoslovakia, France, Belgium, Great Britain, Italy and Spain (ex. 2.5). Although some recordings of *Pierrot* last barely half an hour,[33] on the 1912 tour it was performed alone with intermissions between its three parts. This befitted the semi-theatrical character of each event, with Zehme's white costume and make-up, her reported physical gestures, and her separation from the screened-off instrumentalists.[34] But as further performances took place, other works were programmed alongside *Pierrot*, whether to acknowledge the country in which the concert was being held (hence the premiere of Alfredo Casella's Op. 40 in Italy) or to represent better the breadth of Schoenberg's repertoire with works of equally challenging musical language but less notoriety.

This story of some of *Pierrot*'s earliest performances, from its first tour to those of the interwar period, is remarkable for the variety of performing styles that were adopted and the patchy reception history it reflects. Its trajectory is significant enough to our understanding of *Pierrot*'s performance and criticism, but after the realization that the work need not stand alone in concert, composers and concert programmers were encouraged to experiment. Inevitably, these fields coalesce since *Pierrot* attracted a cluster of composer-conductors and performer-theorists. Along with Scherchen and Steuermann, two of the earliest to be drawn to the work were Erwin Stein, its conductor at the *Verein für musikalische Privataufführungen* in Vienna and Prague (1921-22) and again in London in the 1930s, and Louis Fleury, its flautist in Paris and London without Schoenberg (1922-23) then across Italy with the composer at the helm (1924). Each musician, Fleury especially, chronicled their own experiences and those of their audiences and fellow performers:

> When we were applauded it was with some diffidence, and when we were hissed there was always an emphatic opposition camp … the only thing that no one thought of "Pierrot Lunaire" was that it was insignificant.[35]

Across cities, countries and continents, a cycle of anticipation and reaction was born that shaped *Pierrot* as a divisive yet momentous work. Stein and Scherchen, both members of Schoenberg's circle, fed this frenzy. In different countries, both musicians wrote articles excitedly previewing revivals of *Pierrot* to be performed under their direction.[36]

Several of the personnel of Pierrot ensembles in the 1920s travelled widely for its promotion, none more so than Steuermann, who returned for its 'Verein' performances and the Italian tour. But Stein did most to spark *Pierrot*'s revival. Made director of the *Verein für musikalische Privataufführungen* in 1921, he oversaw three *außerordentlicher Vereinsabend* performances of *Pierrot* in eight days in April and May. The work appeared relatively late in the history of the society (which was founded in 1918) because Schoenberg was loath to be seen to promote his own works, although he did twice conduct *Pierrot* after Stein in Vienna. Most memorable of these was the final concert in that city's series. However, the first time Schoenberg revisited *Pierrot*, in Concert 99, marked another notable revival: Webern's *Sechs Stücke für großes Orchester*, Op. 6, whose arrangement by the composer for flute doubling piccolo, oboe, clarinet doubling bass clarinet, string quintet, percussion, piano and harmonium had already been premiered by the *Verein*. (Interestingly, nowhere in the literature is an oboist for this concert listed, and only cues – not parts – for cello and double bass are extant.) Its significance lies in being one of approximately twenty-five works

Concerts 95-99

Festsaal der Schwarzwaldschen Schulanstalten, Nibelungengasse, Vienna
Saturday, 30 April 1921 Concert 95 †
Tuesday, 3 May 1921 Concert 97 †
Saturday, 7 May 1921 Concert 98 †
Thursday, 12 May 1921 Concert 99 ‡

Concert 113 (*final* Verein *concert in Vienna*)

Festsaal des Ingenieur- und Architektenvereins (IAV),
Eschenbachgasse, Vienna
Monday, 5 December 1921 Concert 113 ‡

Pierrot was performed alone in Concerts 95, 97, 98 and 113. Anton Webern's chamber-ensemble arrangement of his *Sechs Stücke für großes Orchester*, Op. 6 (1909, arr. 1920) introduced Concert 99. The numbering of concerts in Vienna follows Szmolyan's comprehensive list of *Verein* events held there. See Walter Szmolyan, 'Die Konzerte des Wiener Schönberg-Vereins' in: *Schönbergs Verein für musikalische Privataufführungen (Musikkonzepte* 36), ed. Heinz-Klaus Metzger and Rainer Riehn (Munich: Text und Kritik, 1984), 101-14. Ivan Vojtěch catalogues the Prague concerts in Metzger and Riehn (eds.), 115-18.

Saturday, 25 May 1922 – Mozarteum, Prague

Concert 1 (*first* Verein *concert in Prague*)

Claude Debussy
Sonata for Violoncello and Piano (1915)

Arnold Schoenberg
Pierrot lunaire (Albert Giraud, trans. Otto Erich Hartleben), Op. 21 ‡

Erika [von] Wagner (*Sprechsängerin*),
Erwin Stein († conductor), Arnold Schoenberg (‡ conductor)

Ensemble

FLUTE / PICCOLO Franz Wangler	PIANO Eduard [Edward] Steuermann
CLARINET / BASS CLARINET	VIOLIN / VIOLA Rudolf Kolisch
Viktor [Victor] Polatschek	CELLO Wilhelm Winkler

Example 2.6   Notable Performances of Pierrot lunaire, *1921-25*
(i) Vienna and Prague

16 January 1922, 9pm – Salle Gaveau, 45 Rue la Boétie, Paris

3ème Concert Jean Wiéner

Arnold Schoenberg
Pierrot lunaire (Albert Giraud, trans. Otto Erich Hartleben,
re-trans. Jacques Benoist-Méchin), Op. 21

Marya Freund (*Sprechsängerin*), Darius Milhaud (conductor)

FLUTE / PICCOLO Louis Fleury   VIOLIN / VIOLA Alexandre Roëlens
CLARINET / BASS CLARINET Henri Delacroix   CELLO Louis Feuillard
PIANO Jean Wiéner

*At the previous concert in the series (15 December 1921) Milhaud's ensemble played the first part of
Pierrot (and repeated it at the end of the evening). The same players also performed Pierrot at the
'4ème Concert Jean Wiéner' on 10 March 1922.*

---

19 November 1923, 8.30pm – Kensington Town Hall, London

Federation of Music Clubs Concert
(Kensington New Music Club)

Robert Schumann
Four Songs from *Liederkreis*, Op. 39 (1840) †
Leonardo Vinci
Sonata in D Major for Flute and Basso Continuo (c. 1715) ‡
Arnold Schoenberg
Pierrot lunaire (Albert Giraud, trans. O.E. Hartleben,
re-trans. Jacques Benoist-Méchin), Op. 21 ‡

Marya Freund (‡ *Sprechsängerin* / † soprano)
Darius Milhaud (conductor)

FLUTE / PICCOLO Louis Fleury ‡   VIOLIN / VIOLA H. Denayer
CLARINET / BASS CLARINET Henri Delacroix   CELLO Paul Mas
PIANO Jean Wiéner † ‡

Example 2.6   (ii) Paris and (iii) London

4 February 1923 – Klaw Theater, New York

International Composers' Guild

Charles Koechlin
Sonata pour deux flutes, Op. 75 (1920)
Erik Satie
Sports et divertissements (1914)
Darius Milhaud
Three Numbers from *Saudades do Brazil*, Op. 67 (1920)
Arnold Schoenberg
Pierrot lunaire (Albert Giraud, trans. O.E. Hartleben), Op. 21 ‡

Greta Torpadie (*Sprechsängerin*) ‡, Louis Gruenberg (conductor)

FLUTE / PICCOLO George R. Possell	PIANOS LeRoy B. Shield [Shields],
FLUTE II Sarah Possell	E. Robert Schmitz
CLARINET / BASS CLARINET Robert Lindemann	VIOLIN Jacob Mestechkin
[Lindeman]	CELLO William Durieux

---

28 March 1924 – Accademia di Santa Cecilia, Rome

Corporazione delle Nuove Musiche

Alfredo Casella
Concerto per due violini, viola e violoncello, Op. 40 (1924) WP †
Arnold Schoenberg
Pierrot lunaire (Albert Giraud, trans. O.E. Hartleben), Op. 21 ‡

Erika Wagner (‡ *Sprechsängerin*), Arnold Schoenberg (‡ conductor)

FLUTE / PICCOLO Louis Fleury	VIOLIN (I in †, absent in ‡) Alphonse Onnou
CLARINET / BASS CLARINET Henry Delacroix	VIOLIN (II in †, soloist in ‡) Laurent Halleux
PIANO Edward Steuermann	VIOLA Germain Prévost
	CELLO Roberto Maas

The same performers toured Italy hereafter: Rome (28-29 March), Naples (30 March), Florence (1 April),
Venice (3 April), Padua (5 April), Milan (7 April), Turin (8 April).

Example 2.6 (iv) New York and (v) Rome

29 April 1925 – Palau de la Música Catalana, Barcelona

Festival de la Musica Viennesa,
presented by the Associació de Música de Camara

Arnold Schoenberg, arr. Anton Webern
Chamber Symphony No. 1, Op. 9 (1906, arr. for Pierrot ensemble 1922-23) *WP*
Arnold Schoenberg
Acht Lieder, Op. 6, Nos. 4, 8, 1, 6 only (1903-05) NP* †
'Verlassen', 'Der Wanderer', 'Traumleben', 'Am Wegrand'
Pierrot lunaire (Albert Giraud, trans. Otto Erich Hartleben), Op. 21 NP ‡

Marya Freund (‡ *Sprechsängerin* / † soprano),
Arnold Schoenberg (conductor)

FLUTE (‡ / PICCOLO) Franz Wangler   PIANO Friedrich Wüllner †
CLARINET (‡ / BASS CLARINET) Viktor Polatschek   VIOLIN Rudolf Kolisch
                                             CELLO Joachim Stutschewsky

*   NP signifies a national premiere.

Example 2.6   (vi) Barcelona

that various composers arranged for the society.[37] It also demonstrates how a *solistischer Instrumentation* aesthetic, epitomized by *Pierrot*, held sway over the society's domesticated orchestra.

After Vienna, *Pierrot* was scheduled to inaugurate the society's next incarnation under Alexander Zemlinsky's aegis in Prague. *Pierrot* also played a defining role on the programmes of several international concert-giving societies and associations besides Schoenberg's. Varèse co-founded the International Composers' Guild (ICG), the body responsible for the American premiere, after hearing a private performance in Berlin; Casella, himself a member of the ICG, brought *Pierrot* to Italy and with it launched the *Corporazione delle Nuove Musiche*; Roberto Gerhard arranged in 1925 for the *Associació de Música de Camara* to stage a *Festival de la Musica Viennesa*; and during the third of the *Concerts Jean Wiéner*, another advocate of soloistic instrumentation in a chamber setting, Darius Milhaud, directed the French premiere with the first ensemble not to be supervised by Schoenberg. No British musician with the same will to promote *Pierrot* could yet be added to the list: according to Elisabeth Lutyens, her husband Edward Clark had observed its rehearsals under Schoenberg and Scherchen in Berlin,[38] but tried in vain to arrange a British performance in the 1920s; and the political turmoil that brought to Britain sympathizers such as Gerhard, Egon Wellesz and Mátyás Seiber was still a decade away. The trend of touring *Pierrot* reached Britain only after Milhaud brought across most of the players that had given the French and Belgian premieres in 1922. Hence the Federation of Music Clubs hosted *Pierrot*'s British premiere in Kensington Town Hall on 19 November 1923, the start of a brief, localised run of concerts across three London districts that took in Westminster (St John's Institute) and Chelsea (Town Hall).

With a fourteen-strong membership from the central London area and local regions, the Federation of Music Clubs had been formed not long before this premiere. It was devoted neither to chamber music nor to contemporary music exclusively, but, in decentralizing musical events, the Federation did improve the conditions of music-making by enabling works to be repeated. The same links between efficiency and standards in performance – especially for new music, the cost of preparation of which might be prohibitive for single performances – had driven the forty rehearsals purported to have been held before *Pierrot*'s first tour.[39] Moreover, contemporary news on how *Pierrot* was greeted in London suggests little sign of outcry. Had the discord provoked elsewhere been brought to a halt? Fleury offers a comparison of his performance under Milhaud in Paris with London's apparently greater appreciation:

> What an impressive calm! How unexpected this inward peace after our stormy meetings at Paris! … [Our audiences] never blenched. They sat there, calm as a boxer who takes punishment with a smile.[40]

Uniquely, *Pierrot* was now heard against a more pleasing backdrop of older music.[41] This apparent reaction (or lack of) should not imply that London's concert-goers were really so progressively minded as to accept the work unreservedly, although the French connections behind these performances offer clues as to why the work's arrival on British shores was received with acquiescence, if not euphoria.

Save for the identity of the string players, the same ensemble had performed *Pierrot* in Paris and Brussels, and their approach to the work was reportedly very different from that ordained by Schoenberg. Another of Fleury's comments, for example, echoes a sentiment Schoenberg would express directly to their ensemble's *Sprechsängerin*, Marya Freund, disclosing that, 'excellent singer that she is, [Freund] cannot quite forget that she is a singer.'[42] Such a performance would certainly have been more palatable than the impenetrable *Sprechstimme* some might have been led to expect.[43] Sung or otherwise, a performance in French marked another departure from

Schoenberg. Freund did not opt for Giraud's original text, but instead used Jacques Benoist-Méchin's (re)translation of Hartleben's German-language version upon which Schoenberg had based his version of *Pierrot lunaire*. Unlike their British counterparts, Parisians heard the work in their mother tongue. It would be ironic if the immediacy in hearing a text permeated with religious imagery and described by some as sacrilegious had provoked audiences more easily. Despite English translations being printed in programmes for two of the London concerts (Westminster was the exception), the distinction is not unthinkable.

Word of Freund's performances was enough to convince Schoenberg that the Polish-born soprano had crossed a line:

> I am anxious to explain to you why I cannot allow any will but mine to prevail in realizing the musical thoughts that I have recorded on paper, and why realizing them must be done in such deadly earnest, with such inexorable severity, because the composing was done just that way.[44]

Freund was no stranger to Schoenberg's music, having sung the Wood-Dove at the February 1913 premiere of the *Gurrelieder* (1900-11), his first work to make use of *Sprechstimme*. The significant difference is that Schoenberg had personally coached the Burgtheater singer and actress Erika Wagner for her *Verein* performances of *Pierrot*. Surprisingly, perhaps, Schoenberg waited eighteenth months to write to Freund: on 10 February 1923 he had witnessed a unique triple performance of *Pierrot* featuring her at the home of their mutual friend, Alma Mahler. *Pierrot* was played first by Stein's ensemble with Wagner, then by Milhaud et al. Alma Mahler wrote:

> To me, two entirely different works seemed to be played on that evening. Schönberg himself hardly recognized his own in Milhaud's conception – which was favoured, however, by a majority of the audience. Schönberg's rhythmicized version of accentuated speech was unquestionably more original as well as, of course, more authentic; in the sung one it was much more noticeable where he had been leaning on Debussy and others. The small orchestra's performance in my room was very effective, and some eighty persons listened with more or less of an effort to the austere wonders of atonality.[45]

As an 'objective yardstick', Steuermann also premiered Stein's piano-duet transcription of *Pierrot* with a young Francis Poulenc, whom Milhaud had invited.[46]

The genesis of *Pierrot*'s American premiere, coincidentally staged six days before this 'triple billing', owed much to its *first* private performance, which was held in Busoni's flat on 17 June 1913.[47] Varèse, who had resided in Berlin since 1907, and, probably, Louis Gruenberg, an American pupil of Busoni, joined there an audience of luminaries that included the pianist Artur Schnabel, violinist Arrigo Serato and violist Egon Kenton.[48] The New York-based International Composers' Guild was launched eight years later as the response of Varèse and a fellow French-born émigré, Carlos Salzedo, to other 'musician cooperatives' such as the *Verein für musikalische Privataufführungen*. Within months, Varèse enlisted Gruenberg to conduct a Pierrot ensemble headed by the Swedish-American singer Greta Torpadie (ex. 2.7). Her performance, ceremonially robed not in white but in black, was so positively received among ICG members that the idea to programme *Pierrot* again was mooted, contradicting a bylaw in the society's charter which disallowed repeat performances. The well-documented fallout from this affair brought into being a rival League of Composers and led Torpadie to resume her role as *Sprechsängerin* alongside Howard Barlow and members of the New York Symphony Orchestra and Chamber Music Art Society on 22 February 1925.[49]

George Gershwin's attendance of this performance garnered much attention, though *Pierrot*'s American premiere drew the more stellar audience, counting Milhaud, Georges Enescu, Leopold Stokowski, Willem Mengelberg and Casella among its number. Stokowski would conduct the next American performance in 1933, but in founding the *Corporazione delle Nuove Musiche* with his *generazione dell'Ottanta* peers Francesco Malipiero and Ildebrando Pizzetti, Casella was quickest to respond to Varèse and Schoenberg.[50] Casella had previously headed the short-lived *Società Italiana di Musica Moderna* (1917-19), and now committed himself to organize *Pierrot*'s Italian premiere and to compose a piece to be heard alongside Schoenberg's: the aforementioned *Concerto per due violini, viola e violoncello*, Op. 40. Thus the first national premiere of *Pierrot* was arranged in which music by a composer from the host country was also heard. Earlier premieres, though not America's 'unauthorized' event, influenced Italy's 'composite' Pierrot ensemble: Fleury and Henri Delacroix, the winds in Paris and London, joined Steuermann and Wagner, by now veterans of *Pierrot*, and the Belgian newcomers, but modern music specialists, the Pro Arte String Quartet.

Conducted by Schoenberg on his first visit to Italy, the Rome premiere on 28 March 1924 introduced an eight-date national tour. The Florentine leg was to prove especially memorable as Giacomo Puccini and Luigi Dallapiccola, the old and new faces of Italian music, travelled to hear *Pierrot*. Puccini's presence especially touched Schoenberg, though no one, understandably, noticed the twenty-year-old Dallapiccola.[51] Some critics were quick to dismiss Schoenberg's melodramas as failing by the revered standards of Italian drama; Casella even pitched in along similar lines, hypothesizing how Schoenberg's art, 'so alien to our [Italian] temperament', faced an 'unbridgeable chasm' – a prelude to a quarrel between the two.[52] Another 'first' of *Pierrot*'s reception in Italy was to indicate how the subject of dodecaphony would colour press coverage of Schoenberg's earlier, atonal works. ('My tonality uses twelve notes instead of seven' was his pointedly simple reply.)[53]

Schoenberg fared better when, twelve months after the Italian tour, *Pierrot* reached Spain. The Catalan composer Roberto Gerhard organized its Barcelona premiere for 29 April 1925, only eighteen months after pleading with Schoenberg for lessons, so becoming his only Spanish pupil.[54] Having compromised in Italy, Schoenberg now reassumed control to direct musicians derived mostly from his and Stein's '*Verein*' Pierrot ensembles. Joachim Stutschewsky replaced Wilhelm Winkler as cellist since the erstwhile *Verein*'s string players had by now formed the Wiener Streichquartett (later known as the Kolisch Quartet). The quartet travelled as one to Spain because their violist and second violinist were also needed to help premiere Schoenberg's entertaining arrangement for flute, clarinet, string quartet and piano of Johann Strauss II's *Kaiser-Walzer*, Op. 437. Although this was designed for the *Festival de la Musica Viennesa* in which the similarly scored *Pierrot* was performed, it is unclear whether the works were heard in the same concert. The programme omits to list either the novelty (though it could feasibly have been an encore) or even the concert's individual performers.

We can at least positively trace Schoenberg's inspiration to 27 May 1921, when the second of the *Verein*'s 'Series B' concerts took place. Schoenberg, Berg and Webern had specially arranged four Strauss waltzes for the evening, though as the concert was a fundraiser for the Society, the harmonium (played by Berg) replaced the winds.[55] Aesthetically, the claim on Schoenberg's bigger *Kaiser-Walzer* arrangement is that its transparency, texturally, is what shapes its 'unblended' modernity.[56] On another arrangement that certainly was heard in Barcelona alongside *Pierrot* and, indeed, was scored for Pierrot ensemble, there are different circumstances to consider. Schoenberg invited Webern to transcribe his Op. 9 *Kammersymphonie* for Pierrot ensemble in 1922, long before the Spanish premiere and, conceivably, for it to be performed in Prague.[57] But there, and earlier in Vienna, the prevailing creative rationale for arranging *new* music was to lay bare the musical values 'beneath' its surface. Webern, especially, was answering criticisms of his alleged over-reliance on striking instrumentation, hence the arrangement of his own Op. 6. Publicly, outside the *Verein*, he followed a similar path by opting to arrange Schoenberg's work for a pared-down Pierrot quintet of

*Example 2.7   The First American Pierrot Ensemble, Klaw Theater, New York
(left to right: LeRoy B. Shield, Greta Torpadie, Jacob Mestechkin,
William Durieux, Louis Gruenberg, Robert Lindemann, George R. Possell)*

flute, clarinet, piano, violin and cello. The original – unlike Strauss's already an 'unblended' work – was certainly left in a more transparent state. Yet, its durable, polyphonic values, which had pleased Schoenberg so in the original, were heightened to the extent that the quintet still required a conductor. Thus Schoenberg and Webern had conspired to initiate a Pierrot-ensemble lineage, just as Schoenberg reasserted his management of *Pierrot*'s performing tradition. This reciprocal pattern of performance and composition would continue but, decisively, something changed: as the permanence of *Pierrot* grew ever more apparent, its ensemble became an attractive option for composers outside Schoenberg's circle to emulate.

Notes

1   See François Lesure (ed.), *Dossier de Presse: Press-book de Pierrot lunaire d'Arnold Schönberg* (Geneva: Minkoff, 1985), 3-45.

2   Schoenberg was famously impatient with his critics, especially in Vienna. Scoring *Verklärte Nacht* for string sextet was a novelty in a city where chamber music was a hallowed tradition, but Schoenberg's memory of a Viennese concert society singling out one chord – bars 41 and 42 – for their refusal to present the work was typically acerbic: 'In my Sextet ... I wrote the inversion of a ninth chord ... without then knowing theoretically what I was doing ... What's worse, I see now that it is none other than that particular inversion which the theorist condemned most resolutely [that the ninth in the bass resolves most simply to a 'forbidden' octave] ... Only now do I understand the objection, at that time beyond my comprehension, of that concert society ... Naturally: inversions of ninth chords simply do not exist; hence, no performance, either, for how can one perform something that does not exist?!' Arnold Schoenberg, *Theory of Harmony* (*Harmonielehre*, 1911), trans. Roy E. Carter (London: Faber, 1978), 345-46.

3   Ravel's designs were even grander than they first appear. His concert, which went ahead without *Pierrot* in January 1914, would originally have included 'pieces for (a) narrator; (b) and (c) voice and: piano, string quartet, 2 flutes, and 2 clarinets.' Ravel admitted that this configuration was a clear vehicle for Stravinsky's *Three Japanese Lyrics* and his own *Trois poèmes de Stéphane Mallarmé* – '(b) and (c)' respectively – both of which augmented *Pierrot*'s line-up and were composed in its immediate aftermath. Maurice Ravel, letter to Alfredo Casella (2 April 1913) in: *A Ravel Reader: Correspondence, Articles, Interviews*, ed. Arbie Orenstein (2nd edn., Minneola, New York: Dover, 2003), 135-36.

4   See Gunther Schuller and Edward Steuermann, 'A Conversation with Steuermann' (20 May 1964), *Perspectives of New Music* 3/1 (Autumn-Winter, 1964), 23.

5   See Reinhold Brinkmann, 'What the Sources Tell Us ... A Chapter of *Pierrot* Philology', *Journal of the Arnold Schoenberg Institute* 10/1 (June, 1987), 11-27.

6   See Chapter 1, notes 11-12.

7   See Reinhold Brinkmann (ed.), *Arnold Schönberg: Sämtliche Werke, Melodramen und Lieder mit Instrumenten*, vol. 1, *Pierrot lunaire, Op. 21, Kritischer Bericht – Studien zur Genesis – Skizzen – Dokumente* (Mainz: Schott; Vienna: Universal, 1995), 225. Translated, part of Webern's letter to Berg (11 February 1912) reads: '[Schoenberg] is writing ... melodramatic music to poems, which [Zehme] recites. Sch. said he had been thinking about something like this for a long time.'

8   '... *Klavierbegleitung, eventuell mit Begleitung von zwei weiteren Instrumenten.*' *Ibid.*, 227.

9   Arnold Schoenberg, letter to Josef Rufer (25 July 1949), *ibid.*, 304. The full quotation reads: '*Sie wollte anfänglich auch, dass ich es für Klavier schriebe, aber ich bestimmte sie nach und nach eins, zwei[,] drei und schliesslich vier Instrumentalisten dazu zu fügen, was sie grosszügigenweise akzeptierte.*'

10   See Hermann Scherchen, *Aus Meinem Leben Rußland in Jenen Jahren: Erinnerungen*, ed. Eberhardt Klemm (Berlin: Henschelverlag Kunst und Gesellschaft, 1984), 32. Unlike Scherchen, Maliniak's principal instrument was violin, not viola. Although his performances were criticized in some reviews, no one suggests he played less convincingly on viola than violin. Whatever inequality there was would have been less exposed than had Scherchen played, since the violin is by far the busier of the two instruments in *Pierrot*. (They are used seventeen and four times respectively.)

11   The full costs are unknown, but Zehme had agreed to pay two of the musicians, Essberger and de Vries, 70DM per engagement. See Zehme's letter (n.d.) to Schoenberg in Reinhold Brinkmann, *Arnold Schönberg: Sämtliche Werke, Melodramen und Lieder mit Instrumenten*, vol. 1, *Pierrot lunaire, Op. 21, Kritischer Bericht – Studien zur Genesis – Skizzen – Dokumente* (Mainz: Schott; Vienna: Universal, 1995), 239.

12   For a more detailed account of this story, see Scherchen, 31-4.

13   We do know Maliniak had led the Blüthner Orchestra, the semi-professional outfit that counted Scherchen among its number and with which Alexander Zemlinsky, Schoenberg and others had cut their teeth in the 1890s. See Edward Steuermann, 'Pierrot lunaire in Retrospect' (1963), *Journal of the Arnold Schoenberg Institute* 2/1 (October, 1977), 50.

14   None of the three mentions exactly when this first encounter occurred, though Steuermann points to the months either side of 1911/12. See Schuller and Steuermann, 22.

15   *Ibid.*, 23.

16   Igor Stravinsky and Robert Craft, *Conversations* (London: Faber, 1958), 228; emphasis added.

17   *Ibid.*, 69; emphasis his.

18   Stephen Walsh, *Stravinsky: A Creative Spring – Russia and France 1882-1934* (London: Pimlico, 1999), 190. Before Stravinsky heard *Pierrot*, the first lyric, 'Akahito', was complete in its original guise for voice and piano, and a projected instrumentation was sketched. Stravinsky added clarinets and reduced the number of violas from two upon his return from Berlin. Richard Taruskin detects greater significance in the second and third lyrics, 'Mazatsumi' and 'Tsaraiuki', and their shift from octatonicism to a more atonal domain. More convincing is Stravinsky's post-*Pierrot* 'general inclination toward spare linearity' ('Mazatsumi', especially, is noticeably soloistic in its conception) in spite of his 'shade more opulent' ensemble. Richard Taruskin, *Stravinsky and the Russian Traditions: A Biography of the Works through Mavra*, 2 vols. (London: Oxford University Press, 1996), vol. 1, 834. Similar textures on a far greater scale in *Le Sacre du printemps* have overshadowed the impression Schoenberg's 'instrumental substance' made. Taruskin, 824.

19   Igor Stravinsky and Robert Craft, *Memories and Commentaries* (London: Faber, 2002), 224.

20   See Hans Keller, 'Arrangement For or Against?', *Musical Times* 110/1511 (January, 1969), 22-5. Britain's Vesuvius Ensemble gave this performance on 20 January 1969 at the Queen Elizabeth Hall.

21   Pierre Boulez, 'Trajectories: Ravel, Stravinsky, Schoenberg' (1949) in: *Stocktakings from an Apprenticeship*, trans. Stephen Walsh (Eng. edn., Oxford: Clarendon, 1991), 191; emphasis his.

22   See Egon Wellesz, 'Schönberg and Beyond', trans. Otto Kinkeldey, *Musical Quarterly* 2/1 (January, 1916), 93.

23   Boulez, 192, 188.

24   Marsh's piece (released 2007, cat. NMC D127) also sets Kay Bourlier's new English translation, sometimes simultaneously with Giraud's text. See also Roger Marsh, '"A Multicoloured Alphabet": Rediscovering Albert Giraud's *Pierrot Lunaire*', *Twentieth-Century Music* 4 (2007), 97-121.

25   Schuller and Steuermann, 24.

26   See Dunsby, 21 and Youens, 103.

27   Hanns Eisler, paper delivered at the Deutsche Akademie der Künste, Berlin, 1954; repr. as 'Arnold Schoenberg', trans. Karin von Abrams in: *Hanns Eisler: A Miscellany*, ed. David Blake (Luxembourg: Harwood, 1995), 179.

28   See, for example, David Blake, 'The Early Music' in: Blake (ed.), 28.

29   Eisler barely mentioned his formative work in his prolific writings, but he did acknowledge Schoenberg's commission: '[*Meine*] *ersten Studien über «Zwölfton-Reihen»* [*habe ich*] *auf Anregungen Schönbergs im Jahre 1925 geschreiben.*' Hanns Eisler, 'Präludium und Fuge über B-A-C-H (mit 12 Tönen)' (1936) in: *Musik und Politik: Schriften 1924-1948*, 2 vols., ed. Günter Mayer (Leipzig: VEB Deutscher Verlag für Musik, 1973), vol. 1, 380. *Palmström*'s date of composition has since been revised to 1924. See Manfred Grabs, *Hanns Eisler: Kompositionen, Schriften, Literatur: Ein Handbuch* (Leipzig: VEB Deutscher Verlag für Musik, 1984), 134. Grabs could not identify the date of its first performance, however. See note 57.

30   See Hanns Eisler, interview with Nathan Notowicz, quoted in: Jürgen Schebera, *Hanns Eisler: Eine Biographie in Texten, Bildern und Dokumenten* (Mainz: Schott, 1998), 31.

31   Richard Kurth, '*Pierrot*'s Cave: Representation, Reverberation, Radiance' in: *Schoenberg and Words: The Modernist Years*, ed. Charlotte M. Cross and Russell A. Berman (New York and London: Garland, 2000), 203.

32   See Arnold Schoenberg, letters to Alexander Siloti (15 June 1914) and Edgard Varèse (23 October 1922) respectively in: *Letters*, ed. Erwin Stein, trans. Eithne Wilkins and Ernst Kaiser (Eng. edn., London: Faber, 1964), 51-2, 78-9.

33   The norm is between 33 and 35 minutes. The briefest official recording to date, at 30' 15", was released by Erika Sziklay with the Budapest Chamber Ensemble under András Mihály (Hungaroton, SLPX 11385, 1971).

34   See Schuller and Steuermann, 23.

35   See Louis Fleury, 'About "Pierrot Lunaire": The Impressions Made on Various Audiences by a Novel Work', trans. Arthur H. Fox Strangways, *Music & Letters* 5/4 (October, 1924), 348.

36   See Hermann Scherchen, 'Pierrot lunaire', *Neue Zeitung* (27 March 1922), 20-1 (trailing *Pierrot*'s Swiss premiere held at a music college in Winterthur that

year); Erwin Stein, 'The Moon-Struck Pierrot Comes to London', *Radio Times* (4 April 1930), 9 (on its performance three days later, its first in London for seven years).

37   The exact authorship of several of these transcriptions is uncertain. Known contributors to this 'occasional' repertory include the likes of Eisler, Stein, Berg, Rudolf Kolisch, Karl Rankl and, of course, Schoenberg and Webern.

38   See Chapter 6, note 1.

39   The figure is disputed: Steuermann recalls only twenty-five rehearsals. The true significance is that such high numbers arise in several accounts and that *Pierrot* inspired a (necessary) tradition of rigorous preparation thereafter. For example, Wiener suggests sixty-two rehearsals were held before the French premiere, while Milhaud remembers six weeks of twice-daily sessions. See Lesure (ed.), 251.

40   Fleury, 348.

41   Fleury surely prompted Leonardo Vinci's flute sonata to be performed; a year earlier he cited the work as proof of how eighteenth-century composers had catered so well for his instrument in their chamber music. Louis Fleury, 'The Flute and Its Powers of Expression', trans. Arthur H. Fox Strangways, *Music & Letters* 3/4 (October, 1922), 392.

42   Fleury, 'About "Pierrot Lunaire": The Impressions Made on Various Audiences by a Novel Work', trans. Arthur H. Fox Strangways, *Music & Letters* 5/4 (October, 1924), 355.

43   Erudite concertgoers were braced for Schoenberg: his reputation in Britain had been forged chiefly by his divisive Proms debut with the world premiere of Five Orchestral Pieces, Op. 16 in September 1912. Cecil Gray had also recently documented Schoenberg's career to date, acclaiming *Pierrot* especially. See Henry J. Wood, *My Life of Music* (London: Purnell, 1938), 134; Cecil Gray, 'Arnold Schönberg: A Critical Study', *Music & Letters* 3/1 (January, 1922), 83-4.

44   Arnold Schoenberg, letter to Marya Freund (16 August 1924), in: *Letters*, ed. Erwin Stein, trans. Eithne Wilkins and Ernst Kaiser (Eng. edn., London: Faber, 1964), 74.

45   Alma Mahler-Werfel, *And the Bridge is Love* [trans. E.B. Ashton] (London: Hutchinson, 1959), 148.

46   See Schuller and Steuermann, 31.

47   Busoni had missed *Pierrot*'s premiere while touring England, so arranged this performance himself. See Delia Couling, *Ferruccio Busoni: A Musical Ishmael* (Lanham, Md. and Oxford: Scarecrow, 2005), 267-68.

48   Schnabel also went on to perform *Pierrot*, under Fritz Stiedry (Erika Wagner's future husband) and with Marie Gutheil-Schröder, another singer-actress, as *Sprechsängerin*. Also notable for launching Gregor Piatigorsky's career, this revival of *Pierrot* took place in Berlin in January 1924, with other players plucked from the Berlin Philharmonic.

49   See R. Allen Lott, '"New Music for New Ears": The International Composers' Guild', *Journal of the American Musicological Society* 36/2 (Summer, 1983),

273-74; David Metzer, 'The League of Composers: The Initial Years', *American Music* 15/1 (Spring, 1997), 46; Carol J. Oja, *Making Music Modern: New York in the 1920s* (New York: Oxford University Press, 2000), 186, 217.

50   Casella announced the name of his new society by letter to Varèse. See Louise Varèse, *A Looking-glass Diary, Volume 1: 1883-1928* (London: Davis-Poynter, 1973), 206.

51   See Arnold Schoenberg, 'My Public', *Style and Idea*, 97; Luigi Dallapiccola, 'On the Twelve-note Road' ('Sulla strada della dodecafonia', 1951), trans. Deryck Cooke, *Music Survey* 4/1 (October, 1951), 318-32.

52   Alfredo Casella, 'Schoenberg in Italy', *Modern Music* 1/1 (1924), 7-8. An opinion Casella expressed in 1934, hailing the independence of the Italian national spirit, so riled Schoenberg that although a decade had passed since their tour together, he sarcastically cited *Pierrot*, and Casella's *Concerto* and *Serenata*, Op. 46 (1927), by reply. Among his rebuttals, Schoenberg illuminated the debt *Serenata* owed him: that is, how its mixed quintet of clarinet, bassoon, trumpet, violin and cello (a clear *Pierrot* take off) helped to delineate its structure timbrally (also in the manner of *Pierrot*). See Alfredo Casella, 'Modern Music in Italy', *Modern Music* 12/1 (1934), 19-20; Arnold Schoenberg, '"Fascism is No Article of Exportation"' (c. 1935) in: Joseph Auner (ed.), *A Schoenberg Reader: Documents of a Life* (New Haven and London: Yale University Press, 2003), 268-75. Incidentally, Schoenberg's Mussolini-quoting article title was not meant to reflect on Casella as an individual, and it is worth remembering how the Italian's education in Paris had once established him as among the most outward looking of the post-Puccini generation.

53   Arnold Schoenberg, quoted in Renzo Massarini, 'Arnold Schönberg in Italy', trans. G.A. Pfister, *Sackbut* 4/12 (July, 1924), 364.

54   See Joaquim Homs, *Roberto Gerhard and His Music*, ed. Meirion Bowen, trans. Agustín Prunell-Friend (Eng. edn., Sheffield: Anglo-Catalan Society, 2000), 28. Homs (1905-90) was Gerhard's only regular pupil. See also Roberto Gerhard, letter to Arnold Schoenberg (21 October 1923), repr. *ibid.*, 91-5. Schoenberg's positive reply (4 November 1923) is repr. in Stein (ed.), 102.

55   Ostensibly, 'Series B' existed to grant better performances to non-contemporary music, but in light of post-war inflation it was economically sensible, too. The *Walzer-Abend* comprised Schoenberg's arrangement for piano, string quartet and harmonium of *Rosen aus dem Süden*, Op. 388 and *Lagunenwalzer*, Op. 411, Webern's arrangement of *Schatzwalzer*, Op. 418, and Berg's take on 'Wein, Weib und Gesang', Op. 333. See Bryan R. Simms, 'The Society for Private Musical Performances: Resources and Documents in Schoenberg's Legacy', *Journal of the Arnold Schoenberg Institute* 3/2 (October 1979), 127-50; Walter Szmolyan, 'Die Konzerte des Wiener Schönberg-Vereins' in: *Schönbergs Verein für musikalische Privataufführungen* (*Musikkonzepte* 36), ed. Heinz-Klaus Metzger and Rainer Riehn (Munich: Text und Kritik, 1984), 101-14.

56   See, for example, Lawrence Kramer, *Musical Meaning: Toward a Critical History* (Berkeley: University of California Press, 2001), 227.

57   Conversely, it is plausible that Schoenberg commissioned Eisler's *Palmström* for the Spanish programme but chose Webern's older arrangement ahead of it; the dates tally. See note 29.

Benjamin Britten (Milein Cosman)

3 Benjamin Britten's Pierrot Ensembles

After Marya Freund's performances in 1923, British audiences would have to wait seven years for *Pierrot lunaire* to return in a more authentic form. On Edward Clark's initiative, its London revival had been provisionally scheduled for 11/12 February 1929, but the intended venue, the Arts Theatre Club, was unavailable.[1] A year later, the BBC succeeded where Clark had failed (ex. 3.1). However reserved its reception in 1923, *Pierrot* had inspired reverence among its listeners: as Percy Scholes put it, the work's 'very great power ... compels respect even when it provokes dislike.'[2] Its new conditions of performance and distinctive personnel made *Pierrot* quite a different spectacle in 1930. Virtually the same ensemble that had performed it several times at the *Verein für musikalische Privataufführungen* and in Spain was brought to Westminster Central Hall for a single broadcast performance – hence their contrived advertisement as the Vienna 'Pierrot Lunaire' Ensemble.[3]

The perils of airing the music-theatrical work to a larger audience was an issue its conductor, Erwin Stein, surely realized, and appeared to ridicule, when he previewed the work for readers of the *Radio Times*:

> Even works of art must bow to destiny, but only few have known
> so much of destiny's caprice as Schönberg's music, and especially
> *Pierrot Lunaire*. The thing has already become an absurd tradition;
> a new work by Schönberg is hailed as incomprehensible and ugly,
> until after a lapse of one or two decades, the public realizes that it
> is beautiful and spiritual.[4]

This did not save *Pierrot* from the critical clique (the BBC's in-house journal *The Listener* excepted). The 'absurdity' of *Pierrot*'s tradition extended to it entirely overshadowing the remainder of the programme: Webern's revived transcription of Schoenberg's First Chamber Symphony and Schoenberg's own Suite for Piano, Op. 25, chosen and performed by Edward Steuermann, an influential voice given his membership of the very first Pierrot ensemble in 1912.

7 April 1930, 8.30pm – Central Hall, Westminster, London

BBC Concert of Contemporary Music:
Contemporary Chamber Music

Arnold Schoenberg, arr. Anton Webern
Chamber Symphony No. 1, Op. 9 (1906, arr. for Pierrot ensemble 1922-23) *NP*
Arnold Schoenberg
Suite for Piano, Op. 25 (1921-23) †
Pierrot lunaire (Albert Giraud, trans. Otto Erich Hartleben), Op. 21 (1912) ‡

Erika Wagner (*Sprechsängerin*), Erwin Stein (*conductor*)

Vienna 'Pierrot Lunaire' Ensemble

FLUTE (‡ / PICCOLO) Franz Wangler   VIOLIN (‡ / VIOLA) Rudolf Kolisch
CLARINET (‡ / BASS CLARINET) Viktor Polatschek   CELLO Benar Heifetz
PIANO Edward Steuermann †

---

24 November 1933, 9pm – Concert Hall, Broadcasting House, London

BBC Concert of Contemporary Music

Arnold Schoenberg
Drei Klavierstücke, Op. 11 (1909) †
Sechs kleine Klavierstücke, Op. 19 (1911) †
Pierrot lunaire (Albert Giraud, trans. Otto Erich Hartleben), Op. 21 ‡

Erika Wagner (*Sprechsängerin*), Constant Lambert (‡ conductor)

Ensemble

FLUTE / PICCOLO Robert Murchie   PIANO Edward Steuermann †
CLARINET Frederick Thurston   VIOLIN / VIOLA Rudolf Kolisch
BASS CLARINET Walter Lear   CELLO Benar Heifetz

---

‡ *Lambert replaced Schoenberg as conductor.*

Example 3.1 The Fourth and Fifth Performances of Pierrot lunaire *in Britain*

Such decisions in concert programming were significant nonetheless. Whereas *Pierrot* was once heard alone with two intermissions, the consensus now was to remove such breaks and to position other works beside it. This was often done to respect the countries in which performances were held, however ideologically difficult this proved in Italy or when *Pierrot* and William Walton's *Façade* were heard side-by-side in London in 1942 (a subject of the next chapter). Another outcome was that Schoenberg's work accrued 'satellites' selected from his repertoire. Steuermann's appearances with several Pierrot ensembles meant these were often scored for solo piano, such as Op. 25 and the sets of three and six piano pieces, Opp. 11 and 19. So it was, both in 1930 and three years later when *Pierrot* returned to Britain. Changes in personnel between its two performances made Robert Murchie, Frederick Thurston and Walter Lear the first Britons to perform *Pierrot* (with Thurston and Lear splitting the usually 'doubled' part for clarinet and bass clarinet). Likewise, Constant Lambert replaced Schoenberg, who had been invited to conduct but rejected the opportunity, having accepted a contract to teach in the United States.[5]

Benjamin Britten: A Cinematic Response (I)

Stephen Pruslin, the only instrumentalist to play with both the Pierrot Players and The Fires of London throughout their twenty-year existence, has argued that

> at the beginning [1967], there was nothing for the [Pierrot] combination of any real consequence except *Pierrot* itself … When Max[well Davies] started writing for the same combination … you began to understand that *Pierrot* was one of those seminal pieces that might not have ever had a progeny.[6]

It is true that only now, nearly a century after its composition, do we begin to recognize a British-led lineage of musical works derived from *Pierrot lunaire*. But the story of how *Pierrot* came to Britain to inspire composers began over a generation earlier. Besides Schoenberg, its improbable cast includes the gasmen and dinner ladies of Britain, an almost forgotten Irish composer, and the first Briton to emulate the Pierrot ensemble in their work – a young Benjamin Britten.[7]

Of all recorded reactions to *Pierrot*'s London performances in the 1930s, Britten's was probably the most enthusiastic.[8] As a seventeen-year-old, he first heard *Pierrot* on the wireless, broadcast from Westminster.[9] Only two days after his twentieth birthday, he delighted in attending a live performance at Broadcasting House for the first time:

> ... the joy of the evening was *Pierrot lunaire*, with Erika Wagner as a divine reciter (amazingly accurate) ... But what a work! The imagination & technique of it. I revelled in the *romanticism* of it.[10]

Those who had derided Schoenberg as an expressionist were invited to do so by what they perceived as his aurally repellent *Sprechstimme* and breakdown in logic and syntax, both harmonic and dramatic. To his defenders, these very same reasons were causes to celebrate a modern masterpiece. Britten belonged to neither faction. His instinctive reaction was to describe *Pierrot* while still a teenager as 'most beautiful' and, consciously or otherwise, to sidestep the theoretical debate the work had stirred. Conversely, he did not acclaim it as an 'impressionistic masterpiece', as Humphrey Searle would, albeit years later.[11] Constant Lambert, similarly, had presciently claimed that *Pierrot* had always belonged to 'the [eighteen] nineties',[12] though this barely amounted to a consensus, even among the more forward-looking of Britten's peers.

Turning to Britten's musical activity in the early 1930s, we see that the timbre and use of a mixed ensemble had already distinguished his first two works with opus numbers (both 1932): *Sinfonietta*, a ten-piece chamber orchestra, and the *Phantasy* quartet for oboe, violin, viola and cello. He went on to write many scores, most for chamber ensemble, as part of his work for the General Post Office (GPO) Film Unit. His role within the thriving British documentary movement of the mid 1930s is best remembered for the W. H. Auden collaborations *Coal Face* and *Night Mail*, both shown in 1936 and acclaimed for their experimental, non-naturalistic approach to narration, dialogue and music.[13] The origin of Britten's choral-chamber music for *Coal Face*, in particular, can be traced to *The King's Stamp*, a less celebrated documentary commissioned for George V's Silver Jubilee and scored just before *Coal Face*. The earlier film's doubled flute and piccolo, pair of clarinets, untuned percussion and piano duet was varied slightly: *Coal Face* undoubled the flute and piccolo, called for a single clarinet, and integrated its commentary through an SATB chorus and the occasional whistler. Refined further, this template would serve Britten well in such films as *6d Telegrams* (adding boys' voices and an oboe, subtracting one piano) and the Auden-scripted account of the slave trade *God's chillun* (with vocal soloists, men's chorus and harp, substituting the flute and clarinet for an oboe doubling cor anglais).[14] *Night Mail*, on the other hand, required ten musicians to accompany its speaker. Britten's 'one of each' scoring for the film – flute, oboe, bassoon, trumpet, untuned percussion, harp, violin, viola, cello, double bass – is a foretaste of his later chamber operas and, nearer the time, the documentaries *Calendar of the Year* and *Men of the Alps* (both scored in 1936), again with minor alterations made to their instrumentation.

To these two approaches we can add a third that shows how *Pierrot* was more than an adolescent fascination to Britten. *Coal Face* and *Night Mail* were separated by a period of intense compositional activity: in the late summer and autumn of 1935 alone, Britten was involved in the production of at least nine other projects, of which two films for the British Commercial Gas Association (BCGA), and possibly a third, were an outlet for his interest in *Pierrot*. These BCGA works reveal their own experimentalism, recycling modern styles from blues to neo-Classicism, and to trace their composition and utility in light of *Pierrot*'s performance history is to uncover the closeness of these two fields. Britten scored his music for *Dinner Hour* (BCGA, 1936) for flute, clarinet in A, piano, violin, cello and percussion: the first use by a Briton of an ensemble derived directly from *Pierrot lunaire* and composed at the age of twenty-two. Moreover, its variation of the line-up, with the addition of triangle and side drum but no voice or instrumental doubling, suggests as an alternative precedent the Schoenberg-Webern transcription Britten had heard in 1930.

How the composer came to belong to, and apparently flourish within, the documentary movement affects our understanding of his music's place within this genre historically and musically. The GPO Film Unit provided the majority of his work in film, but it did not monopolise the movement; the mid 1930s saw the rise of a number of independent film makers. In December 1935, a group of documentary makers formed the Associated Realist Film Producers (ARFP).[15] Earlier that year, two of its founding members, Arthur Elton and Edgar Anstey, had been commissioned to produce and direct respectively a series of five films for the BCGA. Whereas the GPO, essentially a government body, was not in a position to oblige business sponsors, the ARFP was set up for this very purpose, to court industries that saw in film the opportunity to promote their trades.[16]

In the GPO-backed *Coal Face* – a recognizably modernist, collaborative experiment – the director Albert Cavalcanti had involved Britten from the outset of production.[17] There is little, however, to suggest this recurred during the recording processes or narratives of the *Pierrot*-scored BCGA documentaries. For all the innovations in the use of sound John Grierson presided over as Film Officer for the GPO Film Unit, his earliest attitudes towards music itself were surprisingly indifferent. He greeted the installation of recording equipment in the Blackheath studio dispassionately, explaining that 'the producer is his own sound man too … if we want music – and we do not want it much – we find it cheaper to have it written for us.'[18] If this influenced filmmakers such as Elton and Anstey to use Britten's talents sparingly, then it also explains why the inexperienced, 'quiet … and somewhat reserved' composer was their perfect foil.[19] While the one-sidedness of this creative set-up may have devalued or frustrated a lesser composer, the progressive, socially committed politics that emerged within the AFRP also liberated Britten. A distinctive blend of realism and creativity in their films encouraged Britten to experiment stylistically. Against this backdrop, his soundtracks tackle compositional and, by extension, analytical problems: how texture, timbre and cinematic narrative might interrelate, and how to use the Pierrot ensemble successfully.

Dinner Hour

In this documentary about the gas needed 'to cook London's dinner',[20] Britten's role might originally have appeared perfunctory, his only tasks being to write the accompaniment to the opening credits and end titles ('Title Music II', as it is headed on the score; ex. 3.2.i). Anstey, however, reused the title music in a later scene showing food being prepared in a West End restaurant. In the scene, the music begins awkwardly on the second beat of the second bar. Was this simply a mistake in production, or an attempt to persuade the viewer that the players are serenading the diners, as if the documentary has joined them mid-performance? Certainly, the twenty bars Britten composed as 'Title Music II' are never heard in full. At the opening credits only sixteen survive, as bars 13-16 are cut. Far from masking this fact, the soundtrack at this point 'skips'. The contemporary technique for such editing – taking scissors to the tape – emphasizes the cut, though Britten's harmonies otherwise allow the edit to pass by without notice.[21]

The three distinct units (flute and clarinet, strings and percussion, and piano) that emerge within the sextet here and in 'End Title II' (ex. 3.2.iii) also conceal discontinuity. They complement another stylistic allusion. With Anstey's re-use of Britten's material, his group of musicians is suddenly redefined as a salon ensemble playing up-tempo, pastiche palm-court music. The impression is not out of place with the musical style: a triple-time dance for mixed chamber ensemble marked *Allegretto alle Valse* with a clear melody, strumming *pizzicato* and light piano accompaniment. The effect is further underlined when the music drifts in and out of earshot as the camera pans between the tables and kitchen. With such uniform use of timbres, clear but thin textures, and a tonal yet remote, fast-changing harmonic framework, Anstey's palm court ensemble eclipses Britten's nod towards neo-Classicism.[22]

On 16 September 1935, six musicians met at the Blackheath studios to record music for *Dinner Hour, Men Behind the Meters* and another, unidentified BCGA documentary film (ex. 3.3).[23] It is uncertain who brought the players together since the duty was not necessarily Britten's. For this session, it may well have been the flautist John Francis, who organized musicians for later films such as *Men of the Alps* and *Calendar of the Year* (both GPO, 1937). Wherever the responsibility lay, the links between the individual players are clear and provide some clues as to how the ensemble convened. Francis was married to Millicent Silver. Like Britten and Bernard Richards, she had attended the Royal College of Music. Richards belonged to the International String Quartet, whose second violinist in 1935 was Walter Price. Though a clarinettist, Alan Frank's principal employment was his editing for Oxford University Press, Britten's first publisher. Only the identity of the percussionist is unknown. A member of the nearby Blackheath Conservatoire could have been fetched easily, as for earlier recording sessions; the part was not challenging.

Men Behind the Meters

In issuing documentaries, the BCGA sought to advertise the wares of their members, the gas companies, or, in their narrator's words, the 'great world you [the public] call on every time you turn a tap or run a bath.'[24] Another of their films, *Men Behind the Meters*, was commissioned with *Dinner Hour*, and focused on the role of 'gas fitters'. The positioning of music in each film is similar: the only accompaniment of onscreen action is towards the end. The number of times music is heard (three) is also the same, but in the lengthier *Men Behind the Meters* material is not recycled and the scoring is more varied.[25] The clarinettist, for example, now doubles on Bb and A instruments (though swaps only between each section) before being replaced by an oboe for the concluding titles. Once the education of gasmen has been detailed (the majority of the film), an abridged history of gas follows. From the phenomenon of 'inflammable air' noticed nearly two centuries earlier, to the lighting of London's Pall Mall in 1807, the viewer is transported to 1895. A maid sees to the fire and lamps in an opulent, marbled room, while, unusually for such a documentary, apparent pastiche music interrupts the narration for over a minute to accompany the tranquil, Victorian scene. In fact, this is Britten's arrangement for Pierrot ensemble, now with glockenspiel, of 'I dreamt I dwelt in marble halls', a paean to love over status and material worth by the nineteenth-century Irish composer Michael W. Balfe (Document A).[26]

Britten's source was almost certainly Boosey & Co.'s vocal score, one of the many operatic editions made by Arthur Sullivan and Josiah Pittman in the 1860s.[27] His re-scoring strips the aria of its voice, and the melody is first played by the piano as an introduction before the cello (bar 8^3) and violin (bar 16^2) share the first 'verse', the flute and clarinet the second (bar 32^2). The technique is similar to the pairing within *Dinner Hour*, although now a continuous, arpeggio line is shared among the instruments so their roles change frequently. While colourful, this textural exchange was probably not

Example 3.2   (i) Benjamin Britten, Dinner Hour, *'Title Music II'*

Example 3.2   (ii) Benjamin Britten, Dinner Hour, *'End Title II'*

written for its own sake: to fit to the '1895' scene Britten's wordless *Andantino* music is far quicker than Balfe's, and for the purposes of its accurate recording this seamless instrumental play reduced the demands put upon his soloists.[28]

Music for the end titles was recorded by Francis, Frank and the other musicians, but was not used in the film. Either Britten had not finished writing it or he was instructed to compose further music, because on 2 October 1935 an entirely new set of players met to record his completion of *Men Behind the Meters.* Of those present at the first session, we know that the recent schedules of Francis and Richards were busy: they played together as part of another chamber ensemble at the London Contemporary Music Centre the day before the later session. Moreover, there were no pressing aesthetic reasons to recall the original players, and for his score's conclusion, Britten had replaced the clarinet with an oboe. Again, though, the ensemble was replete with past and present students from the Royal College of Music, Olive Richards replacing her brother Bernard, alongside another sister, Eileen, on violin.

16 September 1935 – Bennett Park, Blackheath, London

Men Behind the Meters
Title music I
'I dreamt that I dwelt in Marble Halls' (M.W. Balfe)
End title I (did not make the final cut)

Dinner Hour
Title music II
End title II

$$\left[\begin{array}{c} \textit{How Gas Is Made} \\ \text{Title music III} \\ \text{End title III} \end{array}\right]$$

Benjamin Britten (*conductor*)

FLUTE John Francis	PIANO Millicent Silver
CLARINET Alan Frank	VIOLIN Walter Price
PERCUSSION Unidentified	CELLO Bernard Richards

---

2 October 1935 – Bennett Park, Blackheath, London

Men Behind the Meters
1935 Sequence •
• Only 3½ bars made the final cut (see App. 2)

Benjamin Britten (*conductor*)

FLUTE Arliss Marriott	PIANO Leonard Isaacs
OBOE Sylvia Spencer	VIOLIN Eileen Richards
PERCUSSION Allan Plowman	CELLO Olive Richards

Production credits for the two known documentaries (released 1936):
Made by Associated Realist Film Producers (ARFP): Edgar Anstey (director), Arthur Elton (producer),
Len Page (sound recordist); other crew members not credited.
Commissioned by the British Commercial Gas Association (BCGA).

Example 3.3 Two Recording Sessions for Three of Britten's BCGA Films

The title of the music the group recorded, '1935 Sequence', suggests it was intended to follow 'I dreamt…', where the viewer is brought back to the present to be paraded with various gas-powered appliances found in the modern, 1930s home. As with 'End title I', however, the music was not used. The '1935' scene finds the narrator slowly reeling off the names of household devices with only a picture of each to accompany him. Why Britten's new material was omitted is not known. Certainly, it appears too frenetic and suspenseful to complement such a passive scene. Yet, the allusions to modern trends, especially its bitonally-derived and rhapsodic chromaticism, suited the broader narrative of a present-day timeframe well. Perhaps the juxtaposition of styles between this and 'I dreamt…' was too great to represent the passing of only forty years. Alternatively, the music may simply have been too long. However, the players' efforts were not wholly wasted: to replace 'End Title I', three bars (17-19³) were brusquely extracted from Britten's '1935 Sequence', onto which was tagged a sudden, and rather unconvincing, final chord of E major (Document A).

That Britten had written and recorded further *Pierrot*-scored music for another of the association's documentaries, probably the now unavailable *How Gas is Made*,[29] only confirms how little stylistic consistency there was in his BCGA scores. Further amendments to his Pierrot ensemble were made in the film's 'Title music III' and 'End music III', recorded during the original session in September 1935: a piccolo replaced the flute and the percussionist now played the cymbal and bass drum. The new 'solo' pairing of clarinet and cello (and later 'solo' cymbal), both heavily accented, exhibit a further style in which the youthful Britten dabbled: its stratified texture is highly suggestive of Stravinsky.

Instrumentally, all three scores appear to invoke, if not evoke, *Pierrot lunaire*. If discrepancies remain, then it is historically prescient how the added percussion presages the same modification the Pierrot Players would make forty years later, or how the oboe faintly replaces the clarinet to challenge the configuration of the ensemble it supplements, but only to extend Schoenberg's *Pierrot*-derived ploy of doubling instruments. Britten never commented on his BCGA accomplishments, and must have had to accept his role on the sidelines of the cinematographic process. Only a few years after his elation at gaining such prestigious employment, he belittled his services to film by claiming not to 'take film music seriously qua music anyhow'.[30] A more mature Britten would naturally have had different priorities as a composer, and perhaps this was his reaction to a waning

British documentary movement in which he was no longer employed. Even so, it clearly points to an unequal relationship between his works and that once dominant genre.

Nevertheless, in these interwar years of high unemployment and domestic upheaval, political and social expression through the medium of documentary film inspired Grierson, Anstey, Elton and others. It also enabled Britten to resist a trend in film music that Hanns Eisler was to condemn by deciding to compose *Vierzehn Arten den Regen zu beschreiben*, Op. 70 (1941), for *Pierrot*-derived forces. Indeed, Britten would soon add his own criticism:

> I like to think of the smaller combinations of players, and ... deplore the tendency of present-day audiences to expect only the luscious 'tutti' effect from an orchestra.[31]

In the aftermath of *Pierrot*'s far-reaching performance history, Britten's antithesis was not just any permutation of dissimilar instruments, but the Pierrot ensemble. His BCGA scores are far removed from Schoenberg's melodrama, Eisler's more faithful progenies, or Davies's later post-expressionist works that would definitively set the 'Pierrot' ensemble on a new course. The difference is not only one of shelf life, but also vision. As a touchstone for an early chamber music aesthetic, *Pierrot lunaire* was to Britten more than a notorious beacon of modernism. This attitude, coupled with his freedom from the rigours of the concert hall, led him to emulate *Pierrot*'s soloistic virtuosity in three exercises in colour and style. The possibilities of a nascent medium (the documentary film) spurred another (music for Pierrot ensemble), one hitherto uncultivated by British composers.

Notes

1   Clark also anticipated that the BBC, his employer, would broadcast one of the performances. Some evidence of Clark's procrastination in coordinating this is found his exchanges with the theatre's manager Lionel Barton and Kenneth Wright of the BBC. See Jennifer Doctor, *The BBC and Ultra-modern Music, 1922-1936: Shaping a Nation's Tastes* (Cambridge: Cambridge University Press, 1999), 150-51.

2   Percy Scholes, 'Music and Musicians: Mad Musicians', *The Observer* (25 November 1923), repr. in: *Dossier de Presse: Press-book de Pierrot lunaire d'Arnold Schönberg*, ed. François Lesure (Geneva: Minkoff, 1985), 165.

3   Benar Heifetz had replaced Joachim Stutschewsky as cellist of the Kolisch Quartet – and hence this Pierrot ensemble – since *Pierrot*'s Spanish premiere five years earlier.

4   Erwin Stein, 'The Moon-Struck Pierrot Comes to London', *Radio Times* (4 April 1930), 9.

5   See Hans Heinz Stuckenschmidt, *Arnold Schoenberg: His Life, World and Work*, trans. Humphrey Searle (Eng. edn., London: Calder, 1977), 372; Doctor, 264.

6   Stephen Pruslin, interview with Chris Wines, broadcast as 'Pierrot and Beyond' and taken from a discussion at the interval of a Birmingham Contemporary Music Group concert, BBC Pebble Mill Studios, Birmingham, 23 May 1997 (BLSA, cat. H5918/2).

7   Consciously, perhaps, Pruslin overlooks the claims of those already wooed by *Pierrot*'s mixed ensemble by the time the often sensationalist Pierrot ensembles of their composer-director, Peter Maxwell Davies, reached European audiences. He also echoes the common supposition that, in setting a new benchmark of commitment and attainment in the performance of contemporary music, Davies and his associates may be identified, above all others, as the first British musicians to react inventively to *Pierrot*.

8   Thoughts of Britten and *Pierrot* most commonly evoke his unsuccessful request to the Royal College of Music, while a student there, for its library to purchase a copy of the score. As much as this anecdote has been circulated to expose insular attitudes of the time, or at least its limited provision for uninhibited composers like Britten, it is but one consequence of the work's appeal to the composer in his formative years.

9   See Benjamin Britten, diary entry for 7 April 1930 in: Donald Mitchell and Philip Reed (eds.), *Letters from a Life: The Selected Letters and Diaries of Benjamin Britten 1913-1976* (5 vols.), vol. 1 (London: Faber, 1991), 127.

10   Benjamin Britten, diary entry for 24 November 1933 in: *ibid.*, 129; emphasis added.

11   Humphrey Searle, 'Schoenberg: Prophet and Genius', *Radio Times* (28 December 1951), 32.

12   Constant Lambert, 'Schönberg's "Erwartung"', *Musical Times* 72/1056 (February, 1931), 167. Lambert expounded on this idea after conducting the work, drawing attention to how *Pierrot* marked the 'culmination of the neurasthenia and preciosity of the impressionist or disruptive period.' He purposely reserved judgement on questions of value, however, describing *Pierrot* as a work in which 'the ghost of the German *Lied* meets the ghost of French decadence... [so allowing] those stock figures of fancy-dress ball [to] have for us any meaning.' Constant Lambert, *Music Ho! A Study of Music in Decline* (London: Faber, 1934), 59-60.

13   For a comprehensive record of Britten's time with the GPO, see Philip Reed, *The Incidental Music of Benjamin Britten: A Study and Catalogue of his Music for Film, Theatre and Radio*, 2 vols. (Ph.D. diss., University of East Anglia, 1987), vol. 1, 23-47.

14   This group of scores also invites comparison with Schoenberg's 1901 *Brettl-Lieder*, the last of which ('Nachtwandler') calls for piccolo, muted trumpet, snare drum and piano accompaniment.

15   See interview with Arthur Elton in: Elizabeth Sussex, *The Rise and Fall of British Documentary: The Story of the Film Movement founded by John Grierson* (Berkeley: University of California Press, 1975), 61; Paul Swann, *The British Documentary Film Movement, 1926-1946* (Cambridge: Cambridge University Press, 1989), 111-12.

16   This new commercial offshoot riled the head of the GPO Film Unit, John Grierson, who believed in the public service and financing of film, even though the idea of a guild among documentarists had been his. (His objections did not prevent him resigning from the GPO in June 1937 to create Film Centre, the successor to the ARFP.) The ARFP did not abandon social causes, however, and industry proved no more editorially inhibiting than the governmental pressure put upon the GPO: *Housing Problems* (BCGA, 1935), probably the best known of the five films, advertises no products and covers the clearing of urban slums for new public housing. See Paul Rotha, *Documentary Diary: An Informal History of the British Documentary Film, 1928-1939* (London: Secker and Warburg, 1973), 111; John Gray, 'Soho Square and Bennett Park: The Documentary Movement in Britain in the 1930s', *Screening the Past* 7 (1999), www.latrobe.edu.au/screeningthepast/firstrelease/fr0799/jgfr7a.htm (accessed 7 September 2012).

17   See Philip Reed, 'Britten in the Cinema: *Coal Face*' in: *The Cambridge Companion to Benjamin Britten*, ed. Mervyn Cooke (Cambridge: Cambridge University Press, 1999), 56.

18   John Grierson, 'The GPO Gets Sound', *Cinema Quarterly* 2/4 (January, 1934), 221.

19   Basil Wright, 'Britten and Documentary', *Musical Times* 104/1449 (November, 1963), 779.

20   *Dinner Hour* (BCGA, 1936), opening narration.

21   A chromatically-altered submediant approaches the second-inversion dominant of bar 17 whether the music is edited (in which case it is VI♯) or not (♭VI). According to a co-producer of *Night Mail*, the composer often made such alterations in the cutting room. See Wright, 780.

22   It is reasonable to suggest that responsibilities were split in this way, i.e. Anstey's onscreen direction coupled with Britten's stylistic allusions. Again, we cannot *prove* the extent of the composer's input or the consciousness of his decision to score his music for Pierrot ensemble, notwithstanding the relevance of *Pierrot*'s return to Britain. As we saw earlier, however, other composers have pleaded ignorance of *Pierrot* having written Pierrot ensembles themselves – a case we need not apply to Britten. (At the same time, the inevitable failure of his niche works to shape the future course of the Pierrot ensemble is an issue we shall return to.) The more significant point, then, is that Britten's employment in the film industry guaranteed a group of players would be assembled to record his music when no such British ensemble existed.

23   It was common for music for several films to be recorded in a single day. As part of the industry's prudent 'conveyor-belt' approach to film-making, promotional documentaries shared production teams and session musicians

and were granted little time for recording. The third film is probably *How Gas Is Made* (BGCA, 1936): Britten registered its music with the Performing Right Society. See Britten's correspondence with Harold Walter in Mitchell and Reed (eds.), vol. 1, 525. However, this cannot be corroborated as the British Film Institute does not hold a viewing copy of the film, nor lists Britten among its credits.

24   *Men Behind the Meters* (BCGA, 1936), opening narration.

25   Running times (and extent of music): *Dinner Hour*, 15' 02" (0' 53"), *Men Behind the Meters* 19' 41" (2' 33").

26   Balfe's music is a ballad taken from his grand opera *The Bohemian Girl*, a Drury Lane hit in 1843 and, internationally, beyond. Besides amateur dramatic groups, the job of upholding Balfe's legacy has fallen to Irish folk and pop artists such as Enya, Sinead O'Connor and Brian Kennedy.

27   From this score Britten retained the melody's distinctive second-beat accents, which do not appear in disputed orchestral versions.

28   The same pairing occurs in the opening credits to *Men Behind the Meters*, a march with the same line-up as *Dinner Hour*. 'End Title I' simply restates the opening melodic fragment with greater emphasis, hence the variation of chordal piano and strummed strings.

29   Britten was correcting parts for a 'Gas abstract' in September 1935, though no manuscript matches this title. See Benjamin Britten, diary entry for 3 September 1935, in: *Journeying Boy: The Diaries of the Young Benjamin Britten 1928-1938*, ed. John Evans (London: Faber, 2009), 276. See also note 23.

30   Benjamin Britten, 'Conversation with Benjamin Britten', *Tempo* 6 (February, 1944), 4.

31   Quoted from an answer Britten gave to a questionnaire devised by the film historian Jay Leyda; published as 'On Film Music (c. 1940-41)', in: Paul Kildea (ed.), *Britten on Music* (Oxford: Oxford University Press, 2003), 28. See also Theodor W. Adorno and Hanns Eisler, *Composing for the Films* (1947) (2nd edn., London: Athlone, 1994), 135-65. Kildea also records the influence of Walter Leigh's film music on Britten's experiments with sound effects.

4 'Freak' Works

By the time Benjamin Britten had written for the Pierrot ensemble, Arnold Schoenberg was a figure to whom no one in Germany could safely disclose their allegiance.[1] Schoenberg had already secured his international standing, for better or worse, through word of mouth and by conducting and touring his music, especially *Pierrot lunaire*. But the lineage of modern music would soon be dramatically torn. Living in Los Angeles from 1934, Schoenberg continued to promote *Pierrot*, directing its first recording there in September 1940 with Erika Wagner as reciter. Meanwhile, Britain became home to a stellar cast of émigrés with greater experience of modernist trends than most indigenous musicians had. Over several years, Roberto Gerhard, Mátyás Seiber, Egon Wellesz, Walter Goehr and Berthold Goldschmidt joined musicians such as Erwin Stein (a leading advocate of *Pierrot*, as we have seen), Dea Gombrich, Sela Trau, Oscar Adler and Peter Stadlen – although their efforts were not universally appreciated. Several of these musicians were called upon when, in May 1942, *Pierrot* was performed in Britain for the first time in years. It joined in concert another work for reciter and mixed ensemble, William Walton's *Façade* (1922-29, rev. 1942 and thereafter), to form a collaborative event that bears comparison with *Pierrot*'s most recent 'pan-European' performance in Britain in 1933. This latest concert, and the Boosey & Hawkes series to which it belonged, belied the collapse of international relations in wartime. It could hardly compensate for Britain's cultural isolation, however. During the war, the livelihoods of composers keen to keep abreast of modern developments, and with it the Pierrot ensemble, were to be transformed.

Music-making in Britain during the War

In Britain, concerns about the creative health of the nation gave rise to the Council for the Encouragement of Music and the Arts (CEMA, 1940-45). The virtual cessation of artistic activity during the First World War would not recur. A forerunner of the Arts Council, CEMA famously subsidized Myra Hess's series of midday recitals at the National Gallery. Many similar concerts were organized nationwide, employing hundreds of musicians. Having spent the first years of the war in the United States, Britten and Peter Pears counted among these upon their return in 1942. CEMA joined other British patrons, including the Entertainment National Service Association (ENSA) and the governmental Ministry of Information. Stalwarts such as the BBC also strengthened their commitment to the arts through commissions. Relatively speaking, music-making thrived, although many performers and composers were set on very different paths. Humphrey Searle and Elisabeth Lutyens, Britain's first serialists, were repressed in their prime. Having studied with Anton Webern in 1938, Searle joined the Intelligence Corps. Lutyens was mobilized in another way, spending much of her time working on music for patriotic films such as *Jungle Mariners* (Crown Film Unit, 1944) and as a music copyist. Musically, Lutyens was particularly unlucky. The premiere of *Three Pieces for Orchestra*, Op. 7 (1939-40) marked her Proms debut on 7 September 1940, a date better remembered as the first night of the Blitz.[2]

The war years only deferred Searle's natural musical evolution: his first serial work was the *Intermezzo for Eleven Instruments*, Op. 8 (1946). Lutyens had already aped Webern's Op. 24 concerto for her first such work, the First Chamber Concerto, Op. 8 (1939-40), scored for a very similar nonet. (The bassoon and cello replace the flute and piano.) Robert Mackay has bleakly summarized their predicament:

> The avant-garde, although never a leading force, had virtually atrophied during the war. Lutyens single-mindedly stuck to her serial guns, but not even the arrival in Britain in 1939 of the Catalan, Roberto Gerhard ... was the stimulus it surely would have been in more normal times.[3]

Indeed, Gerhard's music was not performed widely until the mid 1960s, towards the end of the composer's life.[4] As an administrator, too, Gerhard might have contributed much: he had helped organize the 1936 Festival of the International Society for Contemporary Music (ISCM) in Barcelona, and was committed, as in the same city in 1925, to ensuring Schoenberg's music was heard. Gerhard's view of British musical life was graciously balanced. The capabilities of its amateur and semi-professional musicians impressed him, but as a composer used to the musical cosmopolitanism of Barcelona and, earlier, Berlin, he found frustrating the 'strongly conservative taste shown in the overwhelming majority of programmes [in which] contemporary British works hardly appear.'[5]

Gerhard's was not a lone voice. Even in the early war years, there was growing unease at the make-up of programmes heard across London:

Art galleries have been stripped of old masters, the contemporary painter is afforded an unexpected opportunity to exhibit therein, and even to sell his paintings! In music, however, precisely the opposite has happened, and senseless duplication of the classics seems to be the order of the day.[6]

The author of this letter to the *Musical Times* was Alan Frank, a member of Britten's 'studio' Pierrot ensemble in 1935. Frank prefaced his downbeat allusion to self-censorship with a plea to concert artists and programmers to air music 'by living composers – particularly British composers and, more particularly still, by young and lesser-known names.'[7] Diplomatically, this was a hazardous debate: to cite an apparent failure of wartime concerts risked displaying a callow, even unpatriotic, sense of ingratitude for their very existence.

Nevertheless, the foundation of the Boosey & Hawkes Concerts a year later was a fillip to the performance of chamber music in London. The publisher's house newsletter explained that a policy had been agreed to counteract 'the plethora of hackneyed, classical programmes presented … without much thought for anything so seemingly unprofitable as the progressive development of public taste.'[8] The Blech String Quartet gave the inaugural concert (Wigmore Hall, 4 October 1941), performing music by Claude Debussy, Manuel de Falla, Arthur Honegger, Karol Szymanowski and the British composers Ralph Vaughan Williams, Bernard Stevens (then 27) and Alan Rawsthorne (36). Vaughan Williams's now obscure work, *Household Music: Three Preludes on Welsh Hymn Tunes* (1940-41), aptly exemplifies how wartime conditions could guide compositional creativity: *Household Music* was intended to be just that, music for homes whose musicians could play it, if not in the form of a string quartet, then 'by almost any combination of instruments which may be gathered together at one time.'[9] Chamber music had been conspicuously absent from Vaughan Williams's oeuvre in the inter-war period.[10] But when *Household Music* was published he specified four groups of alternative instruments of a roughly corresponding compass and register to the violins, viola and cello, allowing some 2,940 possible combinations.[11] The number is less relevant than the work's *Gebrauchsmusik* aesthetic (notwithstanding the irony of its premiere in the concert hall) and the overwhelming majority of mixed ensembles permutable from it (although not the Pierrot quintet since the popular but immobile piano was omitted).

The Pierrot and Façade Ensembles

While some prospective links between the continent and Britain lay dormant, the war unexpectedly led other pan-European musical relationships to flourish. Like Gerhard, Stein had been taught by Schoenberg, was intimate with his works, and was an adept administrator of concerts (most notably for the *Verein für musikalische Privataufführungen*). Having sought refuge in London in 1938, Stein soon found employment as Senior Editor with Boosey & Hawkes. Here two aspects of his career converged: his evangelism for *Pierrot lunaire* made him at least partly responsible for the concert series in which it was now heard. Precisely how involved he was in the first few months of the Boosey & Hawkes Concerts is uncertain,[12] but it was natural that Stein should once again conduct *Pierrot* when it was programmed alongside Walton's *Façade* in arguably the boldest and most innovative concert of the war (ex. 4.1). It marked the British revival of both works. *Pierrot*'s nine-year absence from Britain is still its longest. Performances of *Façade* were more popular, but not in its original instrumentation for voice and a mixed ensemble that kept intact *Pierrot*'s cello and characteristic doubling of winds, and added saxophone, trumpet and percussion (ex 4.2).[13]

Billed as a collaborative venture with the London Summer Concerts, which ran from 27 May to 11 June, the event nevertheless typified the Boosey & Hawkes Concerts' commitment to exposing enterprising chamber music.[14] Whether this policy was designed to develop the tastes of concertgoers, as Chapman believed, or simply to preserve the union of domestic and foreign music in concert, it obviously called for the public to be sympathetic to the cause.[15] For the ninth concert, it is not clear if this was forthcoming. One columnist noted that *Façade* had amused the audience but denounced both as 'freak works', and on *Pierrot* preserved what was by now almost a tradition in its appraisal: that is, praising the executants, and particularly the *Sprechsängerin* (here Hedli Anderson, more usually a specialist of 'light' music), yet ridiculing the significance of the instrumental parts, if not their performance:

> It does not signify much whether the piano plays three grunts or the piccolo three pips in accompanying the *Sprechgesang* [*sic*], admirably declaimed on this occasion by Miss Hedli Anderson.[16]

Another critic did their best to unpick *significance* from *value* in saluting 'perhaps the most important of the Summer Concerts' (while rubbishing its programme) yet claiming *Pierrot* 'no longer challenges the intellect' (while hailing *Façade* as 'still good fun').[17] One notable dissenter to this pattern of reception was Britten, although his second documented reaction to hearing *Pierrot* in person was markedly different from his first in 1933. Complaining about the 'pretty awful' event, its 'snobby and stupid' audience, and *Façade*'s 'completely inaudible' recitation, his comments were aimed not at *Pierrot*, but instead at the intolerance of its British listeners or, conversely, their uproarious response to *Façade*.[18]

29 May 1942, 6.30pm – Aeolian Hall, London

Boosey & Hawkes Concerts (No. 9)
in conjunction with London Summer Concerts

Arnold Schoenberg
Pierrot lunaire, Op. 21
(Albert Giraud, trans. Otto Erich Hartleben, re-trans. Cecil Gray) †

William Walton
Façade Entertainment (Edith Sitwell) (1922-29, rev. 1942) •

1. Hornpipe [I]
   En Famille [II]
   Mariner Man [III]

2. Trio for two cats and a trombone [IV] ‡
   Through gilded trellises [V]
   Tango: 'I do like to be beside the seaside' [VI]

3. Scotch Rhapsody [XVIII]
   Lullaby for Jumbo [VII]
   Foxtrot: 'Old Sir Faulk' [XX]

4. By the Lake [XI]
   A Man from a Far Countree [X]
   Country Dance [XII]

5. Yodelling Song [XVII]
   Black Mrs. Behemoth [VIII]
   Popular Song [XIX]

6. Polka [XIII]
   Valse [VXI]
   Tarantella [IX]

7. Four in the Morning [XIV]
   Something Lies Beyond the Scene [XV]
   Sir Beelzebub [XXI]

[I-XXI] Subscript numerals denote published order (1951)
‡ Subsequently renamed 'Long Steel Grass'

Hedli Anderson (*Sprechsängerin* †), Constant Lambert (reciter •)
Erwin Stein (conductor †), William Walton (conductor •)

FLUTE / PICCOLO John Francis	PIANO Peter Stadlen († only)
CLARINET / BASS CLARINET	PERCUSSION James [Jimmy] Blades (• only)
Richard Temple Savage	VIOLIN / VIOLA
ALTO SAXOPHONE Frank Johnson (• only)	Anna Amadea [Dea] Gombrich († only)
TRUMPET Richard [Bob] Walton (• only)	CELLO Sela Trau

Non-musicians:
Curtain design: John Piper; Painter: Alick Johnstone, not 'Aleck Johnson' as in programme

Concert repeated 26 June 1942, 6.30pm.

Performers as before except:

ALTO SAXOPHONE	CELLO Sela Trau †
Michael [Mickey] Lewis (• only)	CELLO George Walton •

Example 4.1 Two Wartime Performances of Pierrot lunaire *and* Façade

	Recit.	fl	pic	Bb-cl	A-cl	bcl	alto-sax	tpt	vc	perc
Fanfare			✓	✓			✓	✓	✓	✓
1. Hornpipe	✓	✓	✓	✓				✓	✓	✓	✓
2. En Famille	✓	✓		✓		✓	✓	✓	✓	✓
3. Mariner Man	✓		✓			✓		✓		
4. Long Steel Grass	✓	✓				✓	✓	✓	✓	✓
5. Through Gilded Trellises	✓	✓			✓		✓	✓	✓	✓
6. Tango-Pasodoble	✓	✓		✓			✓	✓	✓	✓
7. Lullaby for Jumbo	✓	✓		✓			✓	✓	✓	✓
8. Black Mrs. Behemoth	✓	✓		✓			✓	✓	✓	✓
9. Tarantella	✓	✓	✓	✓			✓	✓	✓	✓
10. A Man from a Far Countree	✓	✓			✓		✓		✓	✓
11. By the Lake	✓	✓		✓			✓	✓	✓	✓
12. Country Dance	✓	✓			✓					✓
13. Polka	✓	✓		✓			✓	✓	✓	✓
14. Four in the Morning	✓	✓		✓		✓	✓	✓	✓	✓
15. Something Lies Beyond the Scene	✓	✓	✓	✓			✓	✓	✓	✓
16. Valse	✓	✓			✓		✓	✓	✓	✓
17. Yodelling Song	✓	✓		✓			✓	✓	✓	✓
18. Scotch Rhapsody	✓		✓	✓			✓	✓	✓	✓
19. Popular Song	✓	✓	✓	✓		✓	✓	✓	✓	✓
20. Foxtrot: 'Old Sir Faulk'	✓	✓	✓		✓	✓	✓	✓	✓	✓
21. Sir Beelzebub	✓	✓	✓	✓			✓	✓	✓	✓

Example 4.2   Vocal and Instrumental Specification of William Walton's Façade

Why Walton's work outshone *Pierrot* during their first appearance in concert together is telling. Their adjacency promoted their comparison, while alterations made to the usual presentation of each put them in a false position of competition. Cecil Gray specially translated Otto Erich Hartleben's text into English (i.e. not from Albert Giraud directly, 'on account of the musical accentuation'), the same strategy of retranslation Jacques Benoist-Méchin had adopted when preparing for the French premiere in 1923.[19] And Constant Lambert made the new proposal that a seven-sectioned *Façade* could be structured inversely to *Pierrot*'s fêted *dreimal sieben Gedichte* – a 'sort of typically Schoenbergian inversion', as Walton later put it.[20] Yet, in their different ways, both composers consented to these changes. Walton himself conducted the newly structured *Façade* and Lambert's idea became a definitive part of the work thereafter.[21] Meanwhile, Stein passed on news of *Pierrot*'s latest revival to Schoenberg, who suggested by reply that Walter Goehr might be approached to arrange a duplicate, recorded performance – in English.[22]

Such variations to the performance of the two works only added to the likenesses already apparent in their declaimed vocal delivery, poeticised take on cabaret, similar instrumental ensembles and indistinct narratives.[23] But if the illusion of their resemblance was upheld as a consequence, then, paradoxically, their performance together also laid bare their differences. *Pierrot* was a model to Walton in a loosest possible sense: the composer admitted he was 'completely in the dark' about *Pierrot* but pretended to be an expert on Schoenberg.[24] Hearing *Pierrot* in English, followed by an English piece that parodied its ensemble and now structure, would surely lessen the distinction and, potentially, the radicalism of Schoenberg's work. In wartime London, it is no surprise that the more frivolous and entertaining parody *Façade* outclassed the ghoulish, tragicomic *Pierrot*. Schoenberg's parody is much finer and less appreciable, although it is curious that, conceptually, Sitwell's musical genre-evoking, rhythmicized 'patterns in sound' have more in common with *Pierrot* than anyone, Walton included, perhaps realized.[25] Contrary to Britten's candid resentment, then, it is logical to imagine concertgoers and critics instead spotting where the two works diverged most obviously, in their musical language, and reeling from Schoenberg's atonal otherworldliness towards Walton's tonal satire.

Others nevertheless saw success in the two works being offered side by side, and the concert was repeated less than a month later. The same seven musicians, including Stein, reappeared for *Pierrot*. But for *Façade*, still under Walton, there was a new saxophonist and cellist – the latter reportedly due to the composer's dissatisfaction with Trau's playing.[26] Tensions had surfaced elsewhere even before the first concert. The clarinettist Richard Temple

Savage was particularly unimpressed with the painstaking management of rehearsals for *Pierrot*:

> Such intensive coaching [the ensemble allegedly rehearsed for nine months] was totally alien to the British players' approach; we were by tradition brilliant and professional sight-readers … [The] hyper-meticulous preparation of Erwin Stein … was entirely irksome to a British instrumentalist.[27]

Whether he also meant to speak for his compatriot John Francis is unclear; the flautist had greater experience of performing contemporary music and was better prepared for Stein's rigorous approach.[28] During *Pierrot*'s final rehearsal, held at the British Museum, the clarinettist's dismay turned to obduracy when he made the deliberate mistake of playing one number on his clarinet in A.[29] This tale strangely echoes Karl Essberger's confession of the same prank to Schoenberg as a member of his first Pierrot ensemble (albeit Essberger played *Pierrot*'s only number for clarinet in A, 'Der Mondfleck', on the Bb instrument).[30] The difference is that according to Temple Savage, Stein was furious when he found out.

This schism among the musicians' sensibilities had a parallel in the two-part programme; that is, there was a great imbalance in the nationalities of those involved in each half, with an all-British ensemble left to play *Façade*. Lambert again featured in a concert which included *Pierrot* (as he had when replacing Schoenberg as its conductor in 1933), but he had only to recite *Façade*, a role he first assumed in 1926. Frank Johnson, Bob Walton and, most notably, Jimmy Blades were the other Britons to play only for both performances of Walton's work.[31] Temple Savage and Francis were the only British instrumentalists to play with Stein's Pierrot ensemble, although theirs were the parts that so emphasized the instrumental similarity of the two works. For *Pierrot* they joined Stadlen, Gombrich (both Austrian) and Trau (probably Czech), who had each sought sanctuary in Britain.[32] In light of the performance history to which he contributed, Stadlen would revive the difficult issue of authenticity in interpreting *Pierrot*'s speech-song.[33] Later, he used his memory of this performance as an example of Stein's changeable views on *Sprechstimme*, the conductor having done 'his best to get Hedli [Anderson] to give a correct rendering of the written pitches.'[34] Yet the most important historical fact is that the Aeolian Hall concert was Stein's first public performance in Britain since emigrating and, remarkably, also his last. He played no further part in *Pierrot*'s dissemination. Thankfully, two British composers absent from wartime London, Lutyens and Searle, chose again to heed the Second Viennese School in the late 1940s, when the nation's cultural priorities were rewritten once more.

Notes

1   Schoenberg converted back to Judaism in 1933. For a synopsis of how those of his pupils who remained in Germany fared, see Erik Levi, 'Atonality, Twelve-tone Music and the Third Reich', *Tempo* 178 (September, 1991), 17-21.

2   Op. 7 also embodied an unusual *concertante* approach to the orchestra, in which a solo string quintet represented the string family.

3   Robert Mackay, 'Safe and Sound: New Music in Wartime Great Britain' in: '*Millions Like Us*'? *British Culture in the Second World War*, ed. Nick Hayes and Jeff Hills (Liverpool: Liverpool University Press, 1999), 208.

4   Another European conflict, the Spanish Civil War, brought Gerhard to Britain (via France) in 1939.

5   See Roberto Gerhard, 'English Musical Life: A Symposium', *Tempo* 11 (1945), 2-3. Quizzed by the editor of *Tempo* on their impressions of British musical life since moving to Britain, Gerhard, Wellesz and Seiber penned replies that were published consecutively (pp. 2-6); the three composer-musicologists had taken positions at Cambridge, Oxford and Morley College respectively.

6   Alan Frank, 'Why Not Give Living Composers a Chance?' [Letter to the Editor], *Musical Times* 81/1164 (February, 1940), 83.

7   *Ibid.*, 83.

8   E.C. [Ernest Chapman], 'The Boosey & Hawkes Concerts', *Tempo* 6 (February, 1944), 7.

9   Ralph Vaughan Williams, *Household Music: Three Preludes on Welsh Hymn Tunes* (London: Oxford University Press, 1943), preface to the score. Its subtitle is also telling: its Welsh hymn tunes – dutifully patriotic sources – are developed into a fantasia, a scherzo, and a set of variations respectively.

10   Vaughan Williams had already famously written for voice and ensemble (*On Wenlock Edge*, 1908-09) and for the unprecedented mixed quintet of clarinet, horn, violin, cello and piano (Quintet in D Major, 1898). At least three British composers (Hugh Wood, Iain Hamilton and Alan Rawsthorne) have emulated the quintet's unusual line-up, which, incidentally, is very similar to a basic Pierrot quintet.

11   The suggested instrumentation is: 'Violin I, alternatively Oboe, Clarinet, Flute, Recorder, Soprano Saxophone or Cornet; Violin II, alternatively Oboe, Clarinet, Flute, Recorder, Soprano Saxophone or Cornet; Viola, alternatively Violin and Cello (in combination) [in recognition of the scarce ownership of violas, presumably], Clarinet, Recorder, Saxophone in E♭; Cello, alternatively Bassoon, Bass Clarinet, Recorder, Saxophone in B♭ or Euphonium. (A fifth part is also written for horn *ad lib.* [enabling a wind quintet to perform the work].)'.

12   Credit for the stewardship of the series is attributed to Keith Douglas, the conductor and impresario whose financial intervention had already averted the wartime suspension of the Proms.

13   Indeed, this performance celebrated the twentieth anniversary of its premiere in this form at the home of its poet, Edith Sitwell, on 24 January 1922. Its public premiere was held on 12 June 1923 at the Aeolian Hall, just five months

before *Pierrot*'s first performance in Britain. *Façade* was more usually heard in the form of one of two suites for orchestra Walton had arranged (most recently in 1938) or as a ballet (1929), based on the five numbers used for the First Orchestral Suite (1926).

14   Besides Boosey & Hawkes, the Royal Philharmonic Society, BBC and London Symphony Orchestra (LSO) Concert Society co-promoted the event, although their attachment is likely to have extended only to the release of their orchestral players.

15   This second objective was doubly valuable in light of restrictions on access to music elsewhere, for example in broadcasting. Reluctant to decimate their schedules, the BBC had banned from its airwaves only music hailing from enemy countries that was in copyright (which then subsisted in works until fifty years after a composer's death) and exempted others, most notably Brahms, who had either pre-dated contemporary copyright collection societies or had never joined. For more on the BBC's policy towards 'alien' composers, see Robert Mackay, 'Leaving Out the Black Notes: The BBC and "Enemy Music" in the Second World War', *Media History* 6/1 (2000), 77-82.

16   Anonymous review of Boosey & Hawkes Concert No. 9, 'Two Freak Works', *The Times* (4 June 1942), 23. Anderson was best known at the time for her role in the Auden-Isherwood Group Theatre piece *The Ascent of F6* (1936), for which Britten wrote incidental music. He proceeded to write *Cabaret Songs* (1937-39) for her.

17   F.B. [identity unknown], 'London Summer Concerts', *Musical Times* 83/1193 (July, 1942), 222.

18   Benjamin Britten, letter to Peter Pears (1 June 1942) in: Donald Mitchell and Philip Reed (eds.), *Letters from a Life: The Selected Letters and Diaries of Benjamin Britten 1913-1976* (5 vols.), vol. 2 (London: Faber, 1991), 1055. The alleged inaudibility of *Façade* was despite, or because of, the text being amplified for the first time by a microphone rather than an authentic Sengerphone (in short, this was a papier-mâché cone, useable without the metallic rasp of a megaphone). See Osbert Sitwell, *Laughter in the Next Room*, vol. 4, *Left Hand, Right Hand* (London: Macmillan, 1949), 137.

19   Edwin Evans, programme notes to each of the concerts detailed in ex. 4.1 (29 May 1942; 26 June 1942), pages unnumbered (CPH). Gray's text meant, uniquely, that three different languages (French, German and English) had been used by the first three reciters of *Pierrot* in Britain (Marya Freund, Erika Wagner and Hedli Anderson respectively). Whatever their reasoning, Benoist-Méchin and Gray would have found it difficult to ignore Hartleben's version because his own translation had been so free.

20   William Walton, interview with Bernard Keeffe, *The Façade Affair*, BBC Radio 3, 12 June 1973, quoted in: Stephen Lloyd, *William Walton: Muse of Fire* (Woodbridge: Boydell Press, 2011), 33. See also note 21.

21   *Façade*'s poetic content had been revised repeatedly since its premiere. Paul Driver explains that the order of the twenty-one poems was settled upon in 1951, the year of *Façade*'s overdue publication, but it was these wartime

performances that fixed their content. See Paul Driver, "'Façade' Revisited', *Tempo* 133/134 (September, 1980), 7.

22 Schoenberg's suspicion was that a version of *Pierrot* in English would outsell his recent recording in the United States. See Arnold Schoenberg, letter to Erwin Stein (23 January 1943) in: *Letters*, ed. Erwin Stein, trans. Eithne Wilkins and Ernst Kaiser (Eng. edn., London: Faber, 1964), 215. The project did not materialize because Walter Goehr was no longer Music Director with Columbia by this time; so began the troubled history of attempts to release an LP of *Pierrot* in Britain. For further details, see Chapter 7, note 12.

23 Optionally including the speaker, *Pierrot* and *Façade* share a quartet of musicians, but the Pierrot and Façade ensembles rarely coalesce: to my knowledge, Walton's line-up has been emulated only once. Dispensing with text, Richard Rodney Bennett's *Commedia I* (1971-72) cast its tuned instruments as characters from the *commedia dell'arte* – flute (Columbine), bass clarinet (Pantaloon), saxophone (Harlequin), trumpet (Punchinello) and cello (Pierrot) – although the flute and bass clarinet are undoubled.

24 Walton, *op. cit.*

25 Edith Sitwell, *Taken Care of – An Autobiography* (London: Hutchinson, 1965), 123.

26 See Richard Temple Savage, *Voice from the Pit: Reminiscences of an Orchestral Musician* (London: Thames, 1965), 97. Trau's replacement was another namesake of the conductor-composer, George Walton. Perhaps recruited by his son, Bob (on trumpet), Walton Sr. retired from the Hallé Orchestra as the war began. On sax, Mickey Lewis replaced Frank Johnson, a fellow regular on the British dance band scene.

27 *Ibid.*, 97-8.

28 For Temple Savage the concert was typically extra-mural: he usually played with the London Philharmonic Orchestra and was also an active conductor. Francis's wartime duties had shifted on medical grounds from policing in London to touring the country playing for CEMA; more significant, however, was his role in recording Britten's *Pierrot*-scored film music a few years earlier.

29 See Temple Savage, 98. On the rehearsal's location, it is probably relevant that the group's violinist-violist, Gombrich, married John Forsdyke, director of the British Museum, that year.

30 See Arnold Schoenberg, diary entry for 23 October 1912, in: *Berliner Tagebuch*, ed. Josef Rufer (Frankfurt: Propyläen, 1974), 34.

31 Blades, then principal percussionist with the London Symphony Orchestra, also worked for ENSA during the war. But it was performance with groups such as the Melos Ensemble, English Opera Group and the *ad hoc Façade* ensemble detailed here that would make his name.

32 See Peter Stadlen, 'Österreichische Exilmusiker in England' in: *Beiträge '90: Österreichische Musiker im Exil-Kolloquium 1988 der Österreichischen Gesellschaft für Musik*, ed. Monica Wildauer (Kassel: Bärenreiter, 1990), 125. Trau's first concert appearance in Britain was in January 1937, after which she performed frequently in London.

33   See Peter Stadlen, 'Schoenberg's Speech-song', *Music & Letters* 62/1 (January, 1981), 1-11. Remembered as much for his music criticism as his performance, Stadlen retired as a pianist in the mid 1950s, after many achievements – premiering Webern's *Variations*, Op. 27, for example, and championing such music across Europe – upon which his second career drew. See Chapter 6, note 8.

34   See Peter Stadlen, 'Österreichische Exilmusiker in England' in: *Beiträge '90: Österreichische Musiker im Exil-Kolloquium 1988 der Österreichischen Gesellschaft für Musik*, ed. Monica Wildauer (Kassel: Bärenreiter, 1990), 132.

5 Two Twelve-note Pierrot Ensembles

For a composer so steeped in the thought of Schoenberg and Webern, it is remarkable that Elisabeth Lutyens claimed to have first heard *Pierrot lunaire* only in 1949.[1] After all, her husband Edward Clark owned a signed copy of the score, had been Arnold Schoenberg's sole British student, and, according to Lutyens, had even witnessed the composer running through *Pierrot* at the piano.[2] Yet, we do know that Lutyens was not resident in London for the wartime performances of *Pierrot* since she evacuated in June 1940 to Blagdon (near Newcastle) and returned only in November 1943. By now middle-aged, she travelled in April 1949 to Palermo, Sicily to attend the twenty-third annual Festival of the ISCM, of which Clark was President. This nine-day event promised Lutyens the rare opportunity of a high-profile premiere: her 'dramatic scena' *The Pit*, Op. 14 (1947) was staged at the Teatro Massimo during the opening weekend (24 April). That event disappointed Lutyens, but another work performed during the festival meant she would remember it fondly. A day earlier she had heard *Pierrot lunaire*, the centrepiece of seventy-fifth birthday celebrations in honour of Schoenberg, with Marya Freund reciting with an ensemble unusually directed from the piano and drawn from the Accademia Filarmonica Romana.

However muted responses to Freund had been during *Pierrot*'s British premiere in 1923, activities after Palermo show a British contingent spurred into action by this veteran of the work's performance. Besides Lutyens, Lennox Berkeley and Humphrey Searle were present at the festival on 28 April to hear performances of their Piano Concerto in Bb Major, Op. 29 (1947) and *Fuga giocoso*, Op. 13 (1948) respectively, conducted by another Briton, Constant Lambert. We have seen how Searle and Lambert had comparable, favourable outlooks on *Pierrot*, but Lutyens was less vocal on how she perceived the piece.[3] She was no less moved by its performance, however. Besides film music, which she regarded as little more than a lucrative chore, the only work she completed during the next eighteen months was the *Concertante for Five Players*, Op. 22 (1950). Furthermore, she scored it for the instrumental specification of *Pierrot lunaire* (ex. 5.1).

	fl	pic	cl	bcl	pf	vn	va	vc
I. Lirico *Allegretto*	✓		✓		✓	✓		✓
II. Drammatico *Allegro moderato*	✓			✓	✓	✓		✓
III. Commodo *Andante*	✓		✓		✓	✓		✓
IV. Scherzando *Allegro moderato*		✓	✓		✓		✓	✓
V. Recitativo *Lento*	✓			✓	✓	✓		✓
VI. Grazioso *Poco allegro*		✓	✓		✓		✓	✓
VII. Adagio *Dolce*	✓			✓	✓		✓	✓

Example 5.1   Instrumental Specification of
Elisabeth Lutyens's Concertante for Five Players, *Op. 22*

This sudden slowdown in Lutyens's prolific output was unusual but reflected her desperate personal circumstances at the time. The death of her close friend Lambert from alcoholism in 1951 persuaded her to seek treatment for the same condition the following year.[4] By then she had already temporarily split from Clark following a mental collapse which had forced her into a hospice, having recently 'found a fifth child en route [but with] neither the health [nor] money to go through with it.'[5] Such crises would appear to render insignificant her artistic dilemmas, but in fact Lutyens never lost sight of her vocation. Tellingly, in 1947-48 she wrote a spate of works whose central concern was to portray victims in various states (*The Pit*, the ballet *Rhadamanthus* and *Requiem for the Living*, Op. 16). Lutyens would abrasively credit her passing interest in the subject to an unnamed friend (probably Clark) who preferred 'failure and grievance to achievement and success'.[6] However disingenuous the claim – Lutyens herself was surely the chief 'victim' – her music was now bound by a heightened, more direct sense of expressivity, a trend that even the non-dramatic *Concertante for Five Players* would continue.[7]

Written a generation before the Second Viennese School reached any kind of general acceptance in Britain, the *Concertante* was the first in a long line of British works for Pierrot ensemble that would be performed in concert alongside *Pierrot*. The prescience of its composition for *Pierrot*'s five players and eight instruments would also eventually go some way to rectifying Lutyens's neglect in Britain. To reveal the true nature of this inchoate, mid-century lineage of Pierrot ensembles, we must question the precise relationship between these works. Notwithstanding the fact that the *Concertante* was originally Lutyens's twenty-first opus, as *Pierrot* had so significantly been to Schoenberg,[8] we ask, did Lutyens's effort extend beyond the notional 'convenience' of the Pierrot ensemble, as visionary as that act was? It is highly unlikely that Lutyens was aware of Benjamin Britten's earlier film music for similar forces: the pieces remain unpublished and unlike his few celebrated works for film that found their way to the concert hall (for example *Night Mail*, *Coal Face* and, indirectly, the choral *Rossini Suite*),[9] *Dinner Hour* and *Men Behind the Meters* did not. Although both composers studied at the Royal College of Music – Lutyens enrolled in 1926, Britten in 1930 – and only seven years in age separated them, relations between the two were never close. Both their personalities were strident, yet they viewed music and life very differently. Lutyens, who saw herself as an unapologetic reformer, could not countenance Britten's more utilitarian aesthetic.[10] However, just as Britten had been aware of another work for the ensemble besides *Pierrot*, so too had Lutyens.

Hanns Eisler: A Cinematic Response (II)

Vierzehn Arten den Regen zu beschreiben (*Fourteen Ways of Describing Rain*), Op. 70 was Hanns Eisler's second work after the Schoenberg-commissioned *Palmström* to be derived timbrally from *Pierrot lunaire* (ex. 5.2). It also was played at the ISCM Festival in Palermo (25 April 1949). After the piano-less *Palmström*, Eisler subtly changed the Pierrot ensemble again: *Vierzehn Arten* does not require doubling between parts (there is no piccolo or bass clarinet), nor even five players specifically, as the violin and viola play separately (but never sound together). The instruments of a traditional string trio may be present, as in *Pierrot*, but they are never used as such; the viola is heard in only three movements.[11] More significantly, as in Lutyens's *Concertante*, Eisler's Pierrot ensemble is voiceless, avoiding the contentious *Sprechstimme*. This is because Eisler wrote the work in 1940-41 as a scholarly response to the film *Regen* (1929), Mannus Franken and Joris Ivens's silent, impressionistic depiction of Amsterdam in the midst of rainfall.[12]

Vierzehn Arten was central to a wider piece of research dubbed the Film Music Project, itself part of the 1947 treatise by the composer and Theodor W. Adorno, *Composing for the Films*. Its purpose was 'to test the most advanced resources and the corresponding complex composing technique in their relation to the motion picture.'[13] Accordingly, Eisler's composition would

	fl	cl	pf	vn	va	vc
Nr. 1 (Anagramm)	✓	✓		✓		✓
Nr. 2 (Introduktion)	✓	✓	✓	✓		✓
Nr. 3 (Choral-Etüde)	✓	✓	✓	✓		✓
Nr. 4 (Scherzando)	✓	✓	✓	✓		✓
Nr. 5	✓	✓	✓		✓	✓
Nr. 6	✓	✓	✓	✓		✓
Nr. 7 (Sonatina)	✓	✓	✓	✓		✓
Nr. 8 (Intermezzo)	✓	✓	✓		✓	✓
Nr. 9	✓	✓	✓		✓	✓
Nr. 10 (Presto Etüde)			✓			
Nr. 11 (Überleitung)	✓	✓		✓		✓
Nr. 12	✓	✓	✓	✓		✓
Nr. 13	✓	✓	✓	✓		✓
Nr. 14	✓	✓	✓	✓		✓
Nr. 15	✓	✓	✓	✓		✓

Example 5.2 Instrumental Specification of Hanns Eisler's
Vierzehn Arten den Regen zu beschreiben, *Op. 70*

experiment with the twelve-note method as, in a more imaginary context, his mentor Schoenberg had a decade earlier in *Begleitungsmusik zu einer Lichtspielszene (Accompaniment to a Cinematographic Scene)*, Op. 34. Eisler's ploy was to shun the type of 'lush' composition for film popular at the time and to co-opt Schoenberg's Pierrot ensemble, with its versatility and quasi-orchestral reach, instead. A micro-structural commentary Eisler provided to accompany his 'Choral Etüde', for example, detailed how the accentuated, 'seeping' (*tropfend*) clusters in the piano herald the cello's 'soft' *pizzicato*, both signalling the first raindrops, as canonic entries of the chorale melody unfurl on the clarinet and cello.[14] Such a literal description shows the extent to which Eisler sought fidelity between his music and the moving image. His analysis, however, did not reach beyond *Vierzehn Arten*'s musico-cinematic design to clarify the broader aesthetic – one that Lutyens's *Concertante for Five Players* happens to share.

Elisabeth Lutyens's Mask

From Schoenberg's twenty-one movements spanning a little over thirty minutes, Eisler aligned his theme and fourteen climatic variations to a film lasting a little under twelve. A decade later, Lutyens wrote the *Concertante* in seven movements, completing an obvious pattern in which the numbers of movements descend from composer to composer in multiples of seven: a number integral to *Pierrot*'s structure, of course. The *Concertante* adopted the same sparse, compartmentalised context, and '[avoided] all superfluities', as Eisler and Adorno had encouraged in *Composing for the Films*.[15] Indeed, Tim Howell's description of *Vierzehn Arten*'s 'mixture of strictly ordered row-forms and freely organized motivic workings' could be applied equally to Lutyens's *Concertante*.[16] The relaxed serial style of the fifth movement ('Recitativo') is typical: a metronomic violin plays crotchets throughout, while, one by one, short utterances of the flute, bass clarinet, cello and piano interrupt each other, interweaving variations of the row (ex. 5.3).

The *concertante* texture duly unfolds just two 'voices' in what is, in effect, an instrumental *recitativo* duet.[17] The solo violin's colourfully double-stopped accompaniment is stable, for all the redundant changes in time signature. To modern listeners, its 'drone' may sound a little naïve in the serial context, yet the tonal centricity it effects is reconciled, however technically, with the serial method.[18] Both Eisler and Lutyens, then, followed Schoenberg in seeking the maximum dramatic contrast from minimal means. Their common choice of the Pierrot ensemble and, relatedly, their gestural and dramatic effects was what realized this, not *Pierrot*'s varied breadth of timbres. The timbral variation between Lutyens's movements was purposely limited: all seven movements are quintets, no player is compelled to swap instruments within a movement, yet the complete '*Pierrot* palette' is used across the piece. Within these constraints, only eight permutations were available to Lutyens, and only four are found in the piece.

This is surprising given its genesis in *Pierrot*, in which the number and combination of instruments are famously varied. Timbrally, Eisler had also been more consistent than Schoenberg in *Vierzehn Arten*. Five of the six instruments are heard in every movement except the 'Anagramm' theme and the 'Presto Etüde', whose solo piano belongs with its neighbouring 'Überleitung' ('Transition', bar 361), as the flute, clarinet, violin and cello re-orchestrate and develop the etude's material. A relevant parallel in *Pierrot*, with the same forces, is the single-bar piano transition between 'Raub' and 'Rote Messe'. Indeed, Lutyens imitated the same scheme in her 'Commodo' movement, in which the piano's sixteen-bar introduction precedes the entry of the same instruments.

Example 5.3   Elisabeth Lutyens, Concertante for Five Players, *V. 'Recitativo'*

How the presentation of the *Pierrot* and *Vierzehn Arten* changed over time would also appear to have influenced Lutyens. In part, both works shed the 'authentic' designs that had been present at their inception to assume different meanings in performance. By 1949 a costumed and/or acted *Pierrot* had long given way to more popular performances without these theatrical elements. And whether or not Lutyens was aware of the cinematic genesis of *Vierzehn Arten* – it would be ironic if so, given her attitude towards film music – that work, too, survived autonomously in concerts at Palermo and elsewhere. But for all that Lutyens was inspired by her sojourn to Palermo and clearly engaged with this early heritage in Pierrot ensemble composition, the *Concertante for Five Players* did not make spectacular inroads in Britain. Much like Britten's film music for similar forces, a schism existed between any appreciation of how these early British examples envisioned the genre and how the musical community, let alone the public, received them. Britten's works, however 'invisible' their performance on screen, were at least recorded, and his advantage of writing for an industry-backed sponsor meant the films were additionally toured using roadshows and mobile projectors.[19]

Despite its prescience, the first British concert work to emulate *Pierrot*'s ensemble fell victim to one of Lutyens's many wrangles with her various publishers, and the *Concertante* was unavailable commercially for over twenty years after its composition.[20] This may explain why neither of the two studies devoted to Lutyens – Harries and Harries (1989) and Tenant-Flowers (1991) – mentions the work. Her biographers exacerbate the omission, claiming that, '[over] the next few years [after her breakdown] Liz wrote a succession of pieces which made no advances or were so feeble she instantly scrapped them'.[21] In fact, the inventive *Concertante* was a defiant act of a composer overlooking her problems to furrow an almost lone serial path in Britain. The work was certainly not at that time 'typical of [her] employment of serial technique',[22] and although Lutyens did not mention it, her brand of serialism bore comparison with the innovations of composers held in much greater esteem, such as Ernst Krenek or her friend, Igor Stravinsky, whom she may have met through her husband, Edward Clark.

What must not be overlooked, either, is how unconventional the *Concertante* would have appeared in Britain at that time. As Lutyens was to say of her musical rebellion: 'One generally begins by reacting against the previous generation.'[23] Which names had she in mind? Representatives of the so-called Establishment, such as Ralph Vaughan Williams and Arnold Bax, whom she criticized elsewhere in her autobiography, are likely suspects. So too, startlingly, is Schoenberg, whose music Lutyens professed to dislike. Herein, at the feet of their composers, lies another reason for the obscurity of the earliest British Pierrot ensembles. Britten and, especially, Lutyens each propagated defensive judgments and accounts that served only to mask their achievements. Soon after writing so prolifically for the GPO and other sponsors, Britten belittled his efforts, as we have seen.[24] In what was surely a reference to his experiences in film and documentary, he would endorse this view by warning against the use of music 'just as a sound-effect, or to fill up the gaps during the talking' – exactly the functions his music for *Dinner Hour* and *Men Behind the Meters* had served.[25]

Lutyens's obfuscation was more elaborate. Despite being the first Briton to write serially, she resolutely, if incredibly, denied that Schoenberg was her inspiration. This is where Eisler and Lutyens differed most: *Vierzehn Arten* was written in honour of Schoenberg (as its dedication goes) and used his initials to form the beginning of its principal theme in 'Anagramm'. Instead, Lutyens eccentrically credited the equal part-writing of Henry Purcell's string fantasias as her precedent. When an interviewer put it to her that she '*chose* to become a student in the Viennese school of composition, stemming from Schoenberg', her response was typically caustic:

> Well I certainly didn't come to it from any knowledge of Schoenberg, Berg or Webern. I come from an unmusical family.[26] ... The thing which I think precipitated me towards what is now called serialism was the rediscovery in performance of the Purcell fantasias, where you heard four equal parts, coupled with the feeling I should scream if I heard a cadence again ... I remember being shown a score of Schoenberg in the war and saying, "Oh, he's done this too" ... I'd heard one piece of Webern at a contemporary concert,[27] never having heard the name before and thinking, "What marvellous music but how very strange from the composer of *Der Freischütz*." ... Well, I never get names right, you see.[28]

What Robert Saxton calls a 'complex psychological smoke-screen' is also a suspiciously well-evidenced argument,[29] and probably a defence mindful of a 'musical public conditioned to regard any deviations from tonal harmony as somehow un-English and not quite nice.'[30]

While this may conveniently recall Lutyens's own grievance with British musical life, denials of Schoenberg's influence recurred more troublingly throughout her career. This particular anecdote, for example, arose long after British hostility towards serialism had largely expired. Few, therefore, sought to question the extent of that influence. To describe it less charitably than Saxton, Lutyens's apologia became a rehearsed ruse: to cite Purcell in an improbable British lineage and, in turn, to hoodwink her audience. Nevertheless, an explicit instrumental companion to *Pierrot lunaire*, and a serial one at that, could hardly persuade listeners not to reminisce about

Schoenberg. And Lutyens surely knew that with no British group founded upon *Pierrot*'s line-up at the time, the chances of her work being performed hinged on the future success of Schoenberg's work. She took the risk of composing the *Concertante* anyway, and thanks to the efforts of Searle, her ally and fellow Palermo attendee, she was to be rewarded.

Notes

1   See Elisabeth Lutyens, *A Goldfish Bowl* (London: Cassell, 1972), 193.

2   Nevertheless, Lutyens dubiously identified Fritz Kreisler as the violinist Clark saw rehearse with Schoenberg. See *ibid.*, 95. Lutyens's unverifiable account reads: 'A chance reference to Schoenberg would remind Edward [Clark] of the occasion, at which he was present, when the first-ever sounds of *Pierrot Lunaire* emerged from Kreisler's violin as he deciphered the manuscript over Schoenberg's shoulder, sitting at the piano. Schoenberg had wanted Kreisler to undertake the violin/viola part and Kreisler was enthusiastic but unfortunately his international commitments as a soloist prevented him from undertaking this.'

3   See Chapter 3, notes 11-12. Upon his return from Palermo, Searle would also instigate events designed to revitalize the London concert scene with performances of *Pierrot* and a body of other music for mixed chamber ensembles (a subject of the next chapter).

4   See Meirion Harries and Susan Harries, *A Pilgrim Soul: The Life and Work of Elisabeth Lutyens* (London: Faber, 1989), 115-16, 143-45.

5   Elisabeth Lutyens, letter to René Leibowitz (PSS, Sammlung René Leibowitz). This typically unabashed account, though undated, bears the postmark of Eastbourne, home to the hospice where she stayed in early 1948.

6   Elisabeth Lutyens, 'Conceptual Link between *The Pit, Rhadamanthus* and *Requiem for the Living*', paper delivered at the 1951 Canford Summer School, repr. as 'Appendix 11' in: Sarah Jane Tenant-Flowers, *A Study of Style and Techniques in the Music of Elisabeth Lutyens*, 2 vols. (D.Phil. diss., University of Durham, 1991), vol. 2, 69-70.

7   Likewise, the work she credited with rescuing her from 'procrastinating vacillation' in 1952 was the Sixth String Quartet, having told herself 'with some severity, "Well, if you're a composer, bloody well sit down and compose!"' As the first work composed in Blackheath after her escape from the pub-lined streets of Fitzrovia, the quartet is important. But as her direct response to hearing *Pierrot* in Palermo, the *Concertante* saved Lutyens from a period of creative silence earlier still. Lutyens, *A Goldfish Bowl* (London: Cassell, 1972), 212.

8   The correlation between *Pierrot*'s 'three times seven poems' and its opus number is safe to assume; indeed, others have read much more into its numerology. See Colin C. Sterne, 'Pythagoras and Pierrot: An Approach to Schoenberg's Use of Numerology in the Construction of *Pierrot lunaire*',

Perspectives of New Music 21/1-2 (1982-83), 506-34. 'Op. 21' is pencilled in bold on Lutyens's handwritten copy of the *Concertante* (BL, Lutyens Collection, Add. Mss. 64526, vol. 92). Only the later renumbering of her opused works pushed it on to Op. 22.

9   The latter, itself recycled in the orchestral *Soirées musicales* a year later, derived from Britten's music for the animation *The Tocher* (GPO, 1935).

10   Other less deserving criticisms by Lutyens – of the Aldeburgh Festival, Boosey & Hawkes (Britten's publishers), etc. – betray simple resentment of her younger, more successful peer. See Harries and Harries, 249-51.

11   After Eisler's example, many other Pierrot ensembles were scored with separate parts for violin and viola: see Catalogue of Pierrot Ensembles, section 5b: vii. violin and viola undoubled. Although the Pierrot ensemble was certainly Eisler's template, Schoenberg's *Suite*, Op. 29 (1924-26, scored for piccolo, clarinet (or flute), bass clarinet (or bassoon), piano, violin, viola and cello) is a close relation. A more pragmatic coincidence is *Pierrot*'s occasional performance by six players, with a separate violinist and violist.

12   Lou Lichtveld had originally scored *Regen* for flute, string trio and harp.

13   Theodor W. Adorno and Hanns Eisler, *Composing for the Films* (1947) (2nd edn., London: Athlone, 1994), 148.

14   See *ibid.*, 149-51.

15   *Ibid*, 152.

16   Tim Howell, 'Eisler's Serialism: Concepts and Methods' in: *Hanns Eisler: A Miscellany*, ed. David Blake (Luxembourg: Harwood, 1995), 129.

17   We cannot say for certain, but Lutyens was probably aware of Schoenberg's *Harmonielehre* (1911) – Clark was a pupil of Schoenberg as it was being written-which first described a timbrally shared, continuous *Klangfarbenmelodie*. Either way, tone colour is uppermost in Lutyens's vision here, and another precedent is the opening 'Lirico', in which the whole Pierrot ensemble shares a movement-long line.

18   The drone initiates the first row, P4, which the piano continues in bar 2 (D… E♭, D♭, C…), the second row, I4, which the flute takes up in bar 4 (D… D♭, E♭, E♮…), and so forth.

19   See Elizabeth Sussex, *The Rise and Fall of British Documentary: The Story of the Film Movement founded by John Grierson* (Berkeley: University of California Press, 1975), 95.

20   Even relations with the work's eventual publishers, Mills Music, quickly turned sour. By the time the *Concertante* went to print in 1970, Lutyens had launched her self-financed Olivan Press.

21   Harries and Harries, 137.

22   George F. DeVine, 'Chamber Music: Elisabeth Lutyens', *Notes* 27/4 (1971), 806.

23   Elisabeth Lutyens, *A Goldfish Bowl* (London: Cassell, 1972), 213.

24   See Chapter 3, note 30.

25   Benjamin Britten, 'Conversation with Benjamin Britten', *Tempo* 6 (February, 1944), 4.

26   Unmusical, perhaps, but not inartistic: Elisabeth was the daughter of the famous architect Sir Edwin Lutyens.

27   The work was in fact *Das Augenlicht*, Op. 26, Webern's recently composed cantata, which was given its premiere in Britain under Hermann Scherchen at the ISCM Festival in Queen's Hall, London (17 June 1938).

28   Elisabeth Lutyens, interview with Bernard Palmer, BBC Radio 3 (12 September 1969); emphasis added.

29   Robert Saxton, 'Elisabeth Lutyens' in: *New Music 88*, ed. Michael Finnissy, Malcolm Hayes and Roger Wright (Oxford: Oxford University Press, 1989), 10.

30   Susan Bradshaw, 'The Music of Elisabeth Lutyens', *Musical Times* 112/1541 (July, 1971), 653.

6 Rejuvenating Post-war Performance

Upon graduating from General Secretary to President of the ISCM in 1947, Edward Clark enlisted Humphrey Searle – composer, writer, and now BBC 'producer of musical programmes' – to fill his vacancy.[1] Together, they were to be decisive players in the post-war rebirth of contemporary British music. Their efforts also came several years before William Glock and Hans Keller threw the BBC head-first into promoting new music.[2] Arranging for Marya Freund, at the age of 73, to make a rare visit to Britain was one landmark. Just seven months after *Pierrot* was heard at the ISCM Festival in Palermo, and again to mark Arnold Schoenberg's seventy-fifth birthday, Freund and the same Italian ensemble were invited to give its first performance in Britain since the war (ex. 6.1). Unlike its two wartime concerts in 1942, however, no Britons were involved for this presentation by the London Contemporary Music Centre (LCMC, the British Section of the ISCM), which, with no permanent base, was hosted by the galleries of the Royal Society of British Artists (RBA).

For Searle, organizing this and other events was only part of his recognition and promotion of worthy musical trends, as he saw them. Writing in 1949 for the launch of a journal issued by the ISCM, he was quick to document the new attitudes towards instrumental writing that composers had adopted in the early part of the century.[3] Searle believed that standardized combinations in chamber music had reached their height by the end of the nineteenth century, but that recent innovations – from Schoenberg's First Chamber Symphony (1906) to the new *Liriche Greche* (1942-45) by Luigi Dallapiccola (a second-generation serialist, like Searle) – showed a renewed will to experiment with the forces composers chose. Searle himself was practising with unusual ensembles: at the time of this article he was probably completing the *Quartet for Mixed Winds and Strings*, Op. 12, a work dedicated to Clark on his sixtieth birthday and scored for the unusual combination of clarinet, bassoon, violin and viola. *Pierrot* was another work he cited, although it was one of many. Despite his use of the smaller mixed chamber ensemble, he was never to write for Pierrot ensemble. Given the observation that composers in the twentieth century had altogether spurned

8 November 1949, 7.30pm
RBA Galleries, Suffolk Street, Pall Mall, London

London Contemporary Music Centre (LCMC) presents: 'In Celebration of Schoenberg's 75th Birthday'

Arnold Schoenberg
Drei Klavierstücke, Op. 11 (1909) †

Luigi Dallapiccola
Ciaccona, Intermezzo e Adagio (1945) NP ‡

Arnold Schoenberg
Sechs kleine Klavierstücke, Op. 19 (1911) †
Pierrot lunaire (Albert Giraud, trans. Otto Erich Hartleben), Op. 21 (1912) *

[
Ferruccio Busoni
Toccata: Preludio, Fantasia, Ciaccona for Piano, K. 287
]

Marya Freund (*Sprechsängerin*),
Pietro Scarpini († piano / * piano and director),
Pietro Grossi (‡ cello)

Gruppo Musica Insieme dell' Accademia Filarmonica Romana •

Busoni's Toccata was advertised but not performed. It was replaced by Schoenberg's Op. 11.
• On 23 April 1949 the group performed Pierrot at the 23rd ISCM Festival in Palermo.

Ex. 6.1   Arnold Schoenberg 75th Birthday Concert at the RBA Galleries the 'normal' combinations of the past, this is not surprising. What Searle's argument precluded was the possibility that *new* standardized line-ups could emerge. The Pierrot ensemble soon did.

Humphrey Searle's Society for Twentieth Century Music, 1952

Searle's perception is doubly important because upon returning from Palermo he would instigate events designed to rejuvenate the London concert scene in the 1950s. Performances of *Pierrot* and a body of other music for mixed chamber ensembles were central to the ethos. Without Searle, indeed, the first British concert work abiding by *Pierrot*'s instrumental ensemble may never have seen the light of day. In 1952, Elisabeth Lutyens's *Concertante for Five Players*, Op. 22 would help define the capital's newest concert society, the Society for Twentieth Century Music, under whose auspices it was premiered. Formed that year to bring contemporary music to north-west London, the Society was chaired by Searle and used Hampstead Town Hall as its base. A bold agenda allowed for all-contemporary programmes featuring twentieth-century 'classics' alongside new works by young composers, domestic and foreign, with a 'fair general representation of British contemporary works'.[4]

This amounted to the music of one British-born composer being heard in each of the first five concerts: Constant Lambert, Lutyens, Daniel Jones, Peter Racine Fricker and Alan Rawsthorne respectively (ex. 6.2 (i-ii)). Music by Roberto Gerhard and Bernard van Dieren, both now naturalized Britons,[5] was also performed in the third concert (3 March), while in the sixth (26 May) and seventh (8 July, a date not originally planned as part of the series), music by two Britons was heard: Walton's *Façade* on both occasions, with works by Searle and Fricker. The choice of Varèse's *Octandre* as the twentieth-century 'classic' with which to open the inaugural concert (28 January, conducted by Norman Del Mar) proved a remarkable foresight. Programmed with Dallapiccola's recent *Due Liriche di Anacreonte* (1944-45, one third of the *Liriche Greche* Searle had cited three years earlier), the concert displayed a brave dedication to repertoire for mixed ensemble that would characterize the whole series.

Searle's endorsement of Lutyens was a symptom of their broader, natural alliance. At the BBC, he arranged for only the second performance of her aforementioned First Chamber Concerto in November 1947. They were also 'second-generation' serialists, with no British forebears, and were tarred as such: Francis Routh, for example, played a seminal part in acknowledging Britain's latest musical uprising, but would shelve Searle's lifetime's work as 'coloured, and limited, by his creative alignment with the 12-note style of Schoenberg.'[6] Searle had already attributed the rise of mixed ensembles to a parallel interest in counterpoint, to contend that 'only by concentration of their resources could [composers] ensure that each part stood out clearly.'[7] The advent of serialism only fortified the trend. His studies with Anton Webern a decade earlier are instructive here, though not necessarily because of serialism: Searle claimed the subject was raised not once during his six months of lessons; rather, Webern's development (after Schoenberg) of a type of orchestration 'in which each player is a soloist' was noticed above all.[8] Just as Webern's Op. 24 nonet inspired Lutyens to write her chamber concerto, so too is its publication a year before Searle's article probably no coincidence. Certainly, its influence is clear when listening to a work dedicated to Webern's memory, the *Intermezzo for Eleven Instruments*, Op. 8 (1946), another mixed ensemble and Searle's first serial work.

René Leibowitz's support of Searle was mutual, and it was not limited to composition. They exchanged letters in the late 1940s, involving Lutyens and Clark in their correspondence too, while Searle invited Leibowitz to conduct in London in response to his premiere of the *Intermezzo* (which he had also commissioned) with the Chamber Ensemble of the French National Orchestra in Paris. The *Intermezzo*, however, was not performed at any of the Hampstead concerts. Searle's oeuvre was modestly represented by a single work, the new Piano Sonata, Op. 21 (26 May). The repertoire selected placed certain demands on the administration of the concert series and Searle's committee realized measures were needed to sustain their ambitious designs across six concerts. Perhaps looking to the Macnaghten concerts, which had been revived two years earlier, this new series was contrived as a co-operative venture that largely relied on the goodwill of its players. Searle also introduced a novel variation to the norm:

> We ... managed to persuade the BBC to repeat most of our programmes in the studio, so that in most cases the artists were willing to reduce their fees for us; this was necessary because of the small seating capacity of Hampstead Town Hall.[9]

The benevolence of musicians and the BBC was matched by the public, who flocked to the affluent London district for the Monday evening concerts, filling the venue at least twice. On 11 February, at the Society's second concert, the audience spilled into the aisles to hear another contemporary classic, *Pierrot lunaire*.[10]

The performance was its first in Britain since Schoenberg's death a year earlier. Unlike the opening concert's one-off tribute to Lambert, who had also died in 1951, Schoenberg's music was a recurrent feature of the series. Lutyens's *Concertante* was heard with *Pierrot* with two other works written in the 1910s in its aftermath: Igor Stravinsky's *Three Japanese Lyrics*, which augmented its line-up, and Darius Milhaud's *Machines agricoles*, Op. 56,

The Society for Twentieth Century Music

11 February – Hampstead Town Hall, London

Darius Milhaud
Machines agricoles, Op. 56 (1919)

Igor Stravinsky
Three Japanese Lyrics
(Yamabe no Akahito, Masazumi Miyamoto, Ki no Tsurayuki) (1912-13)

Elisabeth Lutyens
Concertante for Five Players, Op. 22 (1950) *WP* •

Arnold Schoenberg
Pierrot lunaire (Albert Giraud, trans. Otto Erich Hartleben), Op. 21 •

Hedli Anderson (*Sprechsängerin*), Margaret Field-Hyde (soprano),
Francis Chagrin (conductor)

The London Symphony Orchestra Chamber Ensemble

FLUTE / PICCOLO Edward Walker	VIOLIN I Lionel Bentley
CLARINET Sidney Fell	VIOLIN II Unidentified †
BASS CLARINET Walter Lear	VIOLA Gwynne Edwards
BASSOON Ronald Waller	CELLO Willem de Mont
PIANO (• / DIRECTOR) Peter Stadlen	DOUBLE BASS George Yates

† Required only for Stravinsky's Three Japanese Lyrics, *the second violinist's identity is not documented. Contemporaneous players in this position, however, included Kenneth Moore, James Soutter and Kenneth Havelock.*
All works except Lutyens's were recorded on 12 February 1952, 7.00pm, for broadcast on 12 March 1952 as 'Chamber Concert', BBC Third Programme, 10.10-11.15pm.

Example 6.2   (i) Second Concert of the Society for Twentieth Century Music, 1952, at 7.30pm, featuring the premiere of Lutyens's Concertante for Five Players, *Op. 22*

28 January – Hampstead Town Hall, London

Edgard Varèse
Octandre (1923)

Constant Lambert
Eight Poems of Li-Po (trans. Shigeyoshi Obata) (1926-29/47)

Luigi Dallapiccola
Due liriche di Anacreonte (*Anacreon*, trans. Salvatore Quasimodo) (1944-45) NP

Constant Lambert
Concerto for Piano and Nine Players (1930-31)

Margaret Field-Hyde (soprano), Martin Boddey (tenor), Kyla Greenbaum (solo piano)
Norman Del Mar (conductor)

London Symphony Orchestra Chamber Ensemble:
Edward Walker (flute, piccolo), Donald Bridger (oboe), Sidney Fell (clarinet), Frank Hughes (piccolo clarinet, *Octandre*; clarinet, *Concerto for Piano*), Patrick Whelan (clarinet), Ronald Waller (bassoon), John Burden (horn), George Eskdale (trumpet), John Ashby (trombone), William Bradshaw (percussion), Sidney Crooke (piano), Gwynne Edwards (viola), Willem de Mont (cello), George Yates (double bass)

3 March – Hampstead Town Hall, London

Arnold Schoenberg
Wind Quintet, Op. 26 (1923-24)

Bernard van Dieren
Four Songs:
'Weep you no more sad fountains' (Anon.), 'Spring Song of the Birds' (King James I), 'Der Asra' (Heinrich Heine), 'Rondel' (Charles I de Valois) (1925-28)

Daniel Jones
Kettledrum Sonata (Sonata for Timpani) (1947) *WP*

Roberto Gerhard
Wind Quintet (1928)

Gilbert Webster (timpani), René Soames (• tenor), Frederick Stone (piano);
• replaced Frederick Fuller (baritone)

Dennis Brain Wind Quintet:
Gareth Morris (flute), Leonard Brain (oboe), Stephen Waters
(clarinet), Dennis Brain (horn), John Alexandra (bassoon)

7 April – Hampstead Town Hall, London

Roman Palester
String Quartet No. 3 (1942-43, later rev.)

Peter Racine Fricker
Four Impromptus, Op. 17 (1950-52) WP

Aaron Copland
Sextet (1937), arr. of *Short Symphony* (1932-33) NP

Peter Warlock
The Curlew (W.B. Yeats) (1920-22)

Trefor Jones (tenor), Lionel Solomon (flute), James MacGillivray (cor anglais),
Frederick Thurston (clarinet), Margaret Kitchin (piano)

New London Quartet:
Eric Gruenberg, Lionel Bentley (violins),
Keith Cummings (viola), Douglas Cameron (cello)

28 April – Hampstead Town Hall, London

Karl Amadeus Hartmann
String Quartet No. 2 (1945-46) NP

Béla Bartók
Contrasts, BB116 (1938)

Alan Rawsthorne
Variations for Two Violins (1937)

Paul Hindemith
Quartet for Piano, Clarinet, Violin and Cello (1938)

Georgina Dobrée (clarinet), Gordon Watson (piano)

Malcolm Latchem String Quartet:
Malcolm Latchem, Régis Plantevin (violins),
Margaret Major (viola), John Cook (cello)

Example 6.2 (ii-v) Other Concerts of the Society for Twentieth Century Music, 1952

26 May – Hampstead Town Hall, London

Arnold Schoenberg
Ode to Napoleon (George Byron), Op. 41 (1942)

Humphrey Searle
Piano Sonata, Op. 21 (1951)

William Walton
Façade Entertainment (Edith Sitwell) (1922-29, rev. 1942)

Hugh Burden (speaker), Gordon Watson (piano), Edith Sitwell (reciter)
George Weldon (conductor)

London Symphony Orchestra Chamber Ensemble Festival Hall, London

8 July – Hampstead Town Hall, London

Jacques Ibert
Concertino da Camera [*Saxophone Concertino*] (1935)

Peter Racine Fricker
Three Sonnets of Cecco Angiolieri, Op. 7 (1947)

Arnold Schoenberg
Pierrot lunaire, Op. 21 ‡

William Walton
Façade Entertainment (Edith Sitwell)

Edith Sitwell (reciter, *Façade*), Walter Lear (saxophone), Hedli Anderson
(*Sprechsängerin*, *Pierrot*), Alexander Young (tenor)
George Weldon (conductor), Peter Racine Fricker (conductor, *Three Sonnets*),
Peter Stadlen (‡ piano / director)

London Symphony Orchestra Chamber Ensemble

The Committee of the Society for Twentieth Century Music comprised:
Humphrey Searle (Chairman), Philip Bate, Maurice Brown, Brian Easdale,
Alan Frank, Sidney Giebel, Leonard Isaacs, Frida Kindler and Frank Winton.

Example 6.2   (vi-vii) Other Concerts of the Society for Twentieth Century Music, 1952

an irreverent setting of a farm-machine catalogue for voice and seven instruments whose only alteration to the template of a classical septet was to replace the horn with a bassoon. Unlike Lutyens and Stravinsky, Milhaud did not write his music in reaction to *Pierrot*, although its inclusion recognized his historical affinity with *Pierrot* as its first conductor in Britain.

At the same time, it was standard for concerts promoted by the Society to be determinedly catholic in style and media. Save for the illustrious appearance of the Dennis Brain Wind Quintet, no two works from any other concert were scored for the same forces (even the quintets of Schoenberg and Gerhard comprised only half of their programme). Some thought was surely given as to how far this inconsistency could be taken during each concert. For example, while Paul Hindemith's quartet for piano, clarinet, violin and cello (28 April) introduced a surprisingly new ensemble – a precursor to Olivier Messiaen's more famous *Quatuor pour la fin du temps* (1940-41) for that line-up – it also required just one more instrument than Béla Bartók's *Contrasts*, BB116. Similarly, a string quartet was required for three-quarters of the fourth concert (7 April), once alone for the Third String Quartet by Roman Palester (a Polish-born émigré to France), and twice within Aaron Copland and Peter Warlock's larger ensembles. Ultimately, however, such innovations were probably a factor in the Society's downfall. To have players either shuffling on or off stage with such regularity, or remaining silently seated while others played, was novel but decidedly inefficient. Despite apparently healthy attendances, big names and assiduous planning, the series was not a financial success. Its first season was also its last.[11]

The London Symphony Orchestra Chamber Ensemble

The performers of Lutyens's momentous Pierrot ensemble did not reflect its title. For in Hampstead, the *Concertante for Five Players* was premiered as a septet. Like the *Concertante*, furthermore, *Pierrot* itself was not conducted. Peter Stadlen, performing the work once more after his wartime concerts under Erwin Stein, instead directed it from the piano. This was unusual, even if Stadlen was following Pietro Scarpini's precedent at the LCMC, and perhaps risky too, since the piano is the busiest of *Pierrot*'s instruments. Nevertheless, the cohesion of ensemble, including Hedli Anderson's *Sprechstimme*, was reportedly unaffected.[12] Ostensibly, the instrumentalists were drawn from the London Symphony Orchestra (LSO), although the presence of Stadlen, a concert pianist, is one indication of the distinct identity and history the ensemble was forging. Another is that their second appearance for the Society for Twentieth Century Music was in a very different guise to their first, without the brass of Edgard Varèse's *Octandre* and Lambert's *Concerto for Piano and Nine Players*. It was again thanks to

14 December 1948 – RBA Galleries, Suffolk Street, Pall Mall, London

Institute of Contemporary Arts (ICA) presents:
'Twelve Note Music Today'

Humphrey Searle
Quartet for Clarinet, Bassoon, Violin and Viola, Op. 12 (1948)

Alois Hába
Toccata quasi una Fantasia, Op. 38 (1931) †

Roberto Gerhard
'Piece for Solo Flute' [*Capriccio*] (1948, later rev.)

Luigi Dallapiccola
Quattro liriche di Antonio Machado (1948, later rev.) •

Serge Nigg
Lied pour Piano (1947) †

Cláudio Santoro
Sonatina for Piano (1948) †

$$\left[\begin{array}{c} \textbf{Hanns Eisler} \\ \textit{Vierzehn Arten den Regen zu beschreiben, Op. 40} \end{array} \right]$$

† Liza Fuchsová (piano)
• Emelie Hooke (soprano), Margaret Kitchin (piano)

London Symphony Orchestra Chamber Ensemble

FLUTE Edward Walker	PIANO Peter Stadlen
CLARINET Sidney Fell	VIOLIN Lionel Bentley
BASSOON Ronald Waller	VIOLA Gwynne Edwards

Eisler's Op. 40, advertised by its subtitle, Variations, *was not performed.*

---

16 December 1948

Discussion

Panel included: Humphrey Searle, Peter Stadlen, Mátyás Seiber,
Roberto Gerhard, Alan Rawsthorne, Benjamin Frankel and Elisabeth Lutyens

Example 6.3 The LSO Chamber Ensemble and 'Twelve Note Music Today'

Searle that the kudos of the LSO was brought to Hampstead. In his position as Librarian and, later, Producer at the BBC, Searle had befriended many of the country's best musicians. His ties with the LSO were especially close. William Walton was its Honorary President and had advised Searle in the mid 1930s. Although thirteen years his junior, Searle returned the favour after the war. It was to the section principals, however, that Searle turned for the Society's inauguration.

In an orchestra run by its members, the custom was to allow players to send a deputy should another more prestigious (or better-paid) engagement arise, such as a solo recital. In reality, this extended to performances with larger groups. Such was the extent of players' moonlighting that various ensembles had been drawn from the orchestra since its earliest days. The trend continues today, of course, with spin-off groups airing mostly staple chamber repertory and 'outreaching' to schools and colleges. In its earliest guise, the Chamber Ensemble of the London Symphony Orchestra (CELSO) served a very different community. As one commentator astutely observed, it had 'come to the rescue of several modern composers who [had] written works for musical combinations.'[13] Devotion to this new repertoire for mixed forces brought with it an obligation, when necessary, to grow as large as fourteen or fifteen strong. Works from this new tradition of British music performed by the ensemble included Benjamin Britten's *Sinfonietta*, Arnold Bax's Nonet, Searle's *Intermezzo* and Lutyens's First Chamber Concerto. Allowing for changes in personnel as players joined or left the LSO, we can see that fostering this type of music meant that membership of the 'chamber' ensemble was inconsistent. Violinists such as Kenneth Moore, James Soutter and Kenneth Havelock were variously drafted in, while Patrick Whelan and Walter Lear swapped duties on bass clarinet. This surely suited musicians used to the accommodating ethos of their orchestra – attitudes that now extended to its derivative ensemble.[14]

Searle's first contact with the group was made several years before events in Hampstead were envisaged. Indeed, their association spoke for a distinct, uninhibited vision of musical life. One of their earlier contributions came on 14 December 1948, when a concert promoted by the newly-formed Institute of Contemporary Arts (ICA) took place (ex. 6.3). A forum for discussion was held a day later on the theme of the concert, 'Twelve Note Music Today'. Lutyens, Searle and Stadlen were again all involved, sitting on a panel with Alan Rawsthorne, Mátyás Seiber, Benjamin Frankel and Roberto Gerhard, although other British modernists, such as Christian Darnton and Denis ApIvor, probably also attended. The programme really stood at the cutting edge of new music. Except for Alois Hába's solo piano work of 1931, every piece had been written within the last two years. The body of composers chosen was also noticeably cosmopolitan: besides Britain, Czechoslovakia,

2 July 1953 – Recital Room, Festival Hall, London

Institute of Contemporary Arts (ICA) presents:
'Contemporary British Chamber Music'

Denis Aplvor
Landscapes (T.S. Eliot), for Tenor, Flute, Clarinet, Horn and String Trio, Op.15
(1950) †

James Iliff
Oboe Sonata (1951) ‡

Humphrey Searle
Quartet for Clarinet, Bassoon, Violin and Viola, Op. 12

Thomas Eastwood
Introduction and Allegro for String Trio (1952) ‡

Wilfrid Mellers
Carmina Felium (Edward Thomas, W.B. Yeats, etc.),
for Soprano, Clarinet, Bassoon, String Trio and Piano (1952, later rev.) ‡

Elisabeth Lutyens
Concertante for Five Players, Op. 22 •

Wilfred Brown (tenor), Pauline Lewis (soprano)

Virtuoso Chamber Ensemble

FLUTE (• / PICCOLO) Edward Walker	HORN John Burden
OBOE Donald Bridger	PIANO Wilfrid Parry
CLARINET Sidney Fell	VIOLIN Lionel Bentley
BASS CLARINET Patrick Whelan	VIOLA Gwynne Edwards
BASSOON Ronald Waller	CELLO Willem de Mont

‡ These were 'SPNM works', premiered that year under its auspices at the Arts Council headquarters
in March (Iliff) and April (Eastwood).

Example 6.4   Concert Debut of the Virtuoso Chamber Ensemble

2 November 1955 – Festival Hall, London ‡

New Era Concert Society

Constant Lambert
Concerto for Piano † and Nine Players

Gail Kubik
Gerald McBoing Boing (Dr. Seuss) (c. 1950) NP

Germaine Tailleferre
Harp Concertino (1926-27) NP

Arnold Schoenberg
Pierrot lunaire (Albert Giraud, trans. Otto Erich Hartleben), Op. 21

Bernard Galais (harp), Ethel Semser (*Sprechsängerin*)
Alvar Liddell (narrator), René Leibowitz (conductor)

Virtuoso Chamber Ensemble

FLUTE / PICCOLO	Edward Walker	PIANO	Wilfrid Parry †
CLARINETS	Sidney Fell	VIOLIN	Lionel Bentley
Douglas Matthews	Unidentified	VIOLA	Gwynne Edwards
BASS CLARINET	Walter Lear	CELLO	Willem de Mont
TRUMPET	George Eskdale	DOUBLE BASS	George Yates
TROMBONE	John Ashby	PERCUSSION	Gilbert Webster

The musicians underlined had recorded Pierrot *for release in Britain and the United States (Argo / Westminster, XWN 18143, 1955) and France (Boîte à Musique, LD 016, 1956).*
‡ Despite the moderate size of the ensemble, there is nothing to suggest the main Festival Hall (rather than one of its smaller spaces) was not used as the venue. Indeed, this concert was the second in the series of six 'orchestral' events promoted by the New Era Concert Society during the 1955/56 season.

Example 6.5   The Virtuoso Chamber Ensemble performs Pierrot lunaire

Spain, Italy, France and Brazil were represented. A German would have been present too, but for an unspecified reason Hanns Eisler could not appear to conduct his *Vierzehn Arten den Regen zu beschreiben* and so the programme's planned centrepiece was dropped.[15] A little over three years passed before the LSO musicians played in *Pierrot* (and *Concertante*) formation. Their activities in the interim, while significant, were sporadically limited by the number of concerts and broadcasts available to them. Their reconstitution as a chamber group was, for now, secondary to their positions in one of the country's leading orchestras.

From 1952, this balance changed. Their performances together became more frequent and paved the way for the reformation of their ensemble. The process began at the Arts Council's London headquarters on New Year's Day. Four of the group's players gave a free recital at a reception to celebrate the renaming of the Committee (now Society) for the Promotion of New Music (SPNM) for its tenth season and beyond. Only the string players were drawn from the LSO – the concert included *Three French Folksongs* (1952) for soprano (Sophie Wyss), flute (Gareth Morris) and string quartet by Peggy Shimmin, a *Scherzo* (1950) for string quartet by Roy Teed and the Third String Quartet (1943-45) by Leonard Salzedo – but fourteen musicians performed the music of Varèse, Lambert and Dallapiccola under the 'CELSO' title in Hampstead just four weeks later (28 January) to inaugurate the Society for Twentieth Century Music. The group made three further appearances during the series and also took part in a Schoenberg Memorial Concert at the Wigmore Hall (5 June), where they played Schoenberg's *Suite*, Op. 29 in its scoring for piano (Stadlen, again directing), a string trio, and flute, clarinet and bassoon (rather than E♭, B♭ and bass clarinets).

This last decision was not taken for the sake of innovation or due to a lack of players; three clarinettists had been called upon for Lambert's *Concerto*. Rather, Schoenberg's alternative septet called for the same instruments now ever-present in the group. That is, despite the changeability of some musicians between and within concerts, a core membership emerged: Edward Walker (flute, sometimes doubling piccolo), Sidney Fell (clarinet), Ronald Waller (bassoon), Lionel Bentley (violin), Gwynne Edwards (viola) and Willem de Mont (cello). Each sat as principals of their sections in the LSO.[16] Only the pianist's recruitment continued to vary within the septet. For their ensemble's second appearance at the Society for Twentieth Century Music they were joined by Walter Lear (bass clarinet), one of the first three Britons to play *Pierrot* in 1933, with Waller required only once for Milhaud's *Machines agricoles*. The bassoonist's usual presence meant the group was not founded exactly on Schoenberg's line-up, as later ensembles would be. Their performances of *Pierrot* (twice in 1952 alone) and the *Concertante for Five Players* nevertheless coincided with the escalation of their activities. Months later, this would manifest itself in the group's reformation, because in 1953 the London Symphony Orchestra Chamber Ensemble was reborn as the Virtuoso Chamber Ensemble.

The name-change brought their awkward former title to an end, but the more significant shift was in the group's greater autonomy.[17] During the summer of 1953, the ICA organized three concerts to showcase 'Contemporary British Chamber Music', for which the Virtuoso Chamber Ensemble gave a second performance of Lutyens's *Concertante* (ex. 6.4). (The group would continue to appear for ICA and SPNM events over the next decade.) In the company of Searle's *Quartet*, the *Concertante* was no longer an infant among continental classics but emphasized Lutyens's experience as a British serialist and composer for mixed ensemble. Two new works for voice and mixed ensemble by younger Britons also featured: *Landscapes*, Op. 50 for tenor, flute, clarinet, horn and string trio, was a song cycle by Denis Aplvor, who had adopted serialism in 1948; and the concert ended with Wilfrid Mellers's *Carmina Felium*, scored for soprano, clarinet, bassoon, string trio and piano in such a way as to suggest the composer's appreciation of the modern chamber song cycle, and Searle's voiceless *Quartet* from the same programme.

The group's regeneration also affected the constitution of the LSO. When, in 1955, it was considered that Fell had absented himself from the orchestra once too often, he was dismissed.[18] In protest, section leaders resigned *en masse*, their outrage doubtless exacerbated by the irony of an institution founded in defiance of Henry Wood's challenge to the deputy system in the Queen's Hall Orchestra sacking its principal clarinettist for the same transgression. As one orchestra was plunged into crisis, another was formed. The Sinfonia of London would not make their concert debut for another two years but its reputation was built from the profitable film work they inherited (or seized) from their previous employers, the LSO.[19] The relevance of the Virtuoso Chamber Ensemble to this episode has not been documented before, but it is clear to see. Over the previous seven years, its players' togetherness had already created an ensemble of increasing purpose in support of contemporary music. This now led to a formal split from the LSO and, with it, full independence.[20]

If performing Lutyens's *Concertante* for a second time compensated for its omission from broadcast a year earlier, then events after the LSO 'affair' would lend the Pierrot ensemble further support. Another performance of *Pierrot* took place in November 1955, conducted by Leibowitz and recited by his wife, Ethel Semser (ex. 6.5). The legacy of the Society for Twentieth Century Music lived on: Lambert's *Concerto* was another of its works to be programmed again, while six of the seven instrumentalists for those original performances of *Pierrot* and the *Concertante* were present in

1955.[21] Completing the programme, the national premieres of Germaine Tailleferre's *Harp Concertino* and Gail Kubik's entertaining *Gerald McBoing Boing*, derived from his music for the eponymous cartoon, set *Pierrot* in light relief. The transatlantic release that year of the Virtuoso Chamber Ensemble's interpretation of *Pierrot* was the first by a British group. Enthusiasm for *Pierrot* had been fired in British composers and ensembles alike. Yet, the next generation of musicians would cause such milestones to seem precursory and almost immaterial. More auspicious designs on the Pierrot ensemble were about to be planned.

Notes

1   Clark was occasionally employed as a composer and conductor but excelled as an administrator: after working for the BBC himself (1927-36) he served the ISCM (1936-52), chaired the London Contemporary Music Centre (1947-52), and advised the Institute for Contemporary Arts (from its inception in 1948).

2   The handling of new music at the BBC is the subject of Leo Black's *BBC Music in the Glock Era and After*, ed. Christopher Wintle (London: Plumbago, 2010).

3   See Humphrey Searle, 'New Instrumental Combinations', *Music Today: Journal of the International Society for Contemporary Music* (1949), 126-31.

4   Quoted from an advertisement for the Society in *Musical Times* 93/1308 (1952), 81. An extended note on the Society (presumably sent to interested parties) elaborated on its objectives: 'The aim of this newly-founded Society is to create an audience for contemporary music, which so far does not exist in any proper sense. It intends to begin its activities with a series of concerts at Hampstead Town Hall ... and to give similar series, supplemented by lectures and gramophone recitals, in future years. ... The works to be performed consist of the outstanding "classics" of our day and represent as many as possible of the very varied kinds of music which have been written in this century. British music is well represented and a number of recent works by young composers will also be performed. The London Symphony Orchestra Chamber Ensemble, many of whose members are Hampstead residents, will take part in three of the concerts.' Quoted from an anonymous typed note located in BL, Ernst Henschel Collection, Add. Henschel, Box 32/i. Searle also gave an account of its formation in his memoirs, *Quadrille with a Raven*. See Chapter 11, 'Lesley and Rosie's Pub', http://www.musicweb-international.com/searle/lesley.htm (accessed 7 September 2012).

5   Van Dieren spent his mature life in London, having left Rotterdam in 1909 aged twenty-one. Gerhard, the exiled Catalan composer, had lived in Cambridge since 1940 but only assumed British citizenship in 1960.

6   Francis Routh, *Contemporary British Music: The Twenty-five Years from 1945 to 1970* (London: Macdonald, 1972), 91.

7   Humphrey Searle, 'New Instrumental Combinations', *Music Today: Journal of the International Society for Contemporary Music* (1949), 127.

8   *Ibid.*, 129. Searle studied harmony with Webern from September 1937 to February 1938. If Webern really avoided the twelve-note technique during these twice-weekly lessons, he did not altogether screen Searle from it: 'On his piano I used to see the twelve transpositions of the note-row ... relating to the piece that he was working on at the time. ... He did not show "work in progress" to his pupils but, towards the end of my stay, he did give me an analysis of his Piano Variations Op. 27 which had recently been published. I was present at its first performance in Vienna, given by the young Viennese pianist Peter Stadlen who now lives in London. ... Webern refused to tell him what the note-row was ("You are a pianist; your job is to play the notes") but he was willing to show it to me as a composition student.' See Searle, *Quadrille with a Raven*, online, *op. cit.*

9   Searle, Quadrille with a *Raven*, online, *op. cit.*

10   Reported by Andrew Porter in his review of the concert. See 'London Concerts', *Musical Times* 93/1310 (April, 1952), 178. Similarly, in the sixth and, as originally scheduled, final concert, Edith Sitwell recited Walton's *Façade* to a sold-out hall yet refused a fee.

11   See Searle, *Quadrille with a Raven*, online, *op. cit.* There is no written evidence to explain why an additional, seventh concert was hastily arranged for 8 July 1952. With the Society's one-off escape from the limited capacity of Hampstead, the objective was probably to reclaim whatever monies had been lost. The programme and personnel were certainly now conspicuously crowd-pleasing, with Edith Sitwell, Hedli Anderson, George Weldon (conductor of the Hallé Orchestra) and others presenting two standout works from the series, *Pierrot* and *Façade*, Jacques Ibert's virtuosic and popular saxophone concertino, and three sonnet settings by Fricker, one of the foremost British composers at that time. The concert duly sold out, though no one, including Searle, recalls it in their assessment of the Society for Twentieth Century Music as a whole.

12   See Porter, 178. It is impossible to verify this. The BBC did record a studio performance of the concert as the Society had agreed, but the tapes were unfortunately destroyed by fire before a master copy was cut. Anderson's next performance of *Pierrot* (8 July) also garnered positive reviews, and since she had starred with London's Group Theatre a decade earlier, we know that the singer, in exile from Berlin, was skilled in the cabaret style of both cities.

13   Anonymous, 'Recitals of the Week', review of the Chamber Ensemble of the London Symphony Orchestra, Kensington Town Hall, London (31 May 1949), *The Times* (6 June 1949), 7.

14   The LSO's self-governing leniency extended especially to Lear, who was a longstanding member of the BBC Symphony Orchestra, not the LSO.

15   The concert's groundbreaking programming was just one example of how Searle used the twelve-note method to drive debate on new music internationally. News of this reached Schoenberg. Writing just a month after 'Twelve Note Music Today', Schoenberg cited in defence of his method its intercontinental appeal and recognized Searle's role: 'There are many composers in South America and in Europe and in other countries who

try this [twelve-note] method, and it seems they become more and more successful. Mr. Humphrey Searle, an Englishman, considers the founding of an international society of composers with twelve tones. I have no idea whether this will succeed and whether it's a good idea, but after all it is significant of the spreading-out of this way of creating coherence in a piece of music.' Arnold Schoenberg, letter to G.F. Stegmann (26 January 1949) in: *Letters*, ed. Erwin Stein, trans. Eithne Wilkins and Ernst Kaiser (Eng. edn., London: Faber, 1964), 267.

16   Bentley led the second violins and occasionally deputized for George Stratton, the Leader from 1933 to 1952. Stratton was never involved with the ensemble.

17   If their old name was something of an oxymoron, then the 'branding' of the new title was also somewhat confused: the Virtuoso Chamber Ensemble was soon known as the Virtuoso Ensemble, but later variously went by the names of the London Virtuoso Ensemble and even the Virtuoso Ensemble of London.

18   See Richard Morrison, *Orchestra – The LSO: A Century of Triumph and Turbulence* (London: Faber, 2004), 109-11.

19   The Virtuoso Ensemble was sometimes conducted by Francis Chagrin, the Romanian-born founder of the CPNM (later SPNM) in 1943. Chagrin organized performances by various *ad hoc* new music groups under the banner of the Francis Chagrin Ensemble. Associates of the Sinfonia of London and Virtuoso Ensemble would, if conducted by Chagrin, happily play under that name, too. I acknowledge here the assistance of Tristram Cary, whose mixed decet *Three Threes and One Make Ten* (1961) was written for the group.

20   Gwynne Edwards later joined the Royal Philharmonic Orchestra but continued to play and record with the Virtuoso Chamber Ensemble.

21   The parallel became even closer when, on 9 May 1958, the group rejoined *Pierrot* and *Façade* in concert at the Oxford Town Hall. Anderson and Stadlen again featured (as in May and June 1942 and July 1952), as did Sitwell (as for the latter 'benefit' performance).

7 The Pierrot Players

Redefining the Young British Composer

In an impassioned and sometimes savage critique of 'new' music in 1950s Britain, a 21-year-old undergraduate named Peter Maxwell Davies invited his compatriots to pass judgement on the customs they held dear.[1] Davies never enjoyed a straightforward relationship with his British peers, Harrison Birtwistle included. Yet, the aesthetic schism within British music at the time was perfectly articulated when Davies took aim at those who were content, as he saw it, to shelter under the 'protective banner of Britishness ... [or] to imitate the most obvious and superficial elements from the Continent'.[2] His harshest words were reserved for the latter group:

> In an effort to be new and different, certain composers resort to innovations which are not implied in the original conception of the piece – perhaps now by serializing something nobody thought worth serializing before ... Among Englishmen, at least, the effect of this sort of thing is usually rather like a self-conscious gentleman doing something slightly indecent.[3]

This is surprising, though only because the dominant and otherwise revered composers of Davies's youth might usually be considered his targets, not outward-looking serialists.[4] The theory is given credence by his well-documented decision to attend Richard Hall's composition seminars at the Royal Manchester College of Music rather than university classes on figures no more contemporary than Edward Elgar and Frederick Delius.[5]

Britain's complicated relationship with Europe looms large here. Driven by the rarely compatible ambitions for parochial and cosmopolitan significance, several of the prominent composers who had cultivated an 'independent' national music had been trained abroad.[6] Which composers had provoked Davies? He did not name names, and besides, this particular passage of his polemic was ill-defined. Quite apart from how serialism could or could not be 'implied in the original conception of the piece',[7] the profile and, indeed, the number of mid-century British serialists was very low. Elisabeth Lutyens and Humphrey Searle must therefore be considered the main culprits. Davies was precocious enough to pen his 'manifesto' but too young to have been aware of Searle's progressive but short-lived Society for Twentieth Century Music. Lutyens's serial works do not live down to the description of the 'self-conscious gentleman [sic]' and their tokenistic approach to the method (even if her brazen national-autonomist rationale of how she adopted it probably does).[8] Circumstances had conspired to devalue her efforts, but Davies was unforgiving of second-generation British serialists who, ultimately, had had no first-generation compatriots to succeed.

For Lutyens, the feeling was mutual. She wryly lamented how the 'adoption of serial techniques by so many young composers – even in England – obliged them to do a spot of homework'.[9] What she and Davies came to share was an interest in *Pierrot lunaire*. By voicing his disquiet at Britain's alleged musical amateurism, a foundation was laid for Davies's breakthrough a decade later. At its heart was an ensemble he was to co-lead, the Pierrot Players, although it is telling that the group never performed Lutyens's Pierrot ensemble piece, the *Concertante for Five Players*. The two composers also recognized the drawbacks of Britain's post-war musical life; only the articulation of their fears varied. Addressing the SPNM in 1959, Lutyens likened the organization to an 'incubation machine [in which] embryo works are hatched before their time … [leaving] the Society in danger of becoming a factory for the artificial insemination of composers.'[10] She was live to the same issues of artificiality and aesthetic retreat, and scolded the same 'language and grammar … so strangely old-fashioned for young men' that Davies had identified three years earlier.

By the time Davies's article had been published, Lutyens had helped secure him and his Manchester-educated colleagues a foothold in London. Her rejuvenation in the early 1950s had been rewarded with a seat on the committee of the ICA Music Section, chaired by William Glock. Malcolm Williamson, Lutyens's first pupil, introduced her to Alexander Goehr, founder and eldest member of the so-called New Music Manchester Group. Together with Glock, she made an offer 'with no directives' to the group to plan a concert at the Arts Council on 9 January 1956 (ex. 7.1).[11] The free rein was probably approved because they saw in the young group – Davies, Birtwistle, Goehr, Elgar Howarth, John Dow and John Ogdon – sympathizers to their progressive cause.[12] Goehr was represented by his *Fantasias* for clarinet and piano (1954), performed for the first time and paired with Lutyens's *Valediction*, Op. 28 (1953-54) for the same line-up. This preceded Davies's Sonata for Trumpet and Piano (1955), while works by Elmer Seidel (a German pupil of Olivier Messiaen) and Nikos Skalkottas (a Greek composer who had studied with Schoenberg) also featured. Richard Hall's *Sonata for*

9 January 1956, 7.30pm – Great Drawing Room,
Arts Council of Great Britain, St. James's Square, London

Institute of Contemporary Arts (ICA): British Section of the ISCM

Elmer Seidel
Fantasie (1953) NP

Nikos Skalkottas
Sonatina (1949) and *Tender Melody* (1949) †

Elisabeth Lutyens
Valediction (1954) WP ‡

Peter Maxwell Davies
Sonata for Trumpet and Piano (1955) WP *

Alexander Goehr
Fantasias, Op. 3 (1955) WP ‡

Anton Webern
Variations, Op. 27 (1936)

Richard Hall
Sonata for Cello and Piano (1955) WP †

New Music Manchester Group

CLARINET Harrison Birtwistle (‡ only)   PIANO John Ogdon
TRUMPET Elgar Howarth (* only)   CELLO John Dow († only)

The advertised order was Webern, Skalkottas, Lutyens, Davies, Hall, Goehr and Seidel.

'New Music Manchester [sic] is a group of young musicians who feel the need for bringing contemporary music to a wider audience, believing that the great ignorance of the achievements and developments in present-day music is caused chiefly by the rarity of concert performances. The group was founded by Alexander Goehr in 1953.' (Quoted from the concert programme.)

Example 7.1 The New Music Manchester Group at the ICA

Cello and Piano (1955) ended the concert, in deference to the group's mentor. The platform gave the group a glimpse of conditions that would accelerate the development of their professional careers; as composer-performers, Davies and Goehr especially could publicize their music and regulate its performance. Yet, the showcase, by definition a one-off event, did not inspire the collective to continue to appear together. After their gathering in London, the New Music Manchester Group gave no further concerts, and for most of their careers Davies and Goehr were to be estranged.

Their very epithet, nowadays identified as the 'Manchester School', is accurate only insofar as it symbolizes the congregation of Birtwistle, Goehr, Davies and Ogdon there under Hall's tutelage. Besides, by the time of their appearance in London, Birtwistle was completing his National Service, Goehr was studying with Messiaen in Paris, and Dow was playing with the Hallé Orchestra. Nor can the convictions they appeared to share – chief among them cooperation in performance and a guarded admiration of activities at another disparate 'school', centred on the German city of Darmstadt – be defined too mutually: each member's responsibilities and rates of progress varied greatly. Still a teenager when he performed at the ICA, Ogdon found celebrity soonest as a recitalist. Birtwistle's decision to focus on composition was still a year away (appreciation of his ability was another decade away). Davies and Goehr were both strong-willed, fledgling composers, but Goehr's seniority, and his greater experience of the trappings of Darmstadt,[13] meant he was *slower* to escape the 'scorn for the past' which had intoxicated it and especially his friends, Pierre Boulez and Luigi Nono.[14] That these British musicians engaged with the European vanguard at all distinguished them from most of their peers, but neither Darmstadt, nor acceptance by the ICA, sated their ambitions. Weeks later, Glock set in motion the next phase of Davies's public introduction by publishing his article.[15] Thus began a far-reaching process that, eventually, would attract responses *from* the continent and make London the musical epicentre of the 1960s.

Towards the Pierrot Players

Music-making also thrived in the regions, which were lifted by a surging number of arts festivals and summer schools in post-war Britain. Annual events at Cheltenham (founded 1945), Aldeburgh (1946), Bryanston (later relocated to Dartington) and Edinburgh (both 1947), Bath (1948), York and King's Lynn (both 1951) enriched the nation's music scene. In 1956, four years after the Society for Twentieth Century Music had resurrected *Pierrot lunaire*, its principal performers were reunited at the Edinburgh Festival for another performance, and once more it was heard alongside William Walton's *Façade* (Freemasons' Hall, 20 August 1956). That Peter Stadlen and

Hedli Anderson were again called upon respectively to conduct and recite *Pierrot* shows their specialist talents were in short supply. The difference in Edinburgh was the Melos Ensemble. Plans to form the group were hatched at a meeting in 1950 between the violist Cecil Aronowitz and the clarinettist Gervase de Peyer. Although young, both musicians were already recognized as soloists and, in this respect, their group would differ from the Chamber Ensemble of the London Symphony Orchestra. The trajectory of de Peyer's career, for example, was the inverse of most of their players: de Peyer replaced Sidney Fell in the LSO after the trauma within its ranks had led the rebranded Virtuoso Ensemble to be unveiled. Three further musicians – flautist Richard Adeney, cellist Terence Weil, and violinist Emanuel Hurwitz – were recruited as founder members.

The Melos Ensemble would 'step outside the normal repertory of trios and quartets', an agenda which did not initially warrant the performance of much music from the twentieth century: Schubert's Octet, Beethoven's Septet, and the clarinet quintets of Mozart and Brahms were the early mainstays of their repertoire.[16] Indeed, the roles of these core members, and the prominence of their mixed quintet of winds and strings, would be no greater than other performers who would augment the line-up. The elastic constitution of the group was in fact quite similar to the Virtuoso Ensemble, except that the Melos's aggregate configuration, fusing a string quintet with a wind quintet and adding a pianist and harpist as the music required, was to become the more recognizable. At the same time, its musicians were more inclined to separate into those standard ensembles during and between concerts. The growth of the group's reputation in the second half of the 1950s coincided with their performance of more modern works, of which *Pierrot* was an early example. It went on to perform music by Alun Hoddinott (Septet, Op. 10), Goehr (*Suite*, Op. 11) and Elizabeth Maconchy (*Reflections*), among others.[17] More famously, Benjamin Britten later scored his *War Requiem*, Op. 66 for the Melos's aggregate line-up (minus piano) as a concertante sub-group to flank the City of Birmingham Symphony Orchestra at the work's premiere in 1962.

International recognition quickly followed. The group was invited to play at festivals in Venice and Warsaw later that same year and a month-long tour of the United States was arranged in 1966. Arguably its most influential, if less glamorous performances, took place in the interim. Located in the grounds of Wiltshire's New Wardour Castle, Cranborne Chase School for Girls employed Birtwistle as Master of Music from 1962. Two years into the post, Birtwistle was inspired to orchestrate something of a reunion with Goehr and Davies. Together, they set about organizing a week-long summer school that would draw on their didactic streaks as much as the desire to hear their music performed better and more often. Michael Tippett, a friend of the Goehr family, was enlisted as President; Birtwistle, Goehr and Davies acted as Musical Directors. Advertisements called for instrumentalists and choral singers and announced concerts supported by the SPNM. In the event, the activities also included composition classes given by each composer, including Tippett and Hugh Wood, and seminars in which compositional problems were discussed.

The first Wardour Castle Summer School was held in mid August 1964.[18] It was a coup to enlist the Melos Ensemble, who at Glock's behest had been a fixture at Dartington since 1960. The ensemble took centre stage only when the school reconvened in 1965, once again in the third week of August. Now, the group commissioned Birtwistle and Davies to write works for its near-complete line-up, emulating the success of their *War Requiem* performance, but autonomously. An incomplete version of Davies's *Seven in Nomine* (1963-65) was premiered alongside Birtwistle's *Tragoedia* (1965), both works scored for a line-up comprising wind quintet, string quartet and harp.[19] The Melos Ensemble, then, was not a rigid Pierrot ensemble; but its performance of *Pierrot lunaire* at the second Wardour Castle Summer School would inspire the most distinguished Pierrot ensemble to form. It was joined there by the American soprano Bethany Beardslee, whose theatrical, costumed performance of *Pierrot* has since become the stuff of legend. Davies's biographer acclaims it for whetting his subject's appetite for music theatre.[20] Others believe her exuberance even crystallized in Davies's mind his expressionist sensibility.[21]

Certainly, in the summer school's aftermath a seminal decision was taken to found an ensemble based closely on the forces of *Pierrot*. The focus on Davies is a consequence of his eventual command of the group (or rather its successor, The Fires of London), when really the initiative behind the newest Pierrot ensemble, as with the summer school itself, was Birtwistle's. This is Alan Hacker's claim, although only Stephen Pruslin's christening of the Pierrot Players is undisputed in light of Birtwistle's unwillingness to discuss the group.[22] The more important observation is how this quartet of young, aspiring reformers saw in the Pierrot ensemble solutions to their grievances with the conditions and nature of modern music in Britain. The Melos Ensemble had briefly 'regularized' their own soloistic line-up; their success hinted that to standardize a mixed ensemble in modern times might be viable. But the return to *Pierrot* gave the Pierrot Players a configuration to emulate.

The membership of this new group would be far more robust than of the mixed ensembles that came before them. By ensuring that its personnel were consistent, it was intended that 'under-rehearsed and uncommitted' performances of new music would become a thing of the past.[23] Birtwistle, Davies, Hacker and Pruslin set about recruiting some of the leading young exponents of contemporary musical performance in Britain at the time. The soprano Mary Thomas had already given an authoritative premiere of Birtwistle's *Entr'actes and Sappho Fragments* at the Cheltenham Festival in 1964 and again later that year under the auspices of the SPNM.[24] Judith Pearce, on flute and piccolo, had performed with the Nash Ensemble since their formation, also in 1964. They were joined by the violinist Sydney Mann, the cellist Jennifer Ward Clarke, and, in a novel but enduring modification of Schoenberg's template, the percussionist Tristan Fry.

The Pierrot Players would make *Pierrot lunaire* a staple of their repertoire, transforming it into their semi-theatrical prototype. The group's flamboyance and youthful drive are significant historically and aesthetically. At their first concert on 30 May 1967 (ex. 7.2), Thomas's Pierrot-clad appearance paid homage to Bethany Beardslee and the group lived up to their promise to rehearse properly: Davies maintains that they held over fifty rehearsals before its performance.[25] Not since the 1920s had such a claim been made. The result was an atypical brand of authenticity that, intentionally or otherwise, recalled aspects of *Pierrot*'s performance history but was deliberately spectacular at the same time. Versed in *commedia dell'arte* gestures, Thomas would '"go off on one" – and quite right, too', as Davies put it.[26]

Decked all in black, the instrumentalists would soon also acquire a modern uniform. When Davies started writing works of music theatre to accompany and, later, replace *Pierrot* in concert, costume 'props' became integral to the Pierrot Players' trademark. The nun's habits of *Revelation and Fall* (1965-66, rev. 1980) and *Missa super L'homme armé* (1968, rev. 1971) and the wedding dress of *Miss Donnithorne's Maggot* (1974) did much to abolish what Pruslin characterized as Britain's overly formal attitude to concert dress and presentation. Being a Pierrot Player would be an 'adventure rather than a chore.'[27] The direct creative input of Birtwistle and Davies, the group's composer-conductors, set the Pierrot Players apart – a legacy of the sympathetic collaborations that had made the Wardour Castle Summer Schools such a success. Dividing its efforts between *Pierrot* and new companion works, the group spawned a lineage of Pierrot ensembles whose breadth and influence are yet to be surpassed.

Harrison Birtwistle's Experiment

The Pierrot Players' first concert embodied this agenda absolutely, although the event was not an entirely auspicious start for the group. Two new progenies to *Pierrot* were premiered, Davies's instrumental *Antechrist* and Birtwistle's *Monodrama* (both 1967). *Pierrot* was almost overshadowed, deliberately so. Yet, the concert's centrepiece, *Monodrama*, is all but forgotten today.[28] It nevertheless set the tone for the Pierrot Players by augmenting the Pierrot ensemble, scoring parts for clarinet in E♭ and alto flute – calling for tripled rather than doubled winds – and doing so theatrically. Davies's much shorter *Antechrist* also modified Schoenberg's line-up. In the context of Pierrot ensembles to date, its piccolo and bass clarinet were normally used as doubling instruments, but here they were used alone as registral opposites. (Indeed, the more telling precedent is *Pierrot*'s eleventh and most controversial number, 'Rote Messe', in which the same instruments mark a similar 'reversal' of instrumentation.)[29] Significantly, the same theme, religious parody, would run through many of Davies's works for Pierrot ensemble, beginning with *Antechrist*, which turned the thirteenth-century motet *Deo confitemini Domino* 'inside-out'.[30] The effect was understandably lost on contemporary critics, for the original effect of its transparent textures, dance-like gestures and opening position in the concert was to cast the piece as an entertaining overture.[31] The absence of the piano from Davies's line-up was another foil for its faux-medievalism: Pruslin instead made his debut with the Pierrot Players as a third percussionist alongside Fry and Birtwistle's wife, Sheila.

Monodrama was Birtwistle's serious but unspecified source-tragedy: a 'tragedy ante-dating all tragedy', according to the composer.[32] A parody of the Greek classical manner, it evoked a more ancient past than *Antechrist* but again marked out *Pierrot* as a distinctly twentieth-century classic. Three painted screens explained that Thomas would undertake three separate roles as Protagonist, Prophetess and Messenger. Unseen but equipped with a megaphone, Pruslin was her interlocutor as the Choregos (chorus-leader). Pruslin also provided the libretto, as he had for *Punch and Judy* (1966-67), a chamber opera Birtwistle was writing for the English Opera Group. That work's violent retelling of the famous, anglicized *commedia dell'arte* story is said to have prompted Benjamin Britten to leave its 1968 Aldeburgh premiere early. The tale is apocryphal, but *Monodrama*, which met with cries of "Rubbish!", certainly fared badly. When it began with the Choregos asking, "Who screamed in pain behind the portal?", the audience may have expected some undetermined crime or accident to be investigated: none would be forthcoming (the full libretto is transcribed as Document 2). Rather, the Protagonist's ambiguous, sung response, "A scream is the portal of pain", pointed towards Birtwistle's post-expressionist intent. More abstractly still, each character's first words – "Silence!" (spoken) and "Speak!" (*Sprechstimme*) – foreshadowed the meta-narrative that would unfold, in which hyper-alliterative phrases and wordplay replaced conventional syntax.

Birtwistle's debt was as much to Milton Babbitt as to Schoenberg. Wardour Castle had hosted the British premiere of another work littered with phonemic associations and inspired by Greek legend: Babbitt's *Philomel* (1963-64) for

30 May 1967, 7.45pm – Queen Elizabeth Hall, London

Anglo-Austrian Music Society

Peter Maxwell Davies
Antechrist (1967) *WP*

Arnold Schoenberg
Pierrot lunaire (Albert Giraud, trans. Otto Erich Hartleben), Op. 21 ‡

Harrison Birtwistle
Monodrama (Stephen Pruslin) (1967) *WP* †

Mary Thomas (‡ *Sprechsängerin* ; † Protagonist, Prophetess, Messenger)
Julian Curry († Choregos)
Peter Maxwell Davies (conductor)
Harrison Birtwistle († conductor)

The Pierrot Players	*Antechrist*	*Pierrot*	*Monodrama*
Judith Pearce	PIC	FL / PIC	FL / AFL / PIC
Alan Hacker	BCL	B♭ CL / A CL / BCL	B♭ CL / E♭ CL / A♭ CL / BCL
Stephen Pruslin	PERC III	PF	PERC II
Sydney Mann	VN	VN / VA	VN / VA
Jennifer Ward Clarke	VC	VC	VC
Tristan Fry	PERC I		PERC I
Sheila Birtwistle	PERC II		

Example 7.2 The Pierrot Players' Launch Concert

voice and tape.[33] *Monodrama* did not emulate the classically expressionist anarchy of, say, 'Heimweh' (*Pierrot*'s fourteenth number), but its tightly controlled web of motifs did echo other numbers.[34] Nor was the (over)clever variation of vocal delivery the only other aspect he took, and developed, after Schoenberg. Familiarly, various combinations of instruments were used in *Monodrama* to delineate its dramatic structure. Though Birtwistle called for four clarinets, a core Pierrot quintet, still with a keyboard-type instrument but here a xylophone, recurred only for the two 'Cryptograms' and the penultimate 'Triumph' scene.[35] The ensemble's completeness contrasted with four solo 'Interstices', each with the same material, that partitioned the work; these would form the basis for the *Four Interludes from a Tragedy* (1967-68), which were later performed independently. The mechanistic, solo xylophone in both Cryptograms, especially, is another example of the type of raw, repetitive textures with which Birtwistle was beginning to experiment. This would become one of his successful hallmarks, but here it was more basic and peripheral, used merely to preface the Choregos's booming revelations that the first and second of the work's 'cycles' had finished.

The second of these scenes had also seen the Choregos announce (that is, promise) "light comes soon". But since the first of the Protagonist's two 'Soliloquies' had already avowed that "If this is false, then where is real? If this is real, then all is false. I confront contradiction of fiction and fact", the audience would (or should) have learned to interpret the Choregos's words figuratively. There were two problems here, however. First, the Choregos's role was blurred, laying somewhere between, or sustaining both, a commentary on the work's structure yet elsewhere playing a dramatic but still non-literal role, all within a virtually static dramaturgy. Second, his promise of clarity would be broken: if the audience's patience was at breaking point when the Choregos appeared to address them to declare "It is you who must connect these links", then it probably snapped in the 'Triumph' scene with the closing statement "Ambiguous endings can anger incite." Quite. Above all else, this might explain *Monodrama*'s lacklustre reception. William Mann complained about the 'obfuscated mandarin style' of the text and considered the megaphoned delivery of Choregos's lines ostentatious.[36] Unimpressed by its vocal aspects, not one of *Monodrama*'s critics noticed its structural or expressionistic parallels, be they with *Pierrot* or, indeed, with Pierre Boulez's *Le Marteau sans maître*, whose British premiere Birtwistle had attended a decade earlier.

Peter Maxwell Davies's Success

Peter Maxwell Davies's agreement to become Composer-in-Residence at the University of Adelaide in 1965/66 delayed the launch of the Pierrot Players, but their initial recruitment of personnel was otherwise trouble-free. The group, however, settled on a definitive line-up only after their debut, when Birtwistle invited Duncan Druce to replace Sydney Mann.[37] Experienced as a freelance musician for the BBC and, crucially, having played *Pierrot* before, Druce first joined the group in Munich for their television debut, which was only their third engagement. The Pierrot Players' next performance was in Cheltenham (17 July 1967), home to the festival mandated to support British contemporary music. Accordingly, the event was an annual draw for voracious critics, but whereas the post-war endeavours of composers such as Iain Hamilton, Malcolm Williamson and Peter Racine Fricker once warranted the most discussion, Cheltenham was now greeted with the brasher, avant-garde styles of such less established peers as Davies and Birtwistle. Their presence gave a new balance to arguments about conservative and progressive trends in British music, even winning over some of the usual naysayers:

> ... where in all this is the vital new voice of English music? Where have we got the power and vitality of Penderecki, the purposeful invention of Serocki's *Segmenti*? ... Is Maxwell Davies our only serious innovator?[38]

To single out Davies for praise was not as commonplace as it is today. Even more striking is that this opinion of E. M. Webster was published in a very traditionalist journal (and one edited by Humphrey Proctor-Gregg).

What impressed this fan of Davies and the Polish School was left unsaid, but it is no coincidence that this was the first concert by the Pierrot Players to feature two of Davies's works and that the only new work to be written for a complete Pierrot ensemble, Birtwistle's *Three Lessons in a Frame* (1967) – a subject of the next chapter – was comprehensively outshone. *Antechrist* was fast becoming the group's 'signature' tune and again introduced the concert; Davies's new *Hymnos* (1967) for clarinet and piano joined it. Davies's violent variations of musical gesture, and Hacker's flamboyantly free interpretation, have made *Hymnos* a touchstone for clarinettists since. Its more intimate instrumentation also held a wider significance: Hacker and Pruslin had already made their London debut together in October 1965, performing Birtwistle's *Verses* (1965), and Davies's Clarinet Sonata had been a breakthrough work for the composer since its 1957 premiere in Darmstadt. The legacy of this history would continue to be felt in the Pierrot Players: *Hymnos* was the first of many 'satellite' works Davies and others composed as offshoots from (and for members of) the Pierrot ensemble.[39]

For its next major concert (ex. 7.3), the group graced the more historic stage of Conway Hall, a venue whose ties with chamber music date back to

26 February 1968 – Conway Hall, London

The Camden Festival:
A Macnaghten Concert

Karlheinz Stockhausen
Zyklus (1959) †

Peter Maxwell Davies
Missa super L'homme armé (Agnus dei; Luke 22) (1968, later rev.) WP

Philip Batstone
John Street (1965) NP ‡

Peter Maxwell Davies
Revelation and Fall (Georg Trakl) (1965-66) WP

Mary Thomas (soprano)
Peter Maxwell Davies (conductor)

The Pierrot Players
FLUTE / PICCOLO Judith Pearce
CLARINET Alan Hacker
CELESTE / HONKY-TONK PIANO / HARPSICHORD / PIANO (‡ only) Stephen Pruslin
VIOLIN / VIOLA Duncan Druce
CELLO Jennifer Ward Clarke
PERCUSSION Tristan Fry †

Unidentified players joined the group to play Revelation and Fall. *A near-complete list of musicians who guested with the group is located at: www.webarchive.org.uk/wayback/archive/20070131163627/ http://www.maxopus.com/organisa/fires4.htm (accessed 7 September 2012). Other 'extras' are positively identified in ex. 9.1-2.*

*Example 7.3   The Pierrot Players at the Conway Hall, 1968,
featuring the premiere of Davies's* Missa super L'homme armé

1879. The new programme included *two* works that may plausibly lay claim to being Davies's first pieces of music theatre for Pierrot ensemble. Composed before the Pierrot Players' debut, *Revelation and Fall* was the earlier of these, but *Missa super L'homme armé* had more in common with *Antechrist*'s closeted subversion. In the later work, Davies conveyed his message more explicitly, through theatre: Thomas's role as a disaffected priest, habited as a nun, would shock some,[40] but it served to emphasize the work's theme of religious betrayal and hypocrisy. It was also steeped in the masquerade traditions of *Pierrot*, in which Schoenberg had transferred Pierrot's gender (as others had before him) yet also confused it with his 'androgynous' use of *Sprechstimme*. And just as *Pierrot* was occasionally performed by a man, beginning with Karl Geibel in Frankfurt in December 1921,[41] *Missa super L'homme armé*'s revision three years after it had been premiered made its crossdressing even more obvious as Murray Melvin, still dressed as a nun, took on Thomas's role.

However macabre *Pierrot*'s make-believe world, it was no match for the confrontation and sensationalism of Davies's Pierrot ensemble. In the final scene, for example, Davies instructed the speaker to point at the audience, to foxtrot off the stage, and to rip off his or her wimple. Musically, a pastiche Victorian hymn heard on the harmonium (another extension of the Pierrot ensemble) accompanied word of Judas's betrayal as the 'priest' declaimed Christ's curse from Luke 22. That this was the last of several transformations of the fifteenth-century popular song from which the work took its name – others include a foxtrot and a Baroque trio sonata – signalled a clear development of *Antechrist*'s more nebulous musical transformations. To these, then, Davies had added two innovative ingredients that were to be the bedrock of his immediate success: stylistic displacement and parody. Since his formative years, Davies had employed old and new techniques of development to distort beyond recognition certain compositional sources.[42] Their absence in the earlier *Revelation and Fall* set it apart, although the most obvious difference, in instrumentation, prevented it from becoming a staple of the group's repertory. The influence of the Melos Ensemble, and specifically the almost contemporaneous *Seven in Nomine*, may have been in Davies's mind when he scored *Revelation and Fall*. Yet, the use of three percussionists was more in keeping with the Pierrot Players' ethos and especially this concert, which interspersed Karlheinz Stockhausen's percussive tour-de-force, *Zyklus*, as one of two solo pieces. (The other was Philip Batstone's *John Street* (1965), a piano piece little known now, but one that inaugurated the group's influential relationship with American composers.)

Zyklus and *Revelation and Fall* also stole the pre-concert limelight in advertisements that spelled out their instrumental innovations:

> Fascinating hardware will be on view when Tristan Fry, young percussion virtuoso, displays his full, glittering kit in Stockhausen's celebrated *Zyklus*. And in Peter Maxwell Davies's new, extraordinary *Revelation and Fall* you will hear anvils, knife-grinders, glass-smashers, cogwheels, glockenspiels and handbells. (Some ordinary instruments, too.)[43]

Revelation and Fall was no less iconoclastic. Davies's setting of Georg Trakl's fervid prose poem 'Offenbarung und Untergang' inspired the bloodstained habit Thomas wore (particularly Trakl's denouement, in which '… the blood ran softly from the silver wound of the nun and rained on me like fire.'). But its similarity with *Missa super L'homme armé* was superficial. The use of a poet so important to Schoenberg's circle, and of a text written just before Trakl's death in 1914, indicated that *Revelation and Fall* was the more expressionistic response to *Pierrot*, and aesthetically truer to Schoenberg. Its familiar mixture of singing and speech-song was as noteworthy as its references to 'wine', 'blood' and 'moon-clad feet that tread the paths of night', i.e. Trakl's debt to the same Giraud-Hartleben text that had inspired Albertine Zehme to commission *Pierrot*. Conversely, the accusatory and exclusive use of speech in *Missa super L'homme armé* was the more melodramatic; even Davies's option to intone the biblical text through plainsong, while simpler, was theatrically derived. Save for one memorable moment when Thomas reached for the megaphone to shriek 'O bitter death', *Revelation and Fall* is remembered, despite its large ensemble, as a 'securely structured … piece of thoroughly developing chamber music.'[44]

Nevertheless, Davies admitted his inspirations at the time were 'often theatrical in the first place rather than purely musical.'[45] Certainly, the historic, (extra)musical and (poly)stylistic resonance of the Pierrot Players' blend of music theatre and 'concert' works was, up to now, their main draw. That *Pierrot lunaire* lay behind the group's formation but featured only occasionally alongside new works, and influenced those works variably, was central to how the Pierrot Players forged a new, distinct profile. If their activities in 1967/68 left some questions of individual and group style lingering, their memorable second season would leave less room for doubt. A year to the day after their debut, the Pierrot Players returned to London's South Bank with their most interesting programme to date (ex. 7.4). Befitting their smaller venue (the Purcell Room) and sponsor (the Redcliffe Concerts),[46] the group gave a recital of all-British music that took the experimentalism of their programming to a new level. Handel's striking, freely-formed 'Lucrezia' cantata, in which Thomas impersonated the eponymous heroine, contrasted with two modern solo works: Birtwistle's juvenilia piece *Oockooing Bird* (1949) and Davies's *Five Little Pieces* (1960-64, first heard at Wardour Castle in 1964). Their composers performed these 'filler' works and with it satisfied their sponsor's desire for British composers to be more active in performance and artistic direction – a spirit they had upheld long before Francis Routh, co-founder and director of the concert series, invited them to appear.

Davies and Birtwistle had used the Pierrot Players in part to explore their fixation with the remote past. After Handel's cantata, the theme was corroborated by *Fantasia on a Ground* (1968). Advertised as a 'realization' by Davies of Henry Purcell's 'Fantazia (Three Parts on a Ground)', it was, taken literally, nothing of the sort. Quite apart from its arrangement for Pierrot ensemble, Davies's rhythmic, melodic and articulative decorations made this a distinctly new work. His languid, inappropriate tenutos put a magnifying glass on incidental motifs, caricaturing a melody already punctuated by short rests, and his doubling of the source material at the twelfth recalled the treatment of *Antechrist*'s earlier source motet, but to wilder effect (now imitating the twelfths of a baroque organ). Written for the whole group, Davies's arrangement-cum-recomposition was as great a departure from Schoenberg's prototype as was possible. Purcell's 'ground' was left intact, save for its re-orchestration for marimba and harpsichord and an inverting interplay between voices that, halfway through, saw it migrate to the 'bell like' flute and clarinet (Davies's instruction). What made the realization more straightforward to the composer was his belief that the music was closer to the 'spirit' of Purcell than most so-called period performances. As such, the new *Fantasia* was an indirect nod to the early music movement, which, despite starting in the 1930s, did not herald the same types of partnership between early and modern music that the Pierrot Players dared to introduce now.

This was as true of performance as it was of composition. The ensemble would soon collaborate with David Munrow's Early Music Consort in concert and film, and, inspired by the *Fantasia*, the groundbreaking conflation of two sound-worlds would recur in varying degrees of rearrangement in such works as Dietrich Buxtehude's cantata *Also hat Gott die Welt geliebet* (Davies), Guillaume de Machaut's *Hoquetus David* and Johannes Ockeghem's *Ut heremita solus* (Birtwistle). Although they must surely have exerted their own influence, the recent efforts of Benjamin Britten to acknowledge his national past, and especially to reconcile Purcell's stylistic starting point with his own in re-settings from *Orpheus Britannicus* and *Harmonia Sacra*, suddenly appeared conservative by comparison. Such was Davies's intention, of course, since his own brand of 'authenticity' was unashamedly simulated.[47]

Entertaining though it was, the *Fantasia* gained its greatest significance, and blew open the black comic value that lay beneath the surface of earlier works such as *Missa super L'homme armé*, only when Davies later added to it two of Purcell's pavans from the same collected edition as the fantasia.

30 May 1968 – Purcell Room, London

Redcliffe Concert of British Music

Peter Maxwell Davies
Antechrist

George F. Handel
Cantata: *O numi eterni* (*La Lucrezia*), HWV 145 (c. 1707)

Peter Maxwell Davies
Five Little Pieces for Piano (1960-64)

Harrison Birtwistle
Oockooing Bird, for piano (1949)

Peter Maxwell Davies
Stedman Caters (1968) WP

Harrison Birtwistle
Ring a dumb carillon (Christopher Logue),
for Soprano (with susp. cymbals), Clarinet and Percussion (1968)

Henry Purcell, arr. **Peter Maxwell Davies**
Fantasia on a Ground (1968) WP

Mary Thomas (soprano)
Peter Maxwell Davies, Harrison Birtwistle (conductors)

The Pierrot Players
[personnel as ex. 7.2]

Example 7.4 The First-anniversary Concert of the Pierrot Players

Davies transformed them into foxtrots, and when he pulled the same trick with John Bull's pavans in the orchestral *St Thomas' Wake* a year later, what arguably began as a show-stopping gimmick became an important aspect of style. This is why commentators have struggled to explain why a composer said to be 'wholly opposed to a notion of art as decoration or entertainment' had composed new and convincing pastiche foxtrots, with and without the prompting of source material such as Purcell's.[48] Indeed, in *Vesalii icones* (1969), arguably Davies's most sober Pierrot ensemble piece (being based formally and conceptually on the Stations of the Cross), Michael Burden reasonably argues that its foxtrots were intended to represent evil among us, or, more subversively, to expose our inability to recognize such evil.[49] As a small-scale ballet, the work was also the first to join dance with the Pierrot ensemble, an innovation Birtwistle had predicted.[50] It is noteworthy, then, that Ballet Rambert had added Glen Tetley's choreographed *Pierrot lunaire* (1962) to their repertory in February 1967.

In the newly-titled *Fantasia on a Ground and Two Pavans*, however, the moralistic significance of resurrecting one popular dance form of the sixteenth and seventeenth centuries as another from the twentieth was submerged beneath its theatricality. Dressed in 'twenties costume, Thomas foxtrotted onto stage accompanied by a railway guard's whistle and football rattle, Ward Clarke strummed her cello as a guitar, and the work was finally brought to a close by a 'side drum scraped around on skin to sound like the centre run-in groove of a scratchy 78rpm disc', to quote Davies's instructions. Every instrument added to the ensemble by Davies's revisions doubled one of those belonging to the *Fantasia*. This is symbolically telling because central to the pavans are an assortment of unpitched percussion, an out-of-tune piano and an optional vocal part with a message more typical of *Missa super L'homme armé* – 'Faith is a virtue whereby that which we cannot see can be believed. Our concern is what it signifies, not whether it is true.'[51]

'A Garland for Dr K', 1969

Davies obsessively wove old and new Pierrot ensemble instruments into the fabric of his works, a process that reached a saturation point in his next piece of music theatre, *Eight Songs for a Mad King* (1969). Davies's stark but heartrending account of George III's derangement also marked a new peak in his exploration of melodrama, parody and vocal and instrumental multiphonic techniques. Given how the *Eight Songs* are remembered today, it is remarkable that they contained little in the way of new areas of musico-dramatic interest, save for their study of madness as a substitute for religion (and even so, Davies's protagonist was obviously also a religious figurehead). *Eight Songs* instead offered new twists on established topics – authenticity, nationality, instrumental theatre – epitomized by the king smashing Druce's violin moments after he had quoted from Handel's *Messiah*. (Druce and his fellow instrumentalists were also housed, bird-like, in Perspex cages.)

What is undeniable is that for the first time since *Pierrot lunaire*, the *Eight Songs* became a defining work within both the lineage of Pierrot ensembles and its wider genre of music theatre. The clamour in response to their premiere catapulted the composer to the forefront of British musical life. Yet, the *Songs'* impact, then as now, stems in part from the reservations harboured by their critics. Jonathan Harvey drew on the audience's divided reaction to their premiere ('wild applause and shouts of "Rubbish" … [so] the work struck home with some, at least')[52] to encapsulate several such anxieties:

> Some said that it was a shame to hold the old boy [George III]
> up to ridicule;[53] for others he was not a historical person but
> an element of the human psyche placed in a historical setting,
> a Beckett clown whose words and actions have less meaning
> as a historical person's than they do as a multi-level poetic-
> psychological fantasy.[54]

In accord with this final remark, Roger Smalley also questioned the *Songs'* apparent revival of Expressionism,[55] while the cohesion of the music itself troubled other critics.[56] Pruslin would nevertheless remember the *Eight Songs'* premiere as a '*succès fou* … generally accepted as the historic moment when music theatre exploded into prominence as a dominant genre' – a claim, once in print, that has been difficult to dislodge.[57]

The Pierrot Players knowingly discarded the trappings of opera in their music-theatrical productions. Three spotlights, one per act, were usually enough for their performances of *Pierrot*, for example. The *Eight Songs* were a grander spectacle, but the 'small-scale' philosophy stayed with Davies when he conceived that each song would be cast as a fragmented monologue, with the king listening to each of his birds 'perform'. Used in role-playing accompaniment, and effectively as instrumental stage props, the entire Pierrot ensemble was dramaticized. Above all, this explains why the *Eight Songs* have received far greater attention than Davies's other Pierrot ensemble pieces. More recent commentators than Pruslin have pined for the halcyon days of the sixties when music theatre flourished, and contemporary critics had, after all, responded volubly to Davies's work. But although Pruslin and others often overlook the equal claims of Luciano Berio, Mauricio Kagel, György Ligeti and even Hans Werner Henze as pioneers of the genre, their nostalgia is set apart by factors they rarely appreciate: first, recognition of the features *Eight Songs* and *Pierrot* share; second, the premiere of the songs themselves, an eclectic, star-studded event, yet one never examined as such.

It is ironic that Davies's inspiration to write his most famous work for the Pierrot Players came not from within the group, but from the poems and vocal pyrotechnics of Randolph Stow and Roy Hart respectively. They lay behind Davies's decision to take the *Sprechstimme* technique to new heights. Spanning four octaves, the king's ravaged voice was a clear development of *Pierrot* and another dramaticized integration of vocal and instrumental forces. The blurring of these roles chimed with Davies's distinctly *Pierrot-esque* confusion of narrative, structure and dramatic personae. Futile though the king's attempts to teach the 'bullfinches' to sing were, in the *Eight Songs* at least, he wisely held court with no more than one bird at a time. In half the songs, he addresses the instruments individually, first the flute (a 'young courtier' in the third poem), then the cello and clarinet in the fourth and sixth, before the seventh's climactic violin-smashing scene. This represents more than the death of a bullfinch; it is a resignation to insanity. It also prefaces a final twist in the storyline, when, in a final aggravation of the problems audiences face in identifying (with) the characters, the 'mad king' announces his own death.

Toying with listeners like this was both playful and thoughtful. Likewise, the *Eight Songs'* emotional range, especially the king's fluctuating self-awareness, makes Davies's portrayal compassionate yet discomforting, too. If the ambiguity of its storytelling and the severity of its music did more to alienate than to entertain,[58] it was because the audience was addressed more directly than ever before. Rather than the morbid fascination with religion, it was *their* latent obsessions, in particular the tendency of us all to 'rubberneck', which were open to review.[59] Are the musicians simply projections from within the king's own mind? How much of the king do we recognize in ourselves? The composer writes:

> The sounds made by human beings under extreme duress, physical and mental, will be at least in part familiar. With Roy Hart's extended vocal range, and his capacity for producing chords with his voice (like the clarinet and flute in this work), these poems presented a unique opportunity for me to exploit these techniques and thus to explore certain extreme regions of experience. Until quite recently 'madness' was regarded as something at which to laugh and jeer. The King's historically authentic quotations from *The Messiah* in the work evoke this sort of mocking response in the instrumental parts – the stylistic switch is unprepared, and arouses an aggressive reaction. I have, however, quoted far more than *The Messiah*: if not the notes, at

22 April 1969 – Queen Elizabeth Hall, London

Music Media / James Murdoch Management

Peter Maxwell Davies
Eight Songs for a Mad King (Randolph Stow, George III) (1969) *WP*

Harrison Birtwistle
Linoi II (1967, rev. 1969) *WP* †

Various: *A Garland for Dr. K.,*
'a tribute to Dr. Kalmus on his 80th birthday,
by composers of Universal Edition':

Henri Pousseur   *Echos II de votre Faust* (1969) *WP*

Cristobal Halffter   *Oda para felicitar a un amigo* (1969) *WP*

David Bedford   *Untitled* (1969) *WP*

Bernard Rands   *Piece for Dr. K.* (1969) *WP*

Roman Haubenstock-Ramati   *Rounds* (1969) *WP*

Hugh Wood   *Untitled* (1969) *WP*

Pierre Boulez   *Untitled (Pour le Dr Kalmus)* (1969) *WP*

Henry Purcell, arr. **Luciano Berio**   *The Modification and Instrumentation of a Famous Hornpipe as a Merry and Altogether Sincere Homage to Uncle Alfred* (1969) *WP*

Harrison Birtwistle   *Some Petals from My Twickenham Herbarium* (1969) *WP*

Richard Rodney Bennett   *Impromptu* (1969) *WP*

Karlheinz Stockhausen   *Dr. K. Sextett* (1969) *WP*

Roy Hart (reciter)
Clover Roope († choreography and dance)
Peter Zinovieff († electronics)
Peter Maxwell Davies, Harrison Birtwistle (conductors)

The Pierrot Players

FLUTES Judith Pearce	VIOLIN / VIOLA Duncan Druce
CLARINETS Alan Hacker	CELLO Jennifer Ward Clarke
KEYBOARDS Stephen Pruslin	PERCUSSION Barry Quinn

*Example 7.5   The Pierrot Players in 'A Garland for Dr. K.', 1969,
featuring the first performance of Davies's* Eight Songs for a Mad King

least aspects of the styles of many composers are referred to, from Handel to Birtwistle.[60]

The crux of the matter lies in the final comment. The *Eight Songs* had squared Davies's hankering after his national past with his quest for authenticity. Such was the extent of this reconciliation that it involved quoting not just Handel, the naturalized Briton, but the British King's actual words. It also took inspiration from a miniature mechanical organ the King once owned and began with asynchronous, clock-like rhythms – an allusion to his co-director's style. Given that Davies's King becomes aware of his predicament moments *after* announcing his own death, it is telling that Birtwistle had tried with a similar idea in *Monodrama*.

Birtwistle's presence was felt in another way: through the planning of the concert in which the *Eight Songs* were premiered (ex. 7.5). Indeed, the average concertgoer might not have anticipated *Eight Songs for a Mad King* as the highlight of the evening. Two works by Birtwistle also contributed to making this the group's most memorable event. *Linoi II* was more than the revision-work its title may have suggested. *Linoi I* had been premiered at the Leeds Festival in October and, unusually for Birtwistle, it had received several follow-up performances. Its success may be attributed to the fact that, scored for clarinet and piano, it joined *Hymnos* in the Pierrot Players' repertory and, temporarily at least, became its successor. (Birtwistle's instructions, for Pruslin only to pluck his piano strings and for Hacker to play his clarinet into the piano, made his work the more theatrical.) *Linoi II* was just as radical, as Birtwistle commissioned Clover Roope to dance to a taped recording of the original. Pruslin, spokesperson for the group once more, explained:

> The composer has long been interested in the idea of an initially self-sufficient musical work which yet could support a further theatrical or choreographical layer should this be desired. The dance is conceived as an emanation of the music … [but is in] no way a pictorial or programmatic treatment of [its Greek] myths, least of all in its danced aspect. It is a piece of 'absolute' music consisting of the generation, the simultaneous flowering and destruction, and the prolonged death agony of a single melodic line.[61]

To this interesting take on musical absolutism we must add that *Linoi II* was as much a commentary on the two levels of activity as the artistic content itself, and that thanks to its choreography, the work belatedly realized Birtwistle's original vision of the Pierrot Players as a multidisciplinary arts troupe.[62]

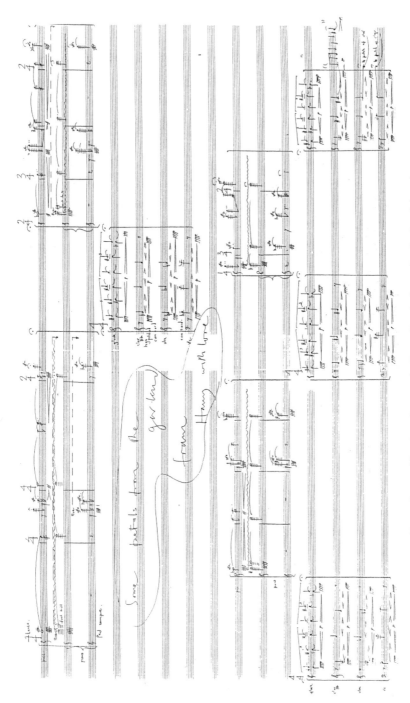

Example 7.6 Harrison Birtwistle, Some Petals from the Garland (1969), advertised and performed as Some Petals from My Twickenham Herbarium

His more conventional other work, the opaquely titled *Some Petals from My Twickenham Herbarium* (ex. 7.6), was a novelty, but one that featured within the illustrious *A Garland for Dr. K.*, to which composers associated with Universal Edition had contributed. This anthology was written to celebrate the eightieth birthday of Alfred Kalmus, who founded the London branch of the publishing house in 1936. However whimsical some of the pieces (Birtwistle and Hugh Wood both quoted the 'Happy Birthday' song), the fact that eleven British and prominent European composers had written works for the Pierrot Players was significant in itself. Few were written for the group's complete line-up, but Stockhausen's *Dr. K. Sextett* was. Its three-minute study of familiar 'moments' of sound in time was experimental in being the first Pierrot ensemble piece to come with an instruction not to be conducted. Also notable was Berio's effort, not just because of its verbose but self-explanatory title, *The Modification and Instrumentation of a Famous Hornpipe as a Merry and Altogether Sincere Homage to Uncle Alfred*, but also for its entertaining, almost Daviesian transformation of Purcell (whose original hornpipe is best known as the song 'There's not a swain').

Davies was not involved with this one-off, celebratory collection, for he was signed to Boosey & Hawkes. Of course, historically, his *Eight Songs* would endure, whereas the *Garland for Dr. K.* was quickly forgotten. Birtwistle, similarly, is little discussed in the history of the Pierrot ensemble. One of his most accomplished works at that point, *Down by the Greenwood Side* (1969), was not even written for the Pierrot Players, but for Alexander Goehr's Music Theatre Ensemble (a bigger group, but one which performed together less often). Meanwhile, Davies's continued fascination with, and transmutation of, the Medieval and Renaissance periods set his musical language apart from other European composers. This synthesis was as alien to the dominant trends of British music during the time of the Pierrot Players as it was during Davies's difficult years at university. What changed in the late 1960s was that, with his group as a vehicle, his use of sources became more overt and parody was put at the heart of his style. The Pierrot Players would give Davies, if not Birtwistle, the platform to compose many more incendiary works for Pierrot ensemble in the line of Schoenberg.

Notes

1   See Peter Maxwell Davies, 'The Young British Composer', *The Score and I.M.A. Magazine* 16 (March, 1956), 84-5.

2   *Ibid.*, 85.

3   *Ibid.*, 85. Incidentally, the article uses 'English' and 'British' interchangeably.

4   As Davies said three years later: 'I suspect the English have been living in a fool's paradise, in complete ignorance of recent and even distant musical

developments. But the smoke screen of polite music, of bygone styles, cannot hide the truth for ever. By this smoke screen I mean most English music by the acknowledged composers of our century.' Peter Maxwell Davies, 'Problems of a British Composer Today', *The Listener* 62/1593 (8 October 1959), 563.

5   Davies's truck was with the Head of Music at Manchester University, Humphrey Procter-Gregg, who thought very little of contemporary music. See Humphrey Procter-Gregg, interview with Brian Gee, 'Professor Humphrey Procter-Gregg: Some Details of His Career', *Musical Opinion* 88/1054 (July, 1965), 599-601.

6   For example: Ralph Vaughan Williams (Berlin, Paris), Delius (Leipzig, via Jacksonville), Cyril Scott and Roger Quilter (both Frankfurt), among others.

7   Given his subsequent qualification of the phrase, this could be interpreted as a put-down of integral serialism, to which his fellow 'Manchester School' member Alexander Goehr had very recently introduced him. See Alexander Goehr, 'Manchester Years' (1990) in: *Finding the Key: Selected Writings of Alexander Goehr*, ed. Derrick Puffett (London: Faber, 1998), 38-9.

8   See Chapter 5, note 28.

9   See Lutyens, *A Goldfish Bowl* (London: Cassell, 1972), 167-68. Regretfully, she went on to say: 'But, as Dallapiccola said to me, "It is not a risk today." Then, it most certainly was.' See also Meirion Harries and Susan Harries, *A Pilgrim Soul: The Life and Work of Elisabeth Lutyens* (London: Faber, 1989), 166-67.

10   Elisabeth Lutyens, 'Sermon Delivered to the S.P.N.M., June 4, 1959', *The Score* 26 (January, 1960), 66. For the record, the composers (and works) involved on this occasion were John Wilks (*Variations for Orchestra*), William Mathias (*Berceuse*, Op. 4, subsequently withdrawn), and Philip Cowlin (Symphony), and it is doubtful they shared Lutyens's sentiment. Without the SPNM, their works may never have graced London's Festival Hall, nor attracted the London Philharmonic Orchestra to play them under Charles Mackerras's direction.

11   Elisabeth Lutyens, *A Goldfish Bowl* (London: Cassell, 1972), 241. Some accounts wrongly suggest the concert took place in 1955. Years later, when the significance of the unique joint appearance of these performers and composers in the capital was apparent, it was enough for one critic to remember how the group had 'burst sensationally upon London'. William Mann, 'British Musical Challenge to Conservative Vienna', *The Times* (24 October 1969), 13.

12   Their roles varied: Goehr was a composer and the group's 'non-playing director'; Davies composed and, like Ogdon, played the piano (though did not perform in London); Howarth (trumpet) and Birtwistle (clarinet) were primarily instrumentalists at the time and made their respective names in conducting and composition only later. Goehr, 37.

13   The Darmstadt School of the late 1950s grew out of the *Internationale Ferienkurse für Neue Musik* (founded 1946); its principal associates were Pierre Boulez, Bruno Maderna, Karlheinz Stockhausen and Luigi Nono. Coined by Nono during a lecture at Darmstadt in 1957, the designation soon came to stand not for a united, collegial aesthetic, but its dissolution: the 'school' could not withstand what seemed then to be widely divergent ideas about

the advancement of serialism, nor the fierce attacks and counterattacks that accompanied them. See Luigi Nono, 'Die Entwicklung der Reihentechnik' (Darmstadt, 1957) in: *Darmstädter Beiträge zur Neuen Musik*, ed. Wolfgang Steinecke (Mainz, 1958), vol. 1, 25-37; Karlheinz Stockhausen, 'Musik und Sprache' (Darmstadt, 1958), *Die Reihe* 6 (1960), 36-58; Luigi Nono, 'Presenza storica nella musica d'oggi' (Darmstadt, 1959) in: *La Rassegna Musicale* 30/1 (1960), 1-8. Goehr had works performed at successive summer courses (Opp. 2 and 4 in 1954/55 respectively). Davies attended in 1956 and later (20 July 1957) accompanied Georgina Dobrée's performance of his Sonata for Clarinet and Piano there, but felt 'constrained and daunted' by the experience. Peter Maxwell Davies, quoted in: Roderic Dunnett, 'Sir Peter Maxwell Davies: On Her Majesty's Service', *The Independent* (15 March 2004), 56.

14   Goehr, 285. In the mid 1950s Goehr befriended Boulez and Nono while studying in Paris and Darmstadt respectively.

15   Glock founded and edited *The Score*, a short-lived but authoritative journal devoted mainly to contemporary music. He stepped down as Chairman of the ICA Music Section to join the BBC as Controller of Music in 1959.

16   Gervase de Peyer, quoted in: 'Problems of a Chamber Music Ensemble', *The Times* (14 January 1963), 12.

17   Premiered by the Virtuoso Ensemble during the inaugural Anglesey Festival (April 1962), Hoddinott's Septet, Op. 10 was scored identically to Stravinsky's recent prototype – both works entered the Melos's repertoire, too. Goehr's *Suite*, Op. 11 was commissioned for the Melos Ensemble by Benjamin Britten and was premiered at the Aldeburgh Festival in 1961. Its line-up is similar to the Pierrot ensemble, replacing the piano with a harp and horn; Maconchy's *Reflections* is one of several works that did the same but without the horn. See Catalogue of Pierrot Ensembles, section 5b: with piano omitted or substituted for percussion and/or harp. The absence of a mixed chamber ensemble in the BBC's portfolio was one inspiration behind the group's formation, and Glock's accession there imposed new demands upon the group. When works for unusual instrumental combinations were broadcast early in his reign, he naturally looked to the Melos Ensemble to join Schoenberg's *Serenade* and Webern's *Concerto for Nine Instruments* with Beethoven's Septet in their pan-Viennese repertoire. All three works were aired live from London's Maida Vale Studios on 24 March 1960.

18   This was not the first event Birtwistle had organized at the school: his *Entr'actes* – later reworked into the *Entr'actes and Sappho Fragments* (1962/64) – were premiered there in the autumn of 1962 by members of the local Bournemouth Symphony Orchestra.

19   Indicating his fondness for instrumental doubling, Birtwistle called for the winds to play claves, while Davies also doubled the flute with piccolo.

20   See Mike Seabrook, *Max: The Life and Music of Peter Maxwell Davies* (London: Gollancz, 1994), 94.

21   See, for example, Michael Burden, 'A Foxtrot to the Crucifixion: The Music Theatre of Peter Maxwell Davies' in: *Perspectives on Peter Maxwell Davies*, ed. Richard McGregor (London: Ashgate, 2001), 52.

22   Alan Hacker, emailed correspondence with the author, 24 April 2004. Just as Birtwistle had befriended Hacker, a young fellow clarinettist, at the Royal Academy of Music, Davies met the American pianist Stephen Pruslin while studying at Princeton. In turn, Pruslin continued his studies in Britain from 1964.

23   Stephen Pruslin, 'Twenty Years of The Fires: A Retrospective Sketch', article from the concert programme for 'The Fires' Farewell and Twentieth Birthday Gala' (Queen Elizabeth Hall, 20 January 1987), pages unnumbered.

24   These concerts were held on 11 June 1964 and 5 October 1964 respectively, both with the Virtuoso Ensemble under John Carewe. The later event, held in the Arts Council Drawing Room, also featured Davies's *Five Little Pieces for Piano* (1960-64), performed by the composer.

25   Peter Maxwell Davies, roundtable discussion with Anthony Payne, Christopher Wintle, Julian Jacobson and Judith Weir, held during a conference on '*Pierrot lunaire* and Its Legacy', 2 March 2006, Kingston University, London.

26   *Ibid.*

27   Pruslin, *op. cit.*

28   The work is difficult to access. Withdrawn before it could be published, its score is held by Universal Edition and the BBC. Only one recording is preserved (BLSA, cat. NP1131W BD 1).

29   Schoenberg's apparently genuine alarm that this should have been interpreted as blasphemous is documented thus: 'In Geneva and Amsterdam I notice for the first time that "Madonna", "Red Mass" and also "Crosses" somehow give religious offence. … I seem to have had an altogether much naiver view of these poems that most people have. … If [listeners] were the faintest bit musical, not a single one of them would give a damn for the words. Instead, they would go away whistling the tunes.' Arnold Schoenberg, letter to Marya Freund (20 December 1922), in: *Letters*, ed. Erwin Stein, trans. Eithne Wilkins and Ernst Kaiser (Eng. edn., London: Faber, 1964), 81-2.

30   Peter Maxwell Davies, programme note to *Antechrist*, Queen Elizabeth Hall, 30 May 1967. The motet is 'broken up and superimposed on related plainsong fragments, which, both musically and with regard to the related implied texts, turns the sense of the motet inside-out. The compositional techniques employed relate more clearly than in any previous work of mine to late medieval techniques, particularly with regard to rhythmic mode and cantus decoration.' For more on Davies's transformational techniques, see Cheryl Tongier, *Pre-existent Music in the Works of Peter Maxwell Davies* (Ph.D. diss., University of Kansas, 1983), esp. 123-83.

31   Typically, Noel Goodwin praised an 'attractive suite … [with] buoyant spirit'. Noel Goodwin, 'Music in London: Pierrot Players', *Musical Times* 108/1493 (July, 1963), 626.

32   Harrison Birtwistle, programme note to *Monodrama*, Queen Elizabeth Hall, 30 May 1967.

33   Based on Ovid's interpretation of the Philomela legend, *Philomel* was written in conjunction with the poet John Hollander. Its allusive wordplay, coupled

with the interplay of live and recorded sound, has made it one of Babbitt's best-known works. See John Hollander, 'Notes on the Text of *Philomel*', *Perspectives of New Music* 6/1 (Autumn-Winter, 1967), 134-41. Like Davies before him, Birtwistle also spent time at Princeton on a Harkness Fellowship in 1966.

34 On *Pierrot*'s motivicism, see Jonathan Dunsby, 'Schoenberg's Pierrot Keeping his *Kopfmotiv*' in: *Pierrot Lunaire: Albert Giraud – Otto Erich Hartleben – Arnold Schoenberg: A Collection of Musicological and Literary Studies*, ed. Mark Delaere and Jan Herman (Louvain: Peeters, 2004), 67-76.

35 Possibly a legacy of the composer's military band days, *Monodrama*'s A♭-clarinet is particularly striking.

36 William Mann, 'Veiled Drama for Pierrot Forces', *The Times* (31 May 1969), 17. Anthony Payne was more circumspect on the music's 'brave failure' but chided Pruslin's 'remarkably naïve collection of clichés in a vein of school-magazine modernism.' Anthony Payne, 'The Problems of Pierrot', *Music & Musicians* 15 (August, 1967), 41.

37 Birtwistle had asked Druce to be on standby to play as early as June, but did not explain to Druce why the vacancy had arisen. Duncan Druce, interview with the author, 28 August 2006. In a further link between the Pierrot Players and the Melos Ensemble, Druce had studied viola with Cecil Aronowitz the previous year. Nevertheless, neither Druce, nor the two original Pierrot Players who assisted my research (Hacker and Ward Clarke), can recall why Mann left the group.

38 E.M. Webster, 'Cheltenham: Blight on the Band-wagon', *Musical Opinion* 90/1080 (September, 1967), 685.

39 For example: Davies's *Ut Re Mi* (after John Bull) for piano (1970); *Solita* for flute and, optionally, musical box (1972); *The Kestrel Paced Round the Sun* for flute (1975, published with *Solita* as *Two Pieces for Flute Alone*; *The Seven Brightnesses* for clarinet (1975); *The Door to the Sun* for viola (1975); *Nocturne* for alto flute (1979); and the monodrama *The Medium* for solo mezzo-soprano (1981). In 1968, Anthony Gilbert also wrote *Spell Respell* for electric basset-clarinet and piano and *The Incredible Flute Music* for flute and piano, two parts of a trilogy of works for the Pierrot Players that included the Pierrot ensemble *Mother* (1969), which pitted a solo cello against the ensemble.

40 'Missa super L'homme armé ... in Conway Hall ... sent shock waves through the London music scene.' Meirion Bowen, 'The Fires Brigade', *The Guardian* (19 January 1987), 9. Or '... the experience [of *Missa super L'homme armé*] is not unlike that of the collage movements of Berio's *Sinfonia*, although Maxwell Davies's use of the cliché and the vulgar is so much more blasphemous.' Elliott Schwartz, review of four scores by Peter Maxwell Davies, *Musical Quarterly* 62/2 (April, 1976), 304. An anonymous review at the time of the concert related the same work's 'perverse spirit of elfin delight', though its revival five years later drew an indignant response from Stanley Sadie: '... "in jokes" like quotations from foreign styles and the effect of a sticking gramophone needle ... may tickle the fancies of camp followers, but it has not much to do with real music.' Respectively: Anonymous, 'Conway Hall', *Musical Opinion*

91/1087 (April, 1968), 368; Stanley Sadie, 'Clever Musical Parodies', *The Times* (19 March 1973), 10.

41   See François Lesure (ed.), *Dossier de Presse: Press-book de Pierrot lunaire d'Arnold Schönberg* (Geneva: Minkoff, 1985), 44.

42   Mensural canon and serialism coexist in *Alma Redemptoris Mater* (1957), for example, yet to all but the analyst its submerged Marian antiphon and eponymous Dunstable motet are undetectable. And not since his youth, with the *Quartet Movement* (1952), had Davies shown his interest in folkloristic writing reminiscent of Bartók, or the witty and parodic flair that would characterize his mature style now. As Davies wrote further works for Pierrot ensemble, often theatrically conceived, his use of sources became clearer and, relatedly, the thinking behind his selection of sources took on extra significance (be it comic or moralistic, as we shall see). Hence, by 'parody' we conflate here its general and idiosyncratic meanings: exaggeration for effect on the one hand, the use of pre-existing material (as in a parody mass) on the other.

43   Quoted from advertisements for the concert.

44   Paul Griffiths, *Peter Maxwell Davies* (London: Robson, 1982), 63.

45   Peter Maxwell Davies, quoted in: Rodney Milnes, 'Towards Music Theatre', *Opera* 23/12 (1972), 1067.

46   The Redcliffe Concerts were founded in 1963/64 to support the performance of modern British music. See Francis Routh, 'The Redcliffe Concerts', *Composer* 26 (1967-68), 24-6.

47   Peceptive critics appeared to appreciate this. The *Fantasia* was praised for its 'outrageously inventive sonorities [that] seemed effectively to underpin the music's ingenious counterpoints and adventurous harmonies.' Robert Henderson, 'Music in London: New Music', *Musical Times* 109/1505 (July, 1968), 644. On its design as a realization, too, William Mann was sympathetic, describing it as 'stimulating and, strangely, more stylish than the revolutionary Purcell realizations with which Britten shocked academics 20 or so years ago', adding that 'anyone who bridled at the Pierrot Players' treatment should try playing this music on a baroque organ.' William Mann, 'Handbells in Concerto', *The Times* (31 May 1968), 15.

48   Griffiths, 13.

49   See Burden, 65.

50   'To our singer, speaker and players, we hope eventually to add a dancer.' Harrison Birtwistle, quoted in: Goodwin, 626.

51   '*Fides est virtus qua credentur quae non viden non videntur nos* [tripping up deliberately on:] *quid* [x4] *significant illud* [x3] *faciamus et quam sit verum non laboremus.*'

52   Jonathan Harvey, 'Maxwell Davies's "Songs for a Mad King"', *Tempo* 89 (Summer, 1969), 2.

53   John Warrack claimed in the *Sunday Telegraph* that Davies was asking the audience to mock the madman and also attacked the work's musical basis: 'Composing madness into the actual technique of music is artistically as self-

defeating as portraying a boring operatic character by writing boring music.'
Quoted in: Seabrook, 111. Davies's rationale is discussed later.

54 Harvey, 2.

55 See Roger Smalley, 'Maxwell Davies and Others', *Musical Times* 114/1565 (July, 1973), 712. See also Epilogue, note 5.

56 Reviewing the premiere, William Mann remarked: '…the musical invention is well sustained, though I did now and then find a sag or two.' William Mann, 'Music in London; Birthday Concerts', *Musical Times* 110/1516 (June, 1969), 645. Attitudes continued to paint the *Eight Songs* as a vital, if deficient, work: '*Eight Songs* is, to be sure, a seriously flawed work, just holding together by the skin of its teeth, but it is nevertheless an indispensable part of my (and I guess many other people's) musical experience.' David Roberts, review of *Ave Maris Stella* and ten other scores by Peter Maxwell Davies, *Contact* 19 (Summer, 1978), 27.

57 Stephen Pruslin, 'Two Portraits of Madness', sleevenotes to Unicorn-Kanchana, DKP(CD)9052 (1987), 3.

58 Writing for *Musical America*, the *Guardian* music critic Edward Greenfield commented: 'Harrowing was the only word to describe the experience, an element of embarrassment deliberately included.' Edward Greenfield, 'London/Brighton: Britten Premiere and a Mad King George', *High Fidelity/Musical America* 19/8 (August, 1969), 27.

59 Nor is it a coincidence that the actual King's reactions to his birds have been likened to the Pierrot character: 'We know from Fanny Burney and other courtiers how the King behaved during his illness and how he reacted to his bullfinches. It was a reaction somewhat similar to that of Pierrot to the moon. The birds were an audience for the King to express his terror of himself and horror at the evils of his age.' Veronica Slater, 'Extended Note [to *Eight Songs for a Mad King*]', www.webarchive.org.uk/wayback/archive/20070131163627/http://www.maxopus.com/works/8songs.htm (accessed 7 September 2012). Peter Maxwell Davies claimed that Olivier Messiaen deemed the *Eight Songs* to be 'cruel to the birds' (*ob. dict.* Oxford, 1971 [ed.]).

60 Peter Maxwell Davies, 'Composer's Note [to *Eight Songs for a Mad King*]', *Ibid.*

61 Stephen Pruslin, programme note to *Linoi II* (Queen Elizabeth Hall, London, 22 April 1969), pages unnumbered.

62 See note 50.

Harrison Birtwistle (David Hockney, 1970),
as reproduced in the 'Spring Song' concert programme (3 March 1970)

8 Rethinking Birtwistle's Role

The Pierrot Players' success masked divisions among their number: Birtwistle left the group during the winter of the 1970/71 season. His reluctance to discuss his time with them has done little to end the speculation surrounding his decision to quit. Particularly in the media, battle lines have been drawn between Birtwistle and Davies ever since the sudden, on-stage announcement of Birtwistle's departure during a concert at the Queen Elizabeth Hall on 19 September 1970. This apparently caught critics unawares.[1] The Lancastrian, working-class backgrounds of the two composers, and their parallel rise through the ranks of British music since the split, have encouraged the notion of rivalry. Such circumstances also inspire the timeworn and rather retroactive proposal that two figures, so ambitious and talented, could not continue to flourish together in such an intimate context as a Pierrot ensemble.

But to draw conclusions about the demise of the Pierrot Players from the grand reputations each composer now enjoys would be to miscalculate their standing in British music in the 1960s. Neither composer received the number of performances or accolades they do today, and Birtwistle, especially, fared considerably worse than his co-director. The composer accused in recent years by Paul Driver of being 'untouchably fashionable [and a] safe-bet avant-gardist' was so dissatisfied with his music for the Pierrot Players that, having already rescinded two works he had written for them, *Monodrama* and *Three Lessons in a Frame*, he also withdrew *Medusa* (1969, rev. 1970) and *Eight Lessons for Keyboards, with Interludes* (1969).[2] This cannot be dismissed, then, as the knee-jerk reaction of a bristly composer, even if around this time, Birtwistle and Davies fell into a dispute that has never since been reliably explained or resolved.

Their frosty relationship was brought into awkward focus by a meeting *The Guardian* managed to engineer a few years ago.[3] This prompted a rare first-hand comment on their schism some thirty-four years earlier, even if it did little to mend relations between the two: Davies's memory that 'Harry [Birtwistle] wanted a larger ensemble' offered nothing new, however.[4] Besides, to obsess over this unsubstantiated quarrel is to perpetuate a line of enquiry that overlooks Birtwistle's musical achievements entirely at a climactic point on the Pierrot ensemble timeline. As Mike Seabrook's garrulous five-page account attests, circumstantial references, often vague in their tenor and recollection, are no adequate substitute for a proper chronicle of the Pierrot Players' unique history, dynamic and ethos.[5] Speculation leads only to conclusions made with false confidence, such as 'no small group was ever going to contain two creative geniuses, two personalities so strong and different, as those of Max and Harry.'[6] Actually, the Pierrot Players thrived for nearly four years.

Birtwistle and the Group Ethos

The grand reputation The Fires of London (the Pierrot Players' successor) secured under Davies's sole control has overshadowed many details in the illustrious, if comparatively short-lived, history of the earlier ensemble. Today, Birtwistle's achievements as co-founder, composer, director and even impresario are all but forgotten. One reason for this is that he became marginalized while still attached to the Pierrot Players. It was at Davies's invitation that James Murdoch became the ensemble's manager in July 1968, having met the Australian during a residency at the University of Adelaide. Previously Secretary of the Melbourne branch of the ISCM, Murdoch had international stature within the new music scene and experience of music theatre, having worked with the Australian Ballet. Murdoch founded Music Media Ltd, the company behind the promotion of the groups' concerts from 1969 until 1974, and also became Davies's personal manager. Birtwistle has never commented on how Murdoch's management of the group he himself had conceived affected his own position, or whether the clear destabilizing potential of this dual administrative role was ever detrimental. Indeed, given the critical failure of *Monodrama*, Birtwistle's debut work for group, we should not focus exclusively on Murdoch's arrival. Yet it is clear that a curious antipathy undermined their working relationship: 'Harry dried up. I had nothing from Harry to market and sell. Inevitable the split.'[7]

Murdoch is abrasive yet consistent: in another drive of the wedge between the two composers, he once justified Birtwistle's exit from the Pierrot Players by claiming to Davies's biographer that the ensemble was 'a music theatre group – the best – and needed music theatre works. Harry didn't write any … Simple!'[8] However one-sided is the criticism that clearly persists here, beyond and behind it lie greater insights. First, Murdoch's expertise came in a field in which Davies, not Birtwistle, had begun to excel. The manager also claims to have crafted the group's soon-to-be iconic image of black outfits and dimly lit staging with which they performed. Exploiting the Pierrot Players' theatrical reputation, these simple devices heralded the start of a new, enduring brand. Second, to say Birtwistle 'dried up' during Murdoch's tenure is plainly untrue. To claim he did not write the type of works the group apparently required, on the other hand, leads to the more remarkable conclusion, implicit in the manager's view, that the composer no longer dictated the direction of his co-led group.

If, after Murdoch's arrival, distinct visions for the very purpose of the Pierrot Players surfaced and collided, then gleaning the composers' own views of its 'brand' (i.e. its audience and profile) would clearly nuance our understanding. In their attitudes to audiences, for example, the similarities between the two composers appear to end. Doubtless Birtwistle's belligerence (e.g. "I can't be responsible for the audience: I'm not running a restaurant.")[9] has hardened with age, although even with the Pierrot Players he emulated aspects of Schoenberg's aloof approach in this area, as we shall see. Conversely, Davies's occasional works for children and his aping of popular styles make him, on balance, the more accessible composer. This second trait, however, is something of an illusion. Davies's militant views on popular music betray its subversive use in his own works,[10] even if he surely knew that pavans reimagined as foxtrots, eighteenth-century parlour songs, Sandy Wilson arrangements and so forth would also attract a bigger audience.[11] Besides, in a similar way to Birtwistle, Davies has declared his wariness of modern conceptions of fandom and celebrity: 'I'm aware of the personality cult that surrounds musical life of today, and I don't want that; I don't want to get in the way of [my] music. ... I don't want to be a personality with a capital P.'[12]

Made long after the Pierrot Players' demise, this statement is nevertheless a defence against the type of situation that apparently arose with them. While the group never systematically probed its fan base, Stanley Sadie's pejorative reference to 'the fancies of camp followers' of Davies's music is startling and relates to the composer's flair for attracting attention, welcome or otherwise.[13] It also endorses an argument recycled by later commentators to explain the breach with Birtwistle, whom Meirion Bowen said felt 'out of sympathy with [the group's] camp sensationalism and occasional aura of meretriciousness.'[14] Michael Hall faithfully repeated this line of reasoning to describe Birtwistle's discomfort 'with the high camp and sensationalism that was developing.'[15] If these were true perceptions, how do they compare with Birtwistle's original vision of the group? Of the two composers, he had been the more specific on the Pierrot Players' ethos, picturing a group that 'resembles the strolling players of old – in fact we intend to travel round the country.'[16] On the group's corporate personality, too, he said 'it had always been at the back of my mind to form some sort of ensemble ... [with the] same players all the time ... so we were a group, like a string quartet.'[17] In fact, both aims were fulfilled, though not without difficulties. The South Bank's Purcell Room and Queen Elizabeth Hall became the group's usual venues, yet the Pierrot Players were never tied to one audience. In keeping with Birtwistle's prediction, they often toured as well. The group played at festivals and universities, and the support of the Contemporary Music Network (established 1974) enabled The Fires of London to tour the regions more frequently. Touring different continents, however, would upset the 'robust' principles Birtwistle had set forth, albeit after he had left the group: the fallout over a five-week tour of North America in 1976 precipitated an almost complete change of personnel in the group.[18] Indeed, Davies's subsequent unhappiness with the Arts Council (founders of the Contemporary Music Network) was a factor in the group's dissolution in 1987.[19]

According to Anthony Payne, Birtwistle had publicized a third aim for the Pierrot Players: to present concerts with an air of occasion.[20] This idea also transpired, of course, not just with such a stand-out Pierrot ensemble piece as *Eight Songs for a Mad King*, but also through eclectic, sometimes experimental programming the group's audience could appreciate. As one fan of The Fires of London put it:

> You knew to expect lots of works, lots of different styles. Some [pieces] might have been much better than others – some were terrible! – but because they did this so often [programming in this way and playing so frequently], it didn't matter.[21]

At the same time, Birtwistle's 'air of occasion' became a trademark of the Pierrot Players thanks largely to Davies's iconoclastic streak. Birtwistle was the casualty and knew it:

> Max [Davies] wrote these rather hysterical theatre pieces and I was placed in a false position of competition. I didn't want to write that sort of thing. It's not what I thought the whole thing was about. I think I wrote pieces which were not honest because of that.[22]

Hence, even a former player with the group(s) speaks of 'Twenty Years of The Fires [*sic*]', rendering them synonymous and remembering Birtwistle in a peripheral light, as one never to have 'found a stimulus in the group's small, fixed instrumentation'.[23]

Despite Davies's later achievements with The Fires of London, this account by Stephen Pruslin is disputable: the Pierrot Players' constitution was neither particularly 'small' nor 'fixed'. From the start, with *Monodrama* Birtwistle had shown a keen awareness of contemporary trends, coupled with a resolve to augment the Pierrot ensemble using other forces.[24] He also forged alliances with individual Pierrot Players themselves, especially Alan Hacker, and an audience of a different kind – composers – by engaging the electronic music guru Peter Zinovieff and commissioning young composers such as his pupil Bruce Cole (who wrote the terse *Caesura* for the group), his peers David Bedford (*The Sword of Orion*), David Lumsdaine (*Mandala 2*) and Anthony Gilbert (*Mother*), and such established international figures as Morton Feldman (*the viola in my life I*). These relationships were not incidental: The Fires of London would not only develop them, but also establish a proud reputation for helping the next generation of composers and for fastening Anglo-American ties. If there were credible reasons for Birtwistle deciding some of his works for the Pierrot Players were somehow aesthetically 'dishonest', then we must ask how and why this came about.[25]

Three Lessons in a Frame is the most obscure of the collection. Performed only once and withdrawn before it could be published, its sole catalogued recording is also lost.[26] David Beard's comprehensive study of Birtwistle's instrumental music of this period does not mention the work.[27] What sparse commentary does exist can be traced back to its original reviews, which took their cue from programme notes Birtwistle wrote for the work's premiere (Cheltenham Festival, 17 July 1967). Hall mentions the piece in an appendix, noting that it

> … explores [the] visual image of a mould and its copy. The first two lessons, for piano alone and instruments [flute/piccolo, clarinet, violin, cello] alone respectively, are really the same work twice, except that whatever is implied but missing in one of them is to be found in its complement. In the third lesson the two interlock.[28]

When Robert Adlington speculates that this sculpture-inspired process was too transparent, or that, '[by] the standards of other works which adopt the idea of multiple perspectives on an object, *Three Lessons in a Frame* takes a remarkably simplistic approach',[29] he develops a theme of Stephen Walsh's:

> Birtwistle calls [the lessons] the same piece, related I suppose like positive and negative films. No. 3 combined them into a culminating section … One liked the piece for its amusing source idea, though its content seemed ordinary, and predictably neither of the first two sections said anything that was left unsaid by the third.[30]

Clearly, *Three Lessons in a Frame*, as with *Monodrama*, did not impress. Birtwistle's co-director apparently knew it. Having rehearsed the work as the intended finale for a subsequent concert at the University of Southampton, Davies successfully argued that his flamboyant *Hymnos* should end the programme instead.

At twenty minutes, Birtwistle's work was perhaps overblown if listeners were supposed to 'fill in the gaps' along the way. His developing vision that 'multi-dimensional musical objects [should express] a number of contradictions as well as a number of perspectives' is an inadequate measure of this work, whose reviews tell us that the notional opposition and synthesis of the lessons were either too obvious or did not enable the teleology to be grasped.[31] Reactions to the music would probably have been very different had it accompanied a toy theatre. This, intriguingly, is the original design suggested by Birtwistle's sketches, littered as they are with instructions such as 'P. descend ladder', 'Columbine doll' and 'Pierrot farewell'. As it was, *Three Lessons in a Frame* was saddled with an abstract title and, with only the flute doubling, a simple instrumental ensemble (by the Pierrot Players' standards). When its harshest critic, E. M. Webster, branded Birtwistle as 'a young composer [compared with Davies] whose work never reaches what it set out to find', she made one of the first unfavourable comparisons between the two composers.[32] Armed with similarly discursive themes, Birtwistle found greater success in the coming years, though only once he had turned to larger and more easily *partitioned* line-ups than the Pierrot ensemble – hence the 'stereophonic' subgroups of *Verses for Ensembles* (1968-69) and the orchestral temporal allegory of *The Triumph of Time* (1972).

'Spring Song'

With the critical mauling of *Three Lessons in a Frame* coming so soon after the *Monodrama* debacle, Birtwistle's true breakthrough would, surprisingly, not be enjoyed with the Pierrot Players. The next eighteen months saw Birtwistle take a back seat in the group. The only works of his the Pierrot Players performed in the meantime were the *Four Interludes from a Tragedy*, which he had salvaged from *Monodrama* (Interstices I-IV, as they were in the original work), and the first version of *Linoi*, featuring Alan Hacker and Pruslin. But if Birtwistle was disillusioned either by Murdoch's management or by Davies's conspicuously prolific output, he did not show it. Rather, there are signs that, through composition and event planning, he tried to reassert his leadership and vision of the group in the months before his departure. Planning a unique 'Spring Song' concert on 3 March 1970 was the biggest landmark (ex. 8.1):

Harrison Birtwistle has devised for this concert a programme that can be heard as a total entity, with an overall structure. The concert proceeds until the end without the punctuation of applause, and is arranged symmetrically around the interval, which is also part of the programme.[33]

By silencing its audience, Birtwistle drew a clear parallel with Arnold Schoenberg's *Verein für musikalische Privataufführungen*, whose 'knowledge through familiarity' mantra and subscription-only policy had taken similar steps. Its advertisement saw the sometimes shy composer step out from Davies's shadow. A fold-out, four-page centrespread in the concert programme featuring David Hockney's line-drawn portrait of the composer hit home the message that Birtwistle was back.[34]

'Spring Song' was far from a private event, of course, and it even drew the attention of a new music community abroad. In an unusually vivid and detailed account, the Croatian composer Natko Devčić wrote of his amazement at the 'concrete vision' of the Queen Elizabeth Hall, the sight of 'young girls in trousers and miniskirts, and boys with beards fitting in very well', and the concert's innovations (the article in full is translated in Document C).[35] The latter included the way in which Birtwistle's four spliced interludes for clarinet and tape formed the pillars of the programme, Hacker emerging from darkness into a green spotlight to play each of them. The rest of the programme was designed so that pairs of works, 'correspondent' along lines of chronology, staging and aesthetic, framed the concert: Birtwistle's take on Machaut's *Hoquetus David* had a counterpart in Hacker's *Czardas*; the satirical Satie (*Sports et Divertissements*) and Berners (*Three English Songs*) were both performed on a high podium; and the premieres of works by Bedford and Birtwistle himself were the centrepieces of each half (ex. 8.2).

Devčić turned to electronic music during his year of study in New York, where he collaborated with the Argentine-American composer Mario Davidovsky at the Columbia-Princeton Electronic Music Center (CPEMC). His interest in Birtwistle's 'Spring Song' is a clue to its genesis. Just eight months before Devčić attended the concert, Peter Zinovieff and Tristram Cary had founded the British Society for Electronic Music (BSEM) to gather support for a national studio equipped with tape and processing rooms, a library, an archive, lecture and recital halls and a research laboratory.[36] Davies chaired the new society and was joined on a steering committee that included Zinovieff, Cary, John Woolf, Don Banks, Hugh Davies and Murdoch. Why (Maxwell) Davies was approached is unclear. His experience of electronic music was negligible but his Princeton connections were perhaps useful: the 'godfather' of American electronic music, Milton Babbitt, travelled to London to give an introductory talk to the BSEM's first, SPNM-

3 March 1970, 7.45pm – Queen Elizabeth Hall, London

'Spring Song: A New Concept for a Concert', presented by Music Media Ltd

Harrison Birtwistle   *First Interlude from a Tragedy*
Traditional, arr. **Alan Hacker**   *Czardas* WP
David Bedford   *The Sword of Orion* WP
Erik Satie   *Sports et Divertissements* (staged)
Harrison Birtwistle   *Second Interlude from a Tragedy*

Julie Kendrick   *Chess Piece I* (n.d.) *

Harrison Birtwistle   *Third Interlude from a Tragedy*
Lord Berners   *Three English Songs:*
'Lullaby' (Thomas Dekker),
'The Lady Visitor in the Pauper Ward' (Robert Graves),
'The Green-Eyed Monster' (E.L. Duff)
Harrison Birtwistle   *Medusa* (revised) WP
Guillaume de Machaut, arr. **Harrison Birtwistle**   *Hoquetus David*
Harrison Birtwistle   *Fourth Interlude from a Tragedy*

Mary Thomas (soloist)
Peter Zinovieff (electronics: pre-recorded tapes and realization)
Harrison Birtwistle (conductor)
• Student percussionists from the Royal Academy of Music

The Pierrot Players
FLUTE / PICCOLO Judith Pearce   VIOLIN / VIOLA Duncan Druce
CLARINETS / SAXOPHONE Alan Hacker   CELLO Jennifer Ward Clarke
PIANO / CELESTE Stephen Pruslin   PERCUSSION Barry Quinn

---

* *A programme note instruction concerning this piece read: 'The audience is kindly requested to refrain from applause until the end of the entire concert. There will be musical activity during the 20-minute Interval, and this itself is a part of the planned structure of the concert.'*
Other personnel included: William Alsop (environmental structure design and construction), David Cockerell (special console construction for Medusa*), George Cayford (programme design), David Hockney (artist: line drawing of Harrison Birtwistle in programme centrefold), Hugh Davies (inventor of* Medusa's *shozyg; uncredited in concert programme).*

Example 8.1 'Spring Song, devised and conducted by Harrison Birtwistle'

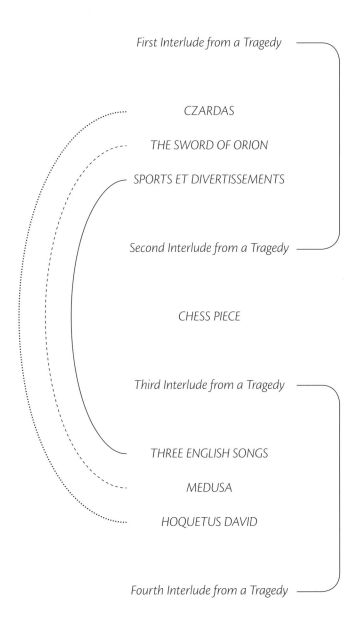

Example 8.2 Natko Devčić's Palindromic Representation of 'Spring Song'

sponsored fundraising concert on 30 June 1969. The Pierrot Players duly performed, although only two of the seven works programmed required most of its players: Davidovsky's *Synchronisms No. 2* (1964) and Justin Connolly's *Obbligati II*, Op. 13 (1967), both scored for flute, clarinet, violin, cello and tape.[37]

If responses to the concert were muted, they only endorsed the BSEM's call for investment in facilities to make possible a more convincing interplay of live and recorded sound. As Hans Keller commented sardonically:

> A National Electronic Studio is a must, especially from the standpoint of those who dislike electronic music and therefore must want to hear it improved.[38]

That the Pierrot Players came to play their small part in the emerging Anglo-American story of electroacoustic music was a significant departure from the norm. The group had flourished in the same 1968/69 season through its string of music theatre works (led by Davies) and concert programming which regularly pitted these works against their prototype, *Pierrot lunaire*. Their involvement with electronic music was a result of a parallel series of events, beginning with an SPNM course held at London University (19-22 July 1968) and leading to a Redcliffe Concert of British Electronic Works (Queen Elizabeth Hall, 10 February 1969). Composers were invited to write short pieces, with 'nine instrumentalists from, and ancillary to, the Pierrot Players' acting as their experimental template.[39] Directed by Don Banks, Anthony Gilbert and David Lumsdaine, one day was devoted to an introduction to the techniques of computerized electronic composition, a medium unfamiliar to most. Of the forty composers and sixteen works that featured during the four-day course, only a few made it to concert.[40] Their 'framing' by Birtwistle's *Interludes* in a version for basset clarinet and tape suggests their composer may have helped plan the concert, although his precise input is unclear.[41] We do know, however, that Birtwistle had replaced Davies as Chairman of the BSEM by the time of 'Spring Song'.

No composer had yet used the whole Pierrot ensemble in the field of electronic music. Birtwistle would address this through 'Spring Song' generally, and *Medusa* specifically. The work was not brand new – it was premiered in Sheffield on 22 October 1969 at the beginning of a tour of universities – but *Medusa* was the catalyst for 'Spring Song' and was revised for the occasion. Ideas for the concert's elaborate structure were jotted in the margins of the work's sketches, while the music, composed in a sequence of symmetrical movements, was a microcosm of the programme's design. Even the staging, a red, octagonal metal construction built by another future celebrity, Will Alsop, was a symbolic nod to Birtwistle's musical title. Julie Kendrick's *Chess Piece*, written not for Pierrot ensemble but for percussionists from the Royal Academy of Music, was the concert's axis of symmetry. Performed during the interval in the foyer, it was also the stray 'tentacle' of the concert, to extend Birtwistle's metaphor:

> [*Medusa*] is one of the names for a jellyfish,[42] and it occurred to me [that] certain things in the form of a jellyfish was [*sic*] like the piece I was writing. ... I have a preoccupation with landscape and I've tended to develop my musical language out of a rather sort of painterly attitude to things. There is no actual separation to me between the things that I make and the things that I see. It's as though I want notes to lose their identity and the piece to gain its identity, and the sound of an instrument, or groups of instruments, to arrive at an identity of its own which are beyond the physical sound of the instrument itself.[43]

Part Greek myth, part jellyfish, Birtwistle's droll inspiration had been explained in his programme notes.[44] But these more recent, if enigmatic, ideas tallied with the multidisciplinary aims of 'Spring Song' and, relatedly, exposed Birtwistle's personal understanding of audio-visual 'identity' – of notes, instruments and works – and the basic relationship between timbre and pitch.

Such views also create problems for scholarship of Birtwistle's music. Michael Nyman, for example, remembers how the composer claimed during an open forum at one of the Wardour Castle Summer Schools that he could 'rewrite his music using different pitches without doing any damage to it'.[45] Given that *Medusa* made use of Hugh Davies's so-called shozyg (ex. 8.3.i), the work's synthesized sounds and sometimes distorted amplification of live instruments demonstrated Birtwistle's 'theory'. But this was also undermined by *Medusa*'s musical symmetry, including the 'medusa' complex itself (ex. 8.3.ii). This peculiarly *visual* representation of a jellyfish invites comparison with the third of Davies's *Eight Songs for a Mad King*, in which the staves are humorously arranged to depict a cage.[46] Birtwistle's 'jellyfish' even came with Schenker-like tentacles – dotted lines to connect his rising and falling sevenths in the piano and xylophone – and was also the work's most important structural sign: in the middle of the work the 'jellyfish' was split in half, with an extended tape interlude sandwiched between.

Separately, *Medusa*'s haunting, semitonal solo motif was another significant element of the work's symmetry, particularly at the start and end of the piece. Its revised scoring for soprano saxophone showed that, like Davies, Birtwistle was writing for his Pierrot Players, not just the Pierrot ensemble: it was Hacker's suggestion to double the clarinet in this way, and it was an important precedent given the saxophone's starring role in *The Triumph of Time*.[47] Yet, tellingly, the full extent of *Medusa*'s polystylism is not reflected in Birtwistle's memory of the piece, and the same 'amusing tonal references' which so pleased one of its first critics probably proved to be its undoing. The experimental parody of the melody to J.S. Bach's *Meine Seele erhebet den Herrn* chorale, coupled with fleeting allusions to a toccata and a 6/8 jig, were highly uncharacteristic of Birtwistle.[48] More typical of Davies, indeed, they would soon also be disowned.

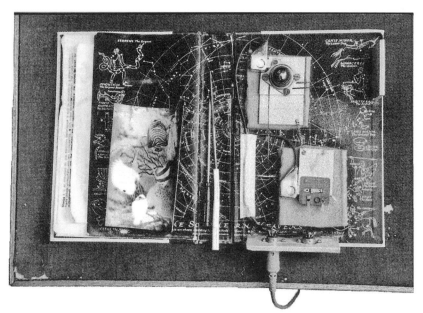

Example 8.3   (i) Hugh Davies's Shozyg, used in Shozyg I *and Birtwistle's* Medusa. *According to Davies, Shozyg I is a stereophonic instrument for live electronic performance, built inside the covers of a book (10" x 7" x 1¾") that also contains the performance instructions. The original instrument was built inside the final volume of an encyclopaedia, SHO-ZYG, hence the title. For performance, Shozyg I needs only to be connected to a stereo amplifier and two loudspeakers. It may be filtered or ring-modulated with the assistance of a second performer. The sounds are produced by the performer's fingers and/or any other small objects such as screwdrivers and electric motors. The objects on the two 'islands' on the right side are amplified by two contact microphones. On the left side a 3-D postcard, played by running fingernails at different speeds over the grooves, rests on the cover and is amplified by the built-in contact microphones.*

Example 8.3   (ii) Harrison Birtwistle, Medusa's *'medusa'*

Notes

1   For example, see William Mann, 'Pierrot Players: Queen Elizabeth Hall', *The Times* (21 September 1970), 11.

2   Paul Driver, 'Is the Game Up for Harrison Birtwistle?', *The Sunday Times*, Culture Supplement (7 November 2004), 30.

3   See Alexander Chancellor, 'How Wonderful to See You', *The Guardian*, G2 Supplement (21 July 2004), 12-13.

4   Peter Maxwell Davies, quoted in: *Ibid.*, 12.

5   See Mike Seabrook, *Max: The Life and Music of Peter Maxwell Davies* (London: Gollancz, 1994), 119-23.

6   *Ibid.*, 121. More nuanced opinions than Seabrook's have been voiced. For Meirion Bowen, Birtwistle's time with the Pierrot Players was 'probably a cul-de-sac in his career [since] … the limitation of the group to the sort of ensemble Schoenberg had employed in *Pierrot lunaire* constituted a considerable strait-jacket.' Meirion Bowen, 'Harrison Birtwistle' in: *British Music Now*, ed. Lewis Foreman (London: Paul Elek, 1975), 62.

7   James Murdoch, interview with the author, 19 February 2004. The full quotation reads: 'Everyone copied the black skivvy outfit I put the Pierrot Players in (really to hide their lumpy bodies) but also to create a new image for modern music. Soon all the others followed. We gave over 200 performances of *Pierrot lunaire* around the traps, all lit by me, sometimes only with two spots. Mary Thomas was riveting. Music poured out of Max [Davies], Harry dried up. I had nothing from Harry to market and sell. Inevitable the split.'

8   James Murdoch, quoted in: Seabrook, 121.

9   Harrison Birtwistle [1996], quoted in: Nicholas Cook, *Music: A Very Short Introduction* (Oxford: Oxford University Press, 1998), 39.

10   For example: 'It is often denied that the old laws of tonality are dead. For "light" or commercial music they are obviously valid. Such music is not meant to awaken the listener, to make him feel deeply and think and increase his awareness – it is meant to soothe him and make money. It is a *drug*.' Peter Maxwell Davies, 'Problems of a British Composer Today', *The Listener* 62/1593 (8 October 1959), 563; emphasis added.

11   Each scored for Pierrot ensemble, the pieces alluded to here, respectively, are the *Fantasia and Two Pavans, Excuse Me* (1986), and the *Suite from 'The Boy Friend'* (1971). The programming of the latter for a one-off Christmas Concert (discussed in the next chapter) and of *Excuse Me* (after Charles Dibdin) for a fundraising concert late in the history of The Fires of London (25 February 1986) proves Davies understood how sellable his music could be. At the same time, after the controversies of engaging, or implicating, concertgoers in *Eight Songs for a Mad King*, his opinions further complicate his relationship with audiences: if popular music was a 'drug', then Davies's use of it was another *Pierrot* take-off, given the hallucinatory theatre into which Schoenberg lured his own listeners.

12   Peter Maxwell Davies, quoted in: John von Rhein, 'Composer Peter Maxwell Davies: Looking for an Audience, Not A Cult', *Chicago Tribune* (22 May 1983), 16. His wild hair, flashing blue eyes and musical histrionics made him an occasional target for satirists, *Private Eye*'s 'Pseuds' Corner' included.

13   See Chapter 6, note 40.

14   Meirion Bowen, 'The Fires Brigade', *The Guardian* (19 January 1987), 9.

15   Michael Hall, *Harrison Birtwistle* (London: Robson, 1984), 50.

16   Harrison Birtwistle, quoted in: Noel Goodwin, 'Music in London: Pierrot Players', *Musical Times* 108/1493 (July, 1963), 626.

17   Harrison Birtwistle, interviewer uncredited, *Music on Two: A Couple of Things about Harry*, broadcast BBC2, 4 April 1971.

18   See Seabrook, 158-60.

19   See Epilogue, note 4.

20   See Anthony Payne, 'The Problems of Pierrot', *Music and Musicians* 15/12 (August, 1967), 41.

21   Chris Heaton (also author of *Changing Platforms: 30 Years of the Contemporary Music Network*), interview with the author, 23 July 2006.

22   Harrison Birtwistle, quoted in: Stephen Moss, 'Sounds and Silence', www.guardian.co.uk/music/2004/jun/19/classicalmusicandopera.proms2004 (accessed 7 September 2012).

23   Stephen Pruslin, 'Twenty Years of The Fires: A Retrospective Sketch', article from the concert programme for 'The Fires' Farewell and Twentieth Birthday Gala' (Queen Elizabeth Hall, 20 January 1987), pages unnumbered.

24   These included percussion, additional singers, electronics (including the pioneering use of computers) and tape.

25   This is not a call for a revival of Birtwistle's music for Pierrot ensemble (or their 'satellites', such as earlier versions of the solo clarinet work *Linoi*), merely a suggestion that despite their withdrawal, they should be looked at again.

26   I am grateful to Robert Adlington for lending copies of notes he took at a time when the score was available to peruse at Universal Edition's London branch. Since moved to their Vienna headquarters, the score is now inaccessible (permission to view the score was denied), although the Paul Sacher Stiftung (Basel) houses some sketches. The BLSA was thought to have the only recording, but it is lost.

27   See David J. Beard, *An Analysis and Sketch Study of the Early Instrumental Music of Sir Harrison Birtwistle (c. 1957-77)* (D.Phil. diss., University of Oxford, 2000).

28   Hall, 159-60.

29   Robert Adlington, *The Music of Harrison Birtwistle* (Cambridge: Cambridge University Press, 2000), 130-31.

30   Stephen Walsh, 'Reports: Cheltenham', *Musical Times* 108/1495 (1967), 826. William Mann, otherwise a staunch supporter of the Pierrot Players, was also unimpressed by the music's anomalous structure, complaining that its 'first two-thirds were not interesting to listen to.' William Mann, 'Williamson's New Sonata in an Earlier Style', *The Times* (18 July 1967), 6.

31   Harrison Birtwistle, quoted in: Paul Griffiths, *New Sounds, New Personalities: British Composers of the 1980s* (London: Faber, 1985), 191.

32   E. M. Webster, 'Cheltenham: Blight on the Band-wagon', *Musical Opinion* 90/1080 (September, 1967), 681. Given that Birtwistle and Davies are the same age, the remarks are also strange, if perhaps indicative of Birtwistle's 'junior' status and his later turn to composition.

33   Quoted from various newspaper advertisements for the concert.

34   Birtwistle's commission of Hockney recalls Schoenberg reaching out to a like-minded artist: the few poster advertisements of the *Verein*'s activities carried Richard Gerstl's nightmarish portraits. Secreting away Hockney's portrait was curious; it bears comparison with the custom of lavish gatefold LPs at the time. Perhaps more relevant is that its layout across four pages (two-by-two) upheld the same sense of symmetry that was enigmatically described overleaf as integral to the concert's experimental programming.

35   Natko Devčić, 'Strukturirani koncert (U povodu jedne nesvakidašnje londonske glazbene priredbe)' (1970) ('Structured Concert (On an Unusual Musical Performance in London)', trans. Sanda Bell) in: *Novi zvuk: Izbor tekstova o suvremenoj glazbi*, ed. Petar Selem (Zagreb: Nakladni Zavod Matice Hrvatske, 1972), 209.

36   The BSEM and Electronic Music Studios Ltd, which counted David Cockerell (designer of *Medusa*'s hardware configuration, i.e. mixer module, tape and

amplifier) and Anthony Rubenstein among their number, operated from the same address in Deodar Road, Putney.

37   The remaining works were Milton Babbitt's *Ensembles for Synthesizer* (1964), Roberto Gerhard's *Audiomobile II*, 'DNA' (c. 1961), James K. Randall's *Mudgett: Monologues by a Mass Murderer* (1965), Richard Orton's *Sampling Afield* (1968) and Vladimir Ussachevsky's *Of Wood and Brass* (1964).

38   Hans Keller, programme note, quoted in: Dominic Gill, 'Music in London: New Music, Recitals: Pierrot Players, Electronics', *Musical Times* 110/1518 (1969), 852-53. Not everyone wanted to hear electronic music improved, however. Elisabeth Lutyens's belief that '[there's] nothing wrong with what they do, so long as we remember that they're electricians, not composers' better represents the schism within British music at the time. Elisabeth Lutyens, quoted in: Philip Oakes, 'Lutyens Clocks In', *The Sunday Times* (27 February 1972), 34.

39   See Anthony Gilbert, 'SPNM Composers' Weekend', *Musical Times* 109/1508 (1968), 946.

40   None used the Pierrot ensemble, however. The works were: the Justin Connolly/Zinovieff collaboration *M-Piriform*, for violin, flute, soprano and tape; Alan Sutcliffe's *Spasmo* for 'composed computer'; Lawrence Casserley's *the final desolation of solitude*, his first electronic piece; Don Banks's *Equation (Part 1)*, a jazz-classical piece for tape and computer; Tristram Cary's *Narcissus* for solo flute; Donald Henshilwood's *Sonata 6* for tape; Hugh Davies's *Shozyg I* (for an instrument discussed later in this chapter); and Ernest Berk's *Synchrome*, Op. 120, again for tape.

41   Similarly, the concert only semi-belonged to the Pierrot Players, despite its genesis. Alan Hacker and Judith Pearce represented the group; the other musicians were Jane Manning (soprano), Pauline Scott (violin), and Edward Walker (flute). John Tilbury and Gavin Bryars also operated the shozyg and oscillators respectively for Hugh Davies's piece.

42   It is also the biological name given to the reproductive stage at which other jellyfish can bud-in some species by detaching one of its parts.

43   Harrison Birtwistle, interviewer uncredited, *Music on Two: A Couple of Things about Harry*, broadcast BBC2, 4 April 1971.

44   '[Like a jellyfish,] this piece consists of material which is either detached and allowed to develop independently, or fixed within its own defined area. All details, large and small, are related to the basic modular shape.' Harrison Birtwistle, programme note to *Medusa*, 'Spring Song', Queen Elizabeth Hall, London, 3 March 1970.

45   Michael Nyman, 'Two New Works by Birtwistle', *Tempo* 88 (Spring, 1969), 50.

46   This was a reference to the instrumentalists'/birds' cages, of course, but also to John Cage, hence the 'J.' at the start of Davies's music and the freedom he gave the flautist to decide how they should navigate through the staves.

47   Alan Hacker, emailed correspondence with the author, 24 April 2004.

48   Howard Rees, 'Birtwistle's "Medusa"', *Tempo* 92 (Spring, 1970), 29.

9 The Fires of London

Soon after Harrison Birtwistle left the Pierrot Players, the remaining members decided it was right to change the group's name: the Pierrot Players was reborn as The Fires of London. It is a measure of their success over the next seventeen years that most fans and commentators remember them by this new title. Its precise origins are uncertain,[1] but by giving up its claim to the piece of music that had inspired their formation, the group was rebranded. The new title brought tangible changes to the group's artistic direction: The Fires, as they became known, performed *Pierrot lunaire* less often, although it remained an intermittent part of the repertoire until they disbanded in 1987, while Birtwistle's absence gave Davies a renewed and more exclusive artistic licence. Davies went on to produce dozens of new works for the group and to advance the policy of commissioning young British composers to write works for Pierrot ensemble. A much broader, more variegated lineage of Pierrot ensembles would be left in The Fires' wake.

By reaching beyond its self-made boundaries, The Fires developed an ethos that, however deliberately, came to challenge the very idea of a feasible, independent Pierrot ensemble. For example, the group occasionally forged links in concert with other ensembles, such as The Early Music Consort, Serenata of London, the Monteverdi Choir, and the Philip Jones Brass Ensemble, the effect of which was often to make explicit the theoretical relationship between 'new' and 'old' music that had been so important to many of Davies's works. Quoting, parodying and pastiching pre-modern music was a hallmark of Davies (and the Pierrot Players) that had set the Pierrot ensemble on a very different course from the one that Schoenberg, Hanns Eisler, Elisabeth Lutyens and others had instigated. Yet, The Fires' expansion to other art forms – dance, mime, film, puppetry – might equally be understood as a logical evolution from the Pierrot ensemble's principles, given its *commedia dell'arte* roots.[2]

Davies was not responsible for what was arguably its most eye-catching manifestation, The Fires' appearance alongside Barry Smith's Theatre of Puppets in Michael Finnissy's *Mr Punch* (1976-77, rev. 1979), but his artistic leadership and development as a composer influenced the direction of the

Pierrot ensemble the most. The increasingly 'symphonic' sound of Davies's musical language is important because wherever the traditions of such a received genre are observed to affect the Pierrot ensemble, the compatibility of the two inevitably remains open to question. In this context, *Pierrot*'s quasi-theatrical, poetry-inspired beginnings make it an acute case, and its ensemble's early heritage only sustained this, from the cinematic experiments of Benjamin Britten and Eisler to its chamber-symphonic aesthetic in Anton Webern's 1924 arrangement of Schoenberg's Op. 9. In light of its purely musical inspiration, the latter example is an exception, but one that invites fruitful comparison with Davies's symphonic-chamber vision half a century later in *Ave Maris Stella* (1975). For just as Schoenberg's heterogeneous means, tightly argued ideas and single-movement design prevail over his work's chamber character, so too did Davies begin to co-opt such symphonic ideals in his Pierrot ensemble pieces.[3]

The same works also flag up more basic taxonomic disparities: Webern's Pierrot quintet and Davies's 'Fires sextet', as it was sometimes designated, are themselves anomalous in the context of The Fires' constitution (if not our understanding of the medium today, as we shall see). There would be far greater variation of instrumental line-ups with the new group, both in its membership and in how the works they performed called on its players. This was more than a product of its longevity. Davies's earliest works for The Fires – *The Devils* and *The Boy Friend* concert suites, *From Stone to Thorn* (all 1971) and *Hymn to St Magnus* (1972) – tinkered with the group's configuration to an unprecedented extent, supplementing or shrinking its line-up on each occasion. Where once the harpsichord or honky-tonk piano was used to extend Schoenberg's ploy of doubling instruments (or to replace the piano), now sporadic appearances of the guitar and, later, the marimba coloured Davies's Pierrot ensembles. Played by Tim Walker, the guitar was usually a straightforward addition to the ensemble, generating a 'Fires septet'. Such timbral innovations undermine the idea that a 'Fires sextet' held sway.[4]

They also have a broader resonance since their introduction coincided with the start of Davies's residence on the Orkney Islands, to which part of the artistic reasoning behind The Fires' instrumentally less uniform Pierrot ensembles can be traced. It would be wrong to suggest that, inspired by the harshness and beauty of his new surroundings, Davies's sense of Orcadian pastoralism altogether replaced sensationalism, melodrama and parody at the heart of his compositional style: his many works for The Fires were too eclectic for that.[5] But at the launch of the annual St Magnus Festival in 1977 and thereafter, Davies's holistic, Brittenesque attitude led to Orcadian-themed works he had written for the group being premiered to the people of Orkney. Appending 'of London' to his ensemble's title had acknowledged its base there while performing as Pierrot Players, but it was far from an inward-looking step.

Having represented Britain as Pierrot Players at festivals in Zagreb, Vienna and Prague during the 1960s, The Fires were fortunate that their home city, London, hosted the ISCM Festival towards the end of their first season in June 1971. There, uniquely, they were joined by members of the London Sinfonietta for a showcase of British music-making that featured alongside *Revelation and Fall* music by the Australian composers Peter Sculthorpe, Nigel Butterley and the conductor of his country's premiere of *Pierrot lunaire*, Richard Meale (*Incredible Floridas*, another Fires commission). Performances in London followed, as did visits to Italy in September and Holland eight months later. The Fires would also conduct repeated Australasian and pan-American tours during the seventies, quickly rekindling its partnership with Morton Feldman and, later, working with Elliott Carter and Pierre Boulez, too.

Its 'new debut' was a more insular affair. A programme crafted entirely from Davies's repertory was compiled for a BBC Invitation Concert at the Queen Elizabeth Hall (12 December 1970), yet the decision to revive works written for variable forces, all of which were greater than the Pierrot Players' usual complement, did little to re-establish a settled line-up in Birtwistle's absence. *Revelation and Fall* was revised for the occasion, as was *Missa super L'homme armé*, which featured the iconic Vanessa Redgrave, robed and crowned with a bald wig.[6] *Seven in Nomine* was another new-old work, pre-dating the Pierrot Players but never having been performed by them (even though, after the Melos Ensemble's premiere at Wardour Castle, the London Sinfonietta had adopted the piece in 1969).

The Fires' next concert (ex. 9.1) was their first to offer new works, and its programme, drawn from more varied sources, was a better marker for their aspirations. As usual, the centrepiece of the event came from within the group, yet neither Davies's *Points and Dances from 'Taverner'* (1970) nor his Purcell 'arrangements' were as elaborate as Duncan Druce's Pierrot ensemble *The Tower of Needles* (1970-71). Primarily a performer, Druce composed relatively little. This work, based on the episode in *War and Peace* in which Natasha bids an affecting farewell to the dying Bolkonsky, was only his sixth. It was also long, at over half an hour, though more episodic than symphonic, and designed, it seems, almost as an exercise in crafting an equally-voiced texture through quick, complicated ostinati. If this stratified approach to the Pierrot ensemble shows Birtwistle's influence, then Mary Thomas's initially wordless appearance is another pointer. Quoting the death scene from *Boris Godunov*, her *Sprechstimme*, marked 'almost spoken', capped the work and upheld the by now traditional idea that the voice is, or can be used as, another instrumental force within the Pierrot ensemble.[7]

20 February 1971 – Queen Elizabeth Hall, London

Guillaume de Machaut, arr. **Peter Maxwell Davies**
Hoquetus David (1968) WP ‡

Guillaume de Machaut, arr. **Harrison Birtwistle**
Hoquetus David (1968)

Gillian Whitehead
Pakuru (Hone Tuwhare) (1967) LP* †

Peter Maxwell Davies
Points and Dances from 'Taverner' – Instrumental Dances and Keyboard
Pieces from the Opera (1962-68, transc. 1970) WP •

Duncan Druce
The Tower of Needles (1970-71) WP

Henry Purcell, arr. **Peter Maxwell Davies**
Fantasia on a Ground and Two Pavans (1968)

Mary Thomas (soprano)
Peter Maxwell Davies (conductor)

The Fires of London

FLUTE / ALTO FLUTE / PICCOLO Judith Pearce   VIOLIN / VIOLA Duncan Druce
CLARINET / BASSET CLARINET / BASS CLARINET /   CELLO Jennifer Ward Clarke
          SAXOPHONE Alan Hacker   GUITAR (Act I of • only) Tim Walker
PIANO / CELESTE / HARPSICHORD / HARMONIUM   PERCUSSION Barry Quinn
          († only) Stephen Pruslin

Guest Musicians (‡ and Act II of • only):
CONTRABASSOON Dominic Weir   TRUMPET Elgar Howarth

• *The interval divided Acts I and II of the* Points and Dances, *which were advertised simply as* Dances
from Taverner.
* *LP indicates a London premiere.*

Example 9.1   Three Premieres of New Works for The Fires of London

Pakuru (1967), by the New Zealand composer Gillian Whitehead, explored a similar idea from a more Daviesian perspective. Her setting of Hone Tuwhare's love poem 'Thine Own Hands Have Fashioned' was named after a customary Maori instrument thought to date from the early nineteenth century. Ethnomusicologists dispute whether the pakuru (a thin strip of resonant wood tapped with a rod) was used as part of the percussive accompaniment of tribal songs or 'a substitute for vocal cords to suggest words.'[8] But the dichotomy is peculiarly relevant to the relationship between the voice and the Pierrot ensemble in contemporary times.[9] *Pakuru*'s prominent pairing of a harmonium and unpitched percussion within its line-up was also new, and perhaps influenced Davies's more dramatic use of the same forces in *Missa super L'homme armé*. Indeed, the composition of *Pakuru* can be traced to Whitehead's studies under Davies in Adelaide and again at Dartington in August 1968, where the first performance was given.

Similarly, Druce's work aside, the programme derived entirely from the time of the Pierrot Players. The first of Davies's pair of works was begun before ideas to form the group had even been conceived: the earliest sketches for *Taverner* date from 1962, and from this opera, based on a since-discredited account of the life and, specifically, the religious conversion of the Tudor composer, the *Points and Dances* were drawn.[10] The irony is that in extracting various dramatically important moments from the opera, Davies had to re-orchestrate for Pierrot ensemble music he had originally written for combinations of authentic period instruments. Centring on the English Reformation, the historic changes played out in the opera have a further musical analogue in that the 'dances' were modelled on Tudor forms (the galliard, march and pavane, for example) yet were parodied by Davies's modern-day broken consort, while the work's interspersed 'points', performed by Pruslin alone, were reworked as variations on plainsong themes. This was a more intelligible, macro-structural version of what *Antechrist* had attempted to convey through the various thematic transfigurations of its 'early music' source.

Davies's next ostensibly new work in the concert was another earlier composition that juxtaposed sound-worlds. The same Machaut hocket Birtwistle had transformed in *Hoquetus David*, also in 1968, was the basis for Davies's version, which had not been performed before. Their partnership here explains why The Fires revived a work by Birtwistle – something they never repeated. Davies's *Hoquetus David* was not for Pierrot ensemble, however, but instead appears to have been scored for the same trio of contrabassoon, trumpet and trombone which joined The Fires to perform Act II of the *Points and Dances*.[11] Nor was his arrangement ever performed again. Machaut's hocket was a shared plaything for the composers, used to inspire a *pièce d'occasion*.[12] This does not mean that their arrangements (or rather, recompositions) were without merit. Their relevance to the ethos of both groups is clear enough, each work adopting a by now familiar meta-compositional approach through which Davies and Birtwistle flaunted their attitudes to music history. Technically, too, it is easy to see why a hocket should have appealed to them as potential source material for their Pierrot ensemble pieces. Its inherent rhythmic-linear design was ripe for the composers' own colourful, hocket-like division of melodic lines between their timbrally distinct instruments. This idea of textural compatibility was not exclusive to *Hoquetus David*, of course, and there are broader conclusions to be drawn from how the composers applied it to their more stratifiable Pierrot ensembles. Birtwistle's version, for example, variously doubled Machaut's melodic line at the octave and the fifth, embroidering and parodying the 'medievalism' of the original. This evoked Davies's *Antechrist*, as did Birtwistle's piquant instrumentation, which featured a clarinet in C, a glockenspiel (replacing the piano) and bells alongside the more usual flute-doubling-piccolo, violin and cello.

If *Hoquetus David* afforded an insight into a three-way relationship between the music of Machaut, Birtwistle and Davies, then it is striking that less than three months later, The Fires' first truly collaborative event included a work that included another intertextual comparison. Recruited as part of a European Broadcasting Union (EBU) initiative, the group travelled to Rome to give the premiere of Hans Werner Henze's *Der langwierige Weg in die Wohnung der Natascha Ungeheuer* on 17 May 1971. The work is not for Pierrot ensemble, although the ensemble, and more importantly its canonic status, occupies an unprecedented role within its narrative. Its premiere brought together some of Europe's pre-eminent exponents of music theatre: The Fires were joined in performance by the American baritone William Pearson and the Japanese percussionist Stomu Yamash'ta; the Philip Jones Brass Ensemble and the Gunther Hempel Free Jazz Ensemble completed the composite instrumentation of a work aimed at the political leftists. Its text, by the Chilean poet Gaston Salvatore, made the eponymous protagonist a 'siren' whose role was to seduce the bourgeoisie into believing in their comfortable but flawed socialistic compromise. By dramaticizing the work's discrete instrumental groups, Henze's setting tried to make theatrical sense of this opaque narrative: the brass, conventionally enough, would represent the military; but The Fires' role was to *be* the 'sick' bourgeoisie, while the jazz ensemble loosely stood for the idea of an artificial Utopia.

Henze's use of The Fires, particularly, was a clue to an additional layer of meaning he brought to Salvatore's text, although the composer studiously avoided discussing specifics:

> [*Der langwierige Weg … is*] about a young man who sets off for Kreuzberg in search of Natascha Ungeheuer and her eponymous

apartment, a sphinx who may be induced to tell people what is to happen to them. Or perhaps she is Utopia personified. Yet Natascha Ungeheuer's apartment ... may also be no more than a whisky bar or simply a cosy, depoliticized garden of delights full of clouds of hashish smoke. Our hero does not reach his destination: but, although he does not find the place, he hears in his head the sirenlike voice of Comrade Natascha, who, far from welcoming and accommodating, reels off a list of objections to him. Attempts to renew his bourgeois connections prove a failure. It is a lone show that our hero stages.[13]

While enigmatic, this précis of the 'plot' does little to conceal the autobiographical message that Henze conveyed well below the work's surface. Its heavy, expressionist vein and Pearson's vocal delivery (singing, speech and *Sprechstimme*) were unambiguously indebted to Schoenberg, yet Henze's (ab)use of the Pierrot ensemble underlines the self-deprecating paradox of the work: that a bourgeois like Henze can never truly abandon his sensibility, socially or mentally, to embrace the revolution without false conscience. The Pierrot ensemble symbolizes his inner struggle since he bears, but cannot eradicate, its stamp. The allegory itself, Henze's heroic 'lone show', situates him within the same nineteenth-century aesthetic paradigm from which *Pierrot lunaire* grew.

Salvatore's text was not distributed to the audience in Rome. Nor was it comprehensible to listeners over the airwaves. If this obscured the work's manifesto, then the failure of one British critic to recognize the Pierrot ensemble as such, registering only 'a quintet [*sic*] of woodwind, strings, and piano', underlines the problem.[14] The issue was resolved only when the work was given a staged performance at the Deutsche Oper in Berlin (without The Fires, incidentally). There it was roundly, if unsurprisingly, booed; this was a symptom of Henze's political point, after all. But changes that were made for this second performance admitted the work's links to *Pierrot* more openly. Part-dressed in bloodstained hospital garb, part-dressed in Pierrot costumes, the Pierrot ensemble was now more than a sideways reference to the sinister fantasies of Giraud and Schoenberg. Moreover, the Berlin street-sounds Henze had incorporated within the work on the Hammond organ and Natascha's pre-recorded tape made for more uncomfortable listening in the city that had hosted *Pierrot*'s premiere decades earlier. As Henze was to write:

> The significance of the two types of costume points to one thing: sickness, the sickness of the bourgeoisie, its music, its morality ... What they have to say has its origins in Schoenberg's construct, but has departed from it and broken with it, beyond the point

of parody towards a new kind of denunciatory analytical music-exercise.[15]

Peter Maxwell Davies: Two Cinematic Responses (III/IV)

By recognizing, if not cherishing, the Pierrot ensemble as a 'received' genre, Henze joined his friend Davies in putting distance between the prototype *Pierrot lunaire* and their own new works. Henze's level of dissociation may have been the greater on this occasion, but the growth in the Pierrot ensemble's autonomy (from and after *Pierrot*) under Davies in the seventies was to be relentless. The next of Davies's works for The Fires is a case in point (ex. 9.2). The focal points of The Fires' Christmas Concert were suites he had derived from music written for two very different films, *The Devils* (1971) and *The Boy Friend* (1972). The programme's other works were more incidental. Zsolt Durkó's semi-aleatory *Fire Music* claimed several firsts: it was the first work specifically commissioned for The Fires,[16] the earliest work to be written apparently in tribute to Davies's group, and the first work to call for The Fires to employ a separate violist (Donald McVay) alongside Druce, as *Fire Music* called for the violin and viola to be played separately, in the vein of Hanns Eisler's *Vierzehn Arten den Regen zu beschreiben*. (The similarities extend to the manner in which Durkó's work comprises sixteen densely motivic miniatures, in which the instruments were often deliberately unsynchronized.)

Druce's more straightforward arrangement of J.S. Bach's *Ich bin vergnügt mit meinem Glücke* (BWV 84) contrasted with Davies's realization-cum-recomposition of Dietrich Buxtehude's 1655 cantata *Also hat Gott die Welt geliebet*. The latter was originally a Pierrot Players work that had been premiered at Dartington a year earlier, a month before the group's final concert, at a time when Hacker was in hospital. Davies took advantage of the clarinet's absence in this work to reproduce the trio-sonata texture of the original, re-scored for flute, violin and cello. More substantial were the two suites. The invitation to score their respective films came from the director Ken Russell. Their collaboration was timely, since both were at a similar point on their creative paths.[17] Russell's version of D.H. Lawrence's *Women in Love* (1969) had won him a worldwide reputation at a time when Davies's star was also in the ascendant, largely thanks to his more melodramatic works for the Pierrot Players.

Arguably the most important aesthetic parallel between the two (beyond their vested interests in music) was their almost schoolboyish delight in courting outrage. *The Boy Friend* indulged this, but subtly. Russell's inspiration was Sandy Wilson's 1954 West End musical of the same name, which was set in a finishing school in the south of France and told the story

11 December 1971 – Queen Elizabeth Hall, London

Media Music presents
The Fires of London Christmas Concert

J.S. Bach, arr. **Duncan Druce**
Cantata: *Ich bin vergnügt mit meinem Glücke* (1971) WP

Zsolt Durkó
Fire Music (1970-71) WP

Dietrich Buxtehude, arr. **Peter Maxwell Davies**
Cantata: *Also hat Gott die Welt geliebet* (1970) WP

Peter Maxwell Davies
Suite from *The Devils* (1971) WP
1. Titles; 2. Sister Jeanne's Vision; 3. Exorcism; 4. Execution and End Titles

Sandy Wilson, arr. **Peter Maxwell Davies**
Suite from *The Boy Friend*,
for Instrumental Ensemble (or Orchestra) (1971) WP
1.Introduction: Honeymoon Fantasy [The Boyfriend [sic] / I could be happy with you]
– piano interlude
2. Sur la Plage – piano interlude
3. A Room in Bloomsbury – piano interlude
4. I Could be Happy with You – piano interlude
5. The You-Don't-Want-to-Play-with-Me Blues – piano interlude
6. Poor Little Pierrette – extended piano interlude
7. Polly's Dream [Free Fantasy on Tunes from *The Boy Friend*]

Mary Thomas (soprano)
Peter Maxwell Davies (conductor)

The Fires of London (for film music, with guests)

FLUTES Judith Pearce		TROMBONES Roger Brenner, Maurice Platt	
CLARINETS Alan Hacker		TUBA / SOUSAPHONE Martin Fry	
KEYBOARDS Stephen Pruslin		PIANO Peter Greenwell	
VIOLIN Duncan Druce		HARP Sidonie Goosens	
VIOLA Donald McVay		UKELELE John Lloyd	
CELLO Jennifer Ward Clarke		PERCUSSION John Donaldson,	
SAXOPHONES Tony Coe,		Peter Greenham, Gary Kettel	
Edward Planas, Kathleen Stobart		VIOLINS Perry Hart,	
CLARINETS Ian Mitchell		Frances Mason, Michael Rennie	
TRUMPETS Ronald Hunt, Ian Wilson		DOUBLE BASS John Steer	

Example 9.2   The Fires of London Christmas Concert, 1971,
featuring the premieres of concert suites from The Devils *and* The Boy Friend

of Polly Browne (played in the film by Twiggy) and her love for toff-in-disguise Tony, with true love conquering in the end. Scored for piano and rhythm accompaniment, each of Wilson's numbers was a fond imitation of 1920s musical theatre. For the film, Davies arranged twelve of these for a line-up he had not used before: an augmented Pierrot ensemble. Though The Fires were present, Davies's chamber-sized orchestra had 'vintage' touches in its employment of various saxophones, a ukulele, a banjo, and, as a nod to Wilson, a prominent piano duet. From the film score sprang the shorter concert suite, now ostensibly for The Fires but still featuring the saxophones and only slightly reducing the brass. Davies also composed new interludes for piano duet (with Mary Thomas on second piano) to link the numbers through modulation. The suite's two outer sections, the 'Honeymoon Fantasy' and a 'free fantasy' entitled 'Polly's Dream', marked the greatest departure from Wilson's originals. The longest interlude introduced the latter with a bluesy variation of the motif from the most memorable number, 'I could be happy with you'. The fantasy itself exhibited many of Davies's parodic hallmarks: violins held like ukuleles, an invented foxtrot and Charleston, and nightingale noises from the toy percussion, among other allusions. On screen, the eponymous heroine dreams up the same dances in a vision not dissimilar to the ritualistic dances of *The Rite of Spring*.

Davies can justifiably be spoken of alongside György Ligeti, Luciano Berio and Mauricio Kagel in a select band of composers that had redefined the genre of music theatre in the post-war era. The amusing yet disturbing vision in this passage alone explains the otherwise puzzling appeal of a frothy piece of English *musical* theatre in the comic vein of Noël Coward and Ivor Novello. This was only possible thanks to Russell's non-literal, glamorized take on Wilson's original story: the film follows a seaside repertory company engaged in their own production of *The Boy Friend*, with a postmodern send-up that on the very night a Hollywood director attends to consider turning their play into a lavish movie musical, the leading lady (Glenda Jackson) has to be replaced by her shy understudy, Polly. While it irritated Wilson, the multi-layered parody implicit in Russell's cinematic 1970s view of his 1950s nostalgic pastiche of 1920s musical theatre was ready-made for Davies, who of course had cloned dance-band music of the inter-war period before.[18] Other techniques Davies preserved from his film score include the 'wailing, pseudo-Indian' clarinets in 'Sur la plage' (evoking the Pierrot Players 'satellite' work *Stedman Doubles*, and a throwback to his student days, when he wrote a thesis on Indian music) and the strings' sickly 'exaggerated vibrato [with] much portamento'. Nor could he resist retaining Wilson's 'Poor Little Pierrette', a short, faux-French song about Pierrot and Pierrette, with a Piaf-like introduction in which the same over-the-top vibrato merges, presciently, with a vocal style halfway between speech and speech-song.

For all *The Boy Friend*'s compelling kitsch, *The Devils*, the other half of the Russell-Davies collaboration, gave the pair far more serious themes to reinterpret. The film – banned by various local authorities but award-winning abroad – and its music were again multiply sourced. Russell's screenplay arose from John Whiting's 1961 play adaptation of Aldous Huxley's 1952 non-fiction novel *The Devils of Loudun*, centring on the French Protestant stronghold of Loudun to recount the alleged demonic possession of its resident Ursuline nuns in 1634. Similarly, The Fires of London were one of two ensembles involved in the recording of the film's soundtrack: David Munrow's Early Music Consort played a small but significant part in the film score (if not Davies's concert suite) by performing both a realization of the *Dies Irae*, upon which Davies composed a fantasia, and Munrow's own arrangements of music by Michael Praetorius and the French Renaissance composer Claude Gervaise. The authentic use of music available at the time of the incident took advantage of the obvious stylistic difference between the groups, so that, unlike The Fires' 'amalgamated' exploits in Henze's showpiece, *The Devils* did not join together its groups as literally. This deliberate juxtaposition had its roots in Russell's cinematic aesthetic of extremes, in which, despite the historically documented event that inspired his film, his characters, the narrative and even the set were presented in a peculiarly unreal, allegorical fashion. The anachronistic appearance of a witch-hunter, dispatched to extract confessions while wearing blue-tinted 'sixties' shades, is perhaps the best visual correspondent to the ongoing disjunctions of the film's soundtrack, and vice versa.

Russell's hard-hitting moral point was to delineate the depths to which the characters go to preserve belief systems. The foreground plot may have detailed the repressed lust of Sister Jeanne (Redgrave again) for Father Urban Grandier (Oliver Reed), but it was her dreams of demonic possession by him, coupled with his religiously motivated, unjust conviction for sorcery that chimed so well with Davies's own artistic impulse. Davies must also have been sensitive to the reality that the only true sin of the charismatic, philandering Grandier was his sexuality. The conversion of many of the townspeople to Catholicism after his execution (not documented in the film but historically accurate) may also have struck a chord, given *Taverner*'s narrative. The controversy the film provoked, even before its release, nevertheless caused Davies problems:

> Russell and I agreed that it would be as interesting to get as much mileage … out of a small group … as to use a full orchestra – and much more economical. … [We] discussed the music at great length before it was written, together with David Munrow … One irritation during composition was constant visits by the

island postmaster with telegrams to say the censor had cut out several more feet of film, which meant constant rethinking and modification of the isorhythmic schemes.[19]

Two of the most contentious scenes were punctuated by Davies's music. 'Sister Jeanne's Vision', as titled by Davies, focussed on Jeanne's erotomanic fantasies, depicting Grandier as Christ, walking on water. Appropriately (if sacrilegiously) enough, Davies's *Dies Irae* fantasia incorporated segments of sung chant – the *Sanctus* and *Benedictus*, both times accompanied by a drawn-out whole-tone scale – alongside music that, by turn, was more elegiac (on screen, romantic) and frenzied (desiring). Later, 'Exorcism' was Davies's musical accessory to Russell's orgiastic, scandalising picture of corruption as the Ursuline nuns are collectively exorcized; much of the scene was cut.

In his concert suite, Davies decided to begin with his core Pierrot ensemble plus wordless soprano and organ, then to entrust the genuine exorcism text ("*Exorciso te, Creatura diaboli ...*") to Thomas. Its resolution in prayer saw Davies transform an invented Victorian hymnal into a foxtrot – another 'corruptive' musical technique familiar to followers of the Pierrot Players. As with *The Boy Friend*, The Fires' line-up was again supplemented, though less drastically so. Davies's intermittent use of sustaining, solo brass mimicked a bleak, orchestral sound to suit the tone of the film well, as did the occasional instruction to Druce to play the regal by holding down a cluster or all of its keys. The suite retained these features intact, but its movements, including those mentioned, comprised only four (under half) of the discrete sections Davies penned for the film. Certainly, 'Titles' and 'Execution and End Music' worked in the film, and the prominence they afforded to the alto flute, coupled with the bass clarinet's association with Jeanne's delusions throughout the film, is also timbrally significant. Equally, the suite's independence from the film, and from Munrow's period input, drew adverse comment upon its premiere. Its 'weightless openendedness', as one critic put it, was a pejorative description of the same music that, on screen, was fittingly and inventively 'primal' and, by its very nature, rhapsodic.[20]

Towards an Orcadian Pierrot Ensemble

Fascinated yet at the same time repelled by religion, Davies conveyed two major anxieties in many of his Pierrot ensemble works: the hypocrisy of institutionalized belief and the betrayal and persecution of innocence. These have never altogether receded, although events in 1971 led to changes in their musical expression. Barely twelve months after his house fire,[21] which took with it the incomplete manuscript of *Vesalii icones* and the last part of *Taverner*, Davies relocated to the Orkney Islands. He soon began to identify himself and his music with Orcadian culture, history and nature, as he often acknowledges:

> These things are very important and … create ideal environmental conditions in which one can work, uninterruptedly, and one's ears, as it were, become completely tuned in to these very fine, small, beautiful sounds … I suppose living here, exploring these new sounds and experiences, has enabled me to explore parallel, new regions … of musical experience.[22]

One of Davies's earliest and most important steps upon reaching Orkney was to befriend the poet and author George Mackay Brown, on whose work he would frequently draw. The association began with *From Stone to Thorn* (1971), which scaled new heights of virtuosity without the theatrical shock tactics of the previous decade. Topically, the work was a clear sequel to *Vesalii icones*. Davies wrote his 'cantata for mezzo-soprano and small instrumental ensemble' to words that set the Stations of the Cross with agricultural analogies (sample: *Scythes are sharpened to bring you down / King Barleycorn*).[23] The musical forces were just as eccentric, appearing in one sense to leave behind the very idea of a Pierrot ensemble – with no flute, violin or cello – yet written for, and premiered by, a quintet drawn from The Fires. *From Stone to Thorn* handed Tim Walker his debut with the group and the significance of his abrasive guitar part, coupled with Barry Quinn's percussion, was that there was no 'percussive' role in Davies's non-theatrical song cycle for Thomas, whose mezzo-soprano was unusually melodic, if typically angular, and entirely sung.

Davies's next Orkney work, the *Hymn to St Magnus* (1972), restored The Fires' line-up to a fuller complement, though the flute, clarinet and viola – increasingly a default choice over the violin – were undoubled. Yet, in the context of Davies's Pierrot ensembles, the piece, described as a 'chamber ensemble with mezzo-soprano obbligato', remains unusual. It took its cue from *The Devils* suite both in its medieval origins and its sparing use of Thomas. Davies's inspiration was the eponymous saint whose martyrdom in 1117 followed a dispute with his cousin, Earl Hakon, over the just division of the Earldom of Orkney. Davies took a twelfth-century hymn written to commemorate Magnus as his source material, although in practice it is barely recognizable after a brief introduction in which successive whispered duets played *tremolo* (flute and glockenspiel, viola and cello) slowly sound the hymn's pitches, if not its rhythms. Over their sustained accompaniment, Thomas's chanted Latin dedication to the saint evoked the mock-ecclesia and textures of *The Devils* and, before it, *Missa super L'homme armé*. The significant difference is that *Hymn to St*

Magnus was derived neither from theatre nor film. Moreover, following this introduction came two sonatas, of which the second accounts for over two-thirds of the work's duration. These sections also raise questions about the work's purpose. Although it could never be called abstract, the aspirational yet strangely disproportioned structure created a work that was almost entirely instrumental in conception. So little had Thomas to do that, after she had intoned her dedication, she switched to being a second percussionist during its performance.

The work also depended far less on driving other styles to their extremes than Davies's earlier comparable works, as though he were aware that such parodic schemes would be unable to sustain interest and momentum sufficiently in such a long piece. In their absence, other more abstractly conceived devices were used – and in some cases invented. With their medieval derivation, isorhythms had long been an important structural device to Davies. But in the ambitiously protracted *Hymn to St Magnus*, their melodic content and the assigned durations were newly dictated by the use of a 'square', extending to 625 notes.[24] It was in this manner that Davies wished to generate, and clarify, the 'structural bones of the music [i.e. the sonata]' – surely a thinly veiled reference to his parallel interest in Schenkerian analysis and its capacity to inform his own less episodic (more symphonic) language.[25]

His take on parametricized, serial principles was nevertheless highly idiosyncratic. This included the use of pre-compositional matrices, yet these alone do not provide the full picture. To recognize other more pragmatic features that exist in Davies's works for Pierrot ensemble is to counteract the type of formalist, 'composition-in-reverse' approach that has made analysis of his music – and, for that matter, Birtwistle's – such a subdued exercise. For example, a small-print 'rhythmic relationship grid' is printed between the staves for most of the third movement of *Hymn to St Magnus*, its purpose being to interlock the differently timed subgroups.[26] None other of Davies's works had gone this far to maintain *ensemble* in performance. The unique relationship between the musicians and the composer-conductor facilitated the procedure, which usually pitted the strings against the rest of the ensemble or otherwise paired off the winds – except that Davies's direction to musicians bracketed into these grids to play in its 'different (but related) tempo' is in itself confusing. To wit, the more significant affect was to render the litany of time signatures redundant (so in another sense overcoming a weakness of traditional musical notation) and to unfurl a stratified texture that was essentially non-discursive yet also denied any single voice the opportunity to dominate. (This caveat upholds the symphonic ideal: 'one massive urgent wave containing smaller flows of forward motion' was Paul Griffiths's more pictorial description of the same idea.)[27] In turn, this left an impressionistic, rhythmically driven movement that captured 'the violence of the martyrdom and the violence of the sea'.[28]

The importance of occasional elements, and of such conceptual links in turn, was underlined when *Hymn to St Magnus* was performed at the Proms in 1974. The concert was devised as a vehicle, not for The Fires, but for Munrow's Early Music Consort, principally to mark the quincentenary of the death of Guillaume Dufay. The *Hymn to St Magnus* was nevertheless heard after its 'preface', the Viking organum *Nobilis humilis* (sung by members of the Consort), which develops into a four-movement chamber composition the same twelfth-century hymn Davies had used for his inspiration. Neither group was suited to the vast venue,[29] but with the Consort on-hand, *The Devils* suite also received its belated 'complete' performance with interspersed arrangements of Praetorius and Gervaise.[30] (This was a unique event, held two years before Munrow's tragic, early death.)

The extended structure of the *Hymn to St Magnus* paved the way for Pierrot ensemble pieces of even greater ambition. The most highly acclaimed of these was the beguiling *Ave Maris Stella* (Hail, Star of the Sea), in which the solo marimba speaks for the percussion section far more sonorously and intimately than had been standard. It was also cast in nine sections but, crucially, these were to be performed without a break. Davies's rehabilitation of symphonic ideals became increasingly clear in the 1970s; indeed, the oft-quoted idea that Schoenberg's Pierrot ensemble is akin to a 'miniature' orchestra was made more plausible by Davies's wide-ranging timbral resources, his polyphonic outlook, and the search for a unified architecture for his ideas. Stylistically, this culminated in the much-hyped First Symphony, premiered in 1978 but begun five years earlier, thus overlapping with *Ave Maris Stella*. Moreover, Davies had dabbled in composing 'symphonically' for orchestra before: concertgoers misunderstood *Worldes Blis* (1966-69), according to the composer, but *Stone Litany* (1973), another work inspired by his move to Orkney, fared better and was a symphony in all but name.[31] Yet, with no apparent connection to The Fires, the symphony still took some commentators by surprise. Those aware that, in the recent past, Davies had seconded a motion by Hans Keller stating 'the extinction of the symphony orchestra is inevitable' had special cause to ponder the composer's motivation for writing such a work.[32] The two actions were not altogether incongruous. Davies did not call for the death of the symphony, nor proclaim it dead. Nevertheless, the few works he had written for orchestra in the 1960s had always arisen as appendages to other compositional and directorial objectives. They had also been (or had appeared to be) subservient to his attachment to the Pierrot ensemble in particular.

This changed in the mid 1970s when, to remarkable effect, Davies's pursuit of such symphonic ideals began to materialize in certain works he wrote for The Fires. The structural and extramusical processes of *Ave Maris Stella* have attracted comment before. Stephen Pruslin had an insider's view on the Beethovenian comparisons to be made, citing the similarly heterogeneous, immense forms of the string quartets Opp. 131 and 135.[33] As with the *Hymn to St Magnus*, Davies was only able to compose longer works for Pierrot ensemble (over and above the episodic structures of his music theatre works) because his style changed. The composer's decree that *Ave Maris Stella* ought to be performed without a conductor should be interpreted not as a contradiction of its symphonism, but, more pragmatically, as a façade to advertise the 'chamberness' of The Fires. This also explains why it was conceived that any one instrument would always give the pulse, a gesture that has invited misguided comparisons with Birtwistle's individual style but which actually mitigated the work's difficulty – and more perceptibly so than the 'rhythmic relationship grid' of *Hymn to St Magnus*.

Davies's new sympathies extended to his programme for *Ave Maris Stella*, in which the piece, seen as a time-cycle, is said to begin and end at the 'hour of the wolf' between night and dawn. Neither the score nor its preface refer to this so-called *Vargtimmen*, and it is significant that Pruslin was the first to reveal this secret derived from Scandinavian folklore, if not one acknowledged as such.[34] Had the piece been written a few years earlier, it is likely that Davies would have made much greater play of the expressionist potential of a time in which, as legend has it, nightmares reach their height and most people are born and die. But *Ave Maris Stella* came without the subversion or parody that had characterized so many of his Pierrot ensemble pieces to date. Instead, this outlandish, lax programme was additionally concealed behind Davies's rendering of two further sources: the eponymous plainsong hymn, worshipping the Virgin Mary, and a setting of a Greek text, printed as a preface to the score, as an invitation 'to travel the path of wisdom and so combat philistinism.' Scored for alto flute, the hymn is heard in its most complete form only towards the very end of the work (a further self-referential link, given the *Hymn to St Magnus*'s similar form). But it is the more abstract manner in which Davies rotated its notes to produce a magic square of values, governing much of the melodic and rhythmic content, that attracted the most attention.[35]

More recently, Joel Lester has explored this same fixation at a foreground level by tracing the nine pitch-class rows that underpin the rapturous cello solo towards the beginning (No. 1, *Andante*).[36] Yet, the continued probing of the individual and corporate virtuosity of The Fires was, and remains, of more immediate aural interest. Greatest among these, for the first time, was the marimba. Its starring role in the work's outstanding section (No. 6, *Lento recitando*) was to unfurl a cadenza whose hurried repetitions of small note-groups was not just knowingly 'theatrical', but also provokes climactic fragments, illustrated as such on the score, from the rest of the ensemble (No. 7, *Presto – Allegro precipitoso – Scorrevole* etc.): an outburst to, or a contradiction of, the artful six-part rhythmic polyphony with which *Ave Maris Stella* began. The work represented a further stage in Davies's post-tonal journey through serialism, and one which positioned him as a pioneer of permutational, non-twelve-note music.[37] Developed from plainsong, Davies's choices were not arbitrary – the nine-sided magic square has been associated with the moon since the Renaissance alchemist and theologian Cornelius Agrippa said so – even if, essentially, they were still artificial. Davies had put such distance between his Pierrot ensemble pieces and *Pierrot lunaire*, but the moon remained.

Notes

1   There are two explanations for the new title. The reference to London's Great Fire is clear enough. Stephen Pruslin has colourfully likened the fireweed that flourished in its aftermath to the similarly renewed ensemble: a 'phoenix arising from the ashes', as he put it. More extravagantly still, Davies has claimed that the group adopted the new identity in 1970 to 'exorcize the devil of fire' that had destroyed his Dorset cottage a year earlier. Tellingly, neither account cites Birtwistle. Stephen Pruslin, interview with Chris Wines, broadcast as 'Pierrot and Beyond' and taken from a discussion at the interval of a Birmingham Contemporary Music Group concert, BBC Pebble Mill Studios, Birmingham, 23 May 1997 (BLSA, cat. H5918/2); Peter Maxwell Davies, interview with Melvyn Bragg, *2nd House*, BBC2, broadcast 2 March 1974.

2   On the importance of mime and dance to British musical theatre, see Robert Adlington, 'Music Theatre since the 1960s' in: *The Cambridge Companion to Twentieth-Century Opera*, ed. Mervyn Cooke (Cambridge: Cambridge University Press, 2005), 236.

3   By 'symphonic', then, we abide by its late nineteenth-century definition in both cases, in which, aptly, the importance of timbre was elevated and the symphony was 'perceived as a work whose very essence emerged from the polyphonic web of all instrumental parts and their distinctive colours.' Mark Evan Bonds, 'Symphony – §II: 19th Century – 1. The Essence of the Genre', *Grove Music Online. Oxford Music Online*, http://www.oxfordmusiconline.com/subscriber/article/grove/music/27254pg2 (accessed 7 September 2012). The four-movements-in-one design of Schoenberg's Op. 9 is particularly relevant to the nine-movements-in-one of *Ave Maris Stella*, which is discussed later in this chapter.

4   The Fires continued to operate with five 'core' musicians; percussionists, singers and guitarist appeared sporadically. Despite several works now requiring a guitar – see Catalogue of Pierrot Ensembles, section 5b: with guitar, banjo or mandolin – Walker was named only as a 'principal guest'.

5   Even then, Davies's pastoralism was resolutely 'hard', paralleling in his music Orkney's often-bloody history or unforgiving terrain, as we shall see. This stands in contrast to a more innocent, idyllic or 'soft' pastoral style, even if Davies found his new working conditions to be ideal. See note 22. For more on this distinction, see Erwin Panofsky, *Meaning in the Visual Arts* (Garden City: Doubleday, 1955), 297. Incidentally, Birtwistle would explore this same trope from a Hebridean perspective in the 'Stark pastoral' (II.) and 'White pastoral' (IV.) of his *Duets for Storab* (1983).

6   See William Mann, 'The Fires of London: Queen Elizabeth Hall', *The Times* (14 December 1970), 6.

7   The Schoenbergian connections extend further. Druce's title refers to Bolkonsky's sensation of a 'strange construction of needles or splinters' rising from his face (Druce, quoting Tolstoy), the prince uncertain, in the manner of Schoenberg's Pierrot, whether his perceptions are real or hallucinatory. Duncan Druce, programme note to *The Tower of Needles*, Queen Elizabeth Hall, London, 20 February 1971.

8   Mervyn McLean, *Maori Music: Records and Analysis of Ancient Maori Musical Tradition and Knowledge* (Auckland: Auckland University Press, 1996), 172.

9   Whitehead's association with The Fires continued throughout the decade, which saw the premieres of the 'dance drama' *Marduk* for Pierrot ensemble with guitar, and the Harpsichord Trio in 1973 and 1975 respectively. She composed further Pierrot ensemble pieces on similar themes but, importantly, did so without The Fires: *Wulf* (1976, commissioned by Themus) was scored for female reciter with a 'Fires sextet' (without doubling); the Pierrot quintet *Manutaki* (1985, written for the Australia Ensemble) followed.

10   See David Josephson, 'In Search of the Historical Taverner', *Tempo* 101 (1972), 40-52.

11   The score was not published, although a recording of the concert was made (BLSA, cat. M3025R TR 2).

12   The memory of the Pierrot Players' 'Spring Song' concert, of which Birtwistle's version had been an integral part, supports this idea.

13   Hans Werner Henze, *Bohemian Fifths: An Autobiography*, trans. Stewart Spencer (London: Faber, 1998), 303.

14   Stanley Sadie, 'Henze: Radio 3', *The Times* (18 May 1971), 12.

15   Hans Werner Henze, *Music and Politics: Collected Writings 1953-81* (London: Faber, 1982), 191.

16   This was at the invitation of Davies, who met the Hungarian composer during their studies together with Goffredo Petrassi at the Santa Cecilia Academy in Rome.

17   The flair of Russell's composer-portrait of Gordon Jacob (*Monitor*, 1959) had first given way to his lyrical, dramaticized 'documentaries' on, inter alia, Elgar (*Monitor: Elgar*, 1962) and Delius (*Omnibus: Song of Summer*, 1968), then, more extravagantly, to his acerbic televisual attack on Richard Strauss (*Dance of the Seven Veils: A Comic Strip in 7 Episodes*) and the Tchaikovsky feature film, *The Music Lovers* (both 1970).

18   Russell had also written the screenplay for the film and set the story in the 1930s, but Wilson failed to recognize this was done deliberately. He also objected to the film's most cavalier interpolation (one which, in the event, did not make the final cut): an 'orgiastic' scene featuring Polly and typical of Russell's fantastical style. Interestingly, Wilson refrained from commenting on how Davies had overhauled his music. See Sandy Wilson, *I Could Be Happy: An Autobiography* (New York: Stein and Day, 1975), 267-71.

19   See Peter Maxwell Davies, quoted in: Paul Griffiths, *Peter Maxwell Davies* (London: Robson, 1982), 155.

20   Gerard McBurney, 'Maxwell Davies', *Tempo* 176 (1991), 33.

21   See note 1.

22   Peter Maxwell Davies, interviewed in *One Foot in Eden: Peter Maxwell Davies*, dir. Gavin Barrie (Arts Council: Platypus, 1978). On Orkney itself, he has been more explicit: 'I wanted to … concentrate on natural sounds, the sounds of the sea and wind. … The waves … [are] like some great Aeolian harp throbbing away out there in the bay.' Davies, quoted in: John von Rhein, 'Composer Peter Maxwell Davies: Looking for an Audience, Not A Cult', *Chicago Tribune* (22 May 1983), 17.

23   See George Mackay Brown, 'Stations of the Cross', *An Orkney Tapestry* (London: Gollancz, 1969).

24   This was first unearthed by Peter Owens in 'Revelation and Fallacy: Observations on Compositional Technique in the Music of Peter Maxwell Davies', *Music Analysis* 13/2-3 (October, 1994), 173-76. See also notes 33 and 35.

25   Peter Maxwell Davies, quoted in: Griffiths, 150. For more on Davies's interest in Schenker, see Richard Duffalo's interview (10 November 1986) with Davies in *Trackings: Composers Speak to Richard Dufallo* (New York: Oxford University Press, 1989), esp. 147.

26   For its first appearance, see page 30 of the published score.

27   Griffiths, 83.

28   Peter Maxwell Davies, sleevenotes to The Fires' LP recording of the *Hymn to St Magnus* (Decca, 1987), DLSO 12.

29   Griffiths complained that the organum's 'finesses were lost, its construction dissolved'. See Paul Griffiths, 'Music in London: Proms', *Musical Times* 115/1580 (October, 1974), 865.

30   According to Stanley Sadie: 'The setting of this music against Renaissance dances … only heightened the grotesqueness [of Davies's music].' Stanley Sadie, 'Early Music Consort/Fires of London: Albert Hall/Radio 3', *The Times* (30 August 1974), 9.

31   Davies was particularly affected by the failure of *Worldes Blis* at the 1969 Proms: The 'audience didn't get the point [many walked out], and in a strange way that threw me off course so that it took me a long time to get to the point. I just left the piece alone.' Peter Maxwell Davies, quoted in: Paul Griffiths, *New Sounds, New Personalities: British Composers of the 1980s in Conversation with Paul Griffiths* (London: Faber, 1985), 33. The more positive slant is that the gap in Davies's symphonic output enabled him to re-channel his energies towards The Fires.

32   See the introduction to *Tempo* 93 (1970), 1. Davies and Keller spoke at a Cheltenham Festival debate chaired by Prof. Alan Peacock, whose Arts Council report on orchestral resources in Great Britain had been published recently.

33   See Stephen Pruslin, 'The Triangular Space: Davies's *Ave Maris Stella*', *Tempo* 120 (1977), 16-22; repr. in: *Peter Maxwell Davies: Studies from Two Decades*, ed. Stephen Pruslin (London: Boosey & Hawkes, 1979), 84-90.

34   *Vargtimmen* is also the subject and title of Ingmar Bergman's 1968 gothic horror film, in which an artist is haunted by, and proceeds to give names to, his demons. From *Eight Songs for a Mad King* to *The Devils*, the parallels with themes in Davies's works at the time are clear.

35   David Roberts first revealed how such matrices are unfurled in Davies's music. See David Roberts, review of *Ave Maris Stella* and ten other scores by Peter Maxwell Davies, *Contact* 19 (Summer, 1978), 28-9. Griffiths explains the process most concisely: 'The [nine-by-nine] grid of rhythmic values is readily obtained, starting from the 1 in the top left corner, adding five successively along the rows and down the columns while also subtracting nine whenever the total exceed that figure [*modulo* 9]. This produces a square in which the same sequence is repeated in rows and columns with progressive rotation.' Griffiths, *Peter Maxwell Davies*, 73-4.

36   See Joel Lester, 'Structure and Effect in *Ave Maris Stella*' in: *Perspectives on Peter Maxwell Davies*, ed. Richard McGregor (Aldershot: Ashgate, 2000), 68-9. Incidentally, the theorist's fascination with the work began with his performance of it in 1980 as violinist with the Da Capo Chamber Players, an American Pierrot ensemble.

37   See Arnold Whittall, *Serialism* (Cambridge: Cambridge University Press, 2008), 228. Davies's time in Princeton was clearly important to how he forged this style: Roger Sessions, Milton Babbitt and Earl Kim taught there, while Charles Wuorinen, another Babbitt follower, developed similar procedures. Davies's earlier studies in Manchester with the unsung Richard Hall surely exerted their own influence, though. To quote Hall from 1956: 'It looks as though a new kind of tonality has been evolved from the old, which is, in reality, not atonal at all, and which will bring with it a new conception of the formal structure of such movements which depended for their shape upon contrasts of key and/or major-minor tonality within their duration … It looks as if composers will have to face up to a reorientation with regard to this and similar problems raised by twelve-note music in the matter of formal structure of music of the future.' Richard Hall, quoted by the New Music Manchester Group in a programme note to their ICA Concert, Arts Council of Great Britain, London, 9 January 1956.

Epilogue

When Elisabeth Lutyens came to write her first piece for Pierrot ensemble in 1950, very few other such pieces existed. Besides, it is likely she knew only two: Arnold Schoenberg's *Pierrot lunaire* and Hanns Eisler's *Vierzehn Arten den Regen zu beschreiben*. When Steve Reich scored his 2009 Pulitzer Prize-winning *Double Sextet* (2007) for Pierrot ensemble, it joined a repertory of literally hundreds. The last twenty-five years, indeed, have seen an outpouring of music for the line-up, written against a richly interconnected backdrop of composition and performance. Yet, the Pierrot ensemble has eluded classification and struggled to enter the lexicon of music criticism. One reason for this is that, as we have seen, *Pierrot*'s line-up has been subjected to continual, if incremental, changes over the years. Some, such as Eisler's scoring for violin *and* viola in *Vierzehn Arten*, are relatively minor. Others are more significant: Peter Maxwell Davies, as we have seen, had long since added percussion to the Pierrot ensemble and taken to tripling the flute with piccolo and alto flute, not to mention doubling the piano with celeste or harpsichord, when he employed a mime artist and children's band in *Le Jongleur de Notre Dame* (1978). In short, three main subcategories of Pierrot ensemble have become standard: the Pierrot quintet, most commonly represented by a fixed format of flute, clarinet, piano, violin and cello, i.e. without voice and doubling; the Pierrot sextet (or Fires sextet), without *Pierrot*'s voice but with percussion; and, most popularly, this same line-up with voice ('*Pierrot*-with-percussion' as it sometimes described).

Conspicuously absent from this list is Schoenberg's original line-up, whose emulation is comparatively, perhaps surprisingly, rare. Notwithstanding Davies's theatrical resurrection of a *Pierrot*-type vocal delivery, *Sprechstimme* proved dispensable to most composers, if not to musicologists. And while the idea of doubling, tripling and even quadrupling the ensemble's winds took hold as alto and bass flutes, contrabass and basset clarinets, recorders, saxophones and even ocarinas entered the fray, the violin and viola were as likely to have been 'undoubled' or to have had one instrument dropped altogether as they were to be doubled in the manner of *Pierrot*.

The accompanying Catalogue of Pierrot Ensembles details these and eight further subcategories of Pierrot ensemble. Each list of works tells its own story of how composers came to view the ensemble after Schoenberg. With Lutyens and Reich, for example, it is clear that they, like many others, were motivated to write for Pierrot ensemble for very different reasons. Whatever her rationale for adopting serialism, Lutyens was faithful to Schoenberg's exotic instrumental template, omitting only the clarinet in A, used just once in *Pierrot*. But the more popular strategy, as in Reich's work, has been to strip away Schoenberg's instrumental doubling and to emulate Davies in adding percussion – commonly tuned percussion, again after Davies. *Tenebrae super Gesualdo* (1972) was Davies's first work for Pierrot ensemble to feature the marimba prominently, although the same feature in *Ave Maris Stella* (1975) is even more pronounced. Reich's *Double Sextet*, meanwhile, lives up to its title: the instrumental sextet, originally the American Pierrot ensemble eighth blackbird [*sic*], plays against its pre-recorded self.

The 'Pierrot ensemble' label withstands these types of variation because, at the most fundamental level, its combination of air and single reeds, and bowed and struck strings, persists. Percussive instruments, voice(s), electronics, plucked strings (guitar, harpsichord, harp), or a combination of these, adorn and characterize it. Its prevalence today attests to its appeal: in the UK, the United States, Canada, most European countries, Australia, Brazil and Japan, among others, more Pierrot ensembles than ever sustain their repertory through performance and commissions. They tread in a tradition modernized by the Pierrot Players and The Fires of London during their twenty years of domestic and foreign tours. Davies's ambassadorial efforts to endorse the Pierrot ensemble were arguably even greater than Schoenberg's. To summarize his groups' main accomplishments, it is clear that their British-led, *Pierrot*-derived lineage was a vehicle for nothing less than a changed condition of music-making and composer behaviour. The ambition to persuade young musicians of the day to form an ensemble dedicated primarily but not exclusively to avant-garde music introduced a new benchmark level of commitment, engagement and attainment.

Stylistically, Davies's legacy, as with Schoenberg's, is less clear. Given the fashion for composing 'basic' Pierrot quintets in the years since his group disbanded, it is telling that all bar one of Davies's works for Pierrot ensemble belong to different categories. *Unbroken Circle* (1984) is anomalous even then, if typical of Davies at the time, in preferring the alto flute and viola to the flute and violin.[1] Besides, by the time of its composition, groups such as Gemini, Lontano (both UK), Joan Towers's Da Capo Chamber Players, the New York New Music Ensemble and California E.A.R. Unit (all USA) had begun to form Pierrot ensembles of their own. Yet the legacy of their undoubted forebears, and of The Fires of London in its final years, still looms large.

In the increasingly 'dislocated' twentieth century, musicologists thought twice when daring to identify cause and effect across the decades. Further, certain manifestations of modernism, whatever the legitimacy of their original designs, are routinely remembered today either as misconceived or, quite simply, mistaken. Famous composer-collective blocs shall not be immune from reassessment. The short-lived Darmstadt School, for example, collapsed under the post-war weight of its interpersonal and aesthetic schisms, and although its music-making inspired the New Music Manchester Group, similar divisions would seep through to Peter Maxwell Davies, Harrison Birtwistle and Alexander Goehr. The Second Viennese School's earlier development and greater collegiality are more straightforward, until we remember how 'affiliated' members such as Erwin Stein, Hanns Eisler and even Roberto Gerhard helped shape new music – and particularly the Pierrot ensemble. Compounded over time, this apparent eclecticism is one reason why Schoenberg's legacy was hotly debated so soon after his death in 1951. Yet the danger of situating Schoenberg within a lineage of hindsight is alleviated by the sweeping geography of *Pierrot*'s 'historical destiny', to recall Jonathan Dunsby. Just as the phenomenon of its international premieres with and without Schoenberg at the helm stands out, so too does the Pierrot ensemble, for which so many composers have written in more recent times. For some, composing for Pierrot ensemble has surely become a validatory act, hence the startling number of young composers who have written for it, buoyed by their peers and teachers doing likewise,[2] and the way in which older composers such as Reich, Louis Andriessen, Elliott Carter and Iannis Xenakis embraced it in their later years.

It is still too early to predict where twenty-first-century music will head, although time may well have been called on the postmodernist cause, which arguably plateaued some years ago. With this came a decisive moment for the Pierrot ensemble, since the story of its international proliferation has evidently led to *Pierrot lunaire* being transcended in the minds of some. Why else would Michael Torke and Judith Weir, two very different composers of a similar generation, deny that *Pierrot* played any part in their own composition of works that are unquestionably *Pierrot*-configured? Weir wrote *King Harald Sails to Byzantium* (1979), based on the life of the eleventh-century king, for The Fires to perform at the third St Magnus Festival. As a light-hearted miniature symphonic poem, it came with typically Daviesian extensions in timbre (alto flute, marimba and glockenspiel) but without the historic histrionics of many of his earlier works. But because many of those same works had cleverly taken on *Pierrot*'s traditional role as a challenging showpiece, Weir and others had new models such as *Eight Songs for a Mad King* to admire and emulate (if they wanted to). Thereafter, it was not unreasonable, nor unexpected, that *Pierrot*'s stylistic language would prove less enduring than its ensemble, even if, curiously, its ability to disturb in a theatrical, narrative sense *has* endured. Should we conclude that the ensemble's post-war champion, if we accept Davies as such, usurped its inventor? Should the Pierrot ensemble, or at least the 'Pierrot-and-percussion' ensemble, perhaps be more accurately named, say, the 'Mad King' ensemble? After all, the *Eight Songs* have their own explicit companions in, say, Paul Dresher's *The Tyrant* (2005), written for the same line-up and even staged similarly, not to mention Davies's own sequel, the sister piece *Miss Donnithorne's Maggot* (1974).

The overriding problem with the naming of any rebranded line-up is the abundance of Pierrot ensembles written during the last forty years, Davies's included. Among his works for Pierrot ensemble Davies counted ballet, music theatre, arrangements-as-recompositions, more introspective 'concert' Pierrot ensembles such as *The Bairns of Brugh* (1981) and *Image, Reflection, Shadow* (1982), as well as his fully-fledged chamber operas *The Martyrdom of St Magnus* (1976) and *The Lighthouse* (1979). Davies had long planned his repositioning of genre: a piece he composed surely with the Pierrot Players in mind, *Notre Dame des Fleurs* (1966), had been labelled a 'mini-opera'. Both operas also had brass-inflected line-ups, although his last large-scale work for The Fires, *The No. 11 Bus* (1983-84), instead augmented the vocal and extramusical resources by calling for one mime artist, two dancers and three singers. With a surreal narrative arc that followed the mocked-up route of the real No. 11 bus from Liverpool Street to Hammersmith – not for the first time, Davies's apocalyptic denouement was World's End – *The No. 11 Bus* furrowed fantastical yet, seemingly, overfamiliar themes. Paul Griffiths openly questioned whether 'so many parodies of parodies betray a lack of confidence in the genre'; and, indeed, the resemblance to earlier works was clear in Davies's 'malleable' Pierrot ensemble and also the same fervid topics of religious righteousness and (ir)rationality he had recently pledged to the same critic to leave behind.[3]

Moreover, the last chapter in The Fires' artistic direction revived, or featured anew, music by a large number of composers. (Relatedly, an unprecedented flurry of conductors, including Nicholas Cleobury, Richard Dufallo, John Carewe, Howard Williams and Günther Bauer-Schenk, often deputized for Davies.)[4] Most were young Britons, such as Richard Emsley (*… from swerve of shore to bend of bay …*), Philip Grange (*Variations*), Brian

Elias (*Geranos*), Michael Finnissy (*Mr Punch*) and Robert Saxton (*Sentinel of the Rainbow*). In other words, the manner in which Davies was increasingly in demand as a figurehead and teacher played its part, although his peers were not forgotten: the debut Pierrot ensembles of relative veterans such as Roger Smalley (*The Narrow Road to the Deep North*), Anthony Payne (*A Day in the Life of a Mayfly*) and Bayan Northcott (Sextet) were also performed.[5]

However, it is Carter's *Triple Duo* (1982-83), which The Fires premiered, that will probably best survive from this era. This clever work had the *subject* of the Pierrot ensemble at its core in a way not seen since Eisler's exercise in cinematic re-scoring, *Vierzehn Arten*. Carter accepted the Fires sextet as his template but separated its three nominal families in the musical discourse. Hence the subdivided duos of its title: flute and clarinet, violin and cello, and piano and percussion. His association with The Fires is significant because of his international prominence and longstanding friendship with Davies.[6] That *Triple Duo* was heard in New York by the likes of Aaron Copland and Leonard Bernstein, and was the first Fires premiere of music by an American composer since Morton Feldman's *I Met Heine on the Rue Fürstenberg* (1971), also testifies to its special position. It also kick-started the 'Anglo-American' strain of Pierrot ensembles (Robert Kyr's *Maelstrom* and Ronald Caltabiano's *Concerto for Six Players* followed) and went on to enjoy a rich performance and recording history that, conspicuously, Pierrot ensemble pieces written by composers of similar or even greater celebrity, for example Pierre Boulez and Karlheinz Stockhausen, did not.

The Pierrot ensemble's successive departures from Schoenberg and Davies might appear to define it as more self-sufficient than ever, but this would be misleading. As a touchstone for composers and performers, *Pierrot lunaire* continues to fascinate and inspire very eclectic responses. The polymath John Zorn has based an entire album, *Chimeras* (2003), on the Pierrot ensemble, while Maria Baptist has written jazz interludes to fit between each of *Pierrot*'s Acts. In 2007, she recorded them within *Pierrot* with her new German Pierrot ensemble, the knowingly titled opus21musikplus. Artists as diverse as Björk and Barbara Sukowa have also performed *Pierrot* in recent years, following in the tradition of singer-actresses such as Hedli Anderson, Cleo Laine (who belatedly fulfilled Schoenberg's wish to have *Pierrot* recorded in English) and, of course, Albertine Zehme. Such revivals still offer the perfect invitations for companion pieces. The latest embodiment of this is the various competitive 'calls for compositions' that Pierrot Lunaire Ensemble Wien (Austria), Jane's Minstrels and the Composers Ensemble (both UK) have issued over the past few years. Most such invitations are relatively unconditional, hence the variations within the thirteen Pierrot ensembles – Tansy Davies (*Patterning*), Jonathan Cole (*Caught*), etc. – of the Composers Ensemble's *The Hoxton 13* (NMC, 2001). Others have been accompanied by well-meaning 'revisionist' caveats, including the now-defunct Schoenberg Institute's commission of William Kraft (*Settings from Pierrot lunaire*), Donald Harris (*GunMar Music*) and others to set poems Schoenberg had omitted from Albert Giraud's *Pierrot lunaire* anthology. (Jane's Minstrels recently did the same in collaboration with the SPNM.)

These initiatives echo those of Schoenberg, Davies and Birtwistle. While the idea that The Fires of London 'were to new music what the Beatles were to pop' may be a little dewy-eyed,[7] the group was unquestionably a catalyst for the UK-based ensembles such as the New Music Players (1990-) and Psappha (1991-), having already influenced such continental groups as Gruppe Neue Musik Berlin and Ars Nova of Cluj.[8] The Fires had pledged one day to reform as a production company for opera and music theatre projects, although, save for a one-off reunion in 1990 during a Davies-themed South Bank festival, this did not come to pass.[9] Rather, it has been left largely to these more recent groups, formed by Ed Hughes and Tim Williams respectively, to prolong the lineage of Pierrot ensembles. Composer-led, the New Music Players have deliberately rekindled aspects unique to the history of their ensemble: Hughes's *Light Cuts Through Dark Skies* (2001), the latest cinematic Pierrot ensemble, was conceived as a multimedia substitute to Eisler's *Vierzehn Arten*. Indeed, if there is a common theme among Pierrot ensembles today, it is their impressive awareness of their heritage – yet, remarkably, Hughes's group does not perform Davies's works.[10] Psappha, conversely, has given a new lease of life not only to Davies's Pierrot ensemble pieces, but also those of Saxton, Elias, Grange, Weir, Piers Hellawell and others – thus it is the only group to have mined The Fires' back catalogue to any significant degree. That these and other groups prosper with quite different visions of the Pierrot ensemble proves, in its centenary year, how sustainable it has become.

Notes

1   Colin Matthews's *Elegiac Chaconne* (1997) replicated Davies's line-up. Of the 65 Pierrot quintets I have identified, only these two works are scored in this way. See Catalogue of Pierrot Ensembles, section 5b: without voice, without doubling: Pierrot quintet.

2   Summoning up memories of his youth, Steven Mackey's prefatory note to *Micro-Concerto for Percussion and Five Instruments* (1999, written for the New York New Music Ensemble) is indicative: 'When I was a young composer in the mid-eighties the so-called *Pierrot* ensemble ... was the

ubiquitous "mod-music" group. It has a certain economic appeal in that you get a little of everything but because of that, every concert you went to had pieces by students and teachers wrestling with this Spartan orchestra in a post-Schoenbergian expressionist idiom. I … felt the need to transform the ensemble into something else, something more sympathetic to my background and interests, something more lively. In *Micro-Concerto,* the featured role of the percussionist playing a combination of toys, kitchen utensils and "legit" instruments makes the ensemble a little more playful.' Steven Mackey, note on *Micro-Concerto,* http://stevenmackey.com/composer (accessed 7 September 2012).

3   Paul Griffiths, 'An Overcrowded Vehicle, Augmented Fires of London', *The Times* (21 March 1984), 17. Davies had recently explained to Griffiths: '1969 was a critical year, and out of it came the music that I started to write in Orkney. I decided I didn't want to go on discussing these [spiritual] things and making these rather extravagant gestures. I wanted to take it much more inside the music. … I realized then [with *Vesalii icones*] that this had got to stop.' Peter Maxwell Davies, quoted in: Paul Griffiths, *Peter Maxwell Davies* (London: Robson, 1982), 113-14. To clarify the debt of *The No. 11 Bus* to its music-theatrical antecedents: its profane resurrection was set to the rhythm of a foxtrot, a dramaturgical contrivance that developed once more out of a set of engraved images (not anatomical drawings as in *Vesalii icones*, but tarot cards); it ended, as *Eight Songs for a Mad King* had, with the emergence of a jailer-drummer to send the audience out into the asylum of the real world; and *Taverner,* that operatic well-spring for several of Davies's works for the Pierrot Players, was answerable for the Pope's exposure to the Preacher's self-delusion.

4   While Davies's role with The Fires lessened slightly during the 1980s, another cause hastened the group's demise: on 20 January 1987, The Fires staged its last concert, a Farewell and Twentieth Birthday Gala, after which Davies gave a bitterly political speech on the Arts Council's inadequate support of the group and the debts he and others had accrued. Mike Seabrook, *Max: The Life and Music of Peter Maxwell Davies* (London: Gollancz, 1994), 221. Interviewed on the eve of the concert, Davies had been more magnanimous: 'A couple of months ago I decided it was time to stop. The group has done its job. … The bigger-scale dramatic works … get done in Switzerland, Germany and the States without my having to cast around to raise the money, which has remained a bugbear with performances here by the Fires.' Quoted in: Meirion Bowen, 'The Fires Brigade', *The Guardian* (19 January 1987), 9.

5   Such role-calls also remind us of how certain British composers were critical friends of The Fires. Smalley's lone voice, for example, had questioned the timeliness of the *Eight Songs'* 'resurrection of the spectre of Expressionism, an artistic movement born or, sustained by (and, I would have said, destroyed by) the social and political climate of another country in another era'. Roger Smalley, 'Maxwell Davies and Others', *Musical Times* 114/1565 (July, 1973), 712. And in performance, too, Emsley co-founded the group Suoraan (line-up: mezzo-soprano, flute, oboe, percussion and piano) in 1979 in part as a reaction

against the Pierrot ensemble by 'excluding the seemingly ubiquitous clarinet and replacing it with the oboe.' Richard Emsley, email communication with the author, 21 August 2006.

6   *Triple Duo* was the fifth of seven works by Carter that the Pierrot Players/Fires of London would perform, a group that included the Cello Sonata (1948), the *Sonata for Flute, Oboe, Cello and Harpsichord* (1952), four of the *Eight Pieces for Kettledrums* (1950-66), the *Duo for Violin and Piano* (1973-74), the solo piano *Night Fantasies* (1980), and the *Canon for 4* (1984). Written in homage to William Glock, the latter was premiered during a private Fires concert held in his honour and was part of a trilogy that included Davies's *Unbroken Circle* and Pierre Boulez's second event-piece Pierrot ensemble, *Dérive I.*

7   Paul Driver, 'The Fires of London', *BBC Music Magazine* 133 (May, 2003), 54.

8   Both ensembles made their British debut within days of each other in early 1970. The Gruppe Neue Musik Berlin appeared at the Purcell Room on February 13. What they missed by employing no clarinettist – their only departure from the Pierrot ensemble – was compensated for by their occasional use of electroacoustics. More distinctively, all of their works had been composed since 1965 and their constitution as a 'composer collective' under the creative direction of one of their number, Gerald Humel, had a familiar ring. Two days earlier, the Romanian ensemble Ars Nova of Cluj had performed at the Queen Elizabeth Hall under the declamatory billing '1 soprano [Agneta Kriza], 10 players, 9 works.' In fact, despite their apparently greater membership, Ars Nova, with its three percussionists, was only slightly larger than the German group. They also paid homage to their hosts by performing the Pierrot Players' signature tune, *Antechrist*, and a trio by Hugh Wood alongside music by their conductor-composer, Cornel Taranu. See David Drew, 'The Berlin New Music Group: A Reminiscence by Way of Introduction', *Musical Times* 111/1524 (1970), 156-57; Dominic Gill, 'Music in London: Park Lane Group, Cluj Ars Nova', *Musical Times* 111/1526 (1970), 408-09.

9   See Stephen Pruslin, 'Fires into Londonflames [*sic*]: The Past and the Future' in: *New Music 88*, ed. Michael Finnissy, Malcolm Hayes and Roger Wright (Oxford: Oxford University Press, 1989), 85-90. Davies also mooted the continuation of Fires of London Ltd to allow others to put on any of the group's repertoire if asked. See Bowen, 9.

10   A list of the group's repertoire can be found at www.newmusicplayers.org.uk (accessed 13 December 2011).

Documents

William Walton (Milein Cosman)

Benjamin Britten, Men Behind the Meters *(1935): Title Music I*

Britten, Men Behind the Meters *(1935): 'I dreamt that I dwelt in Marble Halls', arr. of 'The Dream', a.k.a. 'I Dreamt I Dwelt in Marble Halls', from Michael W. Balfe's* The Bohemian Girl.

Britten, Men Behind the Meters *(1935):*
'Sequence' *(unused except where noted), with* 'End Title I' *(unused)*

[NB. bars 17-19³ etc.
replaced 'End Title I']

[Finished on E major]

End. title — I

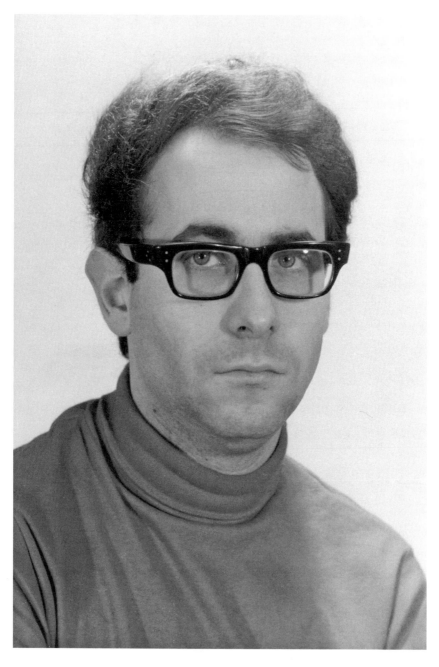

Stephen Pruslin c. 1967 (Roger Holmes)

Document B

Stephen Pruslin's Text for
Harrison Birtwistle's Monodrama (1967)

Harrison Birtwistle did not set the role of the Choregos to music, but wrote the part between the staves for an actor to speak. Stephen Pruslin recalls that, at the post-concert party, the actor admitted he could not decide how to deliver the climactic line of the text: 'Ah! They have struck from within!', and so instead 'sent it up', prompting enormous laughter from the audience at the most serious moment of the piece. In the weeks after the concert, several internationally known writers who attended the concert contacted Pruslin to assure him that his text was a masterpiece. Nevertheless, he has not allowed the text to be published until now.

Parodos

CHOREGOS: Silence … Who screamed in pain behind the portal?

PROTAGONIST: Speak! A scream is the portal of pain.

Oracle I

PROPHETESS: Only the heart of the vision will heal this incision in my visionary heart.

Only the truth of the forecast will cause this holocaust forever to be cast forth.

Only in transfiguration will come the realization of the figure of my trance.

Cryptogram I

PROTAGONIST: This forbidding, foreboding phantasm of fear.

CHOREGOS: CLEAR

PROTAGONIST: This monstrous mystery's myriad maze.

CHOREGOS: AS

PROTAGONIST: This sepulchral secrecy's shudder and swoon.

CHOREGOS: NOON

> CLEAR AS NOON
> ONE CYCLE DONE
> ONE CHANCE GONE

Soliloquy I

PROTAGONIST: Doubting daggers devour the heart,
while ambiguous acids make acrid the head.
If this is false, then where is real?
If this is real, then all is false.
I confront contradiction of fiction and fact.

Interstice I

[Solo instrument I]

Transformula I

CHOREGOS: It is you who must connect these links.
But first you must play another part in this Passion.
Come, rehearse this role that you dare not refuse.

PROTAGONIST: I hear a Herald's factual footstep.
He will substitute speech for silence,
or else – but I dare not, refuse, to speak the substitute.

Interrogation I

HERALD: Sinister stories and terrible tales.

PROTAGONIST: But release comes at last if those terrors you tell,
                and lasting the peace when my fears you dispel.

HERALD: The mirror succeeds where the Messenger fails.

PROTAGONIST: My faith in the Messenger gradually pales.

HERALD: Gnawing guilt and flagrant fault.

PROTAGONIST: But reason would work where a vision had failed,
                and if lurking, unreasoned suspicion were veiled.

HERALD: Mirrors begin after Messengers halt.

PROTAGONIST: My face in this mirror has suddenly palled.

CHOREGOS: Evasive replies can only provoke.
                Erase then her pleas or my anger invoke.

HERALD: Choregos succeeds where Protagonist failed.
                Courageous, I lead now to Agons unveiled.

CHOREGOS: I know not what lies behind the portal!
                What is the source of Protagonist's plight?

HERALD: My message is done. I am shrouded in night.

Interstice II

[Solo instrument II]

Cryptogram II

PROTAGONIST: This secretive, sinister, sepulchral sight.

CHOREGOS: LIGHT

PROTAGONIST: This forbidding foreboding of phantasmic forms.

CHOREGOS: COMES

PROTAGONIST: This myriad menace of mirrors and moon.

CHOREGOS: SOON

                LIGHT COMES SOON
                TWO CYCLES DONE
                TWO CHANCES GONE

Soliloquy II

PROTAGONIST: Suspicious stalactites splinter the mind,
while confounding craters careen in the head.
If this is false, then where is real?
If this is real, then all is false.
I reel and am wracked by fact and fiction.

Interstice III

[Solo instrument III]

Transformula II

CHOREGOS: Is it still you who must unlink these chains.
But now, you must play a previous part in this parody.
Come, repeat this role that you dare not refuse.

PROTAGONIST: I hear an oracle's mantic murmur.
She will replace reason by rhyme,
or else – but I dare not, refuse, to reason in her place.

Transformula III

PROPHETESS: Only the limbo of reason
could unleash this lesion
that freezes in my limbs.

CHOREGOS: Irrational antics can only provoke.

PROPHETESS: Only the mandala's mystery can redeem
this Starry Queen's mastery of mind.

CHOREGOS: Unreasoning mantics can soon be revoked.

Incantation and Chant

PROPHETESS [TO CHOREGOS]:   ENOUGH!

[TO INSTRUMENTALISTS]:   Come then,
Let us merge our acoustic in savage euphony,
till these walls are rubble and this rabble falls.

Madness of moon,
Sanity's sun,
Reason of rain,
Irrational ice,
Tattoo of terror,
Lashing of lymph,
Thrill's tortured threnody.

[Interstice IV]

[Solo instrument IV]

Cryptogram III

CHOREGOS: Autobiography's Accurate Axe.

PROTAGONIST: Fact, facts.

CHOREGOS: Mirror's Merciless Message of Mime.

PROTAGONIST: Chime, chime.

CHOREGOS: Fingerprint's Frank and Prefiguring Form.

PROTAGONIST: Doom, doom.
Clear as Noon,
Light comes soon.
Facts
chime
doom.

Catastrophe

CHOREGOS: Ah! They have struck from within!

PROTAGONIST: Silence ... Who screamed in pain behind the portal?

              Oh, Gods,
              Again, from without!
              They have struck twice!

CHOREGOS: SPEAK! A SCREAM IS THE PORTAL OF PAIN.

Triumph

PROTAGONIST: O radiance and ecstasy of transfiguration!
              Slaying, we are slain.
              Slain, we will slay.
              For who can adjudge these crimson achievements?

CHOREGOS: ONLY A CHOICE CAN SUSPICION REQUITE.

PROTAGONIST: No, my beloved.
              In this circus of suspects, remain circumspect.

CHOREGOS: AMBIGUOUS ENDINGS CAN ANGER INCITE.

PROTAGONIST: Disregard these wrathful whinings.
              Ours is the winning card of truth.

Exodos

CHOREGOS AND PROTAGONIST:

              ONLY AN ULTRA-VIOLENT LIGHT
              WILL INFER ONE RED
              AND IMPLY ONE WHITE.

[The Protagonist slowly turns her back to the audience.]

Stephen Pruslin © 1967

Document C

Natko Devčić's Review of 'Spring Song', 1970.

[Natko Devčić, 'Strukturirani koncert (U povodu jedne nesvakidašnje londonske glazbene priredbe) [1970]' ['Structured Concert (On an Unusual Musical Performance in London)', trans. Sandra Bell] in: Novi zvuk: Izbor tekstova o suvremenoj glazbi, ed. Petar Selem (Zagreb: Nakladni Zavod Matice Hrvatske, 1972), 209-13.]

I found it all a bit unusual, from the venue itself to every other detail, at the Pierrot Players concert that took place on 3 March 1970 in the Queen Elizabeth Hall, London, conducted by Harrison Birtwistle. The venue was a massive concrete building just three years old, situated on the right bank of the River Thames between two bridges, with access on two levels: ground level for visitors in cars that seem to drive underneath the building, and a pedestrian entrance in the shape of a high passage that, as you approach, enables you to see the river, parliament and Westminster Abbey on one side and to get used to the unusual, awe-inspiring building on the other. After this, the visitor enters a very spacious and bright foyer and becomes happily disorientated by the variety of concertgoers. But the concrete vision remains, since it is present inside in the shape of flat, grey vertical lines that interrupt the monotony of the walls and bring to the foyer and hall a specific air of contemporary architecture: a subtle ambience suitable for contemporary music. Moreover, the shape of the hall – oblong with slanted stalls of completely straight, seated rows – is neither sensational nor imposing in itself, but shouts modernity. At the bottom is the stage; above, behind a glass wall, is a room for sound and lighting equipment.

I do not know what an audience wearing their evening clothes might look like in this venue, because tonight's audience were mostly young girls in trousers and miniskirts and boys with beards, but they fitted in very well. Nor did it matter that the only way to get to the seats included jumping over rows of seats as we had to leave our coats and jackets on the floor between rows of seats (the floor is carpeted and the gaps between the seats are wide), A scene in the foyer, during the break, left an impression on me: a girl with a cup of tea in her hand was walking against the stream of people moving towards the bar. She looked happy and nobody complained because there was still enough space in the corridor. Nor do I know how it is when a solo recital or a traditional chamber or orchestral concert, with their more conventional programmes, is heard in the venue. Yet the Pierrot Players suited it perfectly well.

The programme included *The Sword of Orion* for chamber ensemble by David Bedford (b. 1937), *Three English Songs* for voice and piano by Lord Berners (1883-1950), *Four Interludes from a Tragedy* for clarinet and magnetic tape, *Medusa* for chamber ensemble and electronic sounds by Harrison Birtwistle (b. 1934), *Hoquetus David* by Guillaume de Machaut (arranged for chamber ensemble), *Sports et Divertissements* for piano and reciter by Erik Satie (1866-1925), and a Hungarian Czardas! The range was so great that sorting the music alphabetically or arranging it chronologically would not bring order to it (anyway, where would we put the ancient Hungarian Czardas). Nevertheless, the conductor, Birtwistle, managed to make a compact unit out of these various international works, following his own basic ideas [of symmetry, of the jellyfish,] that obviously influenced their choice.

The concert started with the first interlude: a punctuated clarinet combined with complex electronic sound from the magnetic tape. (As with the three remaining interludes, the instrumentalist, standing to the side, emerged from complete darkness into a single, vertical green spotlight, which disappeared as soon as his performance was over.) After this, the Czardas came as a shock, performed by a chamber ensemble fully lit in red and arranged to highlight the typical virtuosity of the piece. Before the final, fourth interlude, there was a perfect antidote to the Czardas, *Hoquetus David* by the great medieval composer Guillaume de Machaut; with bare and unembellished melodic lines and an archaic sonic charm, it completed the programme. However, let me return to the third piece. After the Czardas, the contemporary sound returned in Bedford's *The Sword of Orion*, which found inspiration, formally, in the constellation of Orion. Its counterpart was Birtwistle's *Medusa*, which featured in corresponding position in the second half of the programme – the longest piece of the evening and one in which the composer, as with his interludes, cleverly uses electronic sounds, but now with two magnetic tapes: the first featuring a transformed saxophone sound; the other with artificially produced sounds. Finally, the concert's structure is completed with two contemporary composers, both satirical, ironic and anti-romantic, but hailing from opposite sides of the English Channel and featuring in symmetrically corresponding positions in each half of the programme: Erik Satie with *Sports et Divertissements* and Lord Berners with three solo numbers ('Lullaby', 'The Lady Visitor in the Pauper Ward' and 'The Green-Eyed Monster'). Of course, there are also the third and fourth interludes either side of the interval. All in all, a perfectly balanced unit.

[Devčić's representation of the concert's structure is given here: see ex. 8.2, p. 145]

The works by Satie and Lord Berners were performed on a very high podium at the back of the stage, while the rest of the programme was performed beneath the podium, level with the first row of stalls and under a red metal octagonal construction. Besides reminding us of an octagonal medusa (from the title of the Birtwistle's work), the construction gave a visual frame to a concert that would otherwise have seemed shapeless and disorganized (much like the many unconventionalities that contemporary composers use in almost all their works). I should also mention Julie Kendrick's *Chess Piece*, performed in the foyer during the interval by students from the Royal Academy of Music. It was an unpretentious, aleatory play for percussion instruments that upheld the concert's continuity, and was audible enough above the murmur of the audience but did not need anyone to remind us not to talk, move or listen, as Satie himself once did when his music, written for performance during an interval, turned out to be too audible and interesting.

I do not intend to give too many details about the Bedford and Birtwistle premieres, nor to criticize some parts of *Medusa* that were too traditionally organized, musically and temporally, and whose style did not fit into context; nor to say that the 1392 sounds produced by the percussion instruments at the end of *The Sword of Orion* were too many. However, I would like to point out the significance of the intentional structuring of the concert, which was a proper, creative and artistic intervention that showed extramusical concern for content and order. In its way, it solved the problem of 'concert form', and added another dimension: symmetry (*The Sword of Orion – Medusa; Sports et Divertissements – Three English Songs*); or the balance of contrast between other parts (*Czardas – Hoquetus David*). The balance of the concert as a whole was in contrast with the imbalance within *each* part; this excludes *Czardas*, of course, which, with its square form and entertaining ideas, was a whimsical element in the composition of the 'serious' programme. Hearing *Czardas* in that atmosphere and context makes you laugh and accept it as a good joke.

Clearly, Birtwistle could have structured his concert in other ways, but I think there should always be a 'higher' concept when planning programmes: making that idea work enriches the concert and justifies it as a social and artistic event. This can give the viewer an immediate experience and reach beyond modern means of musical communication which tend only to be transmissive.

I shall go even further than that. Actually, not further but in another direction. It seems that this increasingly popular way of organizing a concert is also connected with the general development of the creative musical idea within the last twenty years. In that time, serial music experienced its beginning, rise and peak, after which its vitality and short existence came to an end. However, its heritage leaves certain rules and perspectives that have reached the consciousness (and subconsciousness) of contemporary composers. In their experiments with statistical forms on the one hand, and reductions of music to its basic elements on the other, we recognize transformations of the serialist school of thought. I would also add that we may want to apply the brave, intelligent and successful planning of 'Spring Song' to the serial music whose heritage was once very neglected.

'Spring Song' – the title Birtwistle gave to the concert – was performed on a very cold evening at the end of winter; only the brightness of the pink sky at the end of the day seemed to indicate spring to the cold visitors walking down the pedestrian passage. I cannot claim it presents the beginning of a new musical movement, but the echoes it created in me, and the thoughts I express in this article which are the result of those echoes, certainly suggest a new spring. [Quoting John Cage, Devčić ends with an aphorism retaining one (italicized) phrase in English. Despite this, it has not been possible to trace the original quote: 'Anyway: "There was a jukebox in the restaurant. Anyone could put money in. I noticed that the music that followed, followed the swimmers as well (*swimming in a lake by the restaurant*) although they could not hear it." (John Cage)'.]

Natko Devčić (1970)

Catalogue of Pierrot Ensembles,
1912-2012

Peter Maxwell Davies (Milein Cosman)

The Pierrot Ensembles: Catalogue

The catalogue falls into two parts, a) alphabetical by composer, and b) categorized according to the following instrumental line-ups:

i)   voice(s) and Pierrot ensemble, with instrumental doubling

ii)   without doubling

iii)   with percussion, irrespective of doubling

iv)   without voice, with instrumental doubling

v)   without voice, without doubling: Pierrot quintet

vi)   without voice, with percussion

vii)   violin and viola undoubled

viii)   with guitar, banjo or mandolin

ix)   with piano omitted or substituted for percussion and/or harp

x)   with tape, multimedia or electronics

xi)   with dancers and/or other extramusical characters

xii)   with miscellaneous additions

a) Alphabetical by Composer

Agnew, Elaine. *Calligraphy* (2002)
[fl/afl, cl/bcl, vib, vn, vc]

Alberga, Eleanor. *Dancing with the Shadow* (1990)
[fl, cl, pf, glock, vn, vc]

Albright, William. *Danse Macabre* (1971)
[fl, cl/bcl, pf, perc, vn, vc]

Alvarez, Javier. *Tientos* (1984)
[fl, cl, pf, vn, vc]

Amy, Gilbert. *Après... D'un désastre obscur* (1971/76, rev. 1996)
[mez/gongs/whip, fl/pic, cl, bcl (or hn), pf, hp (only if hn > bcl), vn, vc]

Andriessen, Louis. *Zilver* (1994)
[fl, cl, pf, 2 perc (vib, mar), vn, vc]

Antunes, Jorge. *Amerika 500* (1992)
[fl, bcl, pf, perc, vn, vc]

Attwood, William. *Cloisonné* (2003)
[fl/pic, bcl/cbcl, pf, vn, vc]

Babbitt, Milton. *Arie da capo* (1973-74)
[fl, cl/bcl, pf, vn, vc]

Baptist, Maria. *Compositions* (2002)
[3 voices, fl, cl, pf, perc, vn, vc]

Barker, Paul. *The Thief of Songs (Nahuatl and Eng. text)* (1991)
[mez, fl, cl, pf, perc, vn, vc]

Barrett, Richard. *Trawl* (1997)
[fl, bcl, pf, vn, vc]

Beamish, Sally. *Commedia* (1990)
[fl/pic, E♭-cl, pf, vn, vc]

Bedford, David. *Music for Albion Moonlight (Kenneth Patchen)* (1965)
[sop, fl, cl, pf, Hohner alto-melodica, vn, vc]

Bedford, David. *A Garland for Dr K.* (1969)
[fl/afl/pic, cl/bcl, pf/hpd, vn/va, vc]

Bedford, David. *The Sword of Orion* (1970)
[fl, cl, 2 perc (32 instrs), vn, vc, 4 metronomes]

Bedford, David. *The OCD Band and the Minotaur (Elisabeth Gorla)* (1990)
[sop, fl, cl, pf, gui, vn, vc]

Bellamy, Mary. *Constellations* (1999)
[fl, cl, pf, vn, va, vc]

Berio, Luciano. *O King* (1967-68)
[mez, fl, cl, pf, vn, vc]

Berio, Luciano. *The Modification and Instrumentation of a Famous Hornpipe as a Merry and Altogether Sincere Homage to Uncle Alfred* (1969)
[fl (or ob), cl, hpd, perc, va, vc]

Berkeley, Michael. *The Mayfly* (1984)
[fl, cl, pf, perc, vn, vc]

Bettison, Oscar. *Preciosa, tira el pandero* (1995)
[fl, cl, pf, vib, vn, va, vc]

Bettison, Oscar. *Cadence* (2000)
[fl, cl, pf, perc, vn, va, vc]

Bibalo, Antonio. *The Savage: 4 Impressions for 6 Players* (1982-83)
[fl/afl/pic, cl/bcl/sax, pf, perc, vn, vc]

Birtwistle, Harrison. *Monodrama (Stephen Pruslin)* (1967, *since withdrawn*)
[sop/finger cymbals, spkr, fl/afl/pic, B♭-cl/A♭-cl/E♭-cl/bcl, 2 perc, vn, vc]

Birtwistle, Harrison. *Three Lessons in a Frame* (1967, *since withdrawn*)
[fl/pic, cl, pf, perc, vn, vc]

Birtwistle, Harrison. *Ut heremita solus (arr. of Johannes Ockeghem)* (1969)
[fl/afl/pic, cl/bcl, pf, glock, va, vc]

Birtwistle, Harrison. *Cantata (Greek text after Sappho etc.)* (1969)
[sop, fl/pic, high-pitched-cl ('Old Eng. pitch'), pf/cel, glock, vn/va, vc]

Birtwistle, Harrison. *Some Petals from the Garland, a.k.a. Some Petals from my Twickenham Herbarium* (1969)
[pic, cl, pf, glock, va, vc]

Birtwistle, Harrison. *Hoquetus David (after Guillaume de Machaut)* (1969)
[fl/pic, C-cl (or E♭-cl)/B♭-cl, glock/bells, vn, vc]

Birtwistle, Harrison. *Medusa* (1969, rev. 1970, *since withdrawn*)
[fl/pic, B♭-cl/A♭-cl/ssax, pf/cel, perc (xylo/vib/glock/tam-tam/gong), va (rev. = vn/va), vc, 2 tapes, shozyg (rev. = synthesizer) – wind and str ampl.]

Boehmer, Konrad. *Qadar* (1997)
[fl, cl, pf, vn, vc]

Bolcom, William. *Whisper Moon (Dream Music No. 3)* (1971)
[afl, cl, pf, vn, vc]

Boulez, Pierre. *Pour le Dr Kalmus* (1969)
[fl, cl, pf, va, vc]

Boulez, Pierre. *Dérive [I]* (1984)
[fl, A-cl, pf, vib, vn, vc]

Boyle, Rory. *Night's Music* (2004)
[fl/pic, bcl, pf, mar, vn, vc]

Bresnick, Martin. *My Twentieth Century (Tom Andrews)* (2002)
[fl, cl, pf, vn, va, vc (musicians also recite poem)]

Britten, Benjamin. *Dinner Hour* (1935)
[fl, cl, pf, perc, vn, vc]

Britten, Benjamin. *Men Behind the Meters* (1935)
[fl, cl (later ob), pf, perc, vn, vc]

Britten, Benjamin. *Title Music III (How Gas is Made)* (1935)
[fl, cl, pf, perc, vn, vc]

Brown, Earle. *Tracking Pierrot* (1992)
[fl, cl/bcl, pf/cel, vib/mar, vn, vc]

Bryars, Gavin. *Non la conobbe il mondo mentre l'ebbe* (2006)
[fl, cl, pf, perc, vn, vc]

Burrell, Diana. *Double Image* (1999)
[fl, cl, pf, vn, vc]

Bush, Alan. *Canzona* (1985)
[fl, cl, pf, vn, vc]

Butler, Martin. *Jazz Machines* (1990)
[fl/afl/pic, cl/bcl, pf, vib, va, vc]

Butler, Martin. *Going with the Grain* (1991)
[fl/pic, cl/bcl, mar, vn, va, vc = mar with fl/pic, cl/bcl, vn, va, vc]

Butler, Martin. *Two Preludes (arr. of J.S. Bach)* (1992)
[fl, cl, mar, vn, va, vc]

Cage, John. *Seven* (1988)
[fl, cl, pf, perc, vn, va, vc]

Caltabiano, Ronald. *Concerto for Six Players* (1987)
[fl/afl, cl/bcl, pf, vib/mar/crotales, vn, vc]

Capyrin, Dmitri. *Scherzo* (2000)
[fl, cl, pf, perc, vn, vc]

Capyrin, Dmitri. *Inside* (2011)
[fl, cl, pf, vn, vc]

Carter, Elliott. *Triple Duo: Free Fantasy* (1982-83)
[fl/pic, Bb-cl/Eb-cl/bcl, pf, perc, va, vc]

Causton, Richard. *Phoenix* (2006)
[fl, cl, pf, vn, vc]

Charlton, Alan. *Quintetto* (1995)
[fl, cl, pf, vn, vc]

Claren, Sebastian. *Fehlstart* (1999)
[fl, cl, pf, perc, vn, vc]

Clark, Philip. *Voice of an Angel* (2000)
[fl/pic, cl/bcl, pf, perc, vn, va, vc = vn, pf with fl/pic, cl/bcl, pf, perc, vn, va, vc]

Clarke, James. *Delirium* (1996)
[fl/bfl, cl, pf, perc, vn, vc]

Clarke, James. *Untitled No. 6* (2010)
[sop, fl/bfl, cl/bcl, pf, vn, vc]

Cohen, Douglas. *Movement through Stasis* (1992)
[fl/pic, bcl, pf, perc, vn, vc]

Cole, Bruce. *Caesura* (1970)
[fl/pic, cl/bcl, pf, perc, vn, vc]

Cole, Jonathan. *Caught* (1998)
[fl, cl, pf, vib, va, vc]

Crane, Laurence. *Five Pieces for Five Instruments* (1992)
[fl/afl, cl/bcl, pf, vn, vc]

Crane, Laurence. *See Our Lake* (1999)
[afl, cl/bcl, vib, vn, vc]

Crane, Laurence. *Seven Short Pieces* (2004)
[bfl, cl, pf, vn, vc]

Currier, Sebastian. *Static* (2003)
[fl, cl, pf, vn, vc]

Dalby, Martin. *The Dancer Eduardova* (1978)
[fl/afl/pic, cl/bcl, pf/cel(ad lib), perc, vn, vc]

Davies, Peter Maxwell. *Sextet* (1958, publ. as *Septet*, 1972)
[fl, A-cl, bcl, pf, vn, vc – gui added 1972]

Davies, Peter Maxwell. *Notre Dame des Fleurs (Peter Maxwell Davies, 'obscene Fr. text')* (1966)
[sop, mez, cten, fl, A-cl, pf/cel, perc, vn, vc]

Davies, Peter Maxwell. *Antechrist* (1967)
[pic, bcl, 2 or 3 perc, vn, vc]

Davies, Peter Maxwell. *Fantasia and Two Pavans (after Henry Purcell)* (1968)
[fl/pic, cl, perc incl. opt. band-kit, hpd/out-of-tune pf, vn, vc, voice (ad lib, pref. female)]

Davies, Peter Maxwell. *Stedman Caters* (1968)
[fl/pic, cl, hpd, perc, va, vc]

Davies, Peter Maxwell. *Vesalii icones* (1969)
[dancer/out-of-tune-honky-tonk-pf (or played by cond), fl/afl/pic, basset-cl (or A-cl), pf/out-of-tune-autoharp/music-box ('unsuitable' tune)/etc., perc (glock/xylo/etc.), va, vc = vc with ensemble listed]

Davies, Peter Maxwell. *Eight Songs for a Mad King (George III, Randolph Stow)* (1969)
[male voice (bar), fl/pic, cl, pf/hpd/dulcimer, perc, vn, vc]

Davies, Peter Maxwell. *Points and Dances from "Taverner"* (1970)
[*Dances from Act I* = afl, cl, gui, hpd, va, vc]
[*Dances from Act II*, with linking keyb movts = pic, cl, cbn, tpt, trb, pos-org, regal, perc (2 drums)]

Davies, Peter Maxwell. *Nocturnal Dances (Miguel Serrano, Corinthians I 13)* (1969-70)
[sop, fl, cl, pf, perc, va, vc - orig. version with dancers]

Davies, Peter Maxwell. *Cantata "Also hat Gott die Welt geliebet" (after Dietrich Buxtehude)* (1970)
[sop, fl, hpd/cel, vn, vc (or chamber org) – NB. no cl]

Davies, Peter Maxwell. *Missa super L'homme armé (Agnus dei and Luke 22)* (1968, rev. 1971)
[spkr, fl/pic, cl, perc, harm, hpd/cel/honky-tonk-pf, vn, vc, tape (boy's voice; rev. = live perf.); cl, vn, vc, harm also play perc]

Davies, Peter Maxwell. *Tenebrae super Gesualdo (after Carlo Gesualdo)* (1972)
[mez, afl, bcl, hpd/cel/chamber org (or harm), mar/glock, gui, vn/va, vc]

Davies, Peter Maxwell. *Hymn to St Magnus* (1972)
[mez (obbligato), fl, A-cl (or basset-cl), pf/hpd/cel, vn, vc]

Davies, Peter Maxwell. *Veni Sancte Spiritus/Veni Creator Spiritus (after John Dunstable)* (1972)
[afl, A-cl/basset cl, hpd/pf, glock, va, vc]

Davies, Peter Maxwell. *Two Preludes and Fugues (arr. of J.S. Bach)* (1972/74)
[fl/afl, A-cl (or basset-cl), hpd, mar, va, vc]

Davies, Peter Maxwell. *Wedding Telegram (for Gary Kettel)* (1973)
[sop, fl, cl, pf, perc, gui, vn, vc]

Davies, Peter Maxwell. *Fantasia upon One Note (arr. of Purcell, Z745)* (1973)
[afl, basset-cl (or A-cl), hpd/open-string-vc/C-sharp brandy glass, perc (crotales/banjo/mar/rototoms), vn, vc]

Davies, Peter Maxwell. *Renaissance Scottish Dances* (1973)
[fl, cl, perc (glock (or other tuned perc)/mar (or bxylo)/tamb/etc.), gui, vn, vc - in final dance, 'Almayne', drone played by melodica or other free-free instr; also, The Fires instr 'may be adapted according to individual requirements.']

Davies, Peter Maxwell. *Four Instrumental Motets from Early Scottish Originals* (1973-77)
[fl/afl, cl/bcl, cel, 2 perc (mar/crotales/etc.), gui, vn/va, vc]

1. Si Quis Diligit Me (after David Peebles, Francy Heagy) (1973)
[afl, cl, cel, crotales, va, vc]

2. All Sons of Adam (after anon.) (1974)
[afl, cl, cel, mar, gui, va, vc]

3. Our Father Whiche in Heaven Art (after John Angus) (1977)
[fl, B♭-cl/E♭-cl (ad lib), cel, mar, vn, vc]

4. Psalm 124 (after Andrew Kemp) (1974)
[fl/afl, bcl, 2 perc, glock/mar, gui, vn/va, vc]

Davies, Peter Maxwell. *Miss Donnithorne's Maggot (Randolph Stow)* (1974)
[female voice (mez), fl/afl/pic, A-cl, pf, perc (glock/mar/etc.), vn, vc]

Davies, Peter Maxwell. *Nach Bergamo* (1974)
[fl, cl, pf, perc, va, vc]

Davies, Peter Maxwell. *Ave Maris Stella* (1975)
[fl/afl, A-cl (or basset-cl), pf, mar, va, vc]

Davies, Peter Maxwell. *My Lady Lothian's Lilt (wordless)* (1975)
[mez (obbligato), afl, bcl, 2 perc (glock, mar), va, vc]

Davies, Peter Maxwell. *The Blind Fiddler (George Mackay Brown)* (1975-76)
[mez/antique-cym, fl/afl/pic, A-cl (or basset-cl)/bcl, cel/hpd, perc, gui, vn, vc]

Davies, Peter Maxwell. *Kinloche his Fantassie (after William Kinloch)* (1976)
[fl, cl, hpd, glock, vn, vc]

Davies, Peter Maxwell. *Runes from a Holy Island* (1977)
[afl, A-cl, cel, perc (mar/glock/etc.), va, vc]

Davies, Peter Maxwell. *Fiftieth Birthday Greeting for Ernst Widner* (1977)
[fl, cl, keybs, perc, vn, vc]

Davies, Peter Maxwell. *Le Jongleur de Notre Dame: A Masque (Peter Maxwell Davies)* (1978)
[bar, mime, fl/afl/pic, A-cl/bcl, pf/cel, perc, vn, vc, children's band (3 fl, ob, 2 cl, 3 tpt, perc)]

Davies, Peter Maxwell. *Dances from 'The Two Fiddlers'* (1978)
[pic, bcl, pf, perc, vn, vc = vn with pic, bcl, pf, perc, vn, vc]

Davies, Peter Maxwell. *The Bairns Of Brugh: Elegy* (1981)
[pic, bcl, pf, mar, va, vc]

Davies, Peter Maxwell. *Take a Pair of Sparkling Eyes (arr. of Arthur Sullivan)* (1982)
[fl, cl, pf, perc, vn, vc]

Davies, Peter Maxwell. *Image, Reflection, Shadow* (1982)
[fl/afl/pic, A-cl/bcl, pf, cimbalom, vn, vc]

Davies, Peter Maxwell. *The No. 11 Bus for Mime, Singers, Dancers and Instrumental Ensemble* (1983-84)
[mez, ten, bar, mime, 2 dancers, fl/pic, cl/bcl, pf/cel, perc (mar/rock-band kit/etc.), vn, vc]

Davies, Peter Maxwell. *Unbroken Circle* (1984)
[afl, bcl, pf, va, vc]

Davies, Peter Maxwell. *Music in Camera* (1986)
[fl, cl, pf/hpd, perc, vn, vc]

Davies, Peter Maxwell. *Winterfold (George Mackay Brown)* (1986)
[mez, afl, bcl, pf, perc (mar/glock/etc.), gui, vn, vc]

Davies, Peter Maxwell. *Excuse Me: Parlour Songs (arr. of Charles Dibdin)* (1986)
[mez, fl, B♭-cl/A-cl, pf, perc (glock/mar/woodblocks/etc.), vn, vc]

Davies, Peter Maxwell. *Farewell - A Fancye (arr. of John Dowland)* (1986)
[afl, bcl, pf, mar, va, vc]

Davies, Peter Maxwell. *A Birthday Card for Hans (Lorenzo da Ponte)* (1996)
[mez, afl, bcl, pf, mar, va, vc]

Davies, Peter Maxwell. *Two Glasses of Wine [= A Glass of Frontignac and A Glass of Shiraz]* (2000/02)
[fl, cl, pf/keybs, perc (incl. mar), vn, vc]

Davies, Peter Maxwell. *A Glass of Frontignac [publ. with A Glass of Shiraz as Two Glasses of Wine]* (2000)
[fl, cl, keybs, perc, vn, vc]

Davies, Peter Maxwell. *A Glass of Shiraz [publ. with A Glass of Frontignac as Two Glasses of Wine]* (2002)
[fl, cl, pf, mar, vn, vc]

Davies, Tansy. *Two Part Invention in Unison* (1999, *since withdrawn*)
[fl/pic, cl, pf, perc, vn, va, vc]

Davies, Tansy. *grind show (electric) / grind show (* unplugged)* (2007)
[fl, cl, pf (prepared [*/processed]), vn, vc, [* sampler = electronics/CD])

Davies, Tansy. *Undertow* (1999, rev. 2000)
[fl, cl, pf, vn, vc]

Davies, Tansy. *Patterning* (2000)
[pic, cl, pf, perc, vn, vc]

Davidovsky, Mario. *Biblical Songs* (1990)
[sop, fl, cl, pf, vn, vc]

Davidovsky, Mario. *Flashbacks* (1995)
[fl/afl/pic, cl/bcl, pf, perc, vn, vc]

Dench, Chris. *eigenmomenta* (2001)
[fl/afl/pic, cl/bcl, pf, vib/crotales, vn, vc]

Denisov, Edison. *La Vie en rouge (Boris Vian)* (1973)
[sop, fl, cl, pf, perc, vn, vc]

Dillon, James. *who do you love* (1980-81)
[voice, fl/pic/bfl, bcl (or cl or ca), perc, vn/va, vc – alternatively, Renaissance instrs.]

Donatoni, Franco. *Etwas Ruhiger im Ausdruck* (1967)
[fl, cl, pf, vn, vc]

Donatoni, Franco. *Lumen* (1975)
[fl, cl, cel, perc, va, vc]

Donatoni, Franco. *Arpége* (1986)
[fl, cl, pf, vib, vn, vc]

Donatoni, Franco. *L'ultima sera* (1980)
[sop, fl, cl, pf, vn, vc]

Dresher, Paul. *The Tyrant (Jim Lewis)* (2005)
[male voice, fl/afl/pic, cls, keybs, perc, vn, vc]

Druce, Duncan. *The Tower of Needles* (1970-71)
[sop, fl/pic, cl, pf, perc, vn/va, vc]

Druce, Duncan. *Märchenzeit* (1974)
[fl, cl, pf, perc, vn, vc]

Druce, Duncan. *The Creator's Shadow* (1975)
[fl, basset-cl, pf, perc (crotales/mar/handbells/gongs), gui, va, vc]

Druckman, Jacob. *Come Round* (1992)
[afl, cl, pf, 1 or 2 perc, vn, vc)

Duddell, Joe. *Grace Under Pressure* (2007)
[fl, bcl, pf, mar, vn, vc]

Durkó, Zsolt. *Fire Music (Sextet)* (1970-71)
[fl/pic/afl.cl/bcl, pf, vn, va, vc]

Edlin, Paul Max. *Five Fantastic Islands* (1993)
[fl/afl, cl, pf, perc, va, vc]

Edwards, Ross. *Laikan* (1979)
[fl, cl, pf, perc, vn, vc]

Eisler, Hanns. *Palmström: Studien über Zwölfton-Reihen* (1924)
[*Sprechstimme*, fl/pic, A-cl, vn/va, vc]

Eisler, Hanns. *Vierzehn Arten den Regen zu beschreiben* (1940-41)
[fl, cl, pf, vn, va, vc]

Elias, Brian. *Geranos* (1985)
[fl/afl/pic, B♭-cl/E♭-cl/bcl(ext. to B♭), pf, perc, vn/va, vc]

Ellis, Nicola. *S.O.S.* (1990)
[fl, cl, pf, vn, vc]

Emsley, Richard. *...from swerve of shore to bend of bay...* (1985)
[afl/pic, E♭-cl, pf, perc, va, vc]

Erb, Donald. *Quintet* (1976)
[fl/harmonica/goblet, cl/goblet, pf/elec-pf-with-phase-shifter/goblet, vn/goblet, vc/goblet]

Erkoreka, Gabriel. *Krater* (1984)
[fl, cl, pf, mar, vn, vc]

Febel, Reinhard. *Sextet* (1977)
[fl, cl, pf, vib, vn, vc = with vib with fl, cl, pf, vn, vc]

Feldman, Morton. *The viola in my life (1)* (1970)
[fl, pf, perc, vn, va, vc = va with fl, pf, perc, vn, vc - NB. no cl]

Feldman, Morton. *The viola in my life (2)* (1970)
[fl, cl, cel, perc, vn, va, vc = va with fl, cl, cel, perc, vn, va, vc]

Feldman, Morton. *I met Heine on the Rue Fürstenberg (wordless)* (1971)
[voice, fl/pic, cl/bcl, pf, perc (vib/chimes/etc.), vn, vc]

Feldman, Morton. *For Frank O'Hara* (1973)
[fl/afl/pic, cl, pf, 2 perc (xylo/glock/vib/chimes/etc.), vn, vc]

Ferneyhough, Brian. *On Stellar Magnitudes (Ferneyhough)* (1994)
[mez, fl/pic, cl/bcl, pf, vn, vc]

Festinger, Richard. *Septet* (1987)
[fl, cl, pf, perc, vn, va, vc]

Festinger, Richard. *A Serenade for Six* (1993)
[fl/pic, cl/bcl, pf, perc, vn, vc]

Festinger, Richard. *After Blue* (1998)
[fl/pic, cl/bcl, pf, perc, vn, vc]

Field, Robin. *Aubade (David Gascoyne)* (1969)
[sop, afl, cl, harp, vn, vc]

Fink, Simon. *Falling* (2001)
[fl, cl, pf, perc, vn, vc]

Fink, Simon. *Swell* (2006)
[fl, cl, pf, vn, vc]

Finnissy, Michael. *Mr Punch* (1976-77, rev. 1979)
[voice (9 roles), fl/pic, E♭-cl (or ob), pf, perc, vn, vc (not if ob used)]

Finnissy, Michael. *Kritik der Urteilskraft* (2001)
[fl, cl, pf, vn, vc]

Finnissy, Michael. *Regen beschreiben* (2001)
[afl, cl, pf, vn, vc]

Fitch, Keith. *Dancing the Shadows* (1994)
[fl/pic, cl/bcl, pf, perc, vn, vc]

Fitkin, Graham. *Ardent* (1993)
[fl, cl, pf, mar, vn, vc]

Fitkin, Graham. *Totti* (2004)
[fl, cl/bcl, pf, mar, vn, vc]

Forbes, Sebastian. *Death's Dominion (Langenheim)* (1971)
[ten, fl, cl, pf, vn, va, vc]

Ford, Andrew. *Chamber Concerto No. 1* (1979)
[fl/pic, cl, pf, vn, va, vc]

Foster, Derek. *The October Country* (1977)
[fl, cl, pf, vn, vc]

Fowler, Jennifer. *"Echoes..."* (2001)
[fl, cl, pf, vn, vc]

Frances-Hoad, Cheryl. *The Glory Tree (6th-8thC. Old Eng. poems on Shamanic rituals)* (2005)
[sop, fl/pic, cl/bcl, pf, vn, vc]

Froom, David. *Chamber Concerto* (1991)
[fl, cl, pf, vib/mar, vn, vc]

Froom, David. *Fantasy Dances* (2000)
[fl, cl, pf, perc, vn, va, vc]

Füssl, Karl Heinz. *Miorita: Altrümanische Volksballade, Op. 1* (1963)
[ten (or sop), female choir (ad lib), fl/afl, cl/bcl, pf/cel, vn/va, vc]

Gervasoni, Stefano. *Due poesie francesi d'Ungaretti* (1994)
[voice, fl, cl, pf, vn, vc]

Gilbert, Anthony. *Mother* (1969)
[wooden-fl/pic, elec.-basset-cl/bcl/sharp-pitch-B♭-cl/E♭-cl, Hammond org (or pf with elec.-keyb attachment), perc, vn/elec.-va, vc (with elec. ampl.) = vc (with elec. ampl.) with ensemble listed]

Gilbert, Anthony. *Calls Around Chungmori* (1979)
[fl, cl, perc, va, vc]

Gordon, Michael Zev. *...by the edge of the forest of desires* (2000)
[fl, cl, pf, vib, cel, vn, va, vc]

Grange, Philip. *Cimmerian Nocturne* (1979)
[pic, bcl, pf, mar, vn, vc]

Grange, Philip. *The Dark Labyrinth* (1986)
[fl/afl, cl/basset-cl, pf, vn, va = vc with fl/afl, cl/basset-cl, pf, vn, va - NB. no vc]

Grange, Philip. *Des fins sont des commencements* (1994)
[fl, cl, pf, perc, vn, vc]

Grange, Philip. *Lament of the Bow* (2000)
[fl, cl, pf, perc, vn, vc]

Grime, Helen. *Quintet* (2002)
[fl, cl, pf, vn, vc]

Grime, Helen. *Blurred Edges* (2004)
[fl/pic, cl/bcl, hp, pf, vn, vc]

Grinberg, Olexander. *House Plant* (1993)
[fl, cl, pf, perc, vn, vc]

Grisey, Gérard. *Taléa* (1986)
[fl, cl, pf, vn, vc]

Grisey, Gérard. *Vortex Temporum I-III* (1996)
[fl, cl, pf, vn, va, vc]

Grossner, Sonja. *Survival: The Story of a Cheetah* (1997)
[fl/afl/pic, cl/bcl, pf, perc, vn, va, vc]

Gustavson, Mark. *A Fool's Journey* (1999)
[fl/afl/pic, cl/bcl, pf, perc, vn, vc]

Hänschke, Bernd. *Changeant I* (1992)
[fl, cl, pf, perc, vn, vc]

Haas, Georg Friedrich. *Sextett* (1992-96)
[fl/bfl/pic, cl/bcl, pf, perc, vn, vc]

Haas, Georg Friedrich. *tria ex uno (after Josquin Desprez)* (2001)
[fl/afl, cl/bcl, pf, perc, vn/va, vc]

Halffter, Cristóbal. *Oda para felicitar a un amigo* (1969)
[afl, bcl, pf/cel, perc, va, vc]

Halle, John. *Vox Pop* (1994)
[fl, cl, pf, perc, vn, vc]

Hannan, Geoffrey. *Centrifugal Bumblepuppy* (1999)
[pic, bcl, pf, perc, vn, vc, db]

Harbison, John. *The Natural World* (1984-86)
[mez, fl, cl, pf, vn, vc]

Harper, Edward. *Quintet* (1974)
[fl, cl, pf, vn, vc]

Harrington, Jeffrey. *KaleidoPsychoTropos* (1995)
[fl, cl, pf, vn, vc]

Harris, Donald. *GunMar Music (Albert Giraud, trans. Otto Erich Hartleben)* (1988)
[sop, fl, cl/bcl, pf, vn/va, vc]

Harrison, Bryn. *time and intervention* (2000)
[fl/afl, cl/bcl, pf, vn, vc]

Harrison, Bryn. *Second In Nomine after William Byrd* (2004)
[afl, cl, pf, vn, va, vc]

Harrison, Sadie. *"and who now will wake the dead?"* (2004)
[fl, cl, pf, vn, va, vc]

Harrison, Sadie. *Quintet: 'No Title Required'* (1994, rev. 1999)
[fl, cl, pf, vn, vc]

Harry, Martyn. *George Meets Arnie for Tennis* (2004)
[fl/pic, cl/bcl, pf/synth, vn, vc]

Hartikainen, Jarkko. *Frankfurt Quintet No. 3* (2009)
[fl, cl, pf, vn, vc]

Hartikainen, Jarkko. *magnetic* (2011)
[fl, cl, pf, vn, vc]

Harvey, Jonathan. *Inner Light 1* (1973)
[fl, cl, pf, perc, vn, va, vc, tape]

Harvey, Jonathan. *Quantumplation* (1973)
[fl, cl, pf, tam-tam, vn, vc]

Haubenstock-Ramati, Roman. *Rounds* (1969)
[fl, cl, pf, vib, va, vc]

Hayden, Sam. *Partners in Psychopathology* (1998)
[afl/pic, bcl/E♭-cl, pf, vib/xylo, va, vc]

Hayes, Morgan. *Snapshots* (1994)
[fl, cl, pf, vn, vc]

Hayes, Morgan. *Alluvial* (1999)
[afl/pic, cl/bcl, pf, perc, vn, vc, db]

Hayes, Morgan. *Buoy* (1999)
[fl/afl/pic, cl/bcl, pf, va, vc]

Hellawell, Piers. *How Should I Your True Love Know?* (1984)
[fl, cl, pf, perc, gui, va, vc]

Hellawell, Piers. *Sound Carvings from the Ice Wall* (1995)
[fl/afl, cl/bcl, pf, perc, va, vc, db]

Hellewell, David. *Synergy* (1970)
[fl, cl, pf, perc, vn, vc]

Henze, Hans Werner. *Sonate für sechs Spieler (derived from L'amour à mort)*
(1984)
[fl/pic, sistra-cl/bcl/dbcl(ad lib)/handbells, pf/cel, perc, vn/handbells, vc/handbells]

Hervig, Richard. *Chamber Music for Six Players* (1976)
[fl, cl/bcl, pf, perc, vn, db]

Hesketh, Kenneth. *Dei Destini Incrociati* (2002)
[fl, cl, pf, perc, vn, vc]

Hesketh, Kenneth. *Fra Duri Scogli* (2002]
[fl, cl, pf, perc, vn, vc]

Hidalgo, Manuel. *Quintett* (1990)
[fl, cl, pf, vn, vc]

Hind, Rolf. *The Horse Sacrifice* (2001)
[fl/bfl/trbrec, B♭-cl/E♭-cl/rec, pf/ratchet/triangles, vn, vc]

Hoyland, Vic. *Seneca / Medea* (1985)
[sop, alt, ten, bass, afl, cl, pf, perc, vn, vc]

Hopkins, John. *Round* (1974)
[fl, cl, pf, va, vc]

Hopkins, John. *Se la face ay pale* (1977)
[fl/afl/pic, cl/bcl, perc, vn, vc]

Hopkins, John. *The Cloud Of Unknowing* (1978)
[fl/afl/pic, cl/bcl, pf/cel, perc, vn/va, vc]

Hopkins, John. *For The Far Journey* (1981)
[sop, fl/afl/pic, B♭-cl/E♭-cl/bcl, hpd, vn, vc]

Hopkins, John. *Fuga Canonica* (1981)
[fl/afl, cl/bcl, hpd, vn, vc]

Horne, David. *Contraries and Progressions* (1991)
[fl, cl, pf, vn/va, vc]

Horne, David. *Concerto for Six Players* (1993)
[fl/pic, cl/bcl, pf, perc (vib (bowed, sticks)/mar/etc.), vn, vc]

Hoyland, Vic. *Crazy Rosa - La Madre* (1988)
[sop, fl/afl, cl, pf, 2 mar, hp, va, vc]

Huber, Nicolaus A. *La Force du Vertige* (1985)
[fl/pic, cl, pf, perc, vn, vc]

Hughes, Edward Dudley. *The Devil's Drum (Roger Morris)* (1998)
[mez, ten, fl, cl, pf, perc, vn, vc]

Hughes, Edward Dudley. *Sextet* (1999)
[fl, cl, pf, mar/vib, vn, vc]

Hughes, Edward Dudley. *Light Cuts through Dark Skies* (2001)
[fl, cl, pf, vn, vc]

Hughes, Edward Dudley. *The Sibyl of Cumae (Tom Lowenstein)* (2001)
[mez, fl/afl/pic, cl/bcl, pf, perc, vn, vc, db]

Hurel, Philippe. *Pour Luigi* (1993)
[fl, cl, pf, vn, vc]

Imbrie, Andrew. *Pilgrimage* (1983)
[fl/afl/pic, Bb-cl/Eb-cl/bcl, pf, perc, vn, vc]

Imbrie, Andrew. *Earplay Fantasy* (1995)
[fl, cl, pf, perc, vn, vc]

Imbrie, Andrew. *Songs of Then and Now* (1998)
[sop, alt, fl, cl, pf, perc, vn, vc]

Ince, Kamran. *Waves of Talya* (1989)
[fl, cl, pf, perc, vn, vc]

Ingoldsby, Tom. *Three Small Litanies (Latin, liturgical)* (1990)
[sop, fl/pic, cl/bcl, pf, vn, vc]

Jarrell, Michael. *Trei II (François le Lionnais, Konrad Bayer, Richard D. Laing)*
(1982-83)
[sop/crotales/chimes, fl/claves/maracas, cl/bcl/maracas/tam-tam, pf/tabla,
vn/woodblock/tam-tam, vc/wood-drum/maracas]

Jarvinen, Arthur. *Isoluminaries* (1995)
[fl, bcl, pf, perc, vn, vc]

Karchin, Louis. *Songs of John Keats* (1984)
[sop, fl, cl, pf, perc, vn, vc]

Karchin, Louis. *Galactic Folds* (1992)
[fl/pic, cl, pf, vn, vc]

Karchin, Louis. *'A Way Separate...' (Ruth Whitman, Hannah Senesh)* (1992)
[sop, fl/pic, cl, pf, vn, vc]

Karchin, Louis. *American Visions: Two Songs on Poems of Yevgeny Yevtushenko* (1998)
[bar, fl/pic, cl/bcl, pf, perc, vn, vc]

Karchin, Louis. *Orpheus: A Masque (Stanley Kunitz)* (2003)
[bar, dancers, fl/pic, cl/bcl, pf, perc, vn, vc]

Kaufmann, Dieter. *Trois Poèmes de Stéphane Mallarmé, Op. 9a* (1967/83)
[sop, fl, cl, pf, vn, vc]

Kay, Alison. *Rat-race* (2000)
[fl, cl, pf, perc, vn, vc]

Kay, Alison. *Godafoss and Breaking Line* (2002)
[fl/pic, cl/bcl, pf, perc, vn, vc, db]

Kay, Alison. *Flux* (2006)
[fl/pic, cl/bcl, pf, vn, vc]

Kee Yong, Chong. *'Mourning the murder of an old banyan tree'* (2002)
[fl/afl/pic, cl/bcl, pf, perc, vn, vc]

Kee Yong, Chong. *'Yuan He': Concerto for Five Chinese Instruments and Five Western Instruments* (2010)
[Sheng, GuZheng, Er-hu, Dizi, Yan Qin / fl, cl, pf, vn, vc]

Kessner, Daniel. *Two Visions* (1991)
[fl, cl, pf, vn, vc]

Kessner, Daniel. *Harmonic Space* (2003)
[fl, cl, perc, vn, vc]

Kessner, Daniel. *A Tempo* (2012)
[fl, cl/bcl, pf, mar/xylo, vn, vc]

King, Alastair. *Ascension (Samuel Beckett)* (1990)
[sop, fl, cl, pf, vn, vc]

Kmitova, Jana. *Kamea* (2000-01)
[fl, cl, pf, perc, vn, vc]

Knussen, Oliver. *Ocean de Terre, Op. 10 (Guillaume Apollinaire)* (1973)
[sop, fl/afl, cl/bcl, pf/cel, 1 or 2 perc, vn, vc, db]

Kolberg, Kåre. *Ennå Er Der Håp* (1978)
[fl, cl, pf, perc, vn, vc]

Kondo, Jo. *Contour Lines* (1999)
[fl, cl, pf, perc, vn, vc]

Kraft, William. *Gallery '83* (1983)
[fl/pic, cl/bcl, pf/cel, perc, vn, vc]

Kraft, William. *Mélange* (1985)
[fl/afl, cl/bcl, pf/cel, perc, vn, vc]

Kraft, William. *Suite from 'Cascando'* (1988)
[fl, cl, pf, vn, vc]

Kraft, William. *Settings from Pierrot Lunaire (Albert Giraud, trans. Otto Erich Hartleben)* (1987-91)
[sop, fl/picc, cl/bcl, pf, vn/va, vc]

Kraft, William. *Vintage Renaissance and Beyond* (2005)
[fl, cl, pf, vn, va, vc]

Kramer, Jonathan. *Atlanta Licks* (1984)
[fl, cl, pf, vn, va, pf]

Kreiger, Arthur. *Meeting Places* (1995)
[fl/afl, cl/bcl, pf, perc, vn, vc, DAT tape]

Kretz, Johannes. *Dynamische Gewächse* (1999)
[fl, cl, pf, vn, vc, electronics]

Kyburz, Hanspeter. *Danse aveugle* (1997)
[fl, cl, pf, vn, vc]

Kyr, Robert. *Maelstrom (Emily Dickinson, Dylan Thomas)* (1983)
[sop, fl, cl, pf, perc, vn, vc]

Lancaster, David. *De rerum naturae* (1982)
[fl/afl, cl, hpd, vib, gui, vn, vc]

Láng, István. *Rhymes* (1972)
[fl, cl, pf, va, vc]

Lash, Hannah. *Subtilior, Lamento* (2011)
[fl, cl, pf, vib/chimes, vn, vc]

Lavenda, Richard. *Alliances* (2003)
[fl, cl, pf, vn, vc]

Leach, Rachel. *Green Plastic, Pink Oil and Water* (1998)
[fl, cl, pf, perc, va, vc]

Lee, Eun Young. *a quiet way (Emily Dickinson)* (2006)
[fl/afl, cl/bcl, pf, perc, vn, vc]

Lee, Joanna. *Pierrot!* (2005)
[female voice, fl/pic, cl/bcl, pf, vn, vc]

Lee, Joanna. *Elephant Woman: A Woman's Love and Life (Jo Shapcott, E.E. Cummings etc.)* (2007)
[voice, fl, cl, pf, va, vc]

LeFanu, Nicola. *The Same Day Dawns* (1974)
[sop, fl/afl, bcl/cl, perc (vib/mar/etc.), vn, vc]

LeFanu, Nicola. *Sextet: A Wild Garden-Fásach* (1996-97)
[fl/afl/pic, cl/bcl, pf, perc, vn, vc]

Lewis, Jeffrey. *Epitaph For Abelard and Heloise* (1979)
[fl/afl, cl, pf, perc, vn, vc]

Lindberg, Magnus. *Quintetto dell'estate* (1979)
[fl, cl, pf, vn, vc]

Lloyd, Jonathan. *Symphony No. 5* (1989)
[fl/pic, cl, pf, perc, vn/va, vc]

Lobbett, Gary. *Resti Euta: Isle of the Dead* (1995)
[fl/pic, cl/bcl, pf, perc, vn, vc]

Lohse, Horst. *A. Schmidts Monde* (1995)
[spkr, fl, cl, pf, vn, vc]

Lorraine, Ross. *Within What Changelessness* (2004)
[fl, cl, pf, vib, vn, vc]

Lumsdaine, David. *Mandala 2 (Catches Catch)* (1969)
[fl/afl/pic, basset-cl (or A-cl), perc, va, vc]

Lumsdaine, David. *Mandala 3* (1978)
[fl, cl, pf, Chinese bell, va, vc = solo pf with fl, cl, Chinese bell, va, vc]

Lumsdaine, David. *Bagatelles* (1985)
[fl, cl, pf, vn, va, vc]

Lutyens, Elisabeth. *Concertante for Five Players* (1950)
[fl/pic, cl/bcl, pf, vn/va, vc]

Mackey, Steven. *Indigenous Instruments* (1989)
[fl/afl/pic, cl, pf, vn, vc]

Mackey, Steven. *Micro-concerto for Percussion and Five Players* (1999)
[fl, cl, pf, perc, vn, vc = solo perc with fl, cl, pf, vn, vc]

MacLeod, Jenny. *For Seven* (1965)
[fl, cl, pf, vib/mar, vn, va, vc]

Martino, Donald. *Notturno* (1973)
[fl/afl/pic, cl/bcl, pf, perc, vn/va, vc]

Mann, Terry. *Quintet* (1998)
[fl, cl, pf, vn, vc]

Mann, Terry. *Quintet for St Swithun* (1999)
[fl/afl, cl/bcl, pf, vn, vc]

Marsh, Roger. *The Wormwood And The Gall: A Lament (Jeremiah)* (1981)
[mez, fl/afl, cl, perc, hp, va, vc]

Martin, Phillip Neil. *Die Fackel* (2003)
[fl/pic, cl/bcl, pf, perc, vn, vc]

Matthews, Colin. *Elegiac Chaconne* (1997)
[afl, bcl, pf, va, vc]

Martland, Steve. *Remembering Lennon* (1981, rev. 1985)
[fl, cl/w̄ine glass, perc, pf/wine glass, vn/wine glass, va, vc]

Maw, Nicholas. *Ghost Dances: Imaginary Ballet for 5 Players* (1988)
[fl/afl/pic/manjeera(= small finger cym), B♭-cl/E♭-cl/A-cl/bcl/manjeera/kazoo (or by flautist), pf/manjeera/kalimba(= Afr. thumb pf), vn/manjeera/strumstick(= Amer. one-string banjo-type instr.), vc/manjeera/flexatone]

Mazulis, Rytis. *Canon mensurabilis* (2000)
[fl, cl, pf, vn, va, vc]

McGarr, Peter. *Vanishing Games* (1995)
[fl/pic/srec/ocarina, cl/bcl/ocarina, pf, perc, vn, vc, off-stage assistant]

McGuire, Edward. *Rebirth* (1974)
[fl/afl, cl/bcl, pf/cel, perc, vn, vc]

McGuire, Edward. *Euphoria* (1980)
[fl/afl/pic, cl/bcl, pf, mar, vn, vc]

McGuire, Edward. *Quintet II* (1987)
[fl, cl, pf, vn, vc]

McNeff, Stephen. *Counting (One)* (2007)
[fl, cl, pf, perc (opt.), vn, vc]

McPherson, Gordon. *Explore Yourself* (2000)
[fl, cl, pf, perc, vn, vc]

Meale, Richard. *Incredible Floridas (Homage to Arthur Rimbaud)* (1971)
[fl/afl/pic, cl/bcl, pf, perc, vn/va, vc]

Metcalf, John. *Dance from Kafka's Chimp* (1993)
[fl, cl, pf, mar, vn, vc]

Moore, Ian. *La Mort des artistes* (1996)
[fl, cl, pf, perc, vn, vc]

Moore, Ian. *Palette de Couleur et de Lumière* (1997)
[fl, cl, pf, perc, vn, vc]

Moore, Timothy. *Sincerest Flattery* (1999)
[fl, A-cl, pf, vn, vc]

Mosko, Stephen L. *Psychotropes* (1993)
[fl/pic, cl/bcl, pf, perc, vn, vc]

Mowitz Ira J. *Shimmerings* (2004)
[afl/pic, cl/bcl, pf, glock, vn, vc, digital soundtrack]

Mozzi, Gustavo. *"the eyes of the night"*
[fl, cl, pf, acc/bandoneón, perc, vn, vc]

Muldowney, Dominic. *Solo/Ensemble* (1974)
[fl/pic, cl, pf, 3 perc, va, vc]

Muldowney, Dominic. *Five Theatre Poems (Bertolt Brecht)* (1980)
[mez, fl, cl, pf, vn, va, vc]

Muldowney, Dominic. *In Dark Times (Bertolt Brecht)* (1981)
[sop, alto, ten, bass, fl/pic, cl/bcl, pf, va, vc]

Mulvey, Grainne. *Sextet Uno* (1997)
[fl/afl/pic, cl/bcl, pf, perc, vn, vc]

Murail, Tristan. *Treize couleurs du soleil couchant* (1978)
[fl, cl, pf, vn, vc, electronics (ad lib)]

Murail, Tristan. *La Barque mystique* (1993)
[fl, cl, pf, vn, vc]

Murail, Tristan. *Winter Fragments* (2000)
[fl, cl, pf, vn, vc, Apple Macintosh, MIDI keyb, amplification, reverberation]

Musgrave, Thea. *Chamber Concerto No. 2* (1966)
[fl/afl/pic, cl/bcl(ext. to Bb), pf, vn/va, vc]

Newland, Paul. *some like horrorshow music for a malenky bit of the old U.V.*
   (Lament for the death of Linus) (1993)
[fl/afl/pic, Bb-cl/Eb-cl/bcl, pf, perc, vn, vc]

Newland, Paul. *time quivers* (2008)
[afl, cl, pf, perc, vn, vc]

Nicholls, David. *Reflections and Refractions* (1978)
[fl, cl, pf, vn, va, vc]

Nicholls, David. *Mosaic 1* (1986)
[fl, cl, pf, vib, vn, vc]

Nicholson, George. *Aubade (Anon.)* (1981)
[sop, afl, cl, pf, va, vc]

Nicholson, George. *Idyll (Thomas Hardy)* (2003)
[sop, fl, bcl, pf, va, vc]

Nicolson, Alistair. *Punch!* (1994)
[fl/pic, cl/bcl, pf, perc, vn, vc]

Northcott, Bayan. *Sextet* (1985)
[fl/pic, cl/bcl, pf, perc, vn, vc]

Nunn, Patrick. *Hextych: Six Impressions on Six Paintings by Philip Core*
   (2001)
[fl/afl, cl/bcl, pf, vn, vc, taped gramophone]

Nunn, Patrick. *Momenta* (2005)
[fl/afl, cbcl, hp, pf, vn, vc]

Nunn, Patrick. *Cruise* (2007)
[fl, cl, pf, vn, vc]

Nyman, Michael. *Acts of Beauty* (2004)
[sop, fl, cl, pf, perc, vn, vc]

Nyman, Michael. *Viola and Piano* (2009)
[fl, cl, pf, vn, vc]

Ocker, David. *Pride and Foolishness* (1986)
[fl, cl/bcl, pf, mar/vib, vn, vc]

Oesterle, Michael. *Urban Canticle* (1995/99)
[fl, cl, pf, perc, vn, vc]

Oliveros, Pauline. *Aeolian Partitions* (1970)
[fl/afl/pic, cl/bcl, pf, vn/va, vc, six assistants (stage hands, stage manager, etc.)]

Pagliarani, Mario. *Pierrot lunatique* (1993)
[voice, fl/pic, cl/bcl, pf, vn/va, vc]

Panufnik, Roxanna. *Colombine, Too* (1995)
[mez, fl, cl, pf, vn, vc]

Parkin, Simon. *Three Pieces for Mixed Sextet* (1991)
[fl, cl, pf, mar, vn, vc]

Parkin, Michael. *Aware (Issa: Jap. haiku)* (1987)
[sop, fl, cl, pf, perc, vn, vc]

Parkinson, Tim. *untitled quintet* (2002)
[fl/pic, cl/bcl, pf, vn, vc]

Patterson, Paul. *Floating Music* (1974)
[fl, cl, pf/cel, perc, vn, vc]

Payne, Anthony. *A Day in the Life of a Mayfly* (1981)
[fl/pic, cl, pf, perc, vn, vc]

Perle, George. *Critical Moments* (1996)
[fl, cl, pf, perc, vn, vc]

Perle, George. *Critical Moments 2* (2001)
[fl, cl, pf, perc, vn, vc]

Poppe, Enno. *Geloschte Lieder* (1997)
[fl, cl, pf, vn, vc]

Powell, Jonathan. *Saturnine* (2000)
[fl, cl, pf, perc, vn, va, vc]

Powell, Mel. *Sextet* (1996)
[fl, cl, pf/cel, perc, vn, vc]

Powers, Anthony. *Another Part of the Island* (1980, rev. 1994)
[fl/afl/pic, B♭-cl/A-cl(or basset-cl), pf/cel, mar/glock/crotales, vn, vc]

Powers, Anthony. *Fast Colours* (1997)
[fl/afl/pic, cl/bcl, pf, vn, vc]

Powers, Anthony. *From Station Island* (2003)
[male spkr, bar, fl/afl/pic, cl/bcl, perc, hp, vn, vc]

Primosch, James. *Sacra conversazione* (1994)
[fl/afl/pic, cl/bcl, pf, perc, vn, vc, tape]

Pritchard, Deborah. *Chanctonbury Ring* (2000)
[fl, cl, pf, perc, vn, vc]

Pritchard, Gwyn. *Ensemble Music for Six* (1976)
[fl, cl, pf, vn, va, vc]

Pritchard, Gwyn. *Chamber Concerto* (1985)
[fl, cl, pf vn, vc]

Ran, Shulamit. *O, The Chimneys* (1969)
[mez, fl, cl/bcl, pf, perc, vc, tape]

Rands, Bernard. *Monotone* (1969)
[fl/afl, cl/bcl, pf, perc (bongos/gong/vib/etc.), va, vc]

Redgate, Roger. *Pierrot on the Stage of Desire* (1998)
[fl, cl, pf, perc, vn, vc]

Reich, Steve. *Double Sextet* (2007)
[fl, cl, pf, vib, vn, vc, pre-recorded tape (of fl, cl, pf, vib, vn, vc) or 2 fl, 2 cl, 2 pf, 2 vib, 2 vn, 2 vc]

Reynolds, Belinda. *Coming Around* (1995)
[fl, cl, pf, vn, vc]

Reynolds, Peter. *Old King Cole* (1994)
[fl/afl, cl, pf, vn, vc]

Rhys, Paul. *Chicago Fall* (1992)
[fl/afl, cl, pf, hpd/cel, vib/bmar, hp, vn, vc, 2 synth/sampler]

Richard, André. *Musique de Rue: Szenische Aktionsmusik* (1987)
[fl, cl, pf, perc, vn, vc, tape = perc with fl, cl, pf, vn, vc, tape]

Roberts, Jeremy Dale. *Reconciliation* (1969)
[spkr, fl/perc, cl/perc, pf, perc, vn, va, vc]

Roberts, Paul. *Fractures (John Ashbery)* (1988)
[sop, afl, cl, pf, perc, va, vc]

Robinson, Paul. *Webernera* (2000)
[fl/pic, cl/bcl, pf, vn, vc]

Rohde, Kurt. *this bag is not a toy – a very short concerto for small mixed ensemble without orchestra* (2011)
[fl/pic, bcl, pf, perc, vn, vc]

Rulon, C. Bryan. *Divine Detours* (1993)
[fl, cl, perc, vn, vc; ensemble and cond. also play music box]

Runchak, Volodymyr. *Time "X..." or farewell no-symphony* (1998)
[fl, cl, pf, vn, vc]

Rzewski, Frederic. *Pocket Symphony* (2000)
[fl, cl, pf, perc, vn, vc]

Santoro, Claudio. *Música de câmera* (1944)
[fl, bcl, pf, vn, vc]

Saxton, Robert. *La Promenade d'automne* (1973)
[sop, fl, cl, pf, perc, vn, va, vc]

Saxton, Robert. *The Sentinel of the Rainbow* (1984)
[fl/afl/pic, B♭-cl/E♭-cl/bcl, pf/cel, vn/va, vc]

Schidlowsky, Leon. *Sextet* (1970)
[fl/pic, cl/bcl, pf, perc, vn, vc]

Schneid, Tobias P.M. *Weird Scenes Inside the Mirror Cages* (2000)
[fl, cl, pf, perc, vn, va, vc]

Schoenberg, Arnold. *Pierrot lunaire, Op. 21 (Albert Giraud, trans. Otto Erich Hartleben)* (1912)
[*Sprechstimme*, fl/pic, B♭-cl/A-cl/bcl, pf, vn/va, vc]

Schwantner, Joseph. *Music of Amber* (1980-81)
[fl, cl/bcl, pf, perc, vn, vc]

Schwehr, Cornelius. *'aber die Schönheit des Gitters'* (1992-93)
[fl, cl, pf, perc, vn, va, vc, film projection (ad lib)]

Shchetynsky, Olexander. *Way to Meditation* (1990)
[fl, cl, pf, vn, vc]

Sherlaw Johnson, Robert. *Triptych* (1973)
[fl, cl, pf, perc, pf, vn, vc]

Simpson, Julia. *A Beast of Burden* (1998)
[fl, cl, pf, vn, va, vc]

Skempton, Howard. *The Witches Wood (Mary Coleridge)* (1990)
[sop, fl, cl, pf, vn, vc]

Skempton, Howard. *Gemini Dances* (1994)
[fl, cl, pf, perc, vn, vc]

Smalley, Roger. *Ceremony II* (1989-90)
[fl/afl/pic, cl/bcl, pf, perc, vn, vc]

Smolka, Martin. *Autumn Thoughts* (1998)
[fl, cl, pf, perc, vn, vc]

Smolka, Martin. *Oh, my admired C Minor* (2000)
[fl, cl, pf, perc, vn, vc]

Stalheim, Jostein. *Glimpses of a Daylight* (1989)
[fl, bcl, pf, perc, pf, vn, vc]

Stankovych, Yevhen. *'What Has Happened in Silence After Echo'* (1944)
[fl, cl, pf, perc, vn, vc]

Stankovych, Yevhen. *Chamber Symphony No. 8* (1997)
[voice, fl, cl, pf, perc, vn, vc]

Stevens, James. *Etymon (James Stevens)* (1972)
[3 voices, fl, cl, pf, perc, vn, vc]

Stockhausen, Karlheinz. *Dr. K-Sextett* (1968-69)
[fl, bcl, perc, pf, va, vc]

Stout, Alistair. *Deep in Your Coral Caves* (2000)
[fl, bcl, pf, vn, va, vc]

Stucky, Steven. *Boston Fancies* (1985)
[fl, cl, pf, perc, vn, va, vc]

Stringer, John. *Hinterland* (1999)
[pic, cl, pf, vn, vc]

Stucky, Steven. *Ad Parnassum* (1998)
[fl/afl, cl/bcl, pf, perc, vn, vc]

Sur, Donald. *Catena III* (1976)
[fl, bcl, 2 perc, vn, vc]

Tann, Hilary. *Winter Sun, Summer Rain* (1986)
[fl, cl, cel, va, vc]

Taylor, Alan. *Midnight Abstract* (2001)
[fl, cl, pf, drum kit, vn, vc]

Thommessen, Olav Anton. *The Uncovering of Slowness (A Paragraph on a Texture)* (1997)
[fl, cl, pf, perc, vn, va, vc]

Toovey, Andrew. *James Purdy Settings* (1999)
[sop, fl, cl, pf, perc, vn, va, vc]

Toovey, Andrew. *Music for the Painter Jack Smith: Version II* (2001)
[fl/pic/afl/bfl, Bb-cl/Eb-cl/bcl, pf/hpd, perc, vn, vc, db]

Torke, Michael. *Ceremony of Innocence* (1983)
[fl, cl, pf, vn, vc]

Torke, Michael. *Telephone Book [incl. The Yellow Pages (1985)]* (1995)
[fl/pic, cl/bcl, pf, vn, vc]

Tower, Joan. *Breakfast Rhythms I and II* (1974-75)
[fl/pic, cl, pf, perc, vn, vc = cl with fl/pic, pf, perc, vn, vc]

Tower, Joan. *Amazon* (1977)
[fl, cl, pf, vn, vc]

Tower, Joan. *Petroushskates* (1980)
[fl, cl, pf, vn, vc]

Tower, Joan. *Noon Dance* (1982)
[fl/afl/pic, cl, pf, perc, vn, vc]

Trainer, Fraser. *Lifelines* (2002)
[fl/afl, cl/bcl/metal windchimes, pf, perc, vn/small whip, vc]

Trunk, Markus. *Spagat* (1997)
[fl, cl, pf, vib/mar, vn, vc]

Uduman, Sohrab [Zohrab]. *In Accord, In Motion* (1997)
[fl, cl, pf, vn, vc]

Vali, Reza. *Folk Songs (Set No. 15)* (1995)
[fl/afl/pic, B♭-cl/E♭-cl/bcl, perc, vn, vc]

Visconti, Dan. *The Clear Light* (2012)
[sop, fl, cl, pf/Vox org, vn, vc]

Walter, Caspar Johannes. *Fünf Ohren* (2003)
[alt, afl, cl, pf, vn, vc]

Waring, Rob. *Concerto for Vibraphone and Chamber Ensemble* (1984)
[fl, bcl, vib, timp, vn, vc = vib with fl, bcl, timp, vn, vc]

Webern, Anton. *Kammersymphonie (Arnold Schoenberg, Op. 9)* (1922-23)
[fl (or vn), cl (or va), pf, vn, vc]

Weeks, James. *Distant Intimacy* (2002)
[fl, bcl, pf, vn, vc]

Weir, Judith. *King Harald Sails to Byzantium* (1979)
[afl/pic, cl/bcl, pf, mar/glock, vn, vc]

Westergaard, Peter. *Variations for Six Players* (1963)
[fl/pic, cl/bcl, pf, perc, vn, vc]

Westlake, Nigel. *Entomology* (1990)
[fl/afl/pic, E♭-cl/bcl, pf, perc, vn, vc, tape]

Whalley, Richard. *Elegy: A Tribute to Colin Nancarrow* (1999)
[fl/pic, cl/bcl, pf, perc, pf, vn, vc, db]

White, Liza. *Grovve III* (2011)
[fl, cl/bcl, pf, vn, vc]

Whitehead, Gillian. *Pakuru (Hone Tuwhare)* (1967)
[sop, fl, cl, harm, perc, va, vc]

Whitehead, Gillian. *Marduk* (1973)
[sop, fl, cl, pf/hpd, perc, gui, vn/va, vc]

Whitehead, Gillian. *Wulf (old Eng. poem, trans. Bill Manhire)* (1976)
[female voice, fl, cl, pf, perc, vn, vc]

Whitehead, Gillian. *Manutaki* (1984)
[fl, cl, pf, vn, vc]

Wiegold, Peter. *Prelude 1* (1978)
[afl, cl, perc, va, vc]

Wilson, Ian. *Tableau* (1970)
[fl/afl, cl/bcl, pf/cel, perc, va, vc]

Wilson, Thomas. *Canti notturni* (1972)
[fl, cl, pf, vn, va, vc]

Wolosoff, Bruce. *Linguistics: Four Poems by Robert Kelly* (1988)
[mez, fl/pic, bcl, pf, vn, vc]

Wolters, Michael. *Departure* (1999)
[fl, cl, pf, perc, vn, va, vc]

Wood, Hugh. *A Garland for Dr K.* (1969)
[fl, cl, pf, vn, vc]

Wood, James. *Crying bird, echoing star* (2002)
[fl/afl/pic, cl, pf, vn, vc]

Woolrich, John. *Le domaine mystérieux* (1981)
[afl/pic, cl/bcl, perc (played by cond), vn/mand, vc/nightingale whistle]

Woolrich, John. *Berceuse* (1990)
[sop/gongs, afl, cl, va, vc]

Woolrich, John. *Envoi* (1997)
[afl, bcl, pf, mar/drums, vn, va, vc = va with afl, bcl, pf, mar/drums, vn, vc]

Wuorinen, Charles. *New York Notes* (1981-82)
[fl, cl, pf, perc, vn, vc, (opt.) tape]

Wuorinen, Charles. *The Great Procession* (1995)
[fl, cl, pf, perc, vn, vc]

Xenakis, Iannis. *Plektó* (1993)
[fl, cl, pf, 5 woodblocks/7 drums, vn, vc]

Yi, Chen. *Near Distance* (1988)
[fl/afl, cl/bcl, pf, perc, vn, vc]

Yi, Chen. *Sparkle* (1992)
[fl, cl, pf, 2 perc, vn, vc, db]

Yiu, Raymond. *Night Shanghai* (2005)
[fl/afl/pic, cl/bcl, acc, pf, vn, vc]

Yiu, Raymond. *Prelude for Five* (1999)
[fl, cl, pf, vn, vc]

Zavala, Mercedes. *La apoteosis nocturna de Andoar* (2001)
[fl/pic, cl/bcl, pf, perc, vn, vc]

Zhou, Long. *Dhyana* (1990)
[fl, cl, pf, vn, vc]

Zorn, John. *Chimeras* (2003)
[2 sop, fl/afl/bfl/pic, cl/bcl, pf/cel/org, perc, vn, vc]

Zwilich, Ellen Taaffe. *Chamber Symphony* (1979)
[fl/pic, cl/bcl, pf, vn, va, vc]

Zwilich, Ellen Taaffe. *Passages (A.R. Ammons)* (1981)
[sop, fl/afl/pic, cl/bcl, pf, vn, va, vc]

Zwilich, Ellen Taaffe. *Intrada* (1983)
[fl/pic, cl, pf, vn, vc]

b) Categorized

i) voice(s) and Pierrot ensemble, with instrumental doubling

Clarke, James. *Untitled No. 6* (2010)
[sop, fl/bfl, cl/bcl, pf, vn, vc]

Davies, Peter Maxwell. *Hymn to St Magnus* (1972)
[mez (obbligato), fl, A-cl (or basset-cl), pf/hpd/cel, vn, vc]

Ferneyhough, Brian. *On Stellar Magnitudes (Brian Ferneyhough)* (1994)
[mez, fl/pic, cl/bcl, pf, vn, vc]

Frances-Hoad, Cheryl. *The Glory Tree (6th-8thC. Old Eng. poems on Shamanic rituals)* (2005)
[sop, fl/pic, cl/bcl, pf, vn, vc]

Füssl, Karl Heinz. *Miorita: Altrümanische Volksballade, Op. 1* (1963)
[ten (or sop), female choir (ad lib), fl/afl, cl/bcl, pf/cel, vn/va, vc]

Harris, Donald. *GunMar Music (Albert Giraud, trans. Otto Erich Hartleben)* (1988)
[sop, fl, cl/bcl, pf, vn/va, vc]

Hopkins, John. *For The Far Journey* (1981)
[sop, fl/afl/pic, B♭-cl/E♭-cl/bcl, hpd, vn, vc]

Ingoldsby, Tom. *Three Small Litanies (Latin, liturgical)* (1990)
[sop, fl/pic, cl/bcl, pf, vn, vc]

Karchin, Louis. *'A Way Separate ...' (Ruth Whitman, Hannah Senesh)* (1992)
[sop, fl/pic, cl, pf, vn, vc]

Kraft, William. *Settings from Pierrot Lunaire (Albert Giraud, trans. Otto Erich Hartleben)* (1987-91)
[sop, fl/picc, cl/bcl, pf, vn/va, vc]

Lee, Joanna. *Pierrot!* (2005)
[female voice, fl/pic, cl/bcl, pf, vn, vc]

Muldowney, Dominic. *In Dark Times (Bertolt Brecht)* (1981)
[sop, alto, ten, bass, fl/pic, cl/bcl, pf, va, vc]

Pagliarani, Mario. *Pierrot lunatique* (1993)
[voice, fl/pic, cl/bcl, pf, vn/va, vc]

Panufnik, Roxanna. *Colombine, Too* (1995)
[mez, fl, cl, pf, vn, vc]

Schoenberg, Arnold. *Pierrot lunaire, Op. 21 (Albert Giraud, trans. Otto Erich Hartleben)* (1912)
[Sprechstimme, fl/pic, B♭-cl/A-cl/bcl, pf, vn/va, vc]

Skempton, Howard. *The Witches Wood (Mary Coleridge)* (1990)
[sop, fl, cl, pf, vn, vc]

Visconti, Dan. *The Clear Light* (2012)
[sop, fl, cl, pf/Vox org, vn, vc]

Wolosoff, Bruce. *Linguistics: Four Poems by Robert Kelly* (1988)
[mez, fl/pic, bcl, pf, vn, vc]

ii) without doubling

Berio, Luciano. *O King* (1967-68)
[mez, fl, cl, pf, vn, vc]

Davidovsky, Mario. *Biblical Songs* (1990)
[sop, fl, cl, pf, vn, vc]

Donatoni, Franco. *L'ultima sera* (1980)
[sop, fl, cl, pf, vn, vc]

Gervasoni, Stefano. *Due poesie francesi d'Ungaretti* (1994)
[voice, fl, cl, pf, vn, vc]

Harbison, John. *The Natural World* (1984-86)
[mez, fl, cl, pf, vn, vc]

Kaufmann, Dieter. *Trois Poèmes de Stéphane Mallarmé, Op. 9a* (1967/83)
[sop, fl, cl, pf, vn, vc]

King, Alastair. *Ascension (Samuel Beckett)* (1990)
[sop, fl, cl, pf, vn, vc]

Lee, Joanna. *Elephant Woman: A Woman's Love and Life (Jo Shapcott, E.E. Cummings etc.)* (2007)
[voice, fl, cl, pf, va, vc]

Lohse, Horst. *A. Schmidts Monde* (1995)
[spkr, fl, cl, pf, vn, vc]

Nicholson, George. *Aubade (anon.)* (1981)
[sop, afl, cl, pf, va, vc]

Nicholson, George. *Idyll (Thomas Hardy)* (2003)
[sop, fl, bcl, pf, va, vc]

Walter, Caspar Johannes. *Fünf Ohren* (2003)
[alt, afl, cl, pf, vn, vc]

iii) with percussion, irrespective of doubling

Baptist, Maria. *Compositions* (2002)
[3 voices, fl, cl, pf, perc, vn, vc]

Barker, Paul. *The Thief of Songs (Nahuatl and Eng. text)* (1991)
[mez, fl, cl, pf, perc, vn, vc]

Birtwistle, Harrison. *Cantata (Greek text, after Sappho etc.)* (1969)
[sop, fl/pic, high-pitched-cl ('Old Eng. pitch'), pf/cel, glock, vn/va, vc]

Davies, Peter Maxwell. *Notre Dame des Fleurs (Peter Maxwell Davies, 'obscene Fr. text')* (1966)
[sop, mez, cten, fl, A-cl, pf/cel, perc, vn, vc]

Davies, Peter Maxwell. *Fantasia and Two Pavans (after Henry Purcell)* (1968)
[voice (ad lib, pref. female), fl/pic, cl, perc incl. opt. band-kit, hpd/out-of-tune pf, vn, vc)

Davies, Peter Maxwell. *Eight Songs for a Mad King (George III, Randolph Stow)* (1969)
[male voice (bar), fl/pic, cl, pf/hpd/dulcimer, perc, vn, vc]

Davies, Peter Maxwell. *Nocturnal Dances (Miguel Serrano, Corinthians I 13)* (1969-70)
[sop, fl, cl, pf, perc, va, vc - orig. version with dancers]

Davies, Peter Maxwell. *Missa super L'homme armé (Agnus dei; Luke 22)* (1968, rev. 1971)
[spkr, fl/pic, cl, perc, harm, hpd/cel/honky-tonk-pf, vn, vc, tape (boy's voice; rev. = live perf.); cl, vn, vc, harm also play perc]

Davies, Peter Maxwell. *Miss Donnithorne's Maggot (Randolph Stow)* (1974)
[female voice (mez), fl/afl/pic, A-cl, pf, perc (glock/mar/etc.), vn, vc]

Davies, Peter Maxwell. *The No. 11 Bus for Mime, Singers, Dancers and Instrumental Ensemble* (1983-84)
[mez, ten, bar, mime, 2 dancers, fl/pic, cl/bcl, pf/cel, perc incl. mar/rock-band kit/ etc., vn, vc]

Davies, Peter Maxwell. *Excuse Me: Parlour Songs (arr. of Charles Dibdin)* (1986)
[mez, fl, B♭-cl/A-cl, pf, perc (glock/mar/woodblocks/etc.), vn, vc]

Davies, Peter Maxwell. *A Birthday Card for Hans (Lorenzo da Ponte)* (1996)
[mez, afl, bcl, pf, mar, va, vc]

Denisov, Edison. *La Vie en rouge (Boris Vian)* (1973)
[sop, fl, cl, pf, perc, vn, vc]

Dresher, Paul. *The Tyrant (Jim Lewis)* (2005)
[male voice, fl/afl/pic, cls, keybs, perc, vn, vc]

Druce, Duncan. *The Tower of Needles* (1970-71)
[sop, fl/pic, cl, pf, perc, vn/va, vc]

Feldman, Morton. *I Met Heine on the Rue Fürstenberg (wordless)* (1971)
[voice, fl/pic, cl/bcl, pf, perc (vib/chimes/etc.), vn, vc]

Finnissy, Michael. *Mr Punch* (1976-77, rev. 1979)
[voice (9 roles), fl/pic, E♭-cl (or ob), pf, perc, vn, vc (not if ob used)]

Hoyland, Vic. *Seneca / Medea* (1985)
[sop, alt, ten, bass, afl, cl, pf, perc, vn, vc]

Hughes, Edward Dudley. *The Devil's Drum (Roger Morris)* (1998)
[mez, ten, fl, cl, pf, perc, vn, vc]

Imbrie, Andrew. *Songs of Then and Now* (1998)
[sop, alt, fl, cl, pf, perc, vn, vc]

Jarrell, Michael. *Trei II (François le Lionnais, Konrad Bayer, Richard D. Laing)* (1982-83)
[sop/crotales/chimes, fl/claves/maracas, cl/bcl/maracas/tam-tam, pf/tabla, vn/woodblock/tam-tam, vc/wood-drum/maracas]

Karchin, Louis. *Songs of John Keats* (1984)
[sop, fl, cl, pf, perc, vn, vc]

Karchin, Louis. *American Visions: Two Songs on Poems of Yevgeny Yevtushenko* (1998)
[bar, fl/pic, cl/bcl, pf, perc, vn, vc]

Kyr, Robert. *Maelstrom (Emily Dickinson, Dylan Thomas)* (1983)
[sop, fl, cl, pf, perc, vn, vc]

Nyman, Michael. *Acts of Beauty* (2004)
[sop, fl, cl, pf, perc, vn, vc]

Parkin, Michael. *Aware (Issa: Jap. haiku)* (1987)
[sop, fl, cl, pf, perc, vn, vc]

Ran, Shulamit. *O, The Chimneys* (1969)
[mez, fl, cl/bcl, pf, perc, vc, tape]

Roberts, Paul. *Fractures (John Ashbery)* (1988)
[sop, afl, cl, pf, perc, va, vc]

Stankovych, Yevhen. *Chamber Symphony No. 8* (1997)
[voice, fl, cl, pf, perc, vn, vc]

Stevens, James. *Etymon (James Stevens)* (1972)
[3 voices, fl, cl, pf, perc, vn, vc]

Whitehead, Gillian. *Wulf (old Eng. poem, trans. Bill Manhire)* (1976)
[female voice, fl, cl, pf, perc, vn, vc]

Zorn, John. *Chimeras* (2003)
[2 sop, fl/afl/bfl/pic, cl/bcl, pf/cel/org, perc, vn, vc]

iv) without voice, with instrumental doubling

Attwood, William. *Cloisonné* (2003)
[fl/pic, bcl/cbcl, pf, vn, vc]

Babbitt, Milton. *Arie da capo* (1973-74)
[fl, cl/bcl, pf, vn, vc]

Beamish, Sally. *Commedia* (1990)
[fl/pic, E♭-cl, pf, vn, vc]

Bedford, David. *A Garland for Dr K.* (1969)
[fl/afl/pic, cl/bcl, pf/hpd, vn/va, vc]

Crane, Laurence. *Five Pieces for Five Instruments* (1992)
[fl/afl, cl/bcl, pf, vn, vc]

Eisler, Hanns. *Vierzehn Arten den Regen zu beschreiben* (1940-41)
[fl, cl, pf, vn, va, vc - NB. vn and va do not sound together]

Erkoreka, Gabriel. *Izaro* (2001)
[fl/pic, cl, pf, vn, vc]

Harrison, Bryn. *time and intervention* (2000)
[fl/afl, cl/bcl, pf, vn, vc]

Harry, Martyn. *George Meets Arnie for Tennis* (2004)
[fl/pic, cl/bcl, pf/synth, vn, vc]

Hayes, Morgan. *Buoy* (1999)
[fl/afl/pic, cl/bcl, pf, va, vc]

Hopkins, John. *Fuga Canonica* (1981)
[fl/afl, cl/bcl, hpd, vn, vc]

Hopkins, John. *For The Far Journey* (1981)
[sop, fl/afl/pic, B♭-cl/E♭-cl/bcl, hpd, vn, vc]

Horne, David. *Contraries and Progressions* (1991)
[fl, cl, pf, vn/va, vc]

Karchin, Louis. *Galactic Folds* (1992)
[fl/pic, cl, pf, vn, vc]

Kay, Alison. *Flux* (2006)
[fl/pic, cl/bcl, pf, vn, vc]

Lutyens, Elisabeth. *Concertante for Five Players* (1950)
[fl/pic, cl/bcl, pf, vn/va, vc]

Mackey, Steven. *Indigenous Instruments* (1989)
[fl/afl/pic, cl, pf, vn, vc]

Mann, Terry. *Quintet for St Swithun* (1999)
[fl/afl, cl/bcl, pf, vn, vc]

Musgrave, Thea. *Chamber Concerto No. 2* (1966)
[fl/afl/pic, cl/bcl (ext. to B♭), pf, vn/va, vc]

Nunn, Patrick. *Hextych: Six Impressions on Six Paintings by Philip Core* (2001)
[fl/afl, cl/bcl, pf, vn, vc, taped gramophone]

Oliveros, Pauline. *Aeolian Partitions* (1970)
[fl/afl/pic, cl/bcl, pf, vn/va, vc, six assistants (stage hands, stage manager, etc.)]

Parkinson, Tim. *untitled quintet* (2002)
[fl/pic, cl/bcl, pf, vn, vc]

Powers, Anthony. *Fast Colours* (1997)
[fl/afl/pic, cl/bcl, pf, vn, vc]

Reynolds, Peter. *Old King Cole* (1994)
[fl/afl, cl, pf, vn, vc]

Robinson, Paul. *Webernera* (2000)
[fl/pic, cl/bcl, pf, vn, vc]

Saxton, Robert. *The Sentinel of the Rainbow* (1984)
[fl/afl/pic, Bb-cl/Eb-cl/bcl, pf/cel, vn/va, vc]

Torke, Michael. *Telephone Book [incl. The Yellow Pages (1985)]* (1995)
[fl/pic, cl/bcl, pf, vn, vc]

White, Liza. *Grovve III* (2011)
[fl, cl/bcl, pf, vn, vc]

Wood, James. *Crying bird, echoing star* (2002)
[fl/afl/pic, cl, pf, vn, vc]

Zwilich, Ellen Taaffe. *Intrada* (1983)
[fl/pic, cl, pf, vn, vc]

v) without voice, without doubling: Pierrot quintet

Alvarez, Javier. *Tientos* (1984)
[fl, cl, pf, vn, vc]

Barrett, Richard. *Trawl* (1997)
[fl, bcl, pf, vn, vc]

Boehmer, Konrad. *Qadar* (1997)
[fl, cl, pf, vn, vc]

Bolcom, William. *Whisper Moon (Dream Music No. 3)* (1971)
[afl, cl, pf, vn, vc]

Boulez, Pierre. *Pour le Dr Kalmus* (1969)
[fl, cl, pf, va, vc]

Burrell, Diana. *Double Image* (1999)
[fl, cl, pf, vn, vc]

Bush, Alan. *Canzona* (1985)
[fl, cl, pf, vn, vc]

Capyrin, Dmitri. *Inside* (2011)
[fl, cl, pf, vn, vc]

Causton, Richard. *Phoenix* (2006)
[fl, cl, pf, vn, vc]

Charlton, Alan. *Quintetto* (1995)
[fl, cl, pf, vn, vc]

Crane, Laurence. *Seven Short Pieces* (2004)
[bfl, cl, pf, vn, vc]

Currier, Sebastian. *Static* (2003)
[fl, cl, pf, vn, vc]

Davies, Peter Maxwell. *Unbroken Circle* (1984)
[afl, bcl, pf, va, vc]

Davies, Tansy. *grind show (electric) / grind show (* unplugged)* (2007)
[fl, cl, pf (prepared [*/processed]), vn, vc, [*sampler=electronics/CD])

Davies, Tansy. *Undertow* (1999, rev. 2000)
[fl, cl, pf, vn, vc]

Donatoni, Franco. *Etwas Ruhiger im Ausdruck* (1967)
[fl, cl, pf, vn, vc]

Ellis, Nicola. *S.O.S.* (1990)
[fl, cl, pf, vn, vc]

Fink, Simon. *Swell* (2006)
[fl, cl, pf, vn, vc]

Finnissy, Michael. *Kritik der Urteilskraft* (2001)
[fl, cl, pf, vn, vc]

Finnissy, Michael. *Regen beschreiben* (2001)
[afl, cl, pf, vn, vc]

Foster, Derek. *The October Country* (1977)
[fl, cl, pf, vn, vc]

Fowler, Jennifer. *'Echoes ...'* (2001)
[fl, cl, pf, vn, vc]

Grime, Helen. *Quintet* (2002)
[fl, cl, pf, vn, vc]

Grisey, Gérard. *Taléa* (1986)
[fl, cl, pf, vn, vc]

Harper, Edward. *Quintet* (1974)
[fl, cl, pf, vn, vc]

Harrington, Jeffrey. *KaleidoPsychoTropos* (1995)
[fl, cl, pf, vn, vc]

Harrison, Sadie. *Quintet: 'No Title Required'* (1994, rev. 1999)
[fl, cl, pf, vn, vc]

Hartikainen, Jarkko. *Frankfurt Quintet No. 3* (2009)
[fl, cl, pf, vn, vc]

Hartikainen, Jarkko. *magnetic* (2011)
[fl, cl, pf, vn, vc]

Hayes, Morgan. *Snapshots* (1994)
[fl, cl, pf, vn, vc]

Hidalgo, Manuel. *Quintett* (1990)
[fl, cl, pf, vn, vc]

Hopkins, John. *Round* (1974)
[fl, cl, pf, va, vc]

Hughes, Edward Dudley. *Light Cuts Through Dark Skies* (2001)
[fl, cl, pf, vn, vc]

Hurel, Philippe. *Pour Luigi* (1993)
[fl, cl, pf, vn, vc]

Kessner, Daniel. *Two Visions* (1991)
[fl, cl, pf, vn, vc]

Kraft, William. *Suite from 'Cascando'* (1988)
[fl, cl, pf, vn, vc]

Kretz, Johannes. *Dynamische Gewächse* (1999)
[fl, cl, pf, vn, vc, electronics]

Kyburz, Hanspeter. *Danse aveugle* (1997)
[fl, cl, pf, vn, vc]

Láng, István. *Rhymes* (1972)
[fl, cl, pf, va, vc]

Lavenda, Richard. *Alliances* (2003)
[fl, cl, pf, vn, vc]

Lindberg, Magnus. *Quintetto dell'estate* (1979)
[fl, cl, pf, vn, vc]

Mann, Terry. *Quintet* (1998)
[fl, cl, pf, vn, vc]

Matthews, Colin. *Elegiac Chaconne* (1997)
[afl, bcl, pf, va, vc]

Maw, Nicholas. *Ghost Dances: Imaginary Ballet for 5 Players* (1988)
[fl, cl, pf, vn, vc]

McGuire, Edward. *Quintet II* (1987)
[fl, cl, pf, vn, vc]

McNeff, Stephen. *Counting (One)* (2007)
[fl, cl, pf, perc (opt.), vn, vc]

Moore, Timothy. *Sincerest Flattery* (1999)
[fl, A-cl, pf, vn, vc]

Murail, Tristan. *Treize Couleurs du soleil couchant* (1978)
[fl, cl, pf, vn, vc, electronics (ad lib.)]

Murail, Tristan. *La Barque mystique* (1993)
[fl, cl, pf, vn, vc]

Murail, Tristan. *Winter Fragments* (2000)
[fl, cl, pf, vn, vc, Apple Macintosh, MIDI keyb, amplification, reverberation]

Nunn, Patrick. *Cruise* (2007)
[fl, cl, pf, vn, vc]

Nyman, Michael. *Viola and Piano* (2009)
[fl, cl, pf, vn, vc]

Poppe, Enno. *Geloschte Lieder* (1997)
[fl, cl, pf, vn, vc]

Pritchard, Gwyn. *Chamber Concerto* (1985)
[fl, cl, pf vn, vc]

Reynolds, Belinda. *Coming Around* (1995)
[fl, cl, pf, vn, vc]

Runchak, Volodymyr. *Time 'X ...' or farewell no-symphony* (1998)
[fl, cl, pf, vn, vc]

Santoro, Claudio. *Música de câmera* (1944)
[fl, bcl, pf, vn, vc]

Shchetynsky, Olexander. *Way to Meditation* (1990)
[fl, cl, pf, vn, vc]

Stringer, John. *Hinterland* (1999)
[pic, cl, pf, vn, vc]

Tann, Hilary. *Winter Sun, Summer Rain* (1986)
[fl, cl, cel, va, vc]

Torke, Michael. *Ceremony of Innocence* (1983)
[fl, cl, pf, vn, vc]

Tower, Joan. *Amazon* (1977)
[fl, cl, pf, vn, vc]

Tower, Joan. *Petroushskates* (1980)
[fl, cl, pf, vn, vc]

Uduman, Sohrab [Zohrab]. *In Accord, In Motion* (1997)
[fl, cl, pf, vn, vc]

Webern, Anton. *Kammersymphonie (Arnold Schoenberg, Op. 9)* (1922-23)
[fl (or vn), cl (or va), pf, vn, vc]

Weeks, James. *Distant Intimacy* (2002)
[fl, bcl, pf, vn, vc]

Whitehead, Gillian. *Manutaki* (1984)
[fl, cl, pf, vn, vc]

Wood, Hugh. *A Garland for Dr K.* (1969)
[fl, cl, pf, vn, vc]

Yiu, Raymond. *Prelude for Five* (1999)
[fl, cl, pf, vn, vc]

Zhou, Long. *Dhyana* (1990)
[fl, cl, pf, vn, vc]

vi) without voice, with percussion

Alberga, Eleanor. *Dancing with the Shadow* (1990)
[fl, cl, pf, glock, vn, vc]

Albright, William. *Danse Macabre* (1971)
[fl, cl/bcl, pf, perc, vn, vc]

Andriessen, Louis. *Zilver* (1994)
[fl, cl, pf, 2 perc (vib, mar), vn, vc]

Antunes, Jorge. *Amerika 500* (1992)
[fl, bcl, pf, perc, vn, vc]

Berio, Luciano. *The Modification and Instrumentation of a Famous Hornpipe as a Merry and Altogether Sincere Homage to Uncle Alfred (after Henry Purcell)* (1969)
[fl (or ob), cl, hpd, perc, va, vc]

Berkeley, Michael. *The Mayfly* (1984)
[fl, cl, pf, perc, vn, vc]

Bibalo, Antonio. *The Savage: 4 Impressions for 6 Players* (1982-83)
[fl/afl/pic, cl/bcl/sax, pf, perc, vn, vc]

Birtwistle, Harrison. *Three Lessons in a Frame* (1967, *since withdrawn*)
[fl/pic, cl, pf, perc, vn, vc]

Birtwistle, Harrison. *Ut heremita solus (arr. of Johannes Ockeghem)* (1969)
[fl/afl/pic, cl/bcl, pf, glock, va, vc]

Birtwistle, Harrison. *Some Petals from the Garland (a.k.a. Some Petals from my Twickenham Herbarium)* (1969)
[pic, cl, pf, glock, va, vc]

Birtwistle, Harrison. *Hoquetus David (after Guillaume de Machaut)* (1969)
[fl/pic, C-cl (or E♭-cl)/B♭-cl, glock/bells, vn, vc]

Birtwistle, Harrison. *Medusa* (1969, rev. 1970, *since withdrawn*)
[fl/pic, B♭-cl/A♭-cl/ssax, pf/cel, perc (xylo/vib/glock/tam-tam/gong), va (rev. = vn/va), vc, 2 tapes, shozyg (rev. = synthesizer) – wind and str ampl.]

Boulez, Pierre. *Dérive [I]* (1984)
[fl, A-cl, pf, vib, vn, vc]

Boyle, Rory. *Night's Music* (2004)
[fl/pic, bcl, pf, mar, vn, vc]

Britten, Benjamin. *Dinner Hour* (1935)
[fl, cl, pf, perc, vn, vc]

Britten, Benjamin. *Men Behind the Meters* (1935)
[fl, cl (later ob), pf, perc, vn, vc]

Britten, Benjamin. *Title Music III (How Gas is Made)* (1935)
[fl, cl, pf, perc, vn, vc]

Brown, Earle. *Tracking Pierrot* (1992)
[fl, cl/bcl, pf/cel, vib/mar, vn, vc]

Bryars, Gavin. *Non la conobbe il mondo mentre l'ebbe* (2006)
[fl, cl, pf, perc, vn, vc]

Butler, Martin. *Jazz Machines* (1990)
[fl/afl/pic, cl/bcl, pf, vib, va, vc]

Caltabiano, Ronald. *Concerto for Six Players* (1987)
[fl/afl, cl/bcl, pf, vib/mar/crotales, vn, vc]

Capyrin [Kapyrin], Dmitri. *Scherzo* (2000)
[fl, cl, pf, perc, vn, vc]

Carter, Elliott. *Triple Duo [Free Fantasy]* (1982-83)
[fl/pic, B♭-cl/E♭-cl/bcl, pf, perc, va, vc]

Clarke, James. *Delirium* (1996)
[fl/bfl, cl, pf, perc, vn, vc]

Cohen, Douglas. *Movement through Stasis* (1992)
[fl/pic, bcl, pf, perc, vn, vc]

Cole, Bruce. *Caesura* (1970)
[fl/pic, cl/bcl, pf, perc, vn, vc]

Cole, Jonathan. *Caught* (1998)
[fl, cl, pf, vib, va, vc]

Claren, Sebastian. *Fehlstart* (1999)
[fl, cl, pf, perc, vn, vc]

Dalby, Martin. *The Dancer Eduardova* (1978)
[fl/afl/pic, cl/bcl, pf/cel (ad lib), perc, vn, vc]

Davidovsky, Mario. *Flashbacks* (1995)
[fl/afl/pic, cl/bcl, pf, perc, vn, vc]

Davies, Peter Maxwell. *Stedman Caters* (1968)
[fl/pic, cl, hpd, perc, va, vc]

Davies, Peter Maxwell. *Fantasia and Two Pavans (after Purcell)* (1968)
[fl/pic, cl, perc incl. opt. band-kit, hpd/out-of-tune pf, vn, vc, voice (ad lib, pref. female)]

Davies, Peter Maxwell. *Veni Sancte Spiritus/Veni Creator Spiritus (after John Dunstable)* (1972)
[afl, A-cl/basset cl, hpd/pf, glock, va, vc]

Davies, Peter Maxwell. *Fantasia upon One Note (arr. of Purcell, Z745)* (1973)
[afl, basset-cl (or A-cl), hpd/open-string-vc/C♯-brandy-glass, perc (crotales/banjo/mar/rototoms), vn, vc]

Davies, Peter Maxwell. *Two Preludes and Fugues (arr. of J.S. Bach)* (1972/74)
[fl/afl, A-cl (or basset-cl), hpd, mar, va, vc]

Davies, Peter Maxwell. *Nach Bergamo* (1974)
[fl, cl, pf, perc, va, vc]

Davies, Peter Maxwell. *Si Quis Diligit Me (after David Peebles, Francy Heagy) (No. 1 of Four Instrumental Motets from Scottish Originals)* (1973)
[afl, cl, cel, crotales, va, vc]

Davies, Peter Maxwell. *Ave Maris Stella* (1975)
[fl/afl, A-cl (or basset-cl), pf, mar, va, vc]

Davies, Peter Maxwell. *Kinloche his Fantassie (after William Kinloch)* (1976)
[fl, cl, hpd, glock, vn, vc]

Davies, Peter Maxwell. *Runes from a Holy Island* (1977)
[afl, A-cl, cel, perc (mar/glock/etc.), va, vc]

Davies, Peter Maxwell. *Fiftieth Birthday Greeting for Ernst Widner* (1977)
[fl, cl, keybs, perc, vn, vc]

Davies, Peter Maxwell. *Our Father Whiche in Heaven Art (after John Angus) (No. 3 of Four Instrumental Motets from Scottish Originals)* (1977)
[fl, B♭-cl/E♭-cl (ad lib), cel, mar, vn, vc]

Davies, Peter Maxwell. *Dances from 'The Two Fiddlers'* (1978)
[pic, bcl, pf, perc, vn, vc = vn with pic, bcl, pf, perc, vn, vc]

Davies, Peter Maxwell. *The Bairns Of Brugh: Elegy* (1981)
[pic, bcl, pf, mar, va, vc]

Davies, Peter Maxwell. *Take a Pair of Sparkling Eyes (arr. of Arthur Sullivan)* (1982)
[fl, cl, pf, perc, vn, vc]

Davies, Peter Maxwell. *Farewell - A Fancye (arr. of John Dowland)* (1986)
[afl, bcl, pf, mar, va, vc]

Davies, Peter Maxwell. *Two Glasses of Wine [= A Glass of Frontignac and A Glass of Shiraz]* (2000/02)
[fl, cl, pf/keybs, perc (incl. mar), vn, vc]

Davies, Peter Maxwell. *A Glass of Frontignac [publ. with A Glass of Shiraz as Two Glasses of Wine]* (2000)
[fl, cl, keybs, perc, vn, vc]

Davies, Peter Maxwell. *A Glass of Shiraz [publ. with A Glass of Frontignac as Two Glasses of Wine]* (2002)
[fl, cl, pf, mar, vn, vc]

Davies, Peter Maxwell. *Music in Camera* (1986)
[fl, cl, pf/hpd, perc, vn, vc]

Davies, Tansy. *Patterning* (2000)
[pic, cl, pf, perc, vn, vc]

Dench, Chris. *eigenmomenta* (2001)
[fl/afl/pic, cl/bcl, pf, vib/crotales, vn, vc]

Donatoni, Franco. *Lumen* (1975)
[fl, cl, cel, perc, va, vc]

Donatoni, Franco. *Arpége* (1986)
[fl, cl, pf, vib, vn, vc]

Druce, Duncan. *Märchenzeit* (1974)
[fl, cl, pf, perc, vn, vc]

Druckman, Jacob. *Come Round* (1992)
[afl, cl, pf, 1 or 2 perc, vn, vc)

Duddell, Joe. *Grace Under Pressure* (2007)
[fl, bcl, pf, mar, vn, vc]

Edlin, Paul Max. *Five Fantastic Islands* (1993)
[fl/afl, cl, pf, perc, va, vc]

Edwards, Ross. *Laikan* (1979)
[fl, cl, pf, perc, vn, vc]

Elias, Brian. *Geranos* (1985)
[fl/afl/pic, B♭-cl/E♭-cl/bcl(ext. to B♭), pf, perc, vn/va, vc]

Emsley, Richard. *...from swerve of shore to bend of bay...* (1985)
[afl/pic, E♭-cl, pf, perc, va, vc]

Erkoreka, Gabriel. *Krater* (1984)
[fl, cl, pf, mar, vn, vc]

Febel, Reinhard. *Sextet* (1977)
[fl, cl, pf, vib, vn, vc = with vib with fl, cl, pf, vn, vc]

Feldman, Morton. *For Frank O'Hara* (1973)
[fl/afl/pic, cl, pf, 2 perc (xylo/glock/vib/chimes/etc.), vn, vc]

Festinger, Richard. *A Serenade for Six* (1993)
[fl/pic, cl/bcl, pf, perc, vn, vc]

Festinger, Richard. *After Blue* (1998)
[fl/pic, cl/bcl, pf, perc, vn, vc]

Fink, Simon. *Falling* (2001)
[fl, cl, pf, perc, vn, vc]

Fitch, Keith. *Dancing the Shadows* (1994)
[fl/pic, cl/bcl, pf, perc, vn, vc]

Fitkin, Graham. *Ardent* (1993)
[fl, cl, pf, mar, vn, vc]

Fitkin, Graham. *Totti* (2004)
[fl, cl/bcl, pf, mar, vn, vc]

Froom, David. *Chamber Concerto* (1991)
[fl, cl, pf, vib/mar, vn, vc]

Gilbert, Anthony. *Mother* (1969)
[wooden-fl/pic, elec.-basset-cl/bcl/sharp-pitch-B♭-cl/E♭-cl, Hammond org (or pf with elec.-keyb attachment), perc, vn/elec.-va, vc (with elec. ampl.) = vc (with elec. ampl.) *with* ensemble listed]

Grange, Philip. *Cimmerian Nocturne* (1979)
[pic, bcl, pf, mar, vn, vc]

Grange, Philip. *Des fins sont des commencements* (1994)
[fl, cl, pf, perc, vn, vc]

Grange, Philip. *Lament of the Bow* (2000)
[fl, cl, pf, perc, vn, vc]

Grinberg, Olexander. *House Plant* (1993)
[fl, cl, pf, perc, vn, vc]

Gustavson, Mark. *A Fool's Journey* (1999)
[fl/afl/pic, cl/bcl, pf, perc, vn, vc]

Haas, Georg Friedrich. *Sextett* (1992-96)
[fl/bfl/pic, cl/bcl, pf, perc, vn, vc]

Haas, Georg Friedrich. *tria ex uno (after Josquin Desprez)* (2001)
[fl/afl, cl/bcl, pf, perc, vn/va, vc]

Halffter, Cristóbal. *Oda para felicitar a un amigo* (1969)
[afl, bcl, pf/cel, perc, va, vc]

Halle, John. *Vox Pop* (1994)
[fl, cl, pf, perc, vn, vc]

Hänschke, Bernd. *Changeant I* (1992)
[fl, cl, pf, perc, vn, vc]

Harvey, Jonathan. *Quantumplation* (1973)
[fl, cl, pf, tam-tam, vn, vc]

Haubenstock-Ramati, Roman. *Rounds* (1969)
[fl, cl, pf, vib, va, vc]

Hayden, Sam. *Partners in Psychopathology* (1998)
[afl/pic, bcl/Eb-cl, pf, vib/xylo, va, vc]

Hellewell, David. *Synergy* (1970)
[fl, cl, pf, perc, vn, vc]

Henze, Hans Werner. *Sonate für sechs Spieler (derived from L'amour à mort)* (1984)
[fl/pic, sistra-cl/bcl/cbcl (ad lib)/handbells, pf/cel, perc, vn/handbells, vc/handbells]

Hervig, Richard. *Chamber Music for Six Players* (1976)
[fl, cl/bcl, pf, perc, vn, db]

Hesketh, Kenneth. *Dei destini incrociati* (2002)
[fl, cl, pf, perc, vn, vc]

Hesketh, Kenneth. *Fra Duri Scogli* (2002]
[fl, cl, pf, perc, vn, vc]

Hind, Rolf. *The Horse Sacrifice* (2001)
[fl/bfl/trbrec, Bb-cl/Eb-cl/rec, pf/ratchet/triangles, vn, vc]

Hopkins, John. *The Cloud Of Unknowing* (1978)
[fl/afl/pic, cl/bcl, pf/cel, perc, vn/va, vc]

Horne, David. *Concerto for Six Players* (1993)
[fl/pic, cl/bcl, pf, perc (vib (bowed, sticks)/mar/etc.), vn, vc]

Huber, Nicolaus A. *La Force du Vertige* (1985)
[fl/pic, cl, pf, perc, vn, vc]

Hughes, Edward Dudley. *Sextet* (1999)
[fl, cl, pf, mar/vib, vn, vc]

Imbrie, Andrew. *Pilgrimage* (1983)
[fl/afl/pic, Bb-cl/Eb-cl/bcl, pf, perc, vn, vc]

Imbrie, Andrew. *Earplay Fantasy* (1995)
[fl, cl, pf, perc, vn, vc]

Ince, Kamran. *Waves of Talya* (1989)
[fl, cl, pf, perc, vn, vc]

Jarvinen, Arthur. *Isoluminaries* (1995)
[fl, bcl, pf, perc, vn, vc]

Kay, Alison. *Rat-race* (2000)
[fl, cl, pf, perc, vn, vc]

Kee Yong, Chong. *'Mourning the murder of an old banyan tree'* (2002)
[fl/afl/pic, cl/bcl, pf, perc, vn, vc]

Kessner, Daniel. *A Tempo* (2012)
[fl, cl/bcl, pf, mar/xylo, vn, vc]

Kmitova, Jana. *Kamea* (2000-01)
[fl, cl, pf, perc, vn, vc]

Kolberg, Kåre. *Ennå Er Der Håp* (1978)
[fl, cl, pf, perc, vn, vc]

Kondo, Jo. Contour Lines (1999)
[fl, cl, pf, perc, vn, vc]

Kraft, William. *Gallery '83* (1983)
[fl/pic, cl/bcl, pf/cel, perc, vn, vc]

Kraft, William. *Melange* (1985)
[fl/afl, cl/bcl, pf/cel, perc, vn, vc]

Kreiger, Arthur. *Meeting Places* (1995)
[fl/afl, cl/bcl, pf, perc, vn, vc, DAT tape]

Lash, Hannah. *Subtilior, Lamento* (2011)
[fl, cl, pf, vib/chimes, vn, vc]

Leach, Rachel. *Green Plastic, Pink Oil and Water* (1998)
[fl, cl, pf, perc, va, vc]

Lee, Eun Young. *a quiet way (Emily Dickinson)* (2006)
[fl/afl, cl/bcl, pf, perc, vn, vc]

LeFanu, Nicola. *Sextet: A Wild Garden-Fásach* (1996-97)
[fl/afl/pic, cl/bcl, pf, perc, vn, vc]

Lewis, Jeffrey. *Epitaph For Abelard and Heloise* (1979)
[fl/afl, cl, pf, perc, vn, vc]

Lloyd, Jonathan. *Symphony No. 5* (1989)
[fl/pic, cl, pf, perc, vn/va, vc]

Lobbett, Gary. *Resti Euta: Isle of the Dead* (1995)
[fl/pic, cl/bcl, pf, perc, vn, vc]

Lorraine, Ross. *Within What Changelessness* (2004)
[fl, cl, pf, vib, vn, vc]

Lumsdaine, David. *Mandala 3* (1978)
[fl, cl, pf, Chinese bell, va, vc = solo pf with fl, cl, Chinese bell, va, vc]

Mackey, Steven. *Micro-concerto for Percussion and Five Players* (1999)
[fl, cl, pf, perc, vn, vc = solo perc with fl, cl, pf, vn, vc]

Martin, Phillip Neil. *Die Fackel* (2003)
[fl/pic, cl/bcl, pf, perc, vn, vc]

Martino, Donald. *Notturno* (1973)
[fl/afl/pic, cl/bcl, pf, perc, vn/va, vc]

Martland, Steve. *Remembering Lennon* (1981, rev. 1985)
[fl, cl/wine glass, perc, pf/wine glass, vn/wine glass, va, vc]

Maw, Nicholas. *Ghost Dances: Imaginary Ballet for 5 Players* (1988)
[fl/afl/pic/manjeera(= small finger cym), B♭-cl/E♭-cl/A-cl/bcl/manjeera/kazoo (or by flautist) pf/manjeera/kalimba (= Afr. thumb pf), vn/manjeera/strumstick(= Amer. one-stringed banjo-type instr.), vc/manjeera/flexatone]

McGarr, Peter. *Vanishing Games* (1995)
[fl/pic/srec/ocarina, cl/bcl/ocarina, pf, perc, vn, vc, off-stage assistant]

McGuire, Edward. *Rebirth* (1974)
[fl/afl, cl/bcl, pf/cel, perc, vn, vc]

McGuire, Edward. *Euphoria* (1980)
[fl/afl/pic, cl/bcl, pf, mar, vn, vc]

McNeff, Stephen. *Counting (One)* (2007)
[fl, cl, pf, perc (opt.), vn, vc]

McPherson, Gordon. *Explore Yourself* (2000)
[fl, cl, pf, perc, vn, vc]

Meale, Richard. *Incredible Floridas (Homage to Arthur Rimbaud)* (1971)
[fl/afl/pic, cl/bcl, pf, perc, vn/va, vc]

Metcalf, John. *Dance from Kafka's Chimp* (1993)
[fl, cl, pf, mar, vn, vc]

Moore, Ian. *La Mort des Artistes* (1996)
[fl, cl, pf, perc, vn, vc]

Moore, Ian. *Palette de Couleur et de Lumiere* (1997)
[fl, cl, pf, perc, vn, vc]

Mosko, Stephen L. *Psychotropes* (1993)
[fl/pic, cl/bcl, pf, perc, vn, vc]

Mowitz, Ira J. *Shimmerings* (2004)
[afl/pic, cl/bcl, pf, glock, vn, vc, digital soundtrack]

Muldowney, Dominic. *Solo/Ensemble* (1974)
[fl/pic, cl, pf, 3 perc, va, vc]

Mulvey, Grainne. *Sextet Uno* (1997)
[fl/afl/pic, cl/bcl, pf, perc, vn, vc]

Newland, Paul. *some like horrorshow music for a malenky bit of the old U.V. (Lament for the death of Linus)* (1993)
[fl/afl/pic, B♭-cl/E♭-cl/bcl, pf, perc, vn, vc]

Newland, Paul. *time quivers* (2008)
[afl, cl, pf, perc, vn, vc]

Nicholls, David. *Mosaic 1* (1986)
[fl, cl, pf, vib, vn, vc]

Nicolson, Alistair. *Punch!* (1994)
[fl/pic, cl/bcl, pf, perc, vn, vc]

Northcott, Bayan. *Sextet* (1985)
[fl/pic, cl/bcl, pf, perc, vn, vc]

Ocker, David. *Pride and Foolishness* (1986)
[fl, cl/bcl, pf, mar/vib, vn, vc]

Oesterle, Michael. *Urban Canticle* (1995/99)
[fl, cl, pf, perc, vn, vc]

Parkin, Simon. *Three Pieces for Mixed Sextet* (1991)
[fl, cl, pf, mar, vn, vc]

Patterson, Paul. *Floating Music* (1974)
[fl, cl, pf/cel, perc, vn, vc]

Payne, Anthony. *A Day in the Life of a Mayfly* (1981)
[fl/pic, cl, pf, perc, vn, vc]

Perle, George. *Critical Moments* (1996)
[fl, cl, pf, perc, vn, vc]

Perle, George. *Critical Moments 2* (2001)
[fl, cl, pf, perc, vn, vc]

Powell, Mel. *Sextet* (1996)
[fl, cl, pf/cel, perc, vn, vc]

Powers, Anthony. *Another Part of the Island* (1980, rev. 1994)
[fl/afl/pic, B♭-cl/A-cl (or basset-cl), pf/cel, mar/glock/crotales, vn, vc]

Primosch, James. *Sacra Conversazione* (1994)
[fl/afl/pic, cl/bcl, pf, perc, vn, vc, tape]

Pritchard, Deborah. *Chanctonbury Ring* (2000)
[fl, cl, pf, perc, vn, vc]

Rands, Bernard. *Monotone* (1969)
[fl/afl, cl/bcl, pf, perc (bongos/gong/vib/etc.), va, vc]

Redgate, Roger. *Pierrot on the Stage of Desire* (1998)
[fl, cl, pf, perc, vn, vc]

Reich, Steve. *Double Sextet* (2007)
[fl, cl, pf, vib, vn, vc, pre-recorded tape (of fl, cl, pf, vib, vn, vc) or 2 fl, 2 cl, 2 pf, 2 vib, 2 vn, 2 vc]

Richard, André. *Musique de Rue: Szenische Aktionsmusik* (1987)
[fl, cl, pf, perc, vn, vc, tape = perc with fl, cl, pf, vn, vc, tape]

Rohde, Kurt. *this bag is not a toy – a very short concerto for small mixed ensemble without orchestra* (2011)
[fl/pic, bcl, pf, perc, vn, vc]

Rzewski, Frederic. *Pocket Symphony* (2000)
[fl, cl, pf, perc, vn, vc]

Schidlowsky, Leon. *Sextet* (1970)
[fl/pic, cl/bcl, pf, perc, vn, vc]

Schwantner, Joseph. *Music of Amber* (1980-81)
[fl, cl/bcl, pf, perc, vn, vc]

Sherlaw Johnson, Robert. *Triptych* (1973)
[fl, cl, pf, perc, pf, vn, vc]

Skempton, Howard. *Gemini Dances* (1994)
[fl, cl, pf, perc, vn, vc]

Smalley, Roger. *Ceremony II* (1989-90)
[fl/afl/pic, cl/bcl, pf, perc, vn, vc]

Smolka, Martin. *Autumn Thoughts* (1998)
[fl, cl, pf, perc, vn, vc]

Smolka, Martin. *Oh, my admired C Minor* (2000)
[fl, cl, pf, perc, vn, vc]

Stalheim, Jostein. *Glimpses of a Daylight* (1989)
[fl, bcl, pf, perc, pf, vn, vc]

Stankovych, Yevhen. *'What Has Happened in Silence After Echo'* (1944)
[fl, cl, pf, perc, vn, vc]

Stockhausen, Karlheinz. *Dr K-Sextett* (1968-69)
[fl, bcl, perc, pf, va, vc]

Stucky, Steven. *Ad Parnassum* (1998)
[fl/afl, cl/bcl, pf, perc, vn, vc]

Taylor, Alan. *Midnight Abstract* (2001)
[fl, cl, pf, drum kit, vn, vc]

Tower, Joan. *Breakfast Rhythms I and II* (1974-75)
[fl/pic, cl, pf, perc, vn, vc = cl with fl/pic, pf, perc, vn, vc]

Tower, Joan. *Noon Dance* (1982)
[fl/afl/pic, cl, pf, perc, vn, vc]

Trainer, Fraser. *Lifelines* (2002)
[fl/afl, cl/bcl/metal windchimes, pf, perc, vn/small whip, vc]

Trunk, Markus. *Spagat* (1997)
[fl, cl, pf, vib/mar, vn, vc]

Weir, Judith. *King Harald Sails to Byzantium* (1979)
[afl/pic, cl/bcl, pf, mar/glock, vn, vc]

Westergaard, Peter. *Variations for Six Players* (1963)
[fl/pic, cl/bcl, pf, perc, vn, vc]

Westlake, Nigel. *Entomology* (1990)
[fl/afl/pic, E♭-cl/bcl, pf, perc, vn, vc, tape]

Wilson, Ian. *Tableau* (1970)
[fl/afl, cl/bcl, pf/cel, perc, va, vc]

Woolrich, John. *Le Domaine mystérieux* (1981)
[afl/pic, cl/bcl, perc (played by cond), vn/mand, vc/nightingale whistle]

Wuorinen, Charles. *New York Notes* (1981-82)
[fl, cl, pf, perc, vn, vc, (opt.) tape]

Wuorinen, Charles. *The Great Procession* (1995)
[fl, cl, pf, perc, vn, vc]

Xenakis, Iannis. *Plektó* (1993)
[fl, cl, pf, 5 woodblocks/7 drums, vn, vc]

Yi, Chen. *Near Distance* (1988)
[fl/afl, cl/bcl, pf, perc, vn, vc]

Zavala, Mercedes. *La apoteosis nocturna de Andoar* (2001)
[fl/pic, cl/bcl, pf, perc, vn, vc]

vii) violin and viola undoubled

Bellamy, Mary. *Constellations* (1999)
[fl, cl, pf, vn, va, vc]

Bettison, Oscar. *Preciosa, tira el pandero* (1995)
[fl, cl, pf, vib, vn, va, vc]

Bettison, Oscar. *Cadence* (2000)
[fl, cl, pf, perc, vn, va, vc]

Bresnick, Martin. *My Twentieth Century (Tom Andrews)* (2002)
[fl, cl, pf, vn, va, vc (musicians also recite poem)]

Butler, Martin. *Going with the Grain* (1991)
[fl/pic, cl/bcl, mar, vn, va, vc = mar with fl/pic, cl/bcl, vn, va, vc]

Butler, Martin. *Two Preludes (arr. of J.S. Bach)* (1992)
[fl, cl, mar, vn, va, vc]

Cage, John. *Seven* (1988)
[fl, cl, pf, perc, vn, va, vc]

Clark, Philip. *Voice of an Angel* (2000)
[fl/pic, cl/bcl, pf, perc, vn, va, vc = vn, pf with fl/pic, cl/bcl, pf, perc, vn, va, vc]

Davies, Tansy. *Two Part Invention in Unison* (1999, *since withdrawn*)
[fl/pic, cl, pf, perc, vn, va, vc]

Durkó, Zsolt. *Fire Music (Sextet)* (1970-71)
[fl/pic/afl.cl/bcl, pf, vn, va, vc]

Eisler, Hanns. *Vierzehn Arten den Regen zu beschreiben* (1940-41)
[fl, cl, pf, vn, va, vc]

Feldman, Morton. *The viola in my life (1)* (1970)
[fl, pf, perc, vn, va, vc = va with fl, pf, perc, vn, vc - NB. no cl]

Feldman, Morton. *The viola in my life (2)* (1970)
[fl, cl, cel, perc, vn, va, vc = va with fl, cl, cel, perc, vn, va, vc]

Festinger, Richard. *Septet* (1987)
[fl, cl, pf, perc, vn, va, vc]

Forbes, Sebastian. *Death's Dominion (Langenheim)* (1971)
[ten, fl, cl, pf, vn, va, vc]

Ford, Andrew. *Chamber Concerto No. 1* (1979)
[fl/pic, cl, pf, vn, va, vc]

Froom, David. *Fantasy Dances* (2000)
[fl, cl, pf, perc, vn, va, vc]

Gordon, Michael Zev. *…by the edge of the forest of desires* (2000)
[fl, cl, pf, vib, cel, vn, va, vc]

Grange, Philip. *The Dark Labyrinth* (1986)
[fl/afl, cl/basset-cl, pf, vn, va = vc with fl/afl, cl/basset-cl, pf, vn, va - NB. no vc]

Grisey, Gérard. *Vortex Temporum I-III* (1996)
[fl, cl, pf, vn, va, vc]

Grossner, Sonja. *Survival: The Story of a Cheetah* (1997)
[fl/afl/pic, cl/bcl, pf, perc, vn, va, vc]

Harrison, Bryn. *Second In Nomine after William Byrd* (2004)
[afl, cl, pf, vn, va, vc]

Harrison, Sadie. *"and who now will wake the dead?"* (2004)
[fl, cl, pf, vn, va, vc]

Harvey, Jonathan. *Inner Light 1* (1973)
[fl, cl, pf, perc, vn, va, vc, tape]

Kraft, William. *Vintage Renaissance and Beyond* (2005)
[fl, cl, pf, vn, va, vc]

Kramer, Jonathan. *Atlanta Licks* (1984)
[fl, cl, pf, vn, va, pf]

Lumsdaine, David. *Bagatelles* (1985)
[fl, cl, pf, vn, va, vc]

MacLeod, Jenny. *For Seven* (1965)
[fl, cl, pf, vib/mar, vn, va, vc]

Mazulis, Rytis. *Canon mensurabilis* (2000)
[fl, cl, pf, vn, va, vc]

Muldowney, Dominic. *Five Theatre Poems (Bertolt Brecht)* (1980)
[mez, fl, cl, pf, vn, va, vc]

Nicholls, David. *Reflections and Refractions* (1978)
[fl, cl, pf, vn, va, vc]

Powell, Jonathan. *Saturnine* (2000)
[fl, cl, pf, perc, vn, va, vc]

Pritchard, Gwyn. *Ensemble Music for Six* (1976)
[fl, cl, pf, vn, va, vc]

Roberts, Jeremy Dale. *Reconciliation* (1969)
[spkr, fl/perc, cl/perc, pf, perc, vn, va, vc]

Saxton, Robert. *La promenade d'automne* (1973)
[sop, fl, cl, pf, perc, vn, va, vc]

Schneid, Tobias P.M. *Weird Scenes Inside the Mirror Cages* (2000)
[fl, cl, pf, perc, vn, va, vc]

Schwehr, Cornelius. *'aber die Schönheit des Gitters'* (1992-93)
[fl, cl, pf, perc, vn, va, vc, film projection (ad lib)]

Simpson, Julia. *A Beast of Burden* (1998)
[fl, cl, pf, vn, va, vc]

Stout, Alistair. *Deep in Your Coral Caves* (2000)
[fl, bcl, pf, vn, va, vc]

Stucky, Steven. *Boston Fancies* (1985)
[fl, cl, pf, perc, vn, va, vc]

Thommessen, Olav Anton. *The Uncovering of Slowness (A Paragraph on a Texture)* (1997)
[fl, cl, pf, perc, vn, va, vc]

Toovey, Andrew. *James Purdy Settings* (1999)
[sop, fl, cl, pf, perc, vn, va, vc]

Wilson, Thomas. *Canti notturni* (1972)
[fl, cl, pf, vn, va, vc]

Wolters, Michael. *Departure* (1999)
[fl, cl, pf, perc, vn, va, vc]

Woolrich, John. *Envoi* (1997)
[afl, bcl, pf, mar/drums, vn, va, vc = va with afl, bcl, pf, mar/drums, vn, vc]

Zwilich, Ellen Taaffe. *Chamber Symphony* (1979)
[fl/pic, cl/bcl, pf, vn, va, vc]

Zwilich, Ellen Taaffe. *Passages (A.R. Ammons)* (1981)
[sop, fl/afl/pic, cl/bcl, pf, vn, va, vc]

viii) with guitar, banjo or mandolin

Bedford, David. *The OCD Band and the Minotaur (Elisabeth Gorla)* (1990)
[sop, fl, cl, pf, gui, vn, vc]

Davies, Peter Maxwell. *Points and Dances from "Taverner"* (1970)
[*Dances from Act I* = afl, cl, gui, hpd, va, vc]
[*Dances from Act I-I*, with linking keyb movts = pic, cl, cbn, tpt, trb, pos-org, regal, perc (2 drums)]

Davies, Peter Maxwell. *Tenebrae super Gesualdo (after Carlo Gesualdo)* (1972)
[mez, afl, bcl, hpd/cel/chamber org (or harm), mar/glock, gui, vn/va, vc]

Davies, Peter Maxwell. *Fantasia upon One Note (arr. of Purcell, Z745)* (1973)
[afl, basset-cl (or A-cl), hpd/open-string-vc/C♯-brandy-glass, perc (crotales/banjo/mar/rototoms), vn, vc]

Davies, Peter Maxwell. *Wedding Telegram (for Gary Kettel)* (1973)
[sop, fl, cl, pf, perc, gui, vn, vc]

Davies, Peter Maxwell. *Renaissance Scottish Dances* (1973)
[fl, cl, perc (glock (or other tuned perc)/mar (or bxylo)/tamb/etc.), gui, vn, vc - in final dance, 'Almayne', drone played by melodica or other free-free instr; also, The Fires instr 'may be adapted according to individual requirements.']

Davies, Peter Maxwell. *Four Instrumental Motets from Early Scottish Originals* (1973-77)
[fl/afl, cl/bcl, cel, 2 perc (mar/crotales/etc.), gui, vn/va, vc]

Davies, Peter Maxwell. *All Sons of Adam (after anon.) (No. 2 of Four Instrumental Motets from Scottish Originals)* (1974)
[afl, cl, cel, mar, gui, va, vc]

Davies, Peter Maxwell. *Psalm 124 (after Andrew Kemp) (No. 4 of Four Instrumental Motets from Scottish Originals)* (1974)
[fl/afl, bcl, 2 perc, glock/mar, gui, vn/va, vc]

Davies, Peter Maxwell. *The Blind Fiddler (George Mackay Brown)* (1975-76)
[mez/antique-cym, fl/afl/pic, A-cl (or basset-cl)/bcl, cel/hpd, perc, gui, vn, vc]

Davies, Peter Maxwell. *Winterfold (George Mackay Brown)* (1986)
[mez, afl, bcl, pf, perc (mar/glock/etc.), gui, vn, vc]

Druce, Duncan. *The Creator's Shadow* (1975)
[fl, basset-cl, pf, perc (crotales/mar/handbells/gongs), gui, va, vc]

Hellawell, Piers. *How Should I Your True Love Know?* (1984)
[fl, cl, pf, perc, gui, va, vc]

Lancaster, David. *De rerum naturae* (1982)
[fl/afl, cl, hpd, vib, gui, vn, vc]

Whitehead, Gillian. *Marduk* (1973)
[sop, fl, cl, pf/hpd, perc, gui, vn/va, vc]

Woolrich, John. *Le Domaine mystérieux* (1981)
[afl/pic, cl/bcl, perc (played by cond), vn/mand, vc/nightingale whistle]

ix) with piano omitted or substituted for percussion and/or harp

Agnew, Elaine. *Calligraphy* (2002)
[fl/afl, cl/bcl, vib, vn, vc]

Babbitt, Milton. *The Head in the Bed (John Hollander)* (1982)
[sop, fl, cl, vn, vc]

Babbitt, Milton. *No Longer Very Clear* (1994)
[sop, fl, cl, vn ,vc]

Bedford, David. *The Sword of Orion* (1970)
[fl, cl, 2 perc (32 instrs), vn, vc, 4 metronomes]

Berio, Luciano. *Différences* (1958-59, rev. 1967)
[fl, cl, hp, va, vc, tape]

Berio, Luciano. *Folk Songs* (1964)
[mez, fl/pic, cl, hp, 2 perc, va, vc]

Birtwistle, Harrison. *Monodrama (Stephen Pruslin)* (1967, *since withdrawn*)
[sop/finger cymbals, spkr, fl/afl/pic, Bb-cl/Ab-cl/Eb-cl/bcl, 2 perc, vn, vc]

Birtwistle, Harrison. *Hoquetus David (after Guillaume de Machaut)* (1969)
[fl/pic, C-cl (or Eb cl)/Bb cl, glock/bells, vn, vc]

Carter, Elliott. *Canon for 4: Homage to William [Glock]* (1984)
[fl, bcl, vn, vc]

Connolly, Justin. *Obbligati II, Op. 13* (1967)
[fl, cl, vn, vc, tape]

Cooke, Arnold. *Harp Quintet, Op. 2* (1932)
[fl, cl, hp, vn, vc = hp with fl, cl, vn, vc]

Crane, Laurence. *See Our Lake* (1999)
[afl, cl/bcl, vib, vn, vc]

Crane, Laurence. *Estonia* (2001)
[afl/bfl, cl, va, vc]

Davidovsky, Mario. *Synchronisms No. 2* (1964)
[fl, cl, vn, vc, electronics]

Davidovsky, Mario. *Romancero* (1983)
[sop, fl/afl/pic, cl/bcl, vn, vc]

Davies, Peter Maxwell. *Antechrist* (1967)
[pic, bcl, 2 or 3 perc, vn, vc]

Davies, Peter Maxwell. *Renaissance Scottish Dances* (1973)
[fl, cl, perc (glock (or other tuned perc)/mar (or bxylo)/tamb/etc.), gui, vn, vc - in
final dance, 'Almayne', drone played by melodica or other free-free instr; also, The
Fires instr 'may be adapted according to individual requirements.']

Davies, Peter Maxwell. *My Lady Lothian's Lilt (wordless)* (1975)
[mez (obbligato), afl, bcl, 2 perc (glock, mar), va, vc]

Denyer, Frank. *Passages* (1984)
[fl/afl/pic, Bb-cl/Eb-cl, vn/va, vc]

Dillon, James. *who do you love* (1980-81)
[voice, fl/pic/bfl, bcl (or cl or ca), perc, vn/va, vc – alternatively, Renaissance instrs.]

Eisler, Hanns. *Palmström: Studien über Zwölfton-Reihen (Christian
Morgenstern)* (1924)
[*Sprechstimme*, fl/pic, A-cl, vn/va, vc]

Eisler, Hanns. *Kammerkantate No. 8, 'Kantate auf den Tod eines Genossen'*
(1937)
[voice, fl, cl, va, vc]

Fox, Christopher. *Dance* (1980)
[afl, cl, va, vc]

Field, Robin. *Aubade (David Gascoyne)* (1969)
[sop, afl, cl, harp, vn, vc]

Gilbert, Anthony. *Calls Around Chungmori* (1979)
[fl, cl, perc, va, vc]

Harbison, John. *Rot und Weiss* (1987)
[fl, cl, vn, vc]

Hopkins, John. *Se la face ay pale* (1977)
[fl/afl/pic, cl/bcl, perc, vn, vc]

Keeling, Andrew. *Quaternaries* (1990)
[fl/afl, cl/bcl, vn, vc]

Kessner, Daniel. *Harmonic Space* (2003)
[fl, cl, perc, vn, vc]

LeFanu, Nicola. *The Same Day Dawns* (1974)
[sop, fl/afl, bcl/cl, perc (vib/mar/etc.), vn, vc]

Lumsdaine, David. *Mandala 2 (Catches Catch)* (1969)
[fl/afl/pic, basset-cl (or A-cl), perc, va, vc]

Musgrave, Thea. *Serenade* (1961)
[fl, cl, hp, va, vc]

Norman, Katherine. *Memory Places* (1990)
[fl/pic, cl/bcl, vn, vc]

Primosch, James. *Four Sacred Songs* (1990)
[sop or mez, fl/pic, cl/bcl, hp, perc, vn, vc]

Rands, Bernard. *Where Are You Going to My Pretty Maid?* (1973)
[sop, fl, cl, hp, gui, vn, vc]

Reeder, Haydn. *Chromatalea* (1973)
[fl/afl, cl/bcl, vn/va, vc]

Roberts, Jeremy Dale. *Vers Libre* (1980)
[fl/afl, cl, vn/va, vc]

Roe, Helen. *Close By The Place* (1978)
[fl/afl/pic, B♭-cl/E♭-cl/bcl, vn/va, vc]

Rulon, C. Bryan. *Divine Detours* (1993)
[fl, cl, perc, vn, vc; ensemble and cond. also play music box]

Sur, Donald. *Catena III* (1976)
[fl, bcl, 2 perc, vn, vc]

Vali, Reza. *Folk Songs (Set No. 15)* (1995)
[fl/afl/pic, B♭-cl/E♭-cl/bcl, perc, vn, vc]

Waring, Rob. *Concerto for Vibraphone and Chamber Ensemble* (1984)
[fl, bcl, vib, timp, vn, vc = vib with fl, bcl, timp, vn, vc]

Wiegold, Peter. *Prelude 1* (1978)
[afl, cl, perc, va, vc]

Woolrich, John. *Berceuse* (1990)
[sop/gongs, afl, cl, va, vc]

Wuorinen, Charles. *Bearbeitungen über das Glogauer Liederbuch* (1962)
[fl/pic, cl/bcl, vn, db]

x) with tape, multimedia or electronics

Berio, Luciano. *Différences* (1958-59, rev. 1967)
[fl, cl, hp, va, vc, tape]

Birtwistle, Harrison. *Medusa* (1969, rev. 1970, *since withdrawn*)
[fl/pic, Bb-cl/Ab-cl/ssax, pf/cel, perc (xylo/vib/glock/tam-tam/gong), va (rev. = vn/
va), vc, 2 tapes, shozyg (rev. = synthesizer) - wind and str ampl.]

Connolly, Justin. *Obbligati II, Op. 13* (1967)
[fl, cl, vn, vc, tape]

Davidovsky, Mario. *Synchronisms No. 2* (1964)
[fl, cl, vn, vc, electronics]

Davies, Peter Maxwell. *Missa super L'homme armé (Agnus dei; Luke 22)*
(1968, rev. 1971)
[spkr, fl/pic, cl, perc, harm, hpd/cel/honky-tonk-pf, vn, vc, tape (boy's voice; rev. =
live perf.); cl, vn, vc, harm also play perc]

Davies, Tansy. *grind show (electric) / grind show (* unplugged)* (2007)
[fl, cl, pf (prepared [*/processed]), vn, vc, [*sampler=electronics/CD])

Erb, Donald. *Quintet* (1976)
[fl/harmonica/goblet, cl/goblet, pf/elec-pf-with-phase-shifter/goblet, vn/goblet, vc/
goblet]

Gilbert, Anthony. *Mother* (1969)
[wooden-fl/pic, elec.-basset-cl/bcl/sharp-pitch-Bb-cl/Eb-cl, Hammond org (or pf
with elec.-keyb attachment), perc, vn/elec.-va, vc (with elec. ampl.) = vc (with elec.
ampl.) *with* ensemble listed]

Harvey, Jonathan. *Inner Light 1* (1973)
[fl, cl, pf, perc, vn, va, vc, tape]

Kreiger, Arthur. *Meeting Places* (1995)
[fl/afl, cl/bcl, pf, perc, vn, vc, DAT tape]

Kretz, Johannes. *Dynamische Gewächse* (1999)
[fl, cl, pf, vn, vc, electronics]

Mowitz Ira J. *Shimmerings* (2004)
[afl/pic, cl/bcl, pf, glock, vn, vc, digital soundtrack]

Murail, Tristan. *Treize Couleurs du soleil couchant* (1978)
[fl, cl, pf, vn, vc, electronics (ad lib.)]

Murail, Tristan. *Winter Fragments* (2000)
[fl, cl, pf, vn, vc, Apple Macintosh, MIDI keyb, amplification, reverberation]

Nunn, Patrick. *Hextych: Six Impressions on Six Paintings by Philip Core* (2001)
[fl/afl, cl/bcl, pf, vn, vc, taped gramophone]

Primosch, James. *Sacra conversazione* (1994)
[fl/afl/pic, cl/bcl, pf, perc, vn, vc, tape]

Ran, Shulamit. *O, The Chimneys* (1969)
[mez, fl, cl/bcl, pf, perc, vc, tape]

Reich, Steve. *Double Sextet* (2007)
[fl, cl, pf, vib, vn, vc, pre-recorded tape (of fl, cl, pf, vib, vn, vc) or 2 fl, 2 cl, 2 pf, 2 vib, 2 vn, 2 vc]

Richard, André. *Musique de Rue: Szenische Aktionsmusik* (1987)
[fl, cl, pf, perc, vn, vc, tape = perc with fl, cl, pf, vn, vc, tape]

Schwehr, Cornelius. *'aber die Schönheit des Gitters'* (1992-93)
[fl, cl, pf, perc, vn, va, vc, film projection (ad lib)]

Westlake, Nigel. *Entomology* (1990)
[fl/afl/pic, E♭-cl/bcl, pf, perc, vn, vc, tape]

xi) with dancers and/or other extramusical characters

Davies, Peter Maxwell. *Vesalii icones* (1969)
[dancer/out-of-tune-honky-tonk-pf (or played by cond), fl/afl/pic, basset-cl (or A-cl), pf/out-of-tune-autoharp/music-box ('unsuitable' tune)/etc., perc (glock/xylo/etc.), va, vc = vc with ensemble listed]

Davies, Peter Maxwell. *Nocturnal Dances (Miguel Serrano, Corinthians I 13)* (1969-70)
[sop, fl, cl, pf, perc, va, vc – orig. version with dancers]

Davies, Peter Maxwell. *Le Jongleur de Notre Dame: A Masque (Peter Maxwell Davies)* (1978)
[bar, mime, fl/afl/pic, A-cl/bcl, pf/cel, perc, vn, vc, children's band (3 fl, ob, 2 cl, 3 tpt, perc)]

Davies, Peter Maxwell. *The No. 11 Bus for Mime, Singers, Dancers and Instrumental Ensemble* (1983-84)
[mez, ten, bar, mime, 2 dancers, fl/pic, cl/bcl, pf/cel, perc incl. mar/rock-band kit/etc., vn, vc]

Karchin, Louis. *Orpheus: A Masque (Stanley Kunitz)* (2003)
[bar, dancers, fl/pic, cl/bcl, pf, perc, vn, vc]

Lutyens, Elisabeth. *One and the Same* (1974)
['sop spkr', actress, 3 mimes/dancers, fl/afl/pic, cl/bcl, pf/cel, 2 perc, vn/va, vc]

McGarr, Peter. *Vanishing Games* (1995)
[fl/pic/srec/ocarina, cl/bcl/ocarina, pf, perc, vn, vc, off-stage assistant]

Oliveros, Pauline. *Aeolian Partitions* (1970)
[fl/afl/pic, cl/bcl, pf, vn/va, vc, six assistants (stage hands, stage manager, etc.)]

xii) with miscellaneous additions

Amy, Gilbert. *Après... D'un désastre obscur* (1971/76, rev. 1996 – follows *D'un désastre obscur* [mez, cl])
[mez/gongs/whip, fl/pic, cl, bcl (or hn), pf, hp (only if hn > bcl), vn, vc]

Arnell, Richard. *The Petrified Princess: Chamber opera – A Puppet Operetta for TV* (1959)
[fl, cl, bn, pf/cel, vn, vc]

Bedford, David. *Music for Albion Moonlight (Kenneth Patchen)* (1965)
[sop, fl, cl, pf, Hohner alto-melodica, vn, vc]

Britten, Benjamin. *Men Behind the Meters* (1935)
[fl, cl (later ob), pf, perc, vn, vc]

Brown, Earle. *Syntagm III* (1970)
[fl, bcl, pf/cel, vib, mar, hp, vn, vc]

Caltabiano, Ronald. *Marrying the Hangman: Chamber Opera (Margaret Atwood)* (1999)
[fl/pic/afl, E♭-cl/bcl, asax/tsax, pf, perc, vn, vc]

Caltabiano, Ronald. *Torched Liberty: Dramatic Cantata No. 2 (Gertrude Stein, Langston Hughes, etc.)* (1986)
[sop, fl/pic, A-cl/E♭-cl/bcl, tpt, pf, perc, vn, vc]

Conyngham, Barry. *Bashō (Basho)* (1980)
[sop, afl/pic, cl/bcl, trb, pf, perc (gong/tam-tam/vib/xylo/etc.), vn, vc]

Davies, Peter Maxwell. *Sextet* (1958, publ. as Septet, 1972)
[fl, A-cl, <u>bcl</u>, pf, vn, vc - gui added 1972]

Davies, Peter Maxwell. *Points and Dances from "Taverner"* (1970)
[Dances from Act I = afl, cl, gui, hpd, va, vc]
[*Dances from Act II*, with linking keyb movts = pic, cl, cbn, tpt, atrb, pos-org, regal, perc (2 drums)]

Davies, Peter Maxwell. *Missa super L'homme armé (Agnus dei; Luke 22)* (1968, rev. 1971)
[spkr, fl/pic, cl, perc, harm, hpd/cel/honky-tonk-pf, vn, vc, tape (boy's voice; rev. = live perf.); cl, vn, vc, harm also play perc]

Davies, Peter Maxwell. *Suite from 'The Devils'* (1971)
[sop, fl/afl/pic, cl/bcl, 2 sax, tpt, trb, Hammond org/out-of-tune-pf/cel, 3 perc, vn/va/regal, vc, db]

Davies, Peter Maxwell. *Suite from 'The Boy Friend' (most arr. of Sandy Wilson)* (1971)
[fl, cl, bcl, 4 sax (ssax, asax/sopranino-sax (or E♭-cl), asax/tsax, t sax), 2 tpt, trb, tb, 2 perc, banjo, uke/mand, hp, 2 keyb (pf/cel/autoharp (or zither), pf/tamb/scraper-inside-pf), str (single or multiple)]

Davies, Peter Maxwell. *The Martyrdom of St Magnus (Peter Maxwell Davies, after George Mackay Brown and the Brennu-Njáls Saga, trans. Mackay Brown)* (1976)
[mez, ten, 2 bar, bass, fl/afl/pic, cl/bcl, hn, 2 tpt, keyb, perc, gui/tabor, va, vc, db]

Davies, Peter Maxwell. *Le Jongleur de Notre Dame: A Masque (Peter Maxwell Davies)* (1978)
[bar, mime, fl/afl/pic, A-cl/bcl, pf/cel, perc, vn, vc, children's band (3 fl, ob, 2 cl, 3 tpt, perc)]

Davies, Peter Maxwell. *The Lighthouse: Chamber Opera (Based on a True Incident in 1900)* (1979)
[ten, bar, bass, fl/afl/pic, A-cl/bcl, hn, tpt, trb, pf/cel/honky-tonk-pf/flexatone/referee's whistle, perc (mar/4 timp/glock/bones/etc.), gui/banjo/drum, vn/tam-tam, va/flexatone, vc, db]

Davies, Peter Maxwell. *Image, Reflection, Shadow* (1982)
[fl/afl/pic, A-cl/bcl, pf, cimbalom, vn, vc]

Dench, Chris. *light-strung sigils* (2002)
[fl/afl/pic, cl/cbcl, ampl. rec, pf, perc, vn, vc = ampl. rec with fl/afl/pic, cl/cbcl, pf, perc, vn, vc]

Elwood, Paul. *Cast Out Devils, Speak with New Tongues* (2006)
[fl, cl, pf, vn, vc with bluegrass band (fiddle, banjo, mand, gui, db)]

Erb, Donald. *Quintet* (1976)
[fl/harmonica/goblet, cl/goblet, pf/elec-pf-with-phase-shifter/goblet, vn/goblet, vc/goblet]

Falla, Manuel de. *Concerto* (1923-26)
[fl, ob, cl, hpd (or pf), vn, vc = hpd (or pf) with fl, ob, cl, vn, vc]

Ferneyhough, Brian. *Flurries* (1997)
[pic, cl, hn, pf, vn, vc]

Goehr, Alexander. *Suite, Op. 11* (1961)
[fl, cl, hn, hp, vn/va, vc]

Grange, Philip. *Variations* (1986)
[fl/afl, cl/basset, hn, pf, perc, vn, vc]

Grime, Helen. *Blurred Edges* (2004)
[fl/pic, cl/bcl, hp, pf, vn, vc]

Hannan, Geoffrey. *Centrifugal Bumblepuppy* (1999)
[pic, bcl, pf, perc, vn, vc, db]

Harrison, Sadie. *Ring the Bells of St Leonard's* (2004)
[children's voices, 4 vn, tpt (procession), fl, cl, vn, vc, pf ('Double Image ensemble'), 10 perc]

Haubenstock-Ramati, Roman. *Credentials or 'Think, think lucky' (Samuel Beckett)* (1960)
[*Sprechstimme*, cl, <u>trb</u>, pf, cel, 2 perc, vib/glock, vn]

Hayes, Morgan. *Alluvial* (1999)
[afl/pic, cl/bcl, pf, perc, vn, vc, db]

Hellawell, Piers. *Sound Carvings from the Ice Wall* (1995)
[fl/afl, cl/bcl, pf, perc, va, vc, db]

Henze, Hans Werner. *Der langwierige Weg in die Wohnung der Natascha Ungeheuer (Gastón Salvatore)* (1971)
[solo bar, solo perc with Pierrot, jazz and brass ensembles, Hammond org = bar, fl/pic, B♭-cl/E♭-cl/bcl, hn, 2 tpt, trb, jazz ens. (fl, ocarina (ampl), bcl, sax, trb, 2 perc, db), pf, Hammond org, perc (timbales/flexaphone/etc.) vn/va (ampl), vc (ampl), tape]

Hind, Rolf. *The Horse Sacrifice* (2001)
[fl/bfl/trbrec, B♭-cl/E♭-cl/rec, pf/ratchet/triangles, vn, vc]

Holloway, Robin. *The Rivers of Hell* (1977)
[fl/afl/pic, ob/ca, E♭-cl/A-cl/bcl, pf, perc, va, vc]

Hoyland, Vic. *Esem* (1975)
[2 fl/bfl, 2 cl/sax, cel/elec.-org, perc, vc, db = db with 2 fl/bfl, 2 cl/sax, cel/elec.-org, perc, vc]

Hoyland, Vic. *Crazy Rosa - La Madre* (1988)
[sop, fl/afl, cl, pf, 2 mar, hp, va, vc]

Hughes, Edward Dudley. *The Sibyl of Cumae (Tom Lowenstein)* (2001)
[mez, fl/afl/pic, cl/bcl, pf, perc, vn, vc, db]

Hughes, Edward Dudley. *Strike Sketches* (2006)
[fl/pic, cl, hn, pf, perc, pf, vn, vc, live electronics]

Kay, Alison. *Godafoss and Breaking Line* (2002)
[fl/pic, cl/bcl, pf, perc, vn, vc, db]

Kee Yong, Chong. *'Yuan He': Concerto for Five Chinese Instruments and Five Western Instruments* (2010)
[Sheng, GuZheng, Er-hu, Dizi, Yan Qin / fl, cl, pf, vn, vc]

Kennea, Evan. *Sextet* (1994 rev, 1997)
[fl, ob, cl, vn, vc, pf]

Knight, Richard. *As Time Goes By* (1985)
[fl, ob, cl, perc, pf, vn, vc]

Knussen, Oliver. *Océan de Terre, Op. 10 (Guillaume Apollinaire)* (1973)
[sop, fl/afl, cl/bcl, pf/cel, 1 or 2 perc, vn, vc, db]

Kraft, William. *The Sublime and the Beautiful* (1979)
[ten, fl/afl/pic/bcl, cl/bcl, pf/cel, 2 perc, 2 vn, 2 vc]

Marsh, Roger. *The Wormwood And The Gall: A Lament (Jeremiah)* (1981)
[mez, fl/afl, cl, perc, hp, va, vc]

Mozzi, Gustavo. *'the eyes of the night'*
[fl, cl, pf, acc/bandoneón, perc, vn, vc]

Nunn, Patrick. *Momenta* (2005)
[fl/afl, cbcl, hp, pf, vn, vc]

Powers, Anthony. *From Station Island* (2003)
[male spkr, bar, fl/afl/pic, cl/bcl, hp, perc, vn, vc]

Reich, Steve. *Double Sextet* (2007)
[fl, cl, pf, vib, vn, vc, pre-recorded tape (of fl, cl, pf, vib, vn, vc) or 2 fl, 2 cl, 2 pf, 2 vib, 2 vn, 2 vc]

Reynolds, Peter. *Borrowed Time* (1988)
[fl, ob, cl, perc, pf, vn, vc]

Rhys, Paul. *Chicago Fall* (1992)
[fl/afl, cl, pf, hpd/cel, vib/bmar, hp, vn, vc, 2 synth/sampler]

Sackman, Nicolas. *Corronach* (1985)
[fl/pic, B♭-cl/E♭-cl, hn, pf, perc, vn, vc]

Toovey, Andrew. *Music for the Painter Jack Smith: Version II* (2001)
[fl/pic/afl/bfl, B♭-cl/E♭-cl/bcl, pf/hpd, perc, vn, vc, db]

Toovey, Andrew. *Self-Portrait as a Tiger!* (2003)
[fl, cl, trb, pf, vn, vc]

Vir, Param. *Contrapulse* (1985)
[fl/pic, ob/ca, cl/bcl, pf/cel, perc, vn, vc]

Weeks, James. *The Catford Harmony* (2008)
[fl, ob, cl, pf, vn, vc]

Whalley, Richard. *The Joy of Melody* (1996)
[fl/pic, cl, tpt, pf, perc, vn, vc]

Whalley, Richard. *Elegy: A Tribute to Colin Nancarrow* (1999)
[fl/pic, cl/bcl, pf, perc, pf, vn, vc, db]

Wilby, Philip. *Et surrexit Christus* (1979)
[3 sop, fl, 2 cl, chamber org/pf, perc, vn/va, vc]

Yi, Chen. *Sparkle* (1992)
[fl, cl, pf, 2 perc, vn, vc, db]

Yiu, Raymond. *Night Shanghai* (2005)
[fl/afl/pic, cl/bcl, acc, pf, vn, vc]

eighth blackbird (Chicago), a Modern Pierrot Ensemble

Bibliography

Lucy Shelton as Pierrot singing 'Nacht', eighth blackbird (Chicago)

Bibliography

ALSO   Archives of the London Symphony Orchestra, London
ASC   Arnold Schönberg Center, Vienna
BFI   British Film Institute, London
BBC   British Broadcasting Corporation
BLSA   British Library Sound Archive, London
BMIC   British Music Information Centre, London
BPA   Britten-Pears Archive, Aldeburgh
CPH   Centre for Performance History, Royal College of Music, London
PSS   Paul Sacher Stiftung, Basel

Sound and Audio Archive

Palmer, Bernard. *Interview with Elisabeth Lutyens*, BBC Radio 3, broadcast 12 September 1969. Also available from the BBC4 Audio Archive: www.bbc.co.uk/bbcfour/audiointerviews/realmedia/lutyense/lutyense2.ram (accessed 20 June 2009).

Wines, Chris. *Pierrot and Beyond*, interview with Stephen Pruslin and Judy Arnold during the interval of a concert by the Birmingham Contemporary Music Group, Pebble Mill, Birmingham. BBC Radio 3, broadcast 23 May 1997; BLSA, H5918/2.

Television

Music on Two: A Couple of Things about Harry. Uncredited interview with Harrison Birtwistle, BBC2, broadcast 4 April 1971; Roy Tipping (dir.), John Amis (ed.).; viewed at BFI.

2nd House. Peter Maxwell Davies, interview with Melvyn Bragg, with performance by The Fires of London. BBC2, broadcast 2 March 1974; Dennis Marks (prod.); viewed at BFI.

Pierrot Lunaire. Ballet Rambert version of Glen Tetley's ballet (1979). BBC; Colin Neers (dir.); viewed at BFI.

Film

Dinner Hour (1935). Edgar Anstey (dir.), British Commercial Gas Association (sponsor); viewed at BFI.

Men Behind the Meters (1935). Edgar Anstey (dir.), British Commercial Gas Association (sponsor); viewed at BFI.

The Devils (1971). Ken Russell (dir.), Warner Bros.

The Boy Friend (1971). Ken Russell (dir.), Russflix / Anglo-EMI / Metro-Goldwyn-Mayer.

One Foot in Eden: Peter Maxwell Davies (1978). Gavin Barrie (dir.); Platypus Films (prod. co.); Arts Council of Great Britain (sponsor); viewed at Goldsmiths College Library, University of London (RV 103).

Selected Concert Programmes

1912-66, various collections incl. Choralion-Saal, Berlin and Society for Twentieth Century Music, Hampstead, London [see www.concertprogrammes.org.uk for further details]. BL, Ernst Henschel Collection, Add. Henschel, incl. Box 32/i.

Boosey & Hawkes Concerts (No. 9), London Summer Concerts, Aeolian Hall, London, 29 May 1942. CPH.

Concert and Recital Programmes for the Royal Festival Hall, Queen Elizabeth Hall and Purcell Room, London. BL, shelfmark W.P.4462.

Books and Articles

Adlington, Robert. *The Music of Harrison Birtwistle* (Cambridge: Cambridge University Press, 2000).

—— 'Music Theatre since the 1960s' in: *The Cambridge Companion to Twentieth-Century Opera*, ed. Mervyn Cooke (Cambridge: Cambridge University Press, 2005), 225-43.

Adorno, Theodor W. and Eisler, Hanns. *Composing for the Films* (1947) (2nd edn., London: Athlone, 1994).

Auner, Joseph (ed.). *A Schoenberg Reader: Documents of a Life* (New Haven and London: Yale University Press, 2003).

Beard, David J. *An Analysis and Sketch Study of the Early Instrumental Music of Sir Harrison Birtwistle (c. 1957-77)* (D.Phil. diss., University of Oxford, 2000).

Black, Leo. *BBC Music in the Glock Era and After*, ed. Christopher Wintle (London: Plumbago, 2010).

Blake, David (ed.). *Hanns Eisler: A Miscellany* (Luxembourg: Harwood, 1995).

Boehmer, Konrad (ed.). *Schönberg and Kandinsky: An Historic Encounter* (Amsterdam: Harwood, 1997).

Bonds, Mark Evan. 'Symphony – §II: 19th Century' in: *Grove Music Online. Oxford*

Music Online, http://www.oxfordmusiconline.com/subscriber/article/grove/music/ 27254pg2 (accessed 11 May 2010).

Boulez, Pierre. 'Trajectories: Ravel, Stravinsky, Schoenberg' (1949) in: *Stocktakings from an Apprenticeship*, trans. Stephen Walsh (Eng. edn., Oxford: Clarendon, 1991).

Bowen, Meirion. 'The Fires Brigade', *The Guardian* (19 January 1987), 9.

Bradshaw, Susan. 'The Music of Elisabeth Lutyens', *Musical Times* 112/1541 (July, 1971), 653-56.

Brinkmann, Reinhold. 'What the Sources Tell Us ... A Chapter of *Pierrot* Philology', *Journal of the Arnold Schoenberg Institute* 10/1 (June, 1987), 11-27.

—— (ed.). *Arnold Schönberg: Sämtliche Werke, Melodramen und Lieder mit Instrumenten*, vol. 1, *Pierrot lunaire, Op. 21, Kritischer Bericht – Studien zur Genesis – Skizzen – Dokumente* (Mainz: Schott, 1995).

—— 'The Fool as Paradigm: Schönberg's *Pierrot Lunaire* and the Modern Artist' in: *Schönberg and Kandinsky: An Historic Encounter*, ed. Konrad Boehmer (Amsterdam: Harwood, 1997), 139-68.

Britten, Benjamin. 'Conversation with Benjamin Britten', *Tempo* 6 (February, 1944), 4-5.

—— *Letters from a Life: The Selected Letters and Diaries of Benjamin Britten, 1913-1976* (5 vols.), ed. Donald Mitchell and Philip Reed (London: Faber, 1991-2012).

Bryn-Julson, Phyllis and Mathews, Paul. *Inside Pierrot lunaire: Performing the Sprechstimme in Schoenberg's Masterpiece* (Lanham: Scarecrow Press, 2009).

Burden, Michael. 'A Foxtrot to the Crucifixion' in: *Perspectives on Peter Maxwell Davies*, ed. Richard McGregor (Aldershot: Ashgate, 2000), 51-65.

Burgess, Martin and Swan, John. *The Triumph of Pierrot: The Commedia dell'Arte and the Modern Imagination* (New York: Macmillan, 1986).

Casella, Alfredo. 'Schoenberg in Italy', *Modern Music* 1/1 (1924), 7-8.

Chagrin, Francis. 'A Quarter-century of New Music', *Composer* 26 (Winter, 1967-68), 4-6.

Chancellor, Alexander. 'How Wonderful to See You', *The Guardian*, G2 Supplement (21 July 2004), 12-3.

Chapman, Ernest. 'The Boosey & Hawkes Concerts', *Tempo* 6 (February, 1944), 7-8.

Cook, Nicholas. *Music: A Very Short Introduction* (Oxford: Oxford University Press, 1998).

Couling, Delia. *Ferruccio Busoni: A Musical Ishmael* (Lanham, Md. and Oxford: Scarecrow, 2005).

Craggs, Stewart. *Peter Maxwell Davies: A Source Book* (Aldershot: Ashgate, 2002).

Cross, Jonathan. *Harrison Birtwistle: Man, Mind, Music* (London: Faber, 2000).

Dallapiccola, Luigi. 'On the Twelve-note Road' ('Sulla strada della dodecafonia', 1951), trans. Deryck Cooke, *Music Survey* 4/1 (October, 1951), 318-32.

Davies, Peter Maxwell. 'The Young British Composer', *The Score and I.M.A. Magazine* 16 (March, 1956), 84-5.

—— 'Problems of a British Composer Today', *The Listener* 62/1593 (8 October 1959), 563-64.

Delaere, Mark and Herman, Jan (eds.) *Pierrot Lunaire: Albert Giraud – Otto Erich Hartleben – Arnold Schoenberg: A Collection of Musicological and Literary Studies*, (Louvain: Peeters, 2004).

Devčić, Natko. 'Strukturirani koncert (U povodu jedne nesvakidašnje londonske glazbene priredbe)' in: *Novi zvuk: Izbor tekstova o suvremenoj glazbi*, ed. Petar Selem (Zagreb: Nakladni Zavod Matice Hrvatske, 1972), 209-13.

DeVine, George F. 'Chamber Music: Elisabeth Lutyens', *Notes* 27/4 (1971), 806.

Doctor, Jennifer. *The BBC and Ultra-modern Music, 1922-1936: Shaping a Nation's Tastes* (Cambridge: Cambridge University Press, 1999).

Driver, Paul. ''Façade' Revisited', *Tempo* 133/134 (September, 1980), 3-9.

—— 'The Fires of London', *BBC Music Magazine* 133 (May, 2003), 54-5.

—— 'Is the Game Up for Harrison Birtwistle?', *The Sunday Times*, Culture Supplement (7 November 2004), 30.

Dromey, Christopher. 'Benjamin Britten's 'Pierrot' Ensembles', in: *British Music and Modernism, 1865-1960*, ed. Matthew Riley (Farnham: Ashgate, 2010), 248-71.

Duff, David. *Modern Genre Theory* (Harlow: Longman, 2000).

Duffalo, Richard. *Trackings: Composers Speak to Richard Dufallo* (New York: Oxford University Press, 1989).

Dunnett, Roderic. 'Sir Peter Maxwell Davies: On Her Majesty's Service', *The Independent* (15 March 2004), 56.

Dunsby, Jonathan. *Schoenberg: Pierrot Lunaire* (Cambridge: Cambridge University Press, 1992).

—— 'Schoenberg's Pierrot Keeping his *Kopfmotiv*' in: *Pierrot Lunaire: Albert Giraud – Otto Erich Hartleben – Arnold Schoenberg: A Collection of Musicological and Literary Studies*, ed. Mark Delaere and Jan Herman (Louvain: Peeters, 2004), 67-76.

Eisler, Hanns. *Musik und Politik: Schriften 1924-1948*, 2 vols., ed. Günter Mayer (Leipzig: VEB Deutscher Verlag für Musik, 1973).

Evans, John (ed.). *Journeying Boy: The Diaries of the Young Benjamin Britten 1928-1938* (London: Faber, 2009).

Fleury, Louis. 'The Flute and Its Powers of Expression', trans. Arthur H. Fox Strangways, *Music & Letters* 3/4 (October, 1922), 383-93.

—— 'About "Pierrot Lunaire": The Impressions Made on Various Audiences by a Novel Work', trans. Arthur H. Fox Strangways, *Music & Letters* 5/4 (October, 1924), 242.

Foreman, Lewis (ed.). *British Music Now* (London: Paul Elek, 1975).

Frank, Alan. 'Why Not Give Living Composers a Chance?' [Letter to the Editor], *Musical Times* 81/1164 (February, 1940), 83.

Frisch, Walter. *German Modernism: Music and the Arts* (Berkeley and Los Angeles: University of California Press, 2005).

Gee, Brian. 'Professor Humphrey Procter-Gregg: Some Details of His Career', *Musical Opinion* 88/1054 (July, 1965), 599-601.

Gerhard, Roberto. 'English Musical Life: A Symposium', *Tempo* 11 (1945), 2-3.

Giraud Albert. *Pierrot lunaire: Rondels bergamasques* (Paris: Alphonse Lemmere, 1884).

Goehr, Alexander. *Finding the Key: Selected Writings of Alexander Goehr*, ed. Derrick Puffett (London: Faber, 1998).

Goodwin, Noel. 'Music in London: Pierrot Players', *Musical Times* 108/1493 (July, 1963), 626.

Grabs, Manfred (ed.). *Hanns Eisler: Kompositionen, Schriften, Literatur: Ein Handbuch* (Leipzig: Deutscher Verlag für Musik, 1984).

Gray, Cecil. 'Arnold Schönberg: A Critical Study', *Music & Letters* 3/1 (January, 1922), 73-89.

Gray, John. 'Soho Square and Bennett Park: The Documentary Movement in Britain in the 1930s', *Screening the Past* 7 (1999), www.latrobe.edu.au/screeningthepast/firstrelease/fr0799/jgfr7a.htm (accessed 7 September 2012).

Grierson, John. 'The GPO Gets Sound', *Cinema Quarterly* 2/4 (1934), 221.

Griffiths, Paul. *Peter Maxwell Davies* (London: Robson, 1982).

—— *New Sounds, New Personalities: British Composers of the 1980s in Conversation with Paul Griffiths* (London: Faber, 1985).

Halfyard, Janet. '*Eight Songs for a Mad King*: Madness and the Theatre of Cruelty', conference paper given at 'A Celebration of the Music of Peter Maxwell Davies' St Martin's College of Performing Arts, Lancaster (31 March to 2 April 2000), www.webarchive.org.uk/wayback/archive/20070131163627/http://www.maxopus.com/essays/8songs_m.htm (accessed 7 September 2012).

Hall, Michael. *Harrison Birtwistle* (London: Robson, 1984).

Hamlin, Peter S. '*Pierrot lunaire*' *and the New Sound World of Twentieth-century Chamber Music* (Ph.D. diss., University of Rochester, Eastman School of Music, 1994).

Hanke, Ken. *Ken Russell's Films* (Metuchen: Scarecrow, 1984).

Harding, James. *The Ox on the Roof: Scenes from Musical Life in Paris in the Twenties* (London: Macdonald, 1972).

Harries, Meirion and Harries, Susan. *A Pilgrim Soul: The Life and Work of Elisabeth Lutyens* (London: Faber, 1989).

Harvey, Jonathan. 'Maxwell Davies's "Songs for a Mad King"', *Tempo* 89 (Summer, 1969), 2-6.

Häusler, Josef (ed.). *Pierre Boulez: eine Festschrift zum 60. Geburtstag am 26. März 1985* (Vienna: Universal Edition, 1985).

Heaton, Chris (ed.). *Changing Platforms: 30 Years of the Contemporary Music Network* (London: Unknown Public, 2001).

Henze, Hans Werner. *Music and Politics: Collected Writings 1953-81* (London: Faber, 1982).

—— *Bohemian Fifths: An Autobiography*, trans. Stewart Spencer (London: Faber, 1998).

Hollander, John. 'Notes on the Text of *Philomel*', *Perspectives of New Music* 6/1 (Autumn-Winter, 1967), 134-41.

Homs, Joaquim. *Roberto Gerhard and His Music*, trans. Agustín Prunell-Friend, ed. Meirion Bowen (Eng. edn., Sheffield: The Anglo-Catalan Society, 2000).

Howell, Tim. 'Eisler's Serialism: Concepts and Methods' in: *Hanns Eisler: A Miscellany*, ed. David Blake (Luxembourg: Harwood, 1995), 103-32.

Hutcheon, Linda. *A Theory of Parody: The Teachings of Twentieth-Century Art Forms* (London: Methuen, 1985).

Jeutner, Renate (ed.). *Peter Maxwell Davies: Ein Komponistenporträt* (Bonn: Boosey & Hawkes, 1983).

Josephson, David. 'In Search of the Historical Taverner', *Tempo* 101 (1972), 40-52.

Keller, Hans. 'Whose Fault is the Speaking Voice?', *Tempo* 75 (Winter, 1965-66), 12-17.

—— 'Arrangement For or Against?', *Musical Times* 110/1511 (January, 1969), 22-5.

Kildea, Paul (ed.)., *Britten on Music* (Oxford: Oxford University Press, 2003).

Kramer, Lawrence. *Musical Meaning: Toward a Critical History* (Berkeley: University of California Press, 2001).

Kurth, Richard. 'Pierrot's Cave: Representation, Reverberation, Radiance' in: *Schoenberg and Words: The Modernist Years*, ed. Charlotte M. Cross and Russell A.

Berman (New York and London: Garland, 2000), 203-41.

—— '*Pierrot lunaire*: Persona, Voice, and the Fabric of Allusion' in: *The Cambridge Companion to Schoenberg*, ed. Jennifer Shaw and Joseph Auner (Cambridge: Cambridge University Press, 2010), 120-34.

Lambert, Constant. *Music Ho! A Study of Music in Decline* (London: Faber, 1934).

Lester, Joel. 'Structure and Effect in *Ave Maris Stella*' in: *Perspectives on Peter Maxwell Davies*, ed. Richard McGregor (Aldershot: Ashgate, 2000), 66-74.

Lesure, François (ed.). *Dossier de Presse: Press-book de Pierrot lunaire d'Arnold Schönberg* (Geneva: Minkoff, 1985).

Levi, Erik. 'Atonality, Twelve-tone Music and the Third Reich', *Tempo* 178 (September, 1991), 17-21.

Lloyd, Stephen. *William Walton: Muse of Fire* (Woodbridge: Boydell Press, 2011).

Lobanova, Marina. *Musical Style and Genre: History and Modernity* (1979), trans. Kate Cook (Amsterdam: Harwood Academic Publishers, 2000).

Lott, R. Allen. '"New Music for New Ears": The International Composers' Guild', *Journal of the American Musicological Society* 36/2 (Summer, 1983), 266-86.

Lutyens, Elisabeth. 'Conceptual Link between *The Pit, Rhadamanthus* and *Requiem for the Living*', paper delivered at Canford Summer School, 1951, repr. 'Appendix 11' in: Sarah Jane Tenant-Flowers, *A Study of Style and Techniques in the Music of Elisabeth Lutyens*, 2 vols. (D.Phil. diss., University of Durham, 1991), vol. 2, 69-70.

—— 'Sermon Delivered to the S.P.N.M., June 4, 1959', *The Score* 26 (January, 1960), 66.

—— *A Goldfish Bowl* (London: Cassell, 1972).

McCalla, James. *Twentieth-century Chamber Music* (New York: Routledge, 2003).

McGregor, Richard (ed.). *Perspectives on Peter Maxwell Davies* (Aldershot: Ashgate, 2000).

Mackay, Robert. 'Safe and Sound: New Music in Wartime Britain' in: '*Millions Like Us? British Culture in the Second World War*, ed. Nick Hayes and Jeff Hills (Liverpool: Liverpool University Press, 1999), 179-208.

—— 'Leaving Out the Black Notes: The BBC and "Enemy Music" in the Second World War', *Media History* 6/1 (June, 2000), 77-82.

McLean, Mervyn. *Maori Music: Records and Analysis of Ancient Maori Musical Tradition and Knowledge* (Auckland: Auckland University Press, 1996).

Mahler Werfel, Alma. *And the Bridge is Love* [trans. E.B. Ashton] (London: Hutchinson, 1959).

Manning, Jane. *Voicing Pierrot* (Amarro, Australia, Southern Voices, 2012).

Marsh, Roger. '"A Multicoloured Alphabet": Rediscovering Albert Giraud's *Pierrot Lunaire*', *Twentieth-Century Music* 4 (2007), 97-121.

Massarini, Renzo. 'Arnold Schönberg in Italy', trans. G.A. Pfister, *Sackbut* 4/12 (July, 1924), 364-65.

Metzer, David. 'The New York Reception of *Pierrot lunaire*: The 1923 Premiere and Its Aftermath', *Musical Quarterly* 78/4 (Winter, 1994), 669-99.

—— 'The League of Composers: The Initial Years', *American Music* 15/1 (Spring, 1997), 45-69.

Milhaud, Darius. *My Happy Life* (1974), trans. Donald Evans, George Hall and Christopher Palmer (Eng. edn., London and New York: Boyars, 1995).

Morrison, Richard. *Orchestra – The LSO: A Century of Triumph and Turbulence* (London: Faber, 2004).

Moss, Stephen. 'Sounds and Silence', www.guardian.co.uk/music/2004/jun/19/classicalmusicandopera.proms2004 (accessed 7 September 2012).

Newlin, Dika. *Schoenberg Remembered: Diaries and Recollections (1938-76)* (New York: Pendragon, 1980).

Nono, Luigi. 'Die Entwicklung der Reihentechnik' (Darmstadt, 1957) in: *Darmstädter Beiträge zur Neuen Musik*, ed. Wolfgang Steinecke (Mainz, 1958), vol. 1, 25-37.

—— 'Presenza storica nella musica d'oggi' (Darmstadt, 1959) in: *La Rassegna Musicale* 30/1 (1960), 1-8.

Northcott, Bayan. 'Peter Maxwell Davies', *Music and Musicians* 17/8 (April, 1969), 36-40, 80-82.

Nyman, Michael. 'Two New Works by Birtwistle', *Tempo* 88 (Spring, 1969), 47-50.

Oja, Carol J. 'Women Patrons and Activists for Modernist Music: New York in the 1920s', *Modernism/Modernity* 4/1 (1997), 129-55.

—— *Making Music Modern: New York in the 1920s* (New York: Oxford University Press, 2000).

Orenstein, Arbie (ed.). *A Ravel Reader: Correspondence, Articles, Interviews* (2nd edn., Mineola: Dover, 2003).

Owens, Peter. 'Revelation and Fallacy: Observations on Compositional Technique in the Music of Peter Maxwell Davies', *Music Analysis* 13/2-3 (October, 1994), 161-202.

Palmer, Russell. *British Music* (London: Robinson, 1947).

Panofsky, Erwin. *Meaning in the Visual Arts* (Garden City: Doubleday, 1955).

Payne, Anthony. 'The Problems of Pierrot', *Music and Musicians* 15/12 (August, 1967), 41.

Porter, Andrew. 'Some New British Composers', *Musical Quarterly* 51/1, *Special Fiftieth Anniversary Issue: Contemporary Music in Europe: A Comprehensive Survey* (January, 1965), 12-21.

Pruslin, Stephen (ed.). *Studies from Two Decades (Tempo Booklet No. 2)* (London: Boosey & Hawkes, 1979).

—— 'Twenty Years of The Fires: A Retrospective Sketch', from the concert programme for 'The Fires' Farewell and Twentieth Birthday Gala' (Queen Elizabeth Hall, 20 January 1987), pages unnumbered.

—— 'Fires into Londonflames [*sic*]: The Past and the Future' in: *New Music 88*, ed. Michael Finnissy, Malcolm Hayes and Roger Wright (Oxford: Oxford University Press, 1989), 85-90.

Ratz, Erwin. 'Hanns Eisler' (*Musikblätter des Anbruch*, 1924) in: *Wer war Eisler: Auffassungen aus sechs Jahrzehnten*, ed. Manfred Grabs (Berlin: Verlag des Europäische Buch, 1983), 28-9.

Reed, Philip. *The Incidental Music of Benjamin Britten: A Study and Catalogue of His Music for Film, Theatre and Radio*, 2 vols. (Ph.D. diss., University of East Anglia, 1987).

—— 'Britten in the Cinema: *Coal Face*' in: *The Cambridge Companion to Benjamin Britten*, ed. Mervyn Cooke (Cambridge: Cambridge University Press, 1999), 54-77.

Reich, Willi. *Schoenberg: A Critical Biography*, trans. Leo Black (Eng. edn., London: Longman, 1971).

Rhein, John von. 'Composer Peter Maxwell Davies: Looking for an Audience, Not A Cult', *Chicago Tribune* (22 May 1983), 16-17.

Roberts, David. Review of *Ave Maris Stella* and ten other scores by Peter Maxwell Davies, *Contact* 19 (Summer, 1978), 26-9.

Rotha, Paul. *Documentary Diary: An Informal History of the British Documentary Film, 1928-1939* (London: Secker and Warburg, 1973).

Routh, Francis. 'The Redcliffe Concerts, *Composer* 26 (1967-68), 24-6.

—— *Contemporary British Music: The Twenty-five Years from 1945 to 1970* (London: Macdonald, 1972).

Saxton, Robert. 'Elisabeth Lutyens' in: *New Music 88*, ed. Michael Finnissy, Malcolm Hayes and Roger Wright (Oxford: Oxford University Press, 1989), 9-21.

Schebera, Jürgen. *Hanns Eisler: Eine Biographie in Texten, Bildern und Dokumenten* (Mainz: Schott, 1998).

Scherchen, Hermann. *Aus Meinem Leben Rußland in Jenen Jahren: Erinnerungen*, ed. Eberhardt Klemm (Berlin: Henschelverlag Kunst und Gesellschaft, 1984).

—— *Werke und Briefe*, ed. Joachim Lucchesi (Berlin: Lang, 1991).

Schoenberg, Arnold. *Theory of Harmony* (*Harmonielehre*, 1911), trans. Roy E. Carter (London: Faber, 1978).

—— *Berliner Tagebuch*, ed. Josef Rufer (Frankfurt: Propyläen, 1974).

—— '"Fascism is No Article of Exportation"' (c. 1935) in: *A Schoenberg Reader: Documents from a Life*, ed. Joseph Auner (New Haven and London: Yale University Press, 2003), 268.

—— 'This is My Fault' (1949) in: *Style and Idea*, ed. Leonard Stein, trans. Leo Black (3rd edn., London: Faber, 1984) 145-47.

—— *Letters*, ed. Erwin Stein, trans. Eithne Wilkins and Ernst Kaiser (Eng. edn., London: Faber, 1964).

Schuller, Gunther and Steuermann, Edward. 'A Conversation with Steuermann' (20 May 1964), *Perspectives of New Music* 3/1 (Autumn-Winter, 1964), 22-35.

Seabrook, Mike. *Max: The Life and Music of Peter Maxwell Davies* (London: Gollancz, 1994).

Searle, Humphrey. 'New Instrumental Combinations' in: *Music Today: Journal of the International Society for Contemporary Music*, ed. Rollo H. Myers (London: Dobson, 1949), 126-31.

—— 'Schoenberg: Prophet and Genius', *Radio Times* (28 December 1951), 32.

—— *Quadrille with a Raven* (1976-82), http://www.musicweb-international.com/searle/titlepg.htm (accessed 7 September 2012).

Simms, Bryan R. 'The Society for Private Musical Performances: Resources and Documents in Schoenberg's Legacy', *Journal of the Arnold Schoenberg Institute* 3/2 (October 1979), 127-50.

—— *The Atonal Music of Arnold Schoenberg 1908-1923* (Oxford: Oxford University Press, 2000).

Slater, Veronica. 'Extended Note [to *Eight Songs for a Mad King*]', www.webarchive.org.uk/wayback/archive/20070131163627/http://www.maxopus.com/works/8songs.htm (accessed 7 September 2012).

Sitwell, Osbert. *Laughter in the Next Room*, vol. 4, *Left Hand, Right Hand* (London: Macmillan, 1949).

Smalley, Roger. 'Some Recent Works of Peter Maxwell Davies', *Tempo* 84 (Spring, 1968), 2-5.

—— 'Maxwell Davies and Others', *Musical Times* 114/1565 (July, 1973), 712-14.

Smallman, Basil. *The Piano Quartet and Quintet: Style, Structure and Scoring* (Oxford: Clarendon, 1994).

Stadlen, Peter. 'Schoenberg's Speech-song', *Music & Letters* 62/1 (January, 1981), 1-11.

—— 'Österreichische Exilmusiker in England' in: *Beiträge '90: Österreichische Musiker im Exil-Kolloquium 1988 der Österreichischen Gesellschaft für Musik*, ed. Monica Wildauer (Kassel: Bärenreiter, 1990), 125-33.

Stein, Erwin. 'The Moon-Struck Pierrot Comes to London', *Radio Times* (4 April 1930), 9.

—— *Orpheus in New Guises*, trans. Hans Keller (London: Rockliff, 1953).

Sterne, Colin C. 'Pythagoras and Pierrot: An Approach to Schoenberg's Use of Numerology in the Construction of *Pierrot lunaire*', *Perspectives of New Music* 21/1-2 (1982-83), 506-34.

Steuermann, Edward. '*Pierrot lunaire* in Retrospect' (1963), *Journal of the Arnold Schoenberg Institute* 2/1 (October, 1977), 49-51.

Stewart, Andrew. 'Restoring the Balance', *Gramophone* (September, 1992), 23.

Stockhausen, Karlheinz. 'Musik und Sprache' (Darmstadt, 1958), *Die Reihe* 6 (1960), 36-58.

Stravinsky, Igor and Craft, Robert. *Conversations* (London: Faber, 1958).

—— *Memories and Commentaries* (London: Faber, 2002).

Stuckenschmidt, Hans Heinz. *Arnold Schoenberg: His Life, World and Work*, trans. Humphrey Searle (Eng. edn., London: Calder, 1977).

Sussex, Elizabeth. *The Rise and Fall of British Documentary: The Story of the Film Movement Founded by John Grierson* (Berkeley: University of California Press, 1975).

Swann, Paul. *The British Documentary Film Movement, 1926-1946* (Cambridge: Cambridge University Press, 1989).

Sweeney-Turner, Steve. 'Resurrecting the Antichrist: Maxwell Davies and Parody-Dialectics or Deconstruction?', *Tempo* 191 (December, 1994), 14-20.

Swinyard, Laurence. 'Hotch Potch', *Musical Opinion* 91/1085 (February, 1968), 253-54.

Szmolyan, Walter. 'Die Konzerte des Wiener Schönberg-*Vereins*' in: *Schönbergs Verein für Musikalische Privataufführungen* (*Musikkonzepte* 36), ed. Heinz-Klaus Metzger and Rainer Riehn (Munich: Text und Kritik, 1984), 101-14.

Taruskin, Richard. *Stravinsky and the Russian Traditions: A Biography of the Works through Mavra*, 2 vols. (London: Oxford University Press, 1996).

Temple Savage, Richard. *A Voice from the Pit: Reminiscences of an Orchestral Musician* (Newton Abbot: David & Charles, 1988).

Tenant-Flowers, Sarah Jane. *A Study of Style and Techniques in the Music of Elisabeth Lutyens*, 2 vols. (D.Phil. diss., University of Durham, 1991).

Tongier, Cheryl. *Pre-existent Music in the Works of Peter Maxwell Davies* (Ph.D. diss., University of Kansas, 1983).

Varèse, Louise. *A Looking-glass Diary, Volume 1: 1883-1928* (London: Davis-Poynter, 1973).

Various. 'Arnold Schönberg 1874-1951', *Music & Letters* 32/4 (October, 1951), 305-23.

Vojtěch, Ivan. 'Die Konzerte des Prager *Vereins*' in: *Schönbergs Verein für Musikalische Privataufführungen* (*Musikkonzepte* 36), ed. Heinz-Klaus Metzger and Rainer Riehn (Munich: Text und Kritik, 1984), 115-18.

Walsh, Stephen. *Stravinsky: A Creative Spring – Russia and France 1882-1934* (London: Pimlico, 1999).

Watkins, Glenn. *Pyramids at the Louvre: Music, Culture, and Collage from Stravinsky to the Postmodernists* (Cambridge, Mass. and London: Harvard University Press, 1994).

Webster, E. M. 'Cheltenham: Blight on the Band-wagon', *Musical Opinion* 90/1080 (September, 1967), 681-85.

Wellesz, Egon. 'Schönberg and Beyond', trans. Otto Kinkeldey, *Musical Quarterly* 2/1 (January, 1916), 76-95.

Whittall, Arnold. 'A Transatlantic Future?', *Music & Letters* 51/3 (July, 1970), 259-64.

—— '*Pierrot* in Context: *Pierrot* as Context' in: *Pierrot Lunaire: Albert Giraud – Otto Erich Hartleben – Arnold Schoenberg: A Collection of Musicological and Literary Studies*, ed. Mark Delaere and Jan Herman (Louvain: Peeters, 2004), 37-46.

—— *Serialism* (Cambridge: Cambridge University Press, 2008).

Wilson, Sandy. *I Could Be Happy: An Autobiography* (New York: Stein and Day, 1975).

Wood, Henry J. *My Life of Music* (London: Purnell, 1938).

Wood, Hugh. 'Reports: Wiltshire – Wardour Castle', *Musical Times*, 106/1472 (October, 1965), 783-84.

Wright, Basel. 'Britten and Documentary', *Musical Times* 104/1449 (November, 1963), 779-80.

Youens, Susan. 'Excavating an Allegory: The Text of *Pierrot Lunaire*', *Journal of the Arnold Schoenberg Institute* 8/2 (November, 1984), 94-115.

Index

Elisabeth Lutyens (Milein Cosman)

Index

Blüthner Orchestra 43
Boccherini, Luigi 19
Boddey, Martin 94
Boosey & Hawkes 65, 68, 74, 87, 129
Boosey & Hawkes Concerts 67, 69
Boulez, Pierre 16-7, 28-9, 110, 116, 126,
  130-31, 155, 177, 180
  Derivé I 180
  Le marteau sans maître 16, 116
  *Untitled (Pour le Dr Kalmus) from A
  Garland for Dr K* 126
Bourlier, Kay 44
Bournemouth Symphony Orchestra 131
Bowen, Meirion 139, 149
Bradshaw, William 94
Brahms, Johannes 19, 74, 111
  String Sextet No. 1, Op. 18 19
  String Sextet No. 2, Op. 36 19
Brain, Dennis 94
Brain, Leonard 94
Brenner, Roger 161
Bridger, Donald 94, 100
Brinkmann, Reinhold 24
British Commercial Gas Association 6,
  18, 53-5, 59-60, 63-4
British Broadcasting Corporation (BBC)
  49, 50, 61, 66, 47, 89, 91-3, 99, 104-05,
  117, 131, 155
BBC Concerts of Contemporary Music
  50
BBC Invitation Concerts 155
BBC Symphony Orchestra 105
British Museum 72, 75
British Society for Electronic Music
  (BSEM) 143, 146, 151
Britten, Benjamin 6, 18-19, 48-68, 71,
  74-5, 79, 84-5, 99, 111, 114, 121, 131, 134,
  154, 183-95
  6d Telegrams 52
  The Ascent of F6 74
  Cabaret Songs 74
  Calendar of the Year 52, 54

Coal Face 52-3, 79
Dinner Hour 53-9, 79, 85
God's chillun 52
Harmonica Sacra 121
How Gas is Made 59-60, 64
The King's Stamp 52
Men Behind the Meters 54-60, 79, 85,
  183-95
Men of the Alps 52, 54
Night Mail 52-3, 79
Orpheus Britannicus 121
Phantasy Quartet 52
Rossini Suite 79
Sinfonietta 52, 99
Soirées musicales 87
The Tocher 87
War Requiem 111-12
Broadcasting House, London 51
Brown, Maurice 96
Brown, Wilfred 100
Bryanston Summer School (see also
  Dartington Summer School) 110
Bryars, Gavin 152
Budapest Chamber Ensemble 44
Bull, John 123
Burden, Hugh 96
Burden, John 94, 100
Burden, Michael 123
Busoni, Ferrucio 10, 27, 39, 45, 90
  Arlecchino 11
  *Toccata: Preludio, Fantasia, Ciaccona,
  K. 287*
Butterley, Nigel 155
Buxtehude, Dietrich 121, 160-61
  Also hat Gott die Welt geliebt 121,
  160-61

Cage, John 152, 206
California E.A.R. Unit 174
Caltabiano, Ronald 177
  Concerto for Six Players 177
Camden Festival 118